HOWARD HODGKIN

To Russ

Happy Christmas

2001

love

Keith

xxx

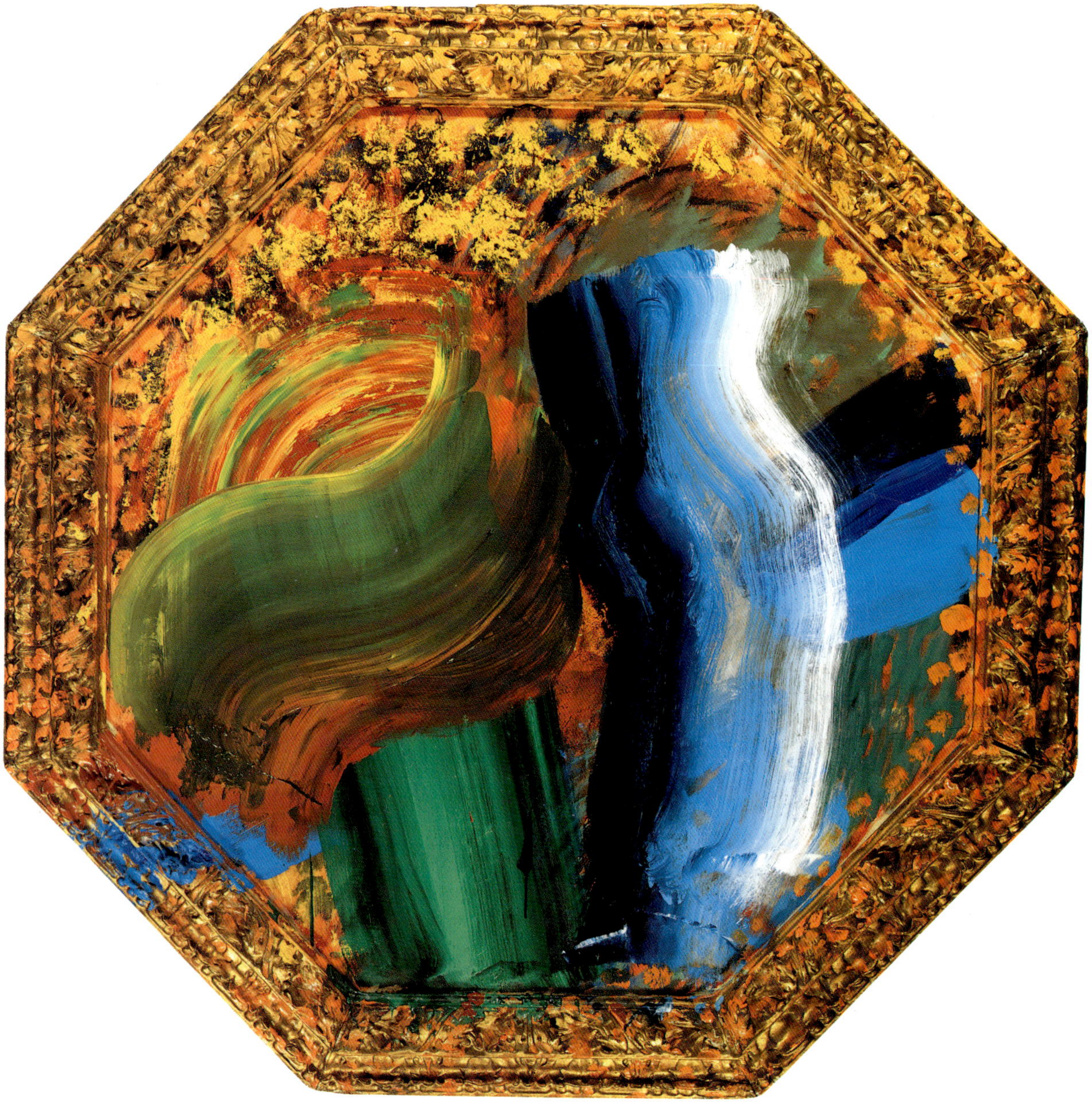

KEITH AND KATHY SACHS
1988 – 91

HOWARD HODGKIN

ANDREW GRAHAM-DIXON

Revised and expanded edition

143 illustrations, 121 in colour

Thames & Hudson

For my family

The Publishers gratefully acknowledge the assistance given by the Artist's Agents Anthony d'Offay Gallery (London) and Knoedler and Company (New York).

Wherever a work of art mentioned in the text is reproduced, a marginal reference indicates the page on which it can be found. Such marginal references have been deemed unnecessary in the case of works reproduced directly opposite the passages in which they are discussed.

First published in Great Britain in 1994 by Thames & Hudson Ltd, London
Revised and expanded edition 2001

British Library Cataloguing-in-Publication Data

A catalogue record for this book is available from the British Library

ISBN 0-500-09298-2

Printed and bound in Singapore

CONTENTS

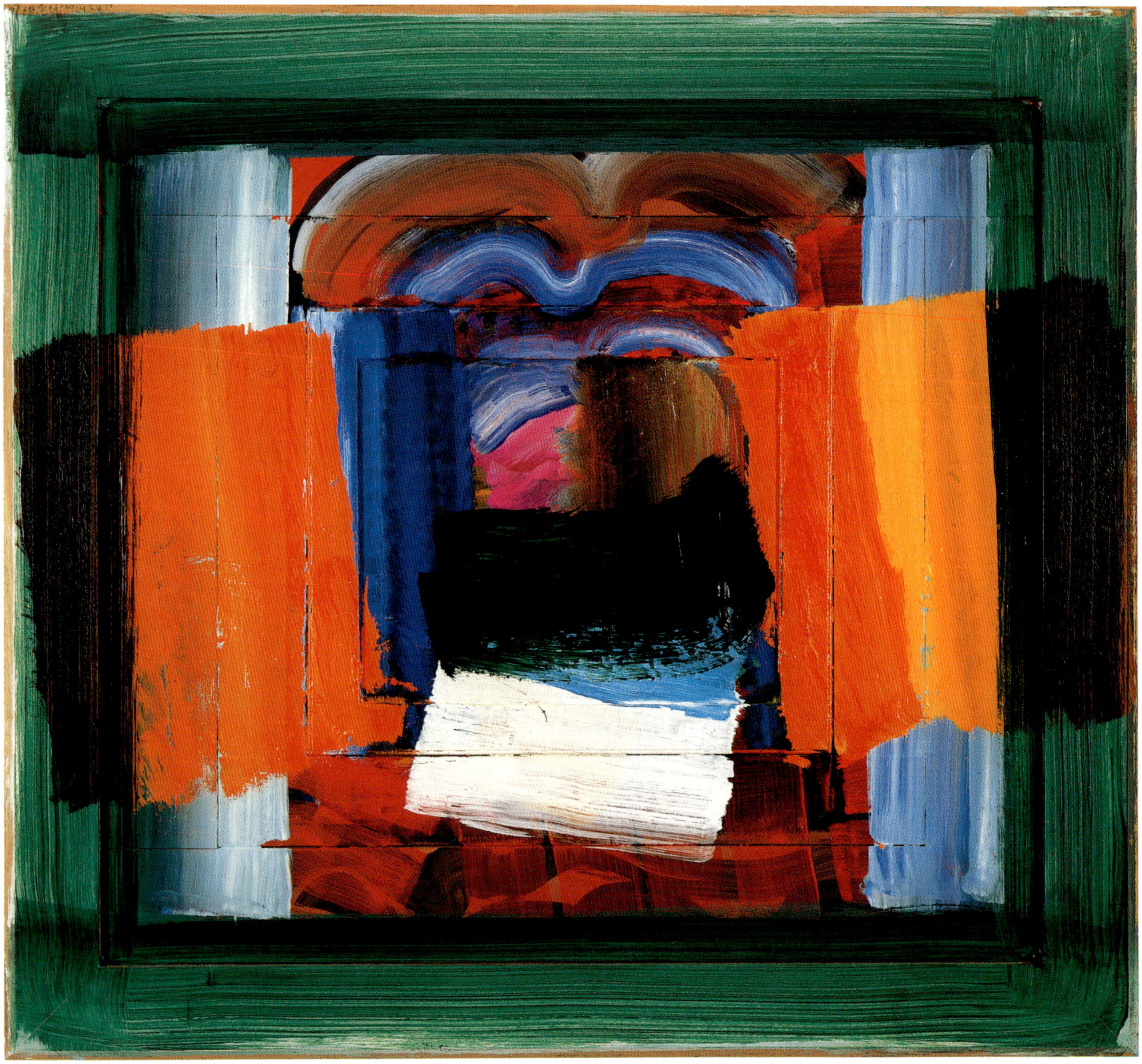

ON THE RIVIERA
1987 – 88

1
BEGINNING

Howard Hodgkin's art is made from an unusual mixture of blatancy and obliqueness, literal statement and suggestion, and the struggle of his career has been the struggle to make its texture of ambiguity compelling. He has said of himself that he is 'a representational painter, but not a painter of appearances. I paint representational pictures of emotional situations'. The remark makes his work sound deceptively straightforward. There it is, the project of a lifetime explained: hundreds of works of art accounted for by a single guiding intention; the disparate products of a painter's heart and mind, hand and eye, suddenly given the willed coherence of a plan. All distilled to five words: 'representational pictures of emotional situations'. But the phrase is a blind alley, an apparent explanation that is nothing of the kind. Howard Hodgkin paints emotional situations. Cézanne painted apples.

It is sometimes a mistake to take on trust what artists have to say about their own work. There is no substitute for looking at the art itself, which usually refutes or complicates their remarks about it. Artists' statements hold out the false promise of a dangled bunch of keys, none of which proves to turn in the lock. But that is no bad thing, since it is also true that whatever residue of inexplicability lodges in a work of art is also its only hope of an afterlife, of an independent existence beyond the confines of the studio. What counts is the quality, the radiance and the urgency of what it is that can never quite be explained or accounted for.

According to the painter himself, he decided to be an artist at the age of five. But he was not a prodigy. His development was tardy, his progress slow towards something like assurance (although that word, suggesting the kind of mastery that can become a source of self-satisfaction and of painting by rote, is at odds with the mobile, intelligently hesitant character of his art). The unusually slow-gathered momentum of Hodgkin's career, which seemed stuck in the low gears for so many years of his life, necessarily unbalances any attempt to treat his work with chronological even-handedness.

The work cannot be divided neatly into periods, sequences or series. For a long time (until as late as the mid-1970s) the paintings seemed unachieved, full of a potential that was yet to be lived up to. Hodgkin was initially a painter of curious, inchoate canvases in which figures often bordering on the caricatural were forever being occluded, blotted out or otherwise diminished by their pictorial surroundings. In *Dancing* (1959), a diagrammatic couple, reduced to the vestigial details of Hodgkin's then shorthand for clothes (a patch of muckily painted stripes) and flesh (a couple of shocking pink fragments, like hung chunks of butcher's meat), are largely obscured by bands of aquamarine paint that seem to have been lowered down the canvas like the slats of a Venetian blind. In *114 Sinclair Road* (1957–58), a group of sitting or reclining figures is swamped by a dreary expanse of red carpeting and brown wallpaper, in an interior infused with a heavy mood of lassitude, of stuck immobility, which is communicated by thickness of paint. *R.B.K.* (1969–70), of around a decade later, is a heavily disguised portrait of the painter R.B. Kitaj – or perhaps it is really an anti-portrait, since its subject has been effectively obliterated – the theme of which, again, is expressed by paint that works to block or imprison. The geometric patterns within the painting make the image read as a box, an interior pictured as a cabinet. But the box is shut, the cabinet is sealed, the room is a prison. It is a picture that speaks of self-inflicted repression, of life lived, cut off, within an emotional or psychological cell.

There is a general air of disaffectedness in many of Hodgkin's earlier pictures, which focus on what was to become one of the central subjects of his subsequent art, the interior with a figure or figures, but which tend to present it as a place of solitary or sociable confinement. The false gaiety of *Small Staff Room* (1965–69), with its bright bars and coils of colour bracketed by expanses of dim maroon and off-white, is loaded with irony: it is a picture about the dismal clutter of an institutional environment, its

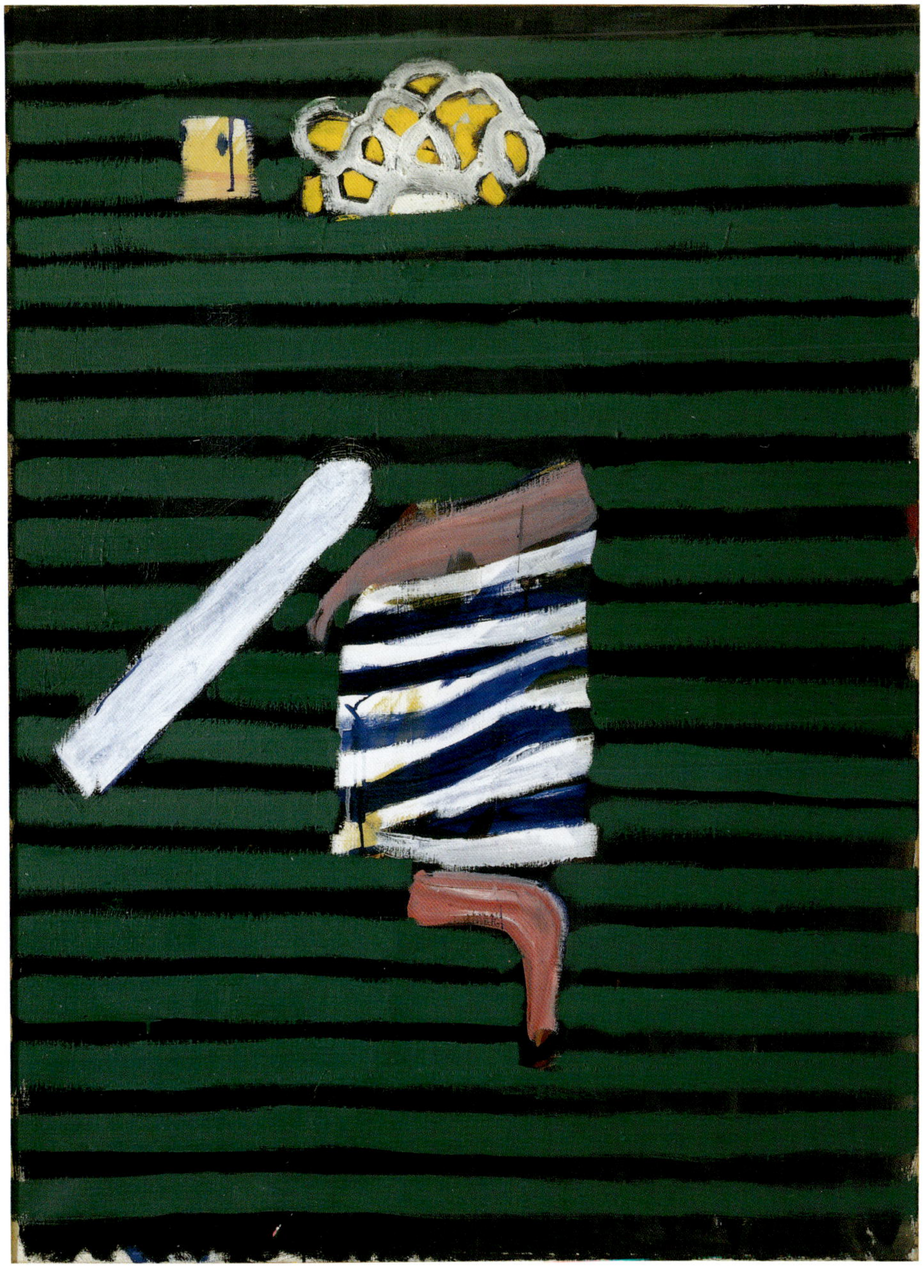

DANCING
1959

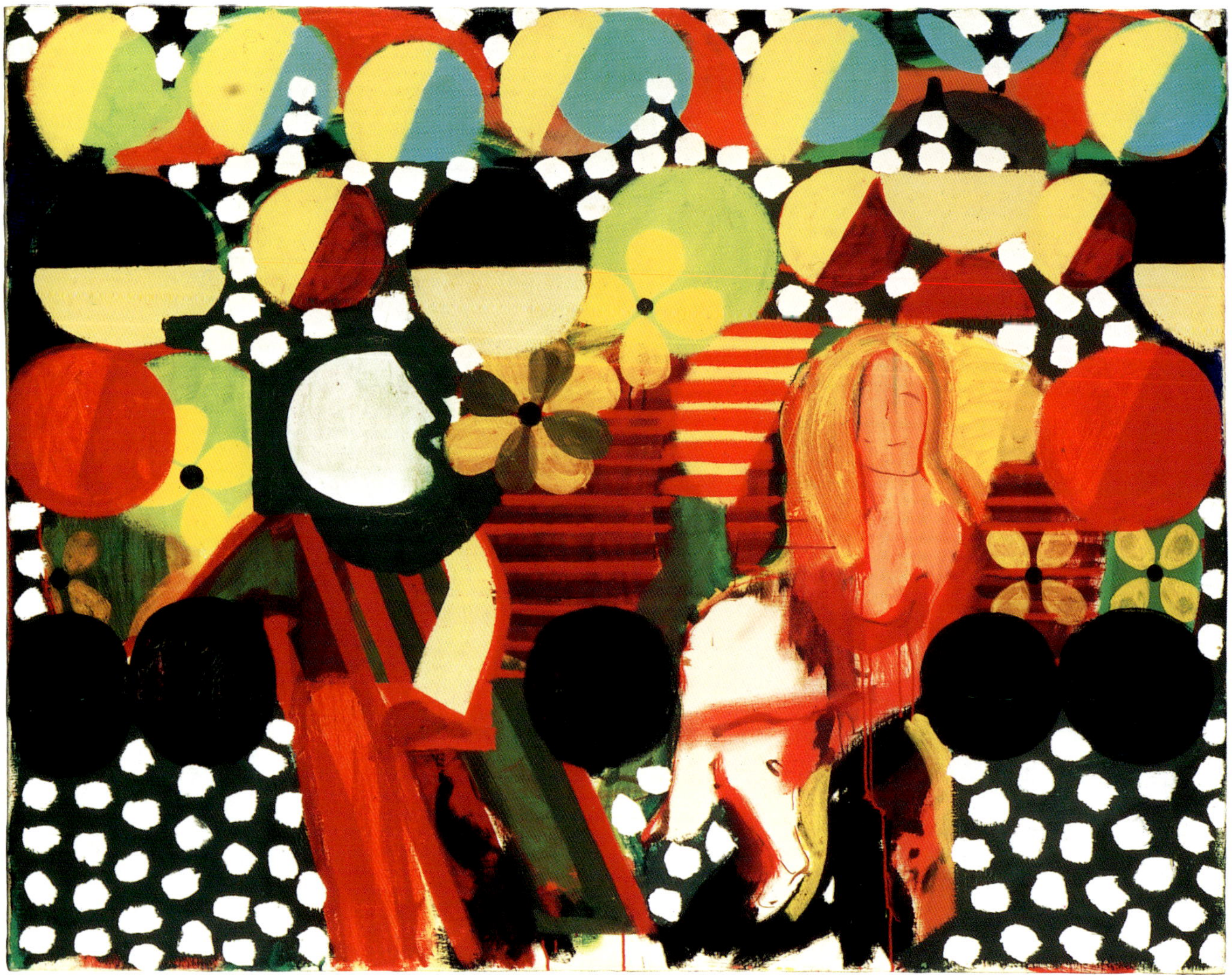

GARDENING
1963

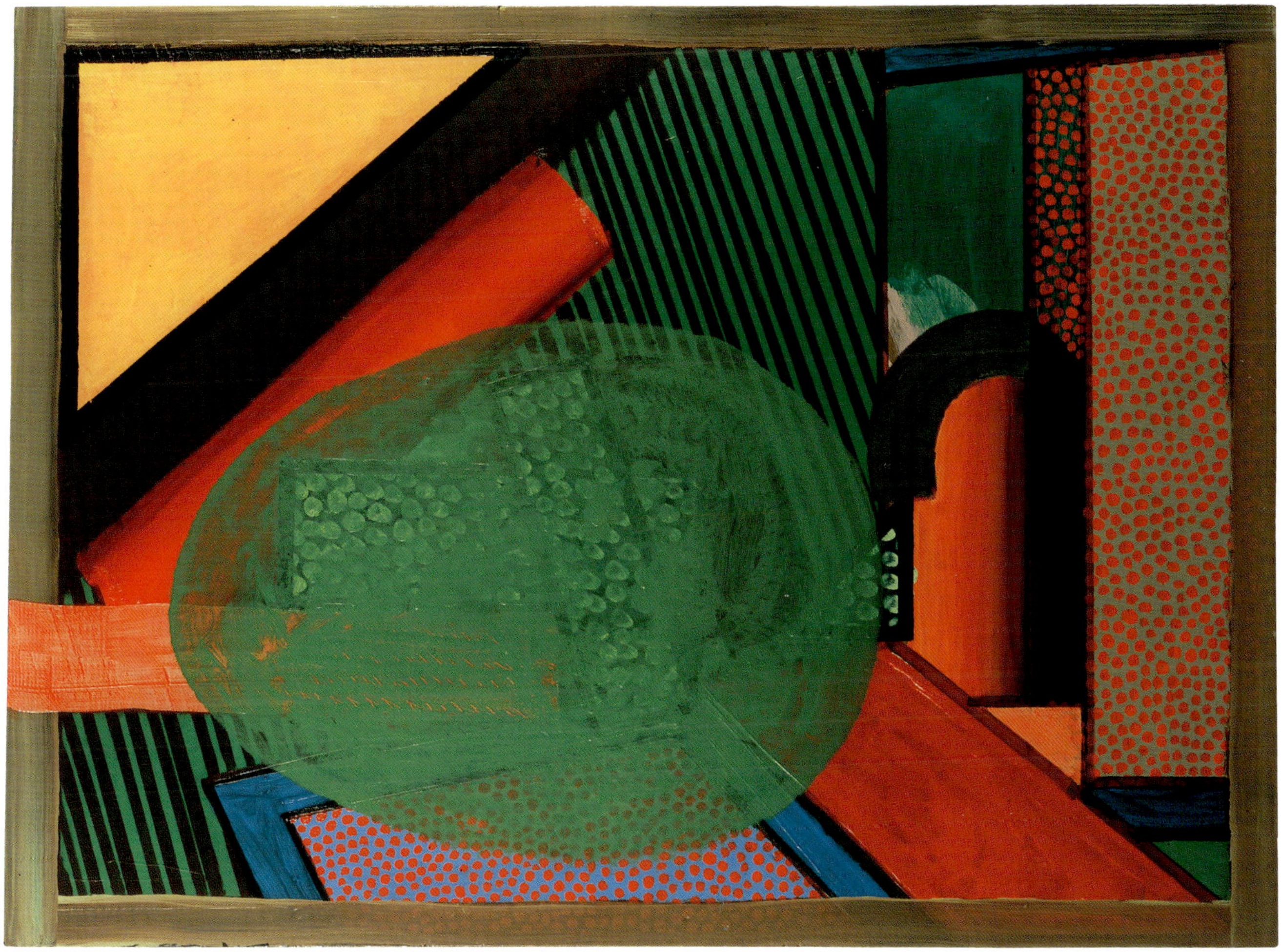

MR AND MRS E.J.P.
1972 – 73

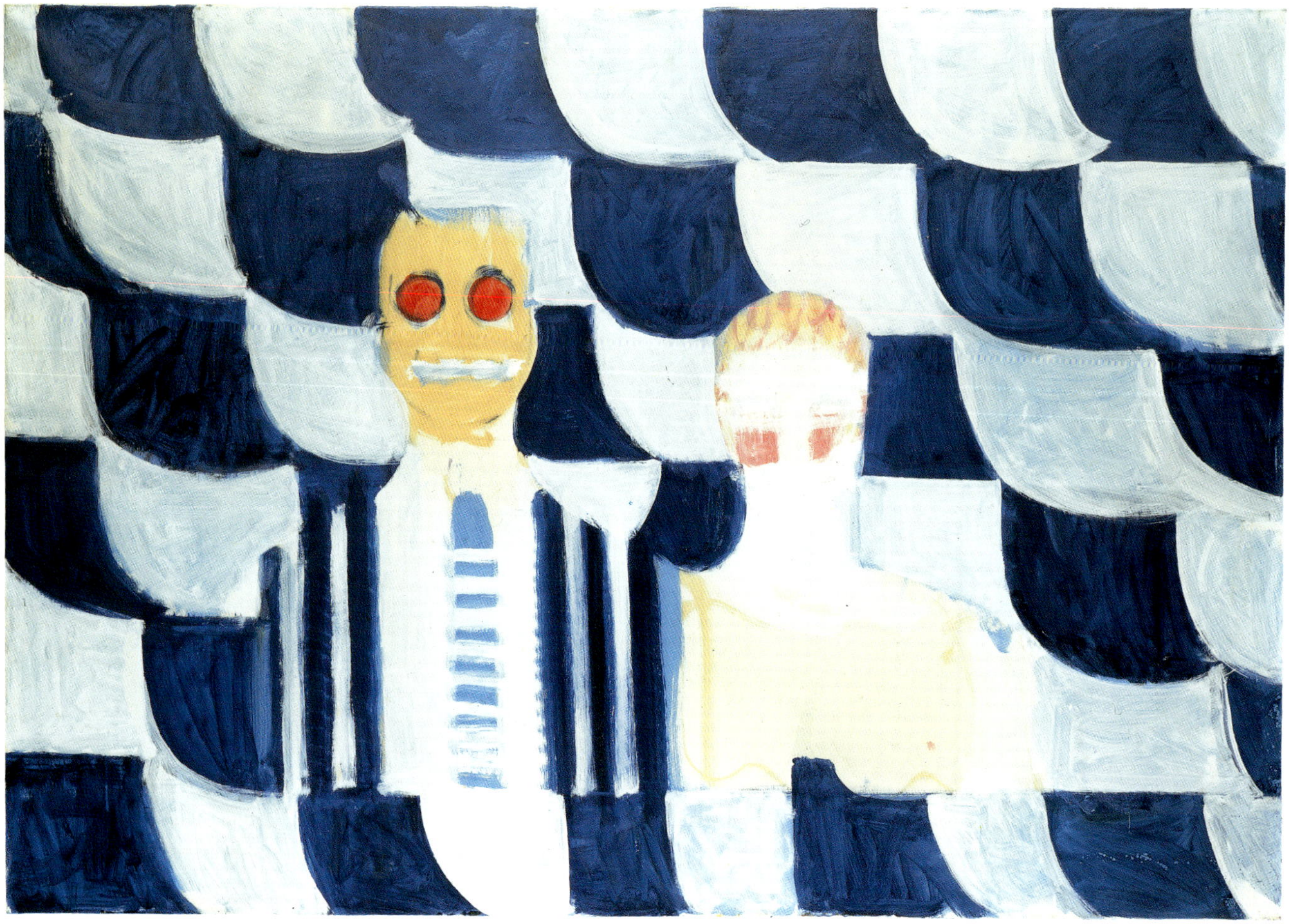

MR AND MRS ROBYN DENNY
1960

P. 11 inability to seem homely. *Mr and Mrs E.J.P.* (1972–73) is another essay in the observation of claustrophobia, but tinged with surrealism: a large green egg-shaped cloud seems to be expanding, like a mist or a fog, to fill a space of cramped and confining pattern. P. 10 The mood spreads outdoors, too, in *Gardening* (1963), a mock-pastoral portrait of a young woman surrounded by spreading floral patterns. Outside, here, feels like inside, nature remade as a form of decor that the painting ironically mimics by emphasizing the extravagance of its own artifice. This *hortus conclusus* is oppressively self-contained. Even the vivid geometries that surround the marionette figures of *Mr and Mrs Robyn Denny* (1960) are, while exuberant, also tyrannical. The artist has invented a scheme of colour and form that serves to fix his subjects (who both stare into space, one through sunglasses, the other with boss-eyed dumbness), to immobilize them like a pair of pinned butterflies. Stranded in these acres of crude pattern, a whole interior condensed to a sign for one, they are people who seem victimized by their own taste for brashness, trapped by their environment.

The sullen mood of an indoors that seems overbearing or unbearable, fraught with P. 15 inexplicable tension, is conjured in the very first painting, *Memoirs* (1949), an image of charged stasis in which an eagle-eyed man fixes the prone, couch-ridden figure of a woman with a stare of cartoon-character intensity. Painted when the artist was seventeen, and the only surviving example of his juvenilia, it is a picture which, despite the miniaturist clarity of its execution (a technique soon abandoned), uncannily prefigures much of the oeuvre that will succeed it. It is small and loaded with both intense feeling and a sense of mystery, like an impenetrable scene preserved, in the form of a single image, from a lost play. The sense of paintings as *mises-en-scène*, staged reconstructions, whether of events or people or things or simply feelings, will endure. The painter makes up his world with the freedom of the stage-set designer, and two decades later the language of his art – in *The Terrace, Delhi* (1967–71), *Reading* (1972) and *Lunch* (1970–72) – will briefly and self-consciously invoke specific parallels with the theatre, arranging bars and bands and stripes of colour like stage flats receding behind a proscenium arch.

Memoirs, as its title indicates, is also the first painting to explore what will become a preoccupation with remembrance, the first picture that begins to define the uneven texture of memory and to find ways of communicating that in the refractory medium of paint. Different registers of style have been allowed to collide: insistently perspectival, in the brick wall seen angling so fiercely away from the viewer out of the window at the back left of the painting; insistently flat, in the red floor and walls that become a single plane of colour, tilting the objects and people in the room forwards. Juxtapositions of vivid and dull colour suggest a deliberate unevenness of attention on the part of the painter, emphasizing certain details (the acid yellow and green lampshade; the reclining woman's bright red fingernails) at the cost of others (the monochrome silhouette of a head in the painting-of-a-painting propped on a table and the blankness of what could be another painting or just a mirror hanging on the wall). Slippages of attention are also suggested by the texture of paint (the proud white dabs that render the ring on one of those dagger-like fingers; the matter-of-fact flatness of floor or wall) and by the abruptness of the composition (the beheading of the couch's occupant by the left edge of the frame). These are methods of talking about the truancy of memory and its enigmatic character, which may be the underlying theme of all the paintings that follow – the way certain things, in retrospect and for no apparent reason, acquire more significance in the mind than others.

Memoirs, although so visually different from the later paintings, defines experience and the quality of memory much as they do. A remembered moment is remade as a collage, an assembling together of parts, the disparateness of which is emphasized by the hard black outline that bounds people and things in the painting. Some elements are vivid, some less so; some distinct, some indistinct. To look at a much later painting like *On the Riviera* (1987–88) is to see the same conception of what a memory is – P. 6 something illogical, subject to the vagaries of feeling and attention – pushed as it so often is in Hodgkin's mature art to the extremes of near-illegibility. Remembered things (flags, sea and sky, perhaps the whitewashed side of a building) merge and blend, melt into each other like the elements of a collage that have been liquefied. The painting phrases itself boldly as a surrogate for an experience that cannot be recaptured, and creates a new world out of the chaos of a memory just as *Memoirs* had done nearly forty years previously. All the paintings will be memoirs, of a kind.

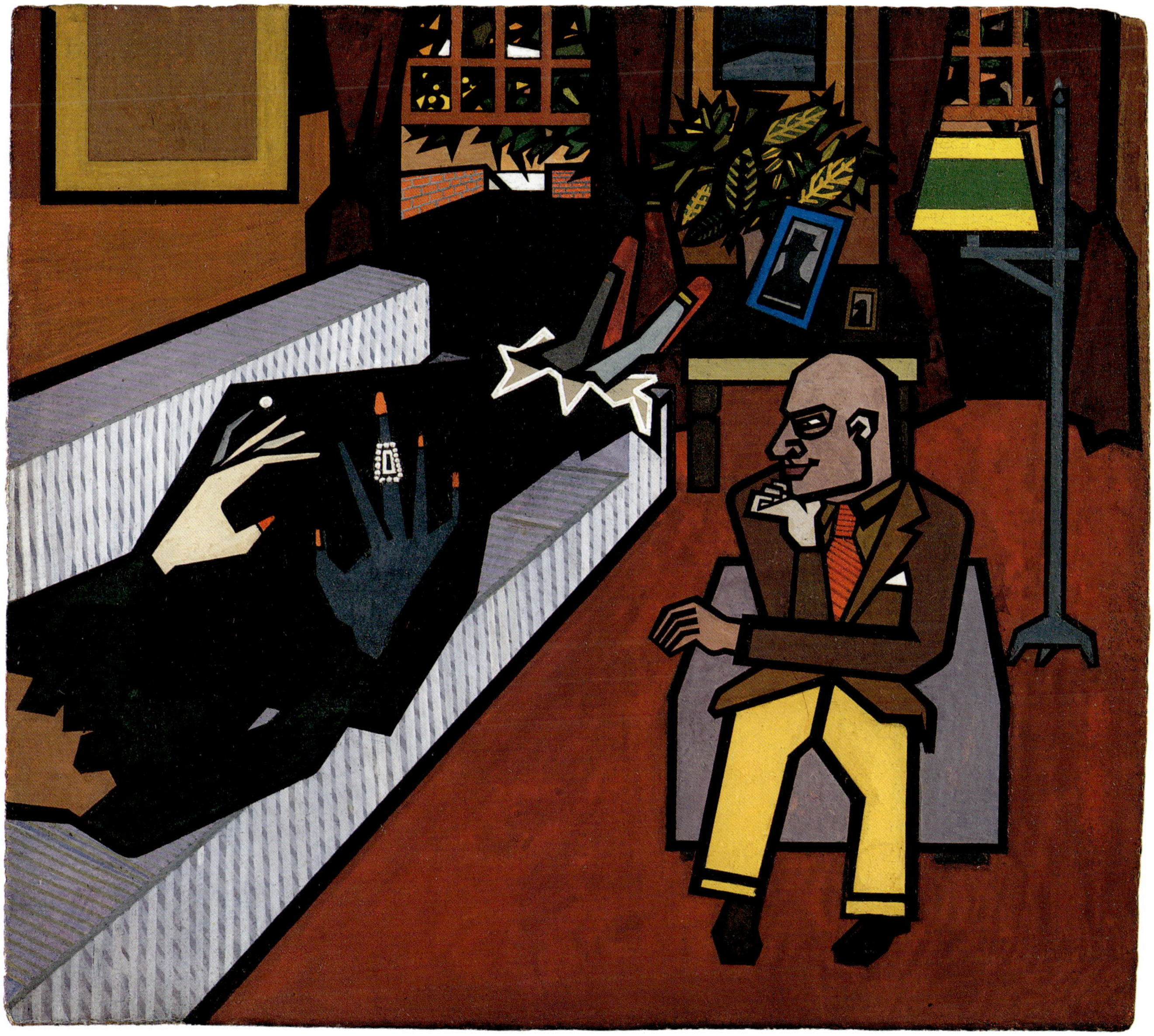

MEMOIRS
1949

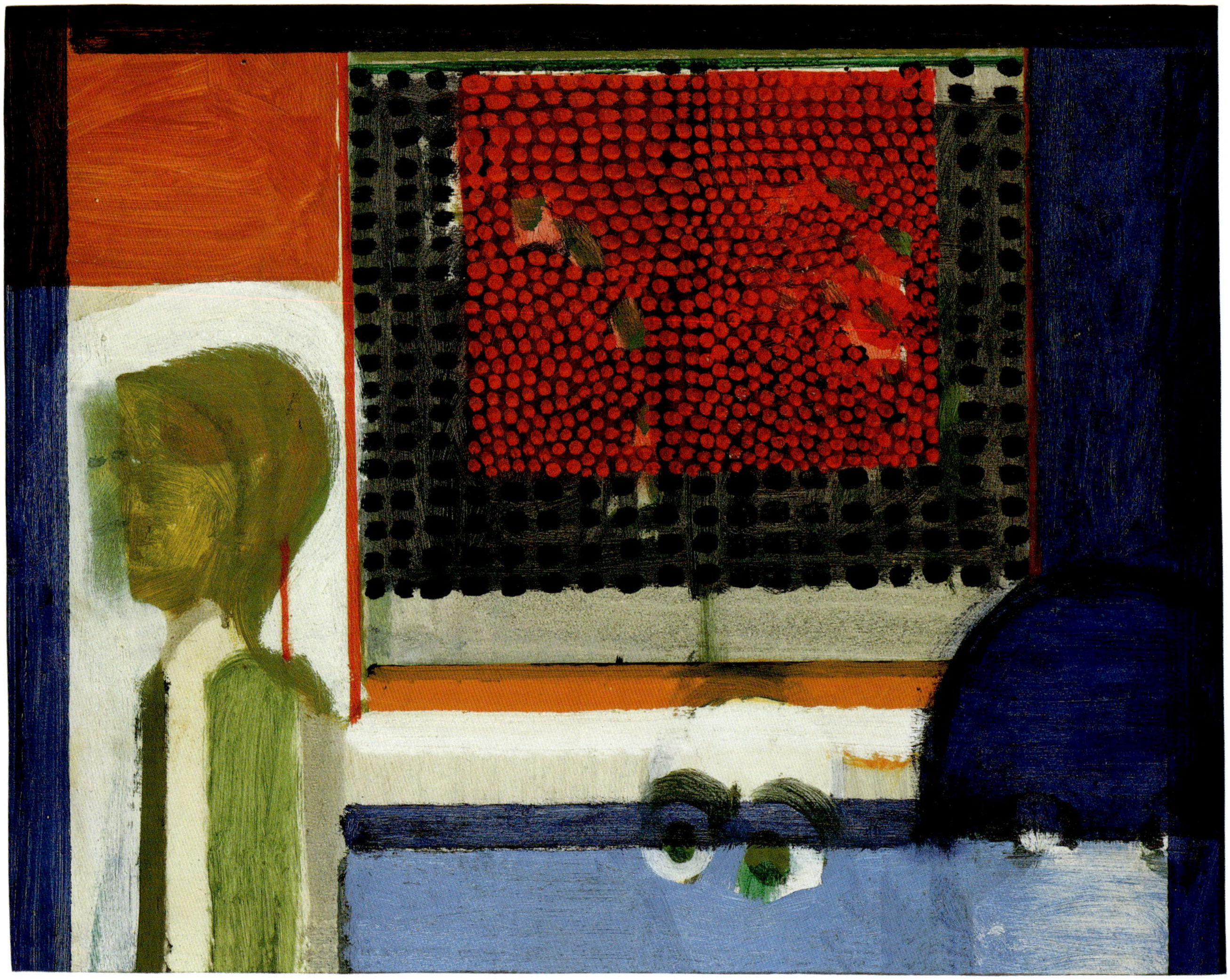

SMALL JAPANESE SCREEN
1962 – 63

Hodgkin has been placed, by numerous writers, within the tradition of painting known as Intimism. The most famous Intimists were French: Matisse, and two other painters of the bourgeois domestic milieu, Bonnard and Vuillard. But Hodgkin's pictorial ancestry is of distinctly mixed blood and cannot be limited to any one school of painting. He has a deep and Catholic interest in art, and his paintings are continual reminders of this, although they wear their learning lightly. Their frequently small scale; their density of colour; their irregular perspective that jumps quickly and often from recession to flatness; their juxtapositions of different codes for things, different registers of realism and non-realism within a single field of artifice – these qualities are certainly to be found in the art of Matisse, Bonnard and Vuillard, but equally (for example) in medieval English manuscript illumination, quattrocento Sienese painting, seventeenth-century Indian Mogul painting, the art of Vermeer and the Synthetic Cubism of Picasso and Braque. Hodgkin's paintings declare, and have done so with increasing boldness down the years, a free and openly eclectic attitude to the art of the past. They have invented their own tradition, to declare their independence from it.

His favoured subjects – the interior, the portrait, scenes from everyday life, admittedly much transmuted – have their origins in a tradition of painting that might be said to run from Dutch genre in the seventeenth century, through to Chardin in France and conversation painting in England in the eighteenth century, and then on to the painters of domestic subject matter in the nineteenth and twentieth centuries. It is only in this broadest sense that Hodgkin can be said to be an Intimist, and when broadened out so far, the term becomes almost meaningless. He is an Intimist only in so far as his concern has always been with the articulation in paint of moments of thought or feeling, discord or harmony, in the lives of human beings.

The earlier work displays a willed conflation of hints and suggestions adapted from a heterogeneous sourcebook of styles, taking from design and fashion as well as from a whole variety of high art ranging from the Old Masters to Seurat and Léger through to Stuart Davis and even, in some passages of monochrome paint applied in expanses, Barnett Newman and Mark Rothko. But the most pressing influences may have had less impact on the forms of this emergent art than its moods. Hodgkin's pictures have never looked *that* much like anyone else's. And many of his early paintings, which seem, with varying degrees of representational literalness, to create worlds of stifled, baffled feeling, are closest in spirit to pictures that bear virtually no physical resemblance to them.

Such early pictures propose their own lineage. Not a lineage of style, however, but a lineage of emotional tenor, an ancestry, in art, of the expression of certain forms of feeling. The ruthless, acerbic observation of *R.B.K.* or *Mr and Mrs Robyn Denny* P. 12
may have its closest antecedent in the imagery of Hogarth, England's harshest painter of

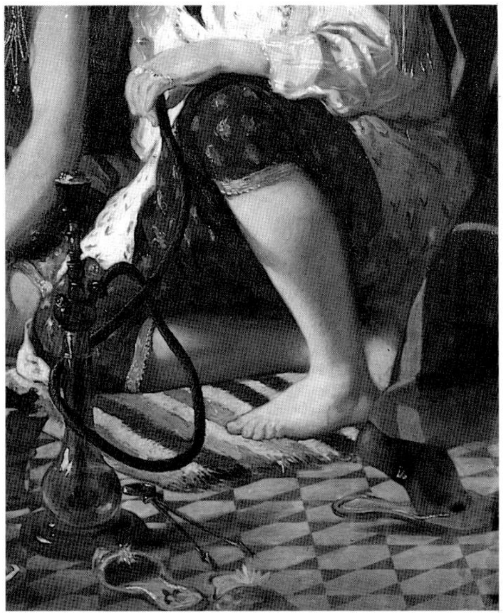

people who have fallen victim to their own tastes and obsessions, people who have made of the rooms which they inhabit boxy traps for the soul. The plush but airless interior of *114 Sinclair Road*, with its static, stultified inhabitants, recalls the mood of Delacroix's *The Women of Algiers*, that great image of stunned, cushioned boredom, of the harem as a beautiful prison. Hodgkin's early works might also be said to have emotional affinities with Degas's portrait of *Hélène Rouart in Her Father's Study*, where the subject is envisaged as part of her father's art collection, metaphorically glass-cased within opulent surroundings. (Hodgkin, in his own *Interior of a Museum* (1956–59), painted a picture of people turning into museum exhibits.) They can also evoke the paintings of drab, ordinary people, leading drab, ordinary lives that Sickert painted in the second decade of this century – paintings like *Ennui*, of whose sad, isolated couple Virginia Woolf once wrote 'It is all over with them, one feels. The accumulated weariness of innumerable days has discharged its burden on them...dull minutes are mounting, old matches are accumulating and dirty glasses and dead cigars; still on they must go, up they must get.'[1]

Yet the pictures also seem to speak implicitly of a desire that runs counter to the realities they evoke: a desire to escape these cloistered confines; a desire to break out; a desire to be somewhere else and perhaps a desire to be *someone* else. Their irony may have been a sign of unease. Between 1962 and 1963, Hodgkin painted a picture
P. 16 called *Small Japanese Screen*. His friend Bruce Chatwin later recalled the circumstances of its making:

> I had recently come back from a desert journey in the Sudan and the sitting room had a monochromatic desert-like atmosphere and contained only two works of art – the arse of an archaic Greek marble kouros, and an early 17th-century Japanese screen. One evening, the Hodgkins and the Welches came to dinner, and I remember Howard shambling round the room, fixing it in his memory with the stare I came to know so well.
>
> The result of that dinner was a painting called *The Japanese Screen* (sic) in which the screen itself appears as a rectangle of pointillist dots; the Welches as a pair of gun-turrets, while I am the acid green smear on the left, turning away in disgust, away from my guests, away from my possessions...and possibly back to the Sahara.[2]

Grim wistfulness is one of the most striking characteristics of the earlier work. The artist may have created, in the 'acid green smear' that was his portrait of Chatwin, that blur of swiped, restive paint, an image of his own dissatisfactions.

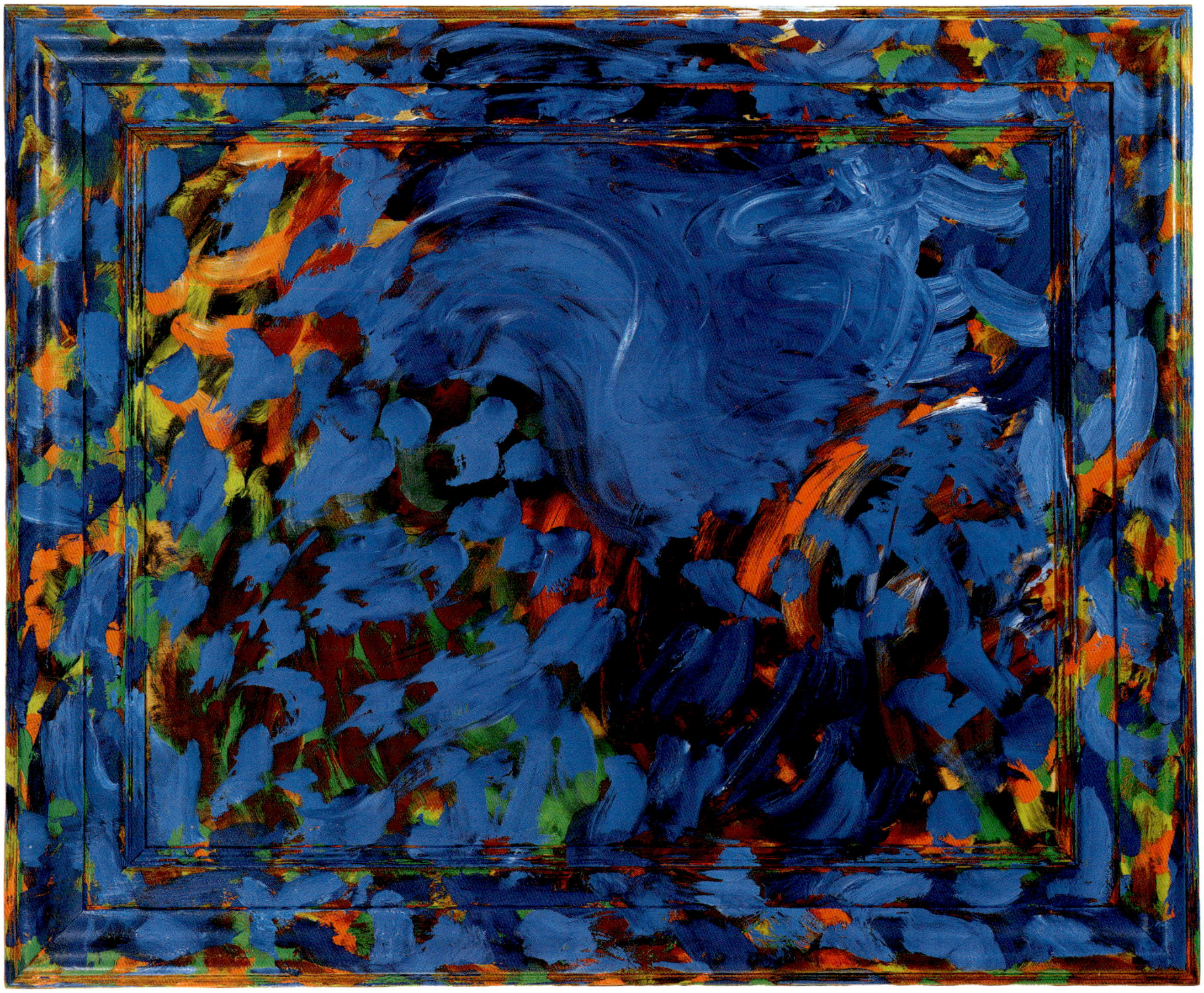

WRITING
1991 – 93

2
REPRESENTATION

Resemblance reproduces the formal aspects of objects but neglects their spirit.[3]
Ching Hao, note on brushwork

In 1966, asked to contribute an artist's statement to *Studio International*, Hodgkin slyly furnished the magazine with a statement by another artist, Henri Matisse – a dissociative strategy which suggests a certain diffidence about his own work, a consciousness that it was not yet adequate to his own intentions for it. 'A work of art', Matisse had said, 'must carry in itself its complete significance and impose it upon the beholder even before he can identify the subject matter. When I see the Giotto frescoes at Padua I do not trouble to recognise which scene of the Life of Christ I have before me, but I perceive instantly the sentiment which radiates from it and which is instinct in every line and colour. The title will serve only to confirm my impression.'[4] Hodgkin seems always to have shared Matisse's faith in the expressive capacities of paint as a carrier of feeling, of intense emotion, linked to, yet also distinct from, its mimetic responsibilities. The problem for him would be how to unlock that capacity in his own art.

If many of the pictures of the first part of his career seem to betray a desire to be elsewhere, the pictures of his maturity see that desire fulfilled. They become new and vivid worlds, no longer so hedged round with irony or so often deflected into satire. They are more naked: their colours are raw and the skin of paint that they present to the world becomes increasingly vulnerable, liquid and membranous. They speak of more (more pleasures and predicaments) and they do so more urgently and eloquently. They can often seem opaque, but their frequent allusiveness and obliqueness, their pictorial veilings and translucencies, are the sources of both ambiguity and authenticity.

The obliqueness of much of Hodgkin's mature art is, also, what has tended to rile people the most about it. One of the standard criticisms levelled against him tends to take the form of a disgruntled rejoinder to his own insistence that his pictures are not abstract. This criticism is worth summarizing here, because it goes to the heart of the painting even though it misses its point.

It runs more or less like this:

Hodgkin says he is a representational painter, but he is nothing of the kind. Look at a picture like *Egypt* (1983–84), or *Goodbye to the Bay of Naples* (1980–82), or P. 109 *Counting the Days* (1979–82), and what do you see? P. 70 A wilful mish-mash of painterly gestures which, when anthologized, are plainly just abstract forms: stripes, blobs, dots and dashes, swathes and coils of disembodied colour, feather-edged bars, wonky lozenges or squares or circles, spreading planes of modulated pigment. They abut one another, mingle with and obscure one another, tangle with and modify and complicate one another endlessly. But there can be no logic to their forms of coexistence, no precise *meaning* to their arrangements, beyond the mysterious and entirely personal rationale of the painter's taste. The passage of forms across these bright surfaces is of no more consequence than the passage of clouds across the sky at sunset. They are as insignificant as weather. A Hodgkin may be beautiful or seductive, there may seem to be a certain rightness about its colour or composition – but these are merely decorative consolations, because he is clearly an artist who has nothing meaningful to say about the world and those who live in it. His insistence that his is an art of Proustian recall is mere rhetoric. *Reality looks nothing like his pictures.*

What this criticism of the paintings fails to account for, in its narrow distinction between the abstract and the representational, is the fact that the paintings themselves test and seek to refute the very categories of thought which such an argument takes for granted. This is an art that sets its face against the notion that the abstract and the representational, the painterly mark *as* mark and the painterly mark as a means to mimetic fidelity, are diametrically opposed. Hodgkin is in many ways a very traditional painter. His art asks old questions. How do we apprehend the world? And how can the ways in which we apprehend it be communicated by a flat, painted image?

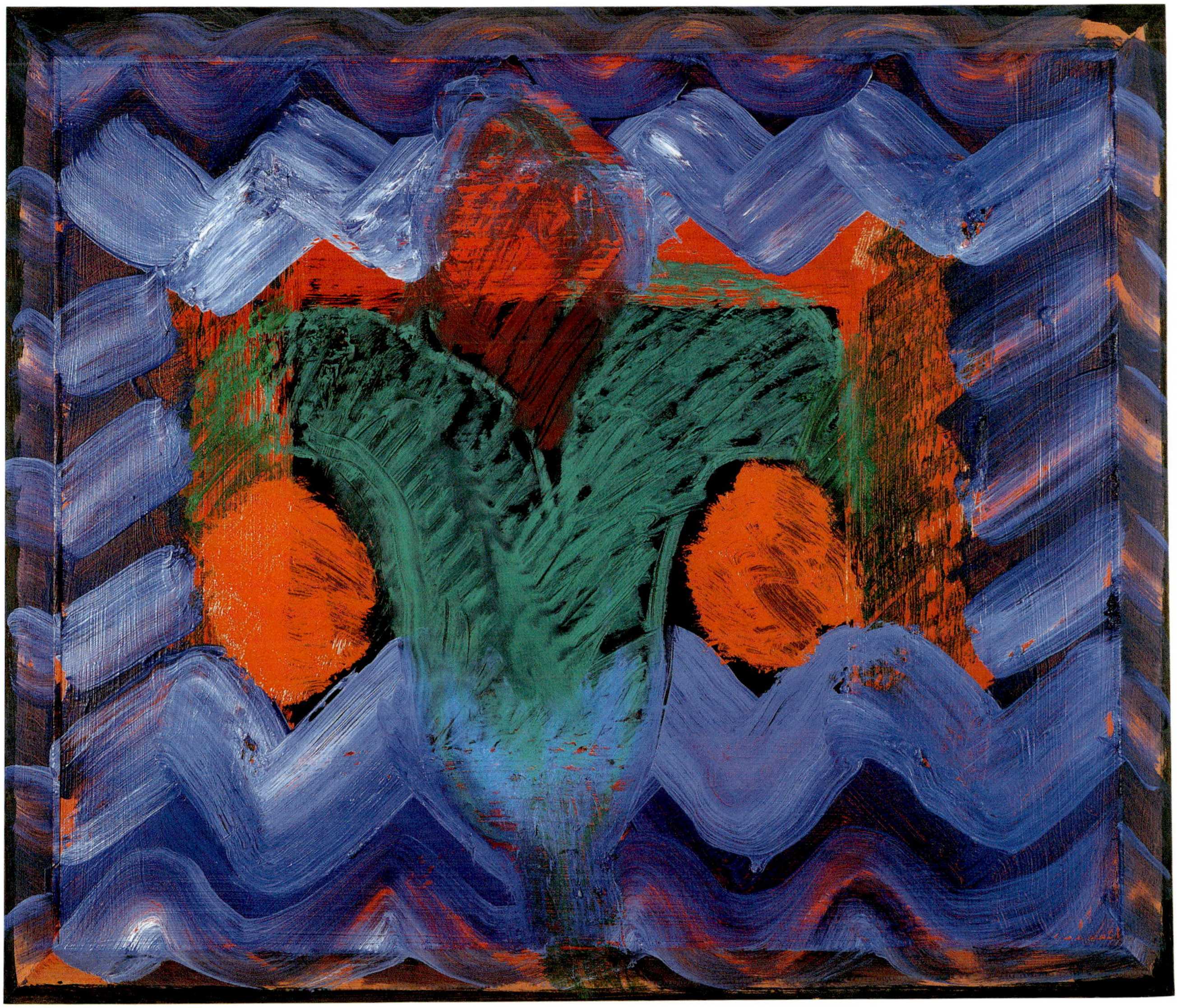

EGYPT
1983 – 84

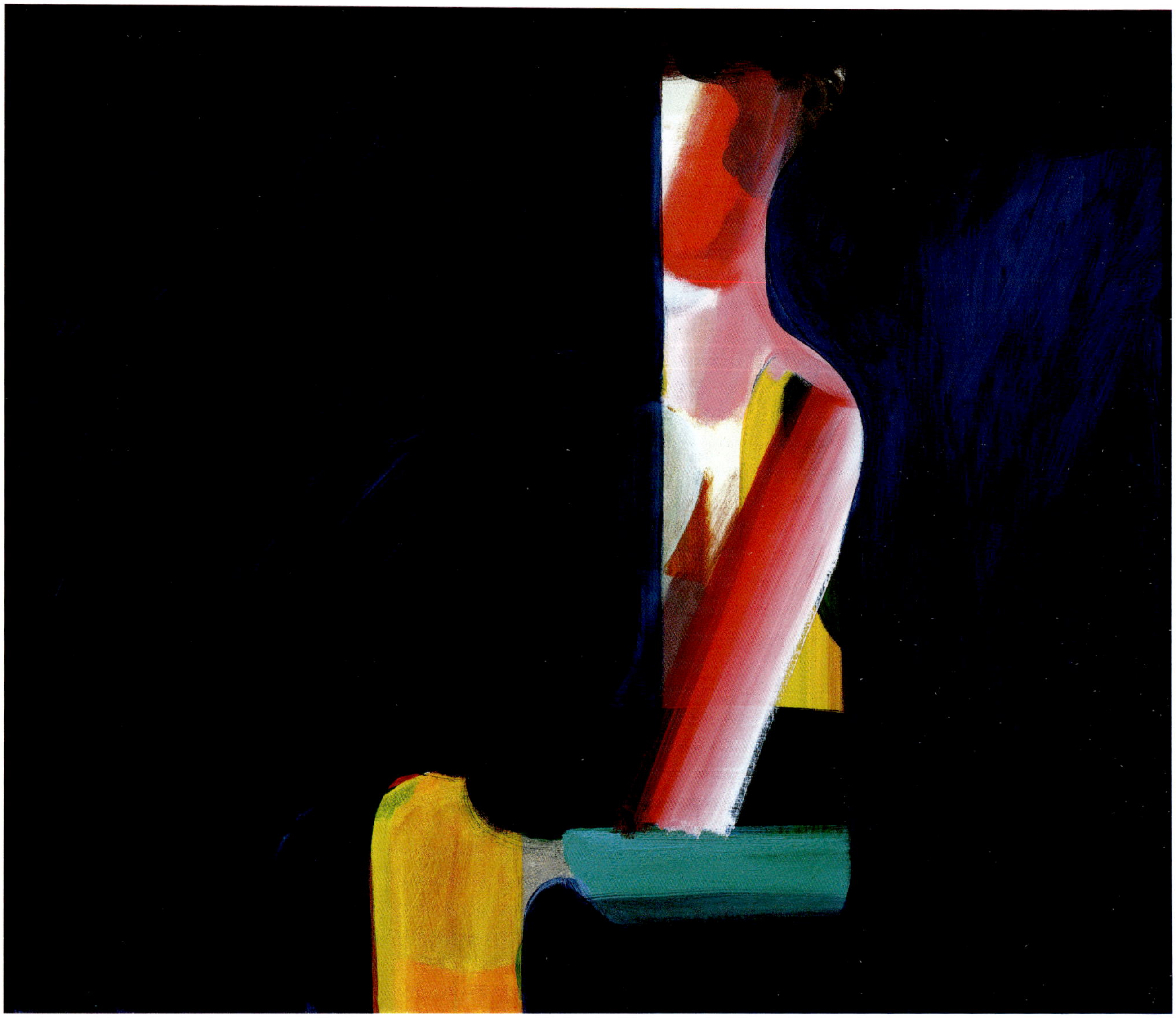

MRS K.
1966 – 67

No painter can exist outside the framework of his own times, and Hodgkin's art can be seen as just one of many responses to the greatest problem facing painters working in the modern period. This might be termed the crisis of representation in Western art. The twentieth century witnessed the breakdown of an age-old collusion between artist and audience, the tearing up of an ancient gentleman's agreement on what it is that a painted likeness of the world might, ideally, be agreed to look like.

The idea that art can achieve or at least should aim at perfect mimesis is deeply rooted. According to the Bible, we are said to be its first example ('And God said, Let us make man in our own image, after our own likeness'). The annals of Western art

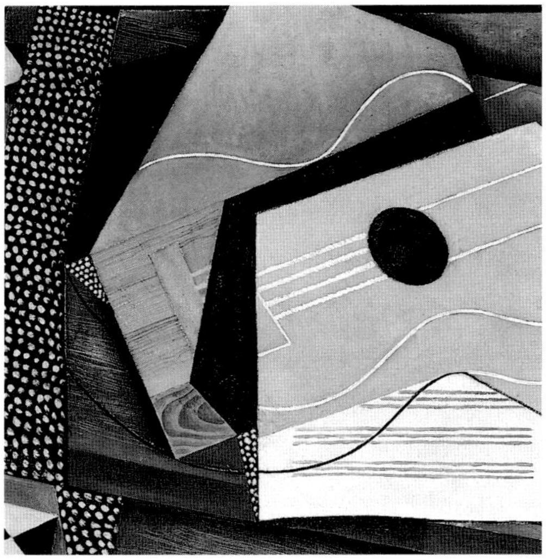

themselves commence with a myth of perfect resemblance, an originary fantasy of faultless mimesis: Pliny tells us that Zeuxis painted a vine with such deceptive lifelikeness that the birds flew down from the trees to eat from his image.

Real (rather than mythical) artists have always known that perfect correspondence between a painting and the reality that it records is an impossibility. But they have known it with a force and an anxiety, in the modern period, unparalleled in earlier times. Modern artists have had to respond to a world whose accelerated pace of change has made the gradual adjustment of pictorial style to new perceptions of reality impossible. The very texture of modern reality is characterized by flux, instability, uncertainty; and the quality of modern experience has been deeply affected by the knowledge that there is far more to know now about the way things are than any one person might ever hope to master. Science has revealed the world under extreme magnification, it has revealed deep space and has investigated the structure of matter, animate and inanimate, in ways that were undreamed of even a century ago.

This has inevitably had an enormous impact on artists' ideas of what realism could or should be, and has been at least partly responsible for the explosion of artistic methods and styles in the nineteenth and twentieth centuries. The Cubists, famously, did away with the fixed perspective of older forms of representational art, but it is quite possible to argue that their pictures are truer to the fractured, truant nature of human perception than those of earlier artists conventionally associated with a tradition of pictorial realism. And it is equally possible, to take a pair of radically differing examples, to make out a case for Paul Klee's wriggling doodles, frequently suggestive of thronged aquatic micro-organisms, as a form of realist art; or for Andy Warhol's numbed replications of silkscreened Campbell's Soup tin labels as a reflection on the extent to which modern reality is a human construction, the product of mass-production. It is no longer possible (if, indeed, it ever has been possible) to speak of anything resembling a single unified tradition of realism. There are only different, competing forms of realism, each expressing different conceptions of different corners of reality. In 1856, the French critic Edmond Duranty observed, correctly, that 'Realism is the opposite of a *school*. "Realist *school*" is a contradiction in terms: Realism means the frank and total expression of individuality; what it attacks is precisely convention and imitation–any kind of *school*'.[5]

The obscurity of much of Hodgkin's art is inseparable from the nature of its realism. The experience of reality which it seeks to communicate is difficult to grasp, erratic and shot through with inconsistencies. 'I want to get the sort of evasiveness of reality into my pictures', he once told David Sylvester. 'Looking at you now, I don't see Ingres' portrait of Monsieur Bertin, for example. Because I'm always seeing something else and

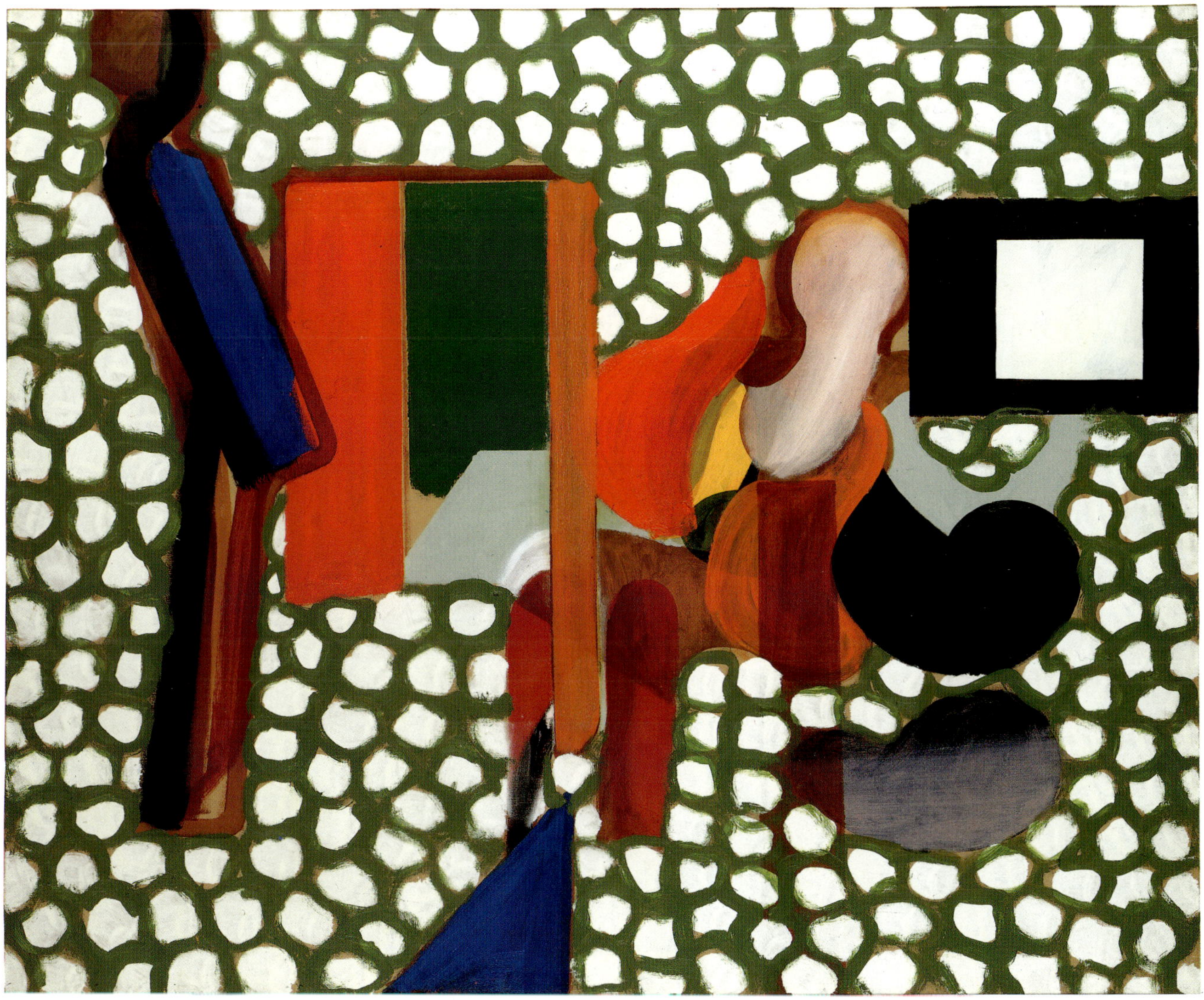

ANTHONY HILL AND GILLIAN WISE
1964 – 66

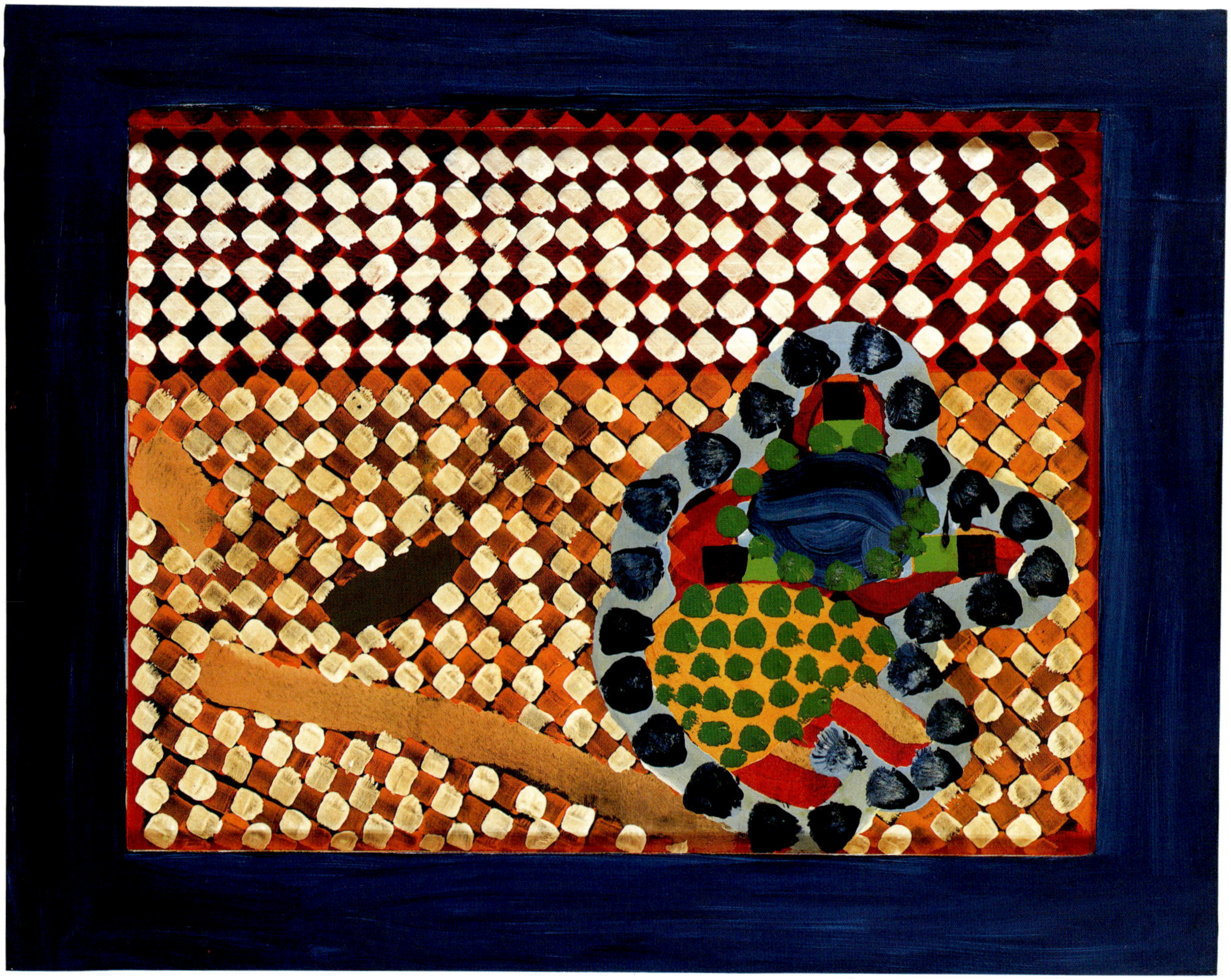

DICK AND BETSY SMITH
1971 – 74

something more. I might be looking past you or looking at the light falling on part of you or thinking of you. So it's my idea of you as well as what I see that's in my mind. But this kind of realism which depends also a lot on illusionism is, of course, evanescent, frail and difficult to establish.'[6]

The portraits in the oeuvre might be said to represent, in microcosm, the artist's odyssey, his quest for a pictorial language appropriate to his perceptions, the way he sees and feels the world. From early on, they announce that what people and things look like, seen through the monocular lens of traditional perspectival illusionism or of the camera, is less the concern of the paintings than how they remain imprinted on the mind as memories. *Mrs Acton in Delhi* (1967–71) is an abstract odalisque occupying a dream world of Matissean *luxe* and *volupté*, not an image of a person so much as the image of an *idea* of a person, indolent in exotic surroundings, as self-consciously decorative as
P. 24 the place she inhabits. *Mrs K.* (1966–67) is recalled, in paint, as a solitary ghost, a blur of flesh and bright candy-coloured clothes occluded by a blue void that could be sky or the wall of a room. The painting belongs within a tradition of female portraits on themes of aloneness and vulnerability which includes, notably, David's *Madame Récamier* and Degas's *Hélène Rouart in Her Father's Study* (a picture which Hodgkin has admired for the way it conveys 'the kind of glancing, slightly dematerialised quality that one does actually see in reality'[7]).

P. 27 *Anthony Hill and Gillian Wise* (1964–66) takes the disembodiment of the human figure further and departs so completely from the traditional form of the portrait that it ends up announcing the painter's apostasy from anything resembling traditional portraiture. Paint supplants and stands in completely for the subjects of its attention, and the result is a busy field of marks that suggests, in its jumpy collision of what could be anatomical fragments or details of dress on a spreading pattern of dots, a memory of people and a place so jumbled and distorted that it can only be remade as a pictorial chaos. It belongs to that group of works in which pictorial settings drown out or obliterate those who tenuously occupy them. But the obliteration, here, seems less claustrophobic than exuberant, the artist declaring his freedom to remake the world in paint as he likes.

Dick and Betsy Smith (1971–74) are reconfigured as unrecognizable marks lost in a paradise garden of painted forms, or tiles in a mosaic of oriental complexity. They are people recalled in a painting that attempts to create an equivalent, perhaps, for the sort of world that might please them. *Robyn Denny and Katherine Reid* (1975) are remade as partially glimpsed, stiff-limbed puppets overcome by the colliding patterns – pink and white blobs, diagonal bars of blue and cream, brown and pink stripes and flat mottled planes of green or black or aquamarine – in which the painting surrounds them. Such pictures mischievously suggest the way in which people, to the painter, can be less memorable than the circumstances in which they are encountered, the way in which essentials can be crowded out of the mind by incidentals. They conjure images, in their frantic collisions of form and pattern, of what John Updike has called (the phrase seems peculiarly well adapted to describe Hodgkin's paintings) the 'blooming, buzzing confusion'[8] of the world. P. 28

The kind of realism represented by such works is so divorced from older pictorial conventions of realism that it ends up amounting to a form of anti-realism. *Mr and Mrs Terence Conran* (1978–81), *Mr and Mrs Michael Chow* (1978–82) and *Keith and Kathy Sachs* (1988–91) are later additions to the family, pictures in which the mingling of painted form and painted gesture seems even more extravagantly detached from the camera's-eye view of the world. *The Spectator* (1984–87), which was briefly titled *Portrait of the Artist*, announces the absolute disengagement of art from attempted likeness. It is a self-portrait conceived as an index of the kinds of marks that the artist uses to paint his world rather than a picture of what he himself looks like: a soft gathering of bars and blobs and liquid veils of paint. What these pictures say is that the world cannot be objectively represented, because objectivity is a myth. They are resolutely personal, defiantly eccentric works of art which supplant mimesis with painted equivalences and metaphors. P. 2

The artist's perpetual adherence to the principle if not the act of collage shows his determination to stay true to the irregularities of perception. One of the most revealing pieces of prose Hodgkin has ever written about his work is not overtly on the subject of his own paintings. It takes the form of a journal that he kept while visiting David

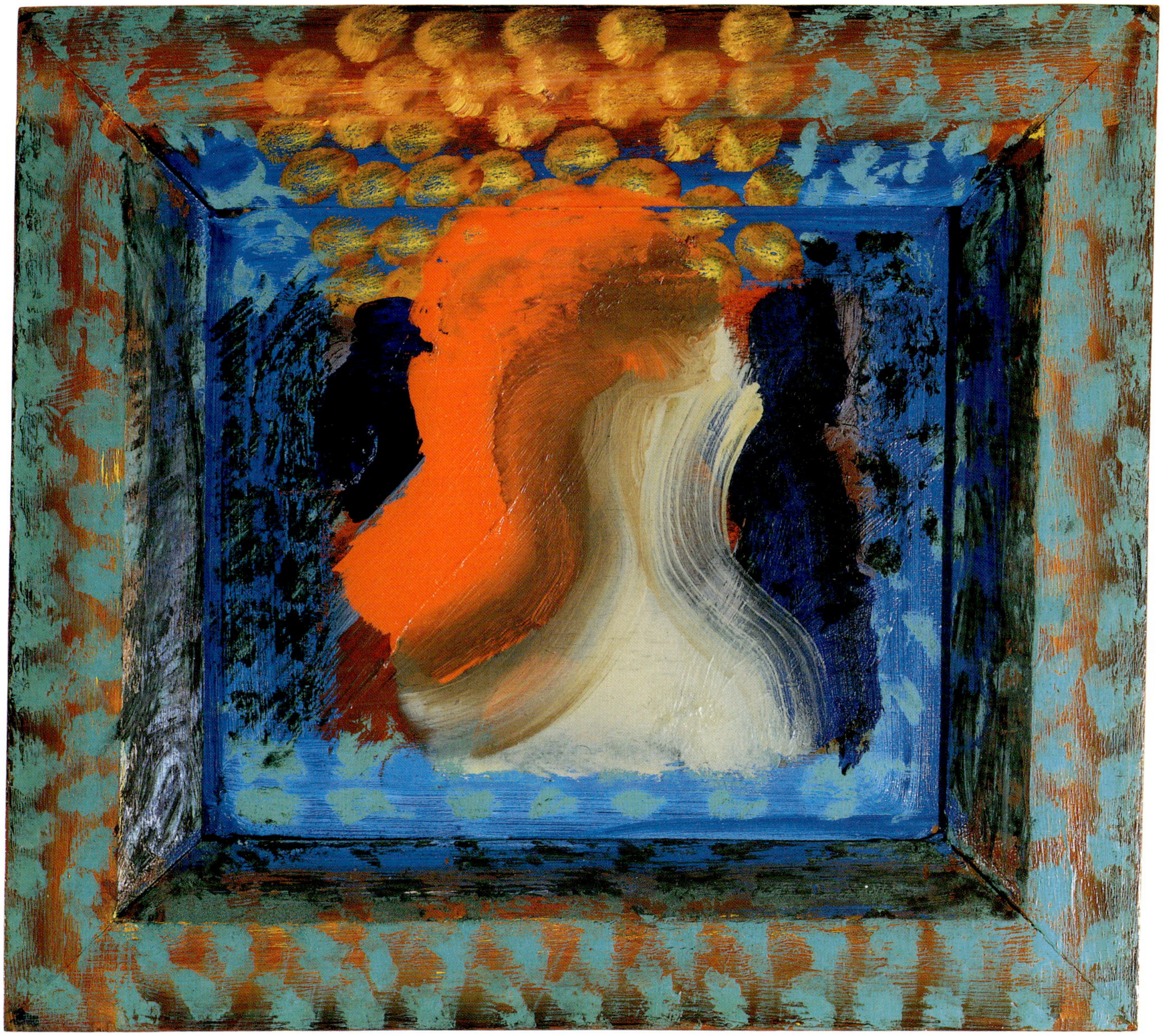

THE SPECTATOR
1984 – 87

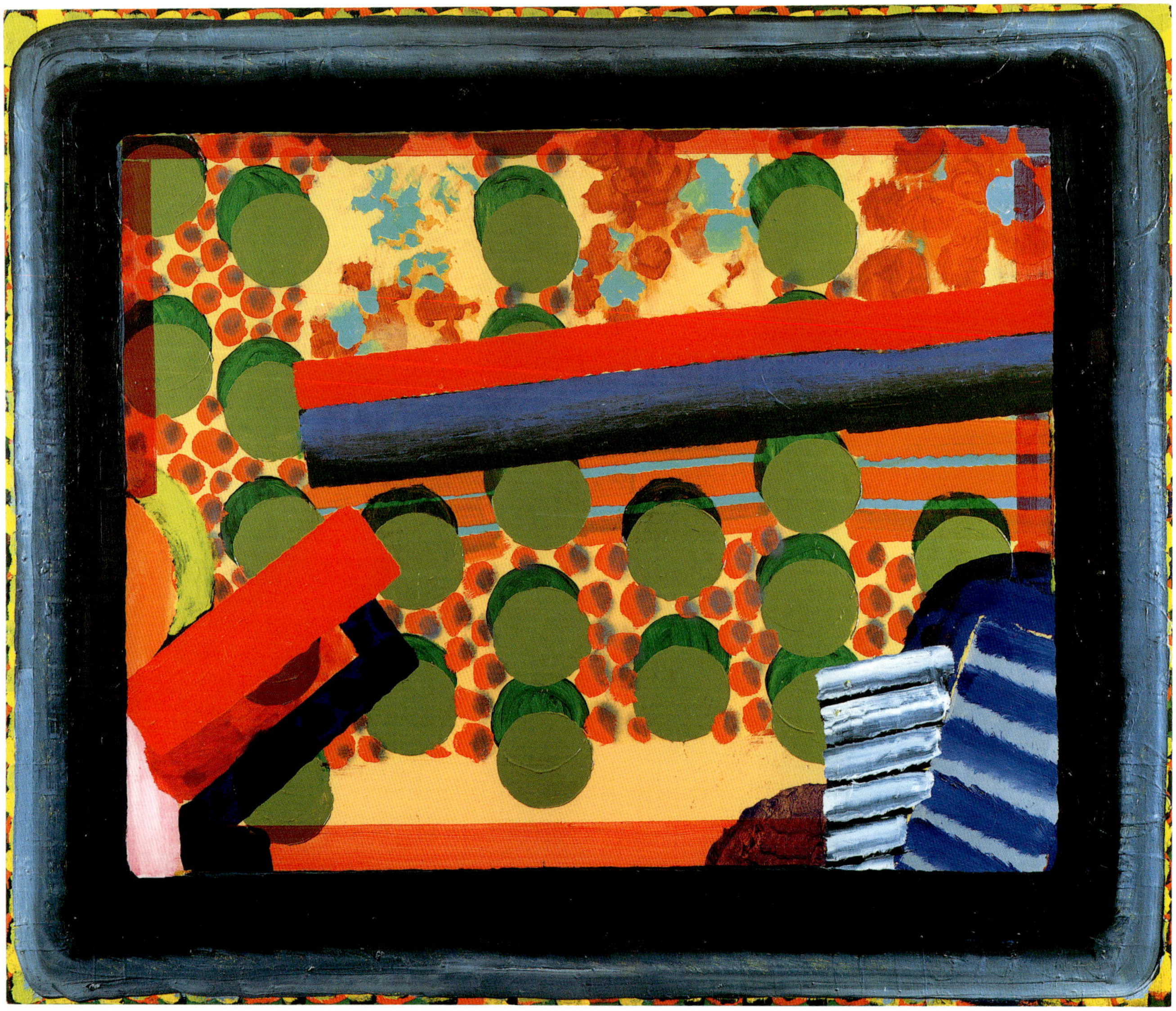

CAFETERIA AT THE GRAND PALAIS
1975

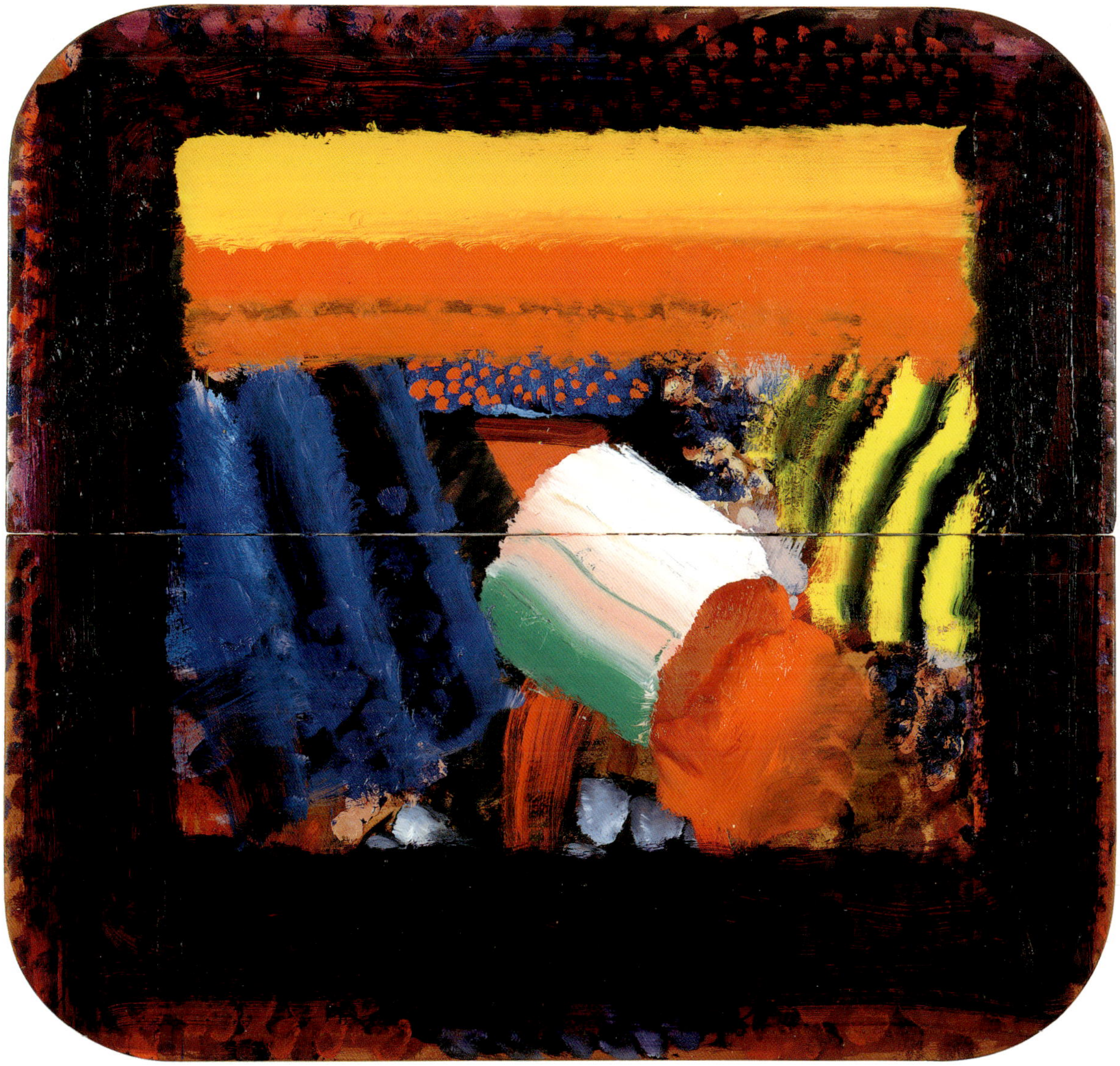

IN A CROWDED ROOM
1981 – 86

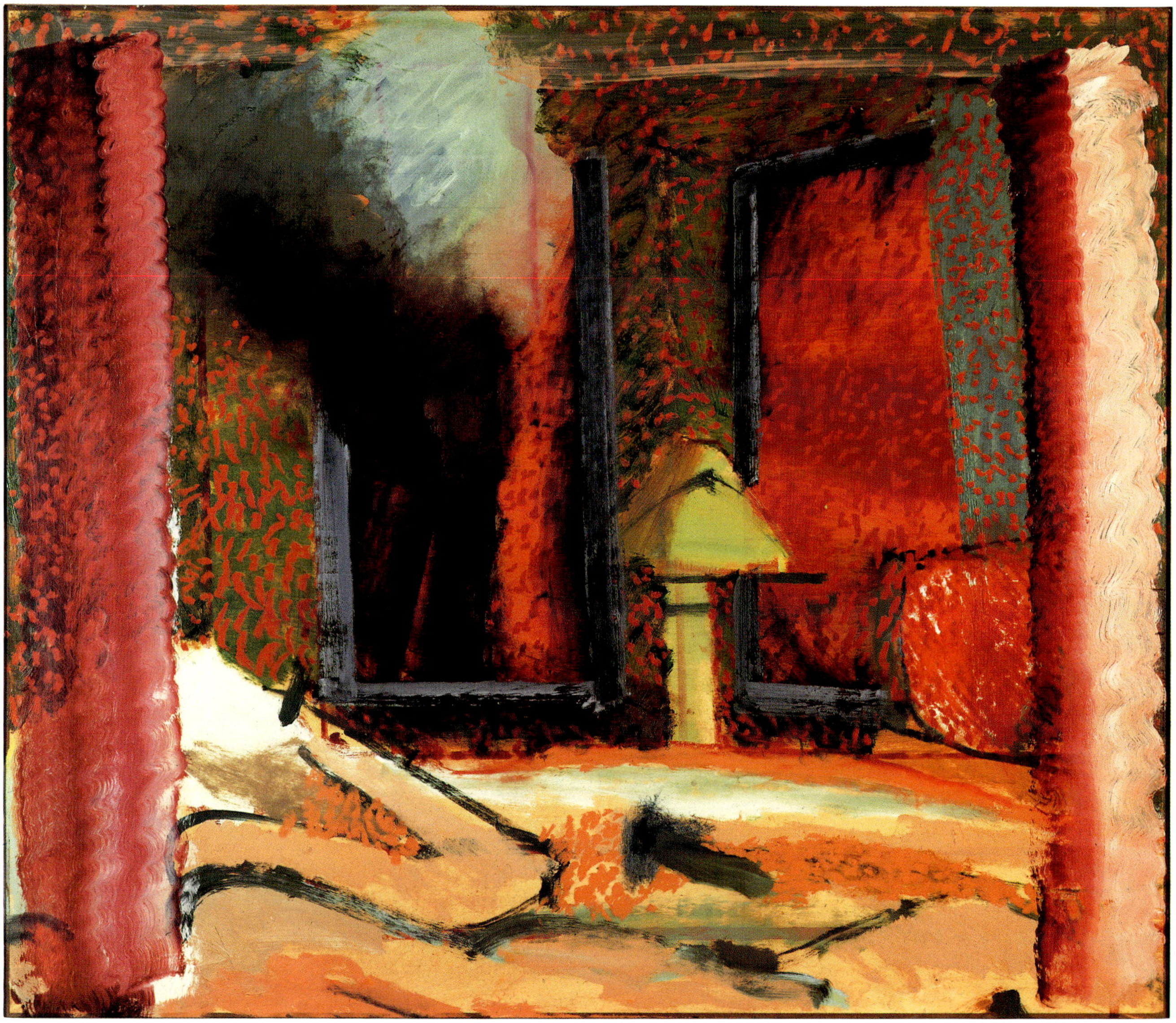

INTERIOR WITH FIGURES
1977 – 84

Hockney in Los Angeles in 1979, although it is not really a diary but, rather, a painter's account of his own epistemology, a description of how he sees the world. The following quotation is extremely partial and fragmented but does, nevertheless, convey a sense of the qualities of the entire text:

> One wall of the bathroom is glass. If you press the wrong switch a little garden beyond lights up. If you continue to press the wrong switch your aching hung-over face is illuminated by 100 watt bulbs surrounding the mirror. When you press the *right* switch everything is bathed in a lovely amber glow. Cold shower, all-bran for breakfast...
>
> DH (David Hockney) and I go for a drive around town, as romantic and artificial as I had hoped and then to his studio in the Versailles Furniture Co. A shop with white washed windows on to the street but with empty transoms through which you can see bits of buildings, the sky, part of a neon sign which says 'NUDE'. A smallish room with a balcony, a Matisse bergere, and many more or less finished paintings in a style which, among others, contains elements of Fauvism and Camden Town and is relentlessly bright in colour...
>
> Back, to sit where I am, beside the pool. The sun shines, there is a smell of vegetation, and from behind the shrubs you can hear the discreet sound of some necessary equipment, perhaps a heater for the pool which is kept at 90 degrees – PB (Peter Blake) sits drawing wearing a shirt of Police blue. Next to him is a red deck chair and a very small palm in a pot...[9]

The world is seen abruptly and discontinuously. Things evoke comparison with art, and works of art are looked at as curious objects. People may survive in the memory more or less vividly than what was around them, a red deck chair and a plant in a pot. Life is made up of sudden apparitions which coalesce into the memory of a place that is both erratic and visionary: the diary is a list of jumbled visual impressions which may eventually spawn their mingled surrogates in a painting.

Cafeteria at the Grand Palais (1975) departs from resemblance to get at another kind of truth – both to reconstruct the haphazardness of experience and, too, to mime the way in which reality is always something every individual makes up for him or herself, in his or her own particular way, as he or she goes along. Painting is no more artificial and arbitrary a construct of eye and mind than the very acts of seeing and remembering. P. 32

So the self-evident artifice of art, its habit of distorting and departing from some notional truth, becomes one of the ways in which it tries to be faithful to actual experience. *In a Crowded Room* (1981–86) looks nothing like a crowded room, but its real P. 33

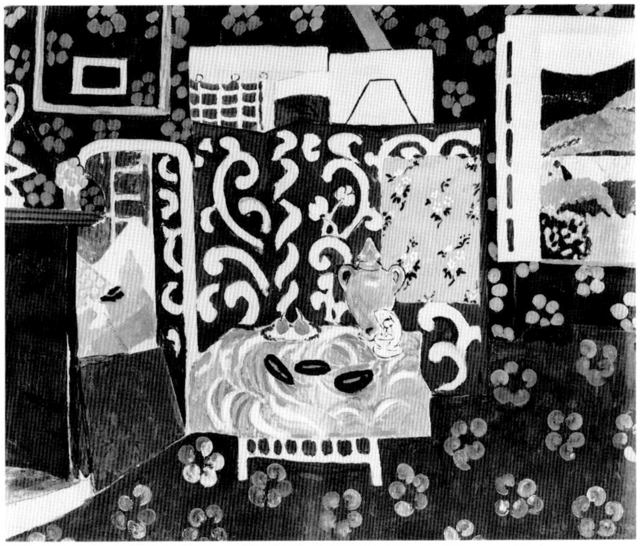

subject may be the crowded room of the mind, where competing impressions fight it out like the warring patterns that have run into one another on this dense and busy surface of flat painted wood. *Interior with Figures* (1977–84) is a painting where things have P. 34 remained, unusually, mimetically distinct. They have done so, however, only to declare their apparitional quality, their dreamy unlikeness (but life *is* dreamlike, the painting says) to anything that a camera might have recorded. A lampshade turns into a firework, a painting catches fire on the far wall, while a patch of shade, in the middle of the picture, has become as independent from what cast it (which is nowhere to be seen) as the truant shadow that Wendy had to sew back to the foot of Peter Pan.

The unreality of art is its way of talking about the real, and its peculiar distortions can speak of the peculiar emphases that the mind can place on things. The impossible spreading pattern of the wallpaper in Matisse's *Still Life with Aubergines*, the way the painter has turned the repeating pattern of a decorative background into a screen of blue blotches that covers everything, makes the picture an image – on one level – of how illogically but insistently a certain shape or a pattern can overwhelm the memory. Hodgkin paints with a similar freedom, and it may be what he owes most both to Matisse and, also, to Vuillard. In *Vuillard: His Life and Work*, Claude Roger Marx wrote a brilliant passage about the liberties which that painter took with facts which can, too, stand as a description of Hodgkin's own truthful departures from the truth:

> He incorporates the persons with the setting to such a degree that one gets the impression that by some law of mimetism, setting and person make only one. A dress appears to be composed of the same material as the wall-paper. A profile seems to be woven. Wall-paper to which Degas assigned so much importance...takes on hallucinatory powers. The background wedges into the foreground. Shadows are denser than solids. Objects have, nearly all of them, more weight and more movement than the living. The perspective seen through a doorway, the hanging lamp, the table laid, become spectacles, I might even say, events, more notable than a company of persons reduced to the rank of dummies little better than still-lifes.[10]

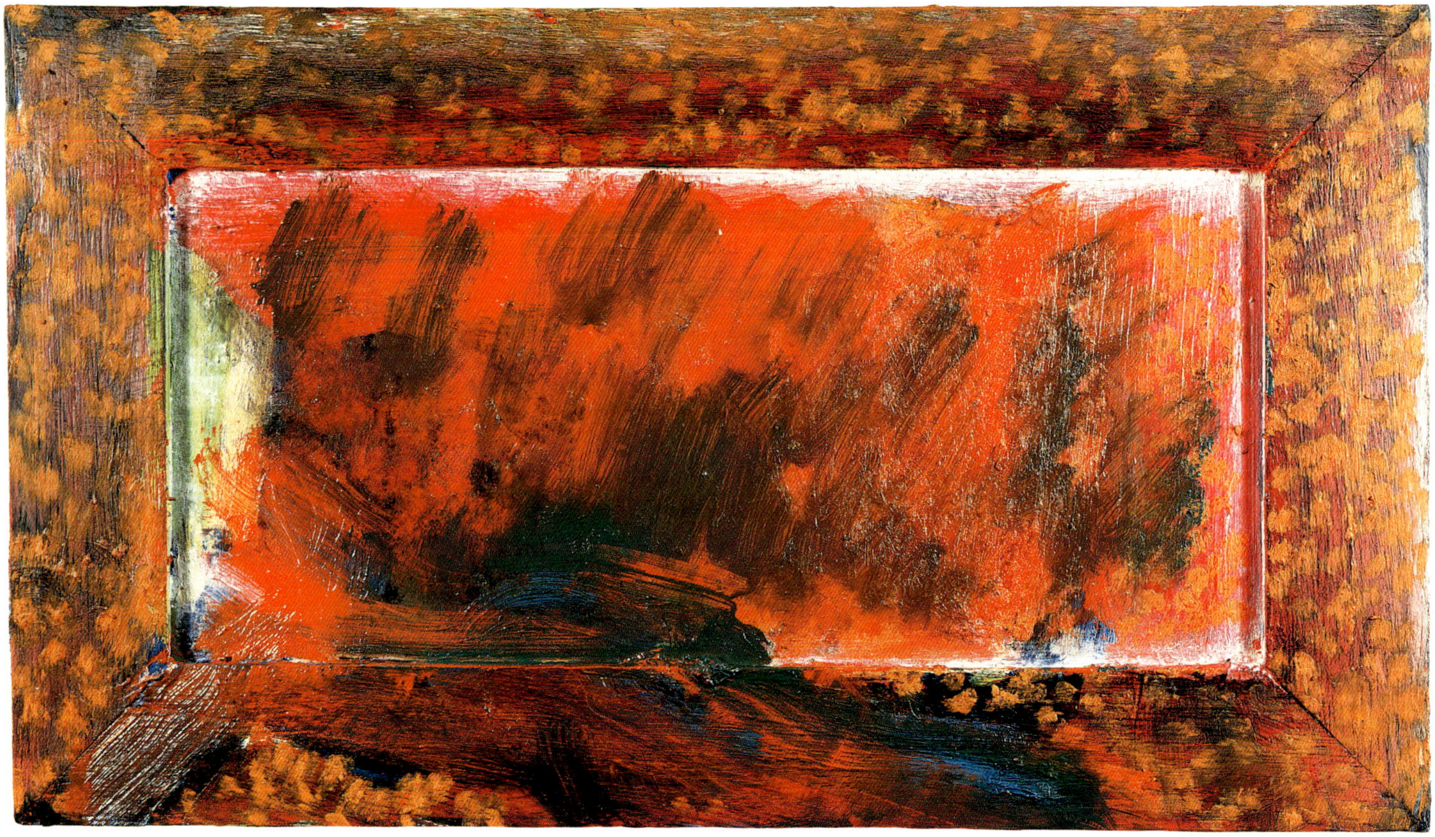

PASSION
1980 – 84

3
FEELINGS

Feelings complicate matters. There are moments in life when emotions exceed P. 41 perceptions, when the world inside takes precedence over the world outside. *Love Letter* (1984–88) is a blue oculus at the centre of which you see what could be a landscape prospect interrupted by a translucent, vertical shimmer of grey that could be a sunbeam breaking through cloud cover or a sudden squall. A flesh-coloured fragment in its foreground could be a detail of a human body, it could be the page of the title's 'letter', or it could be a glimpsed expanse of some sandy beach. But the picture invites such figurative interpretations while simultaneously declaring that they are beside the point. It tempts resolution, into an image of *this* person, in *this* place, but refuses to be easily resolved. It has the quality of a dream that cannot quite be remembered, the precise forms of which remain, tantalizingly, just below the surface of conscious recollection.

Hodgkin's pictures often carry this oneiric charge, often seem loaded with a significance that cannot be exactly articulated – as if what survives, after the transmutation of memory into art, is the intensity of a feeling without the incidental paraphernalia of its narration. *Love Letter*, like many of Hodgkin's paintings, has depth and something like perspectival recession. It can fairly easily be divided into foreground, middle ground and distance. It is full of suggestions of the play of light and shade and of almost meteorological effects. But what is missing is, precisely, the traditional object of such illusionism: the illusion itself. It is as if the language of figurative art has been directed away from its old object, the external world, and turned inwards.

Hodgkin does not set out to paint what the world looks like, but what it feels like. Perhaps it is more accurate to say that his pictures deliberately confuse those two things, and that on their territory vision and feeling, perception and emotion, meet. Hodgkin's apparent imprecision is, in reality, extremely precise. It enables him to picture the waywardness of all recollection, its multiple uncertainties.

One of the most common devices of Hodgkin's art is the image framed within the frame, as if seen through an open window or door (or keyhole). This has a very precise physical effect on the viewer, who responds as if choreographed, stepping close and peering into the picture as if looking into a miniature theatre. It also has a powerful determining effect on the psychology of the encounter between viewer and work of art: looking at a picture like *Love Letter* feels like looking at something private. It feels like looking surreptitiously, even a little furtively. It feels like looking *in on* something. There is a sense in which the paintings make children of those who look at them. They can awaken childhood memories of things seen or felt intensely but obliquely, experienced vividly but not entirely comprehended. Hodgkin's art constantly reincarnates the child's sense of the weirdness of the world.

Many of the paintings have the character of fragments of overheard conversation, suddenly chanced-upon moments of life, loaded with a significance and an urgency that eludes precise definition. Their storylessness is also a form of openness. They require a suspension of one kind of curiosity, the desire for narrative clarity. They require inventiveness on the part of the viewer, a degree of imaginative involvement without which the feelings they seek to invoke cannot come into being. They require that their vulnerability be met and answered by an equivalent vulnerability on the part of whoever engages with them. Their intimacy is demanding.

Jealousy (1977) is a poisonous little painting of a poisonous little emotion. Here is P. 42
a life gone terribly wrong condensed into a single, tiny image that defies analysis, or at least makes it inappropriate. Analyse the painting into its constituent parts, and you are left with nothing much in particular: a red blob silhouetted against a screen of green dots on a yellow ground, triply framed within bands of orange, dark brown and orange again. Analyse the painting into its constituent parts, and you are left with an

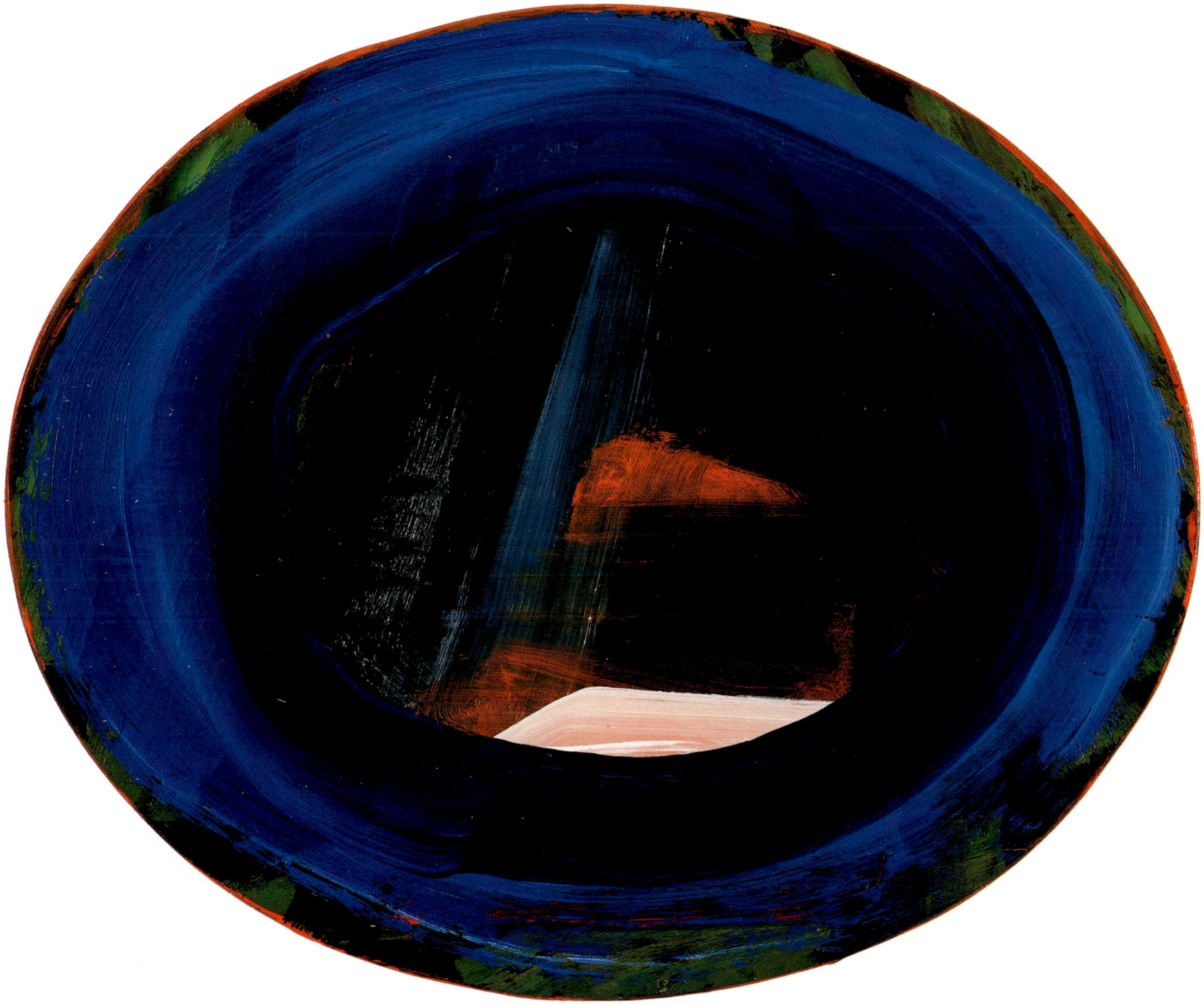

LOVE LETTER
1984 – 88

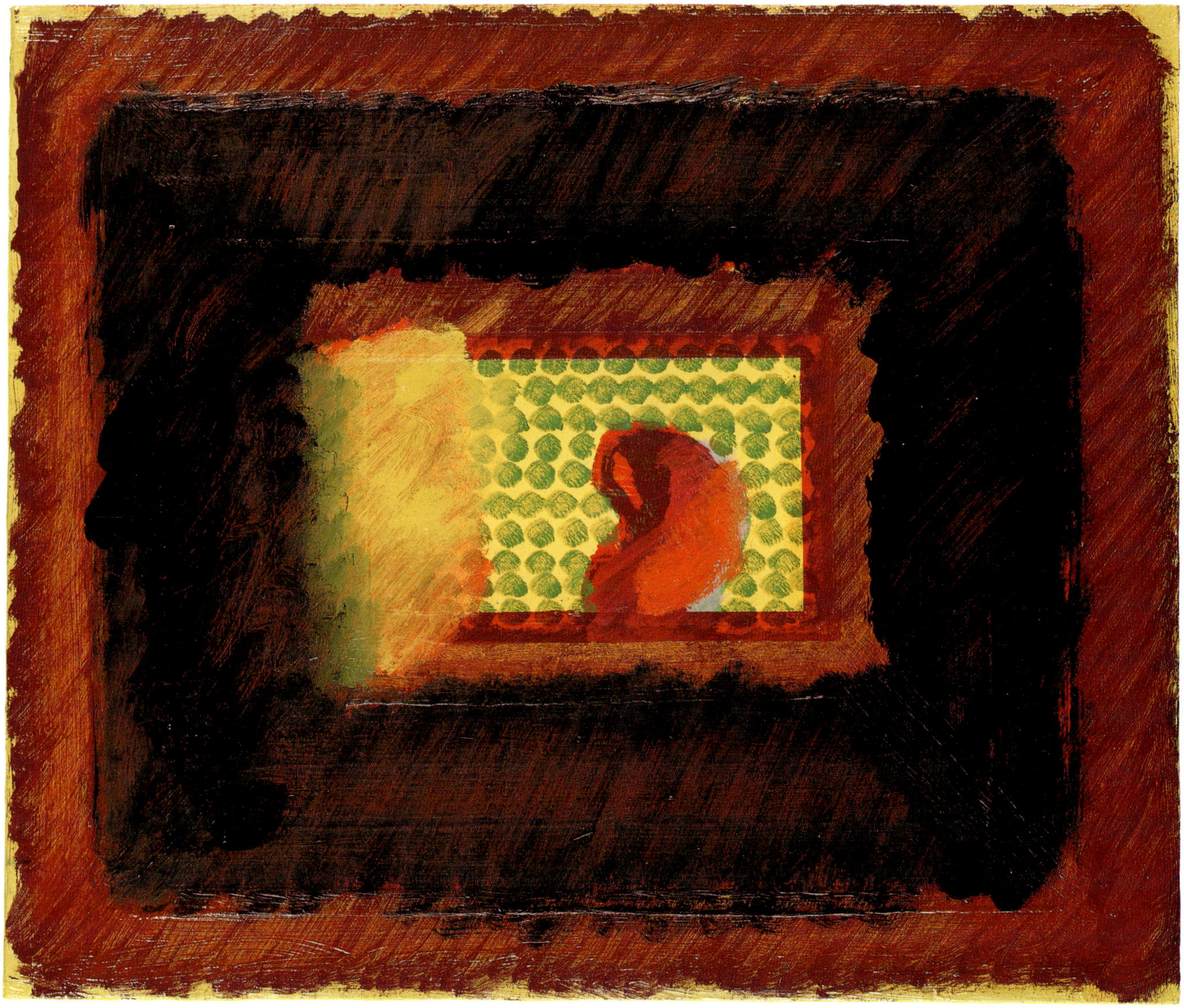

JEALOUSY
1977

abstraction. But enter *into* the painting, and it becomes something different. That blob becomes a human figure, huddled and closed in on itself, locked away in some private room of some private house. The picture is an image of the retentive, uncharitable nature of the emotion that is its subject. It is an image of jealousy as a negative form of self-possession, self-possession transmuted into self-pity; an image, too, of jealousy as an appalling form of loneliness.

This is painting that knows the power of omission. The feelings that are registered are only half-stated, are represented through hints and allusions, which means that the viewer has to meet them half-way and supply the rest from experience. They cannot be conclusively interpreted, but they would fail if it were otherwise. Susan Sontag once described interpretation as the revenge of the intellect upon art. These pictures are art's revenge upon the intellect. They do not make their appeal to the distant, barricaded mentality of the professional exegete. They ask for other forms of response.

P. 38 *Passion* (1980–84) is another awkward rebuke to interpretation, another of Hodgkin's demonstrations of the inadequacy of rigorous formal analysis to his art. It presents a field of unevenly hued red interrupted by patches of swiftly applied paint the colour of blood and framed by a quasi-decorative border of wonkily pointillist dabs. Its true subjects are clouding over and uncontrol and anarchy. It is an image of emotional disorder, phrased as the disordering of a pictorial scheme. A field of glowing colour, framed, is spoiled and invaded and messed up. Nearly all of the action of the painting is situated at its lower edge, where the dark, scribbled obliterations that intermittently cover the rest of the picture take it over and spill out. The picture is about what cannot be defined or contained or refined. It is perhaps Hodgkin's own, miniature answer to Delacroix's *Death of Sardanapalus*, that huge overflowing picture of orgy, murder and affray. *Passion* is about passion, and in this picture (as also in Delacroix's), feeling is displaced from the figure to the paint. It is paint itself, bloody, spilling, obliterating, that has been given the capacity to disturb and to evoke the disturbances of feeling.

Passion and *Jealousy* have the quality of apt metaphors. Their rightness is a rightness of resemblance rather than of exhaustive description. What they call for is not

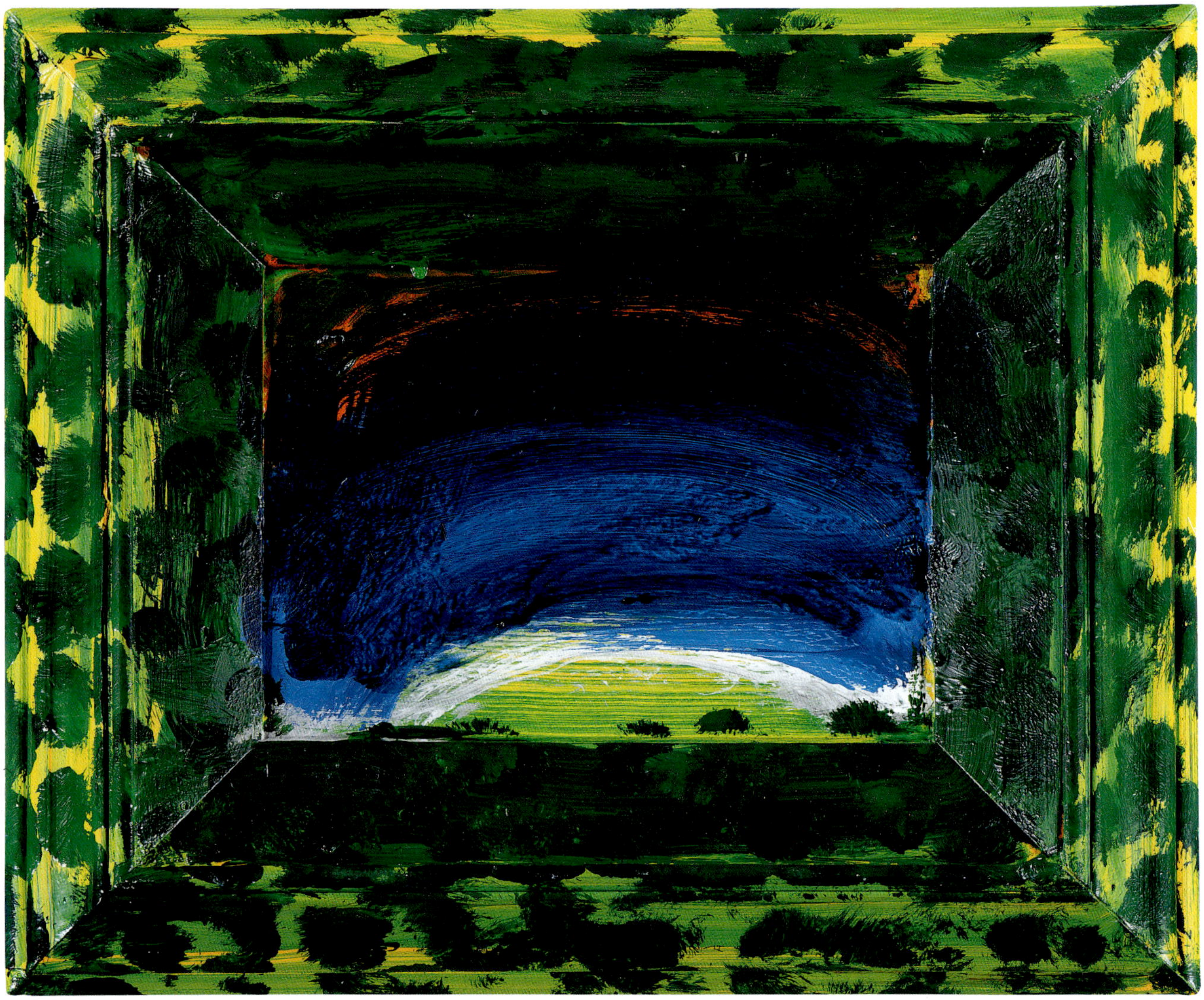

HOME
1988 – 91

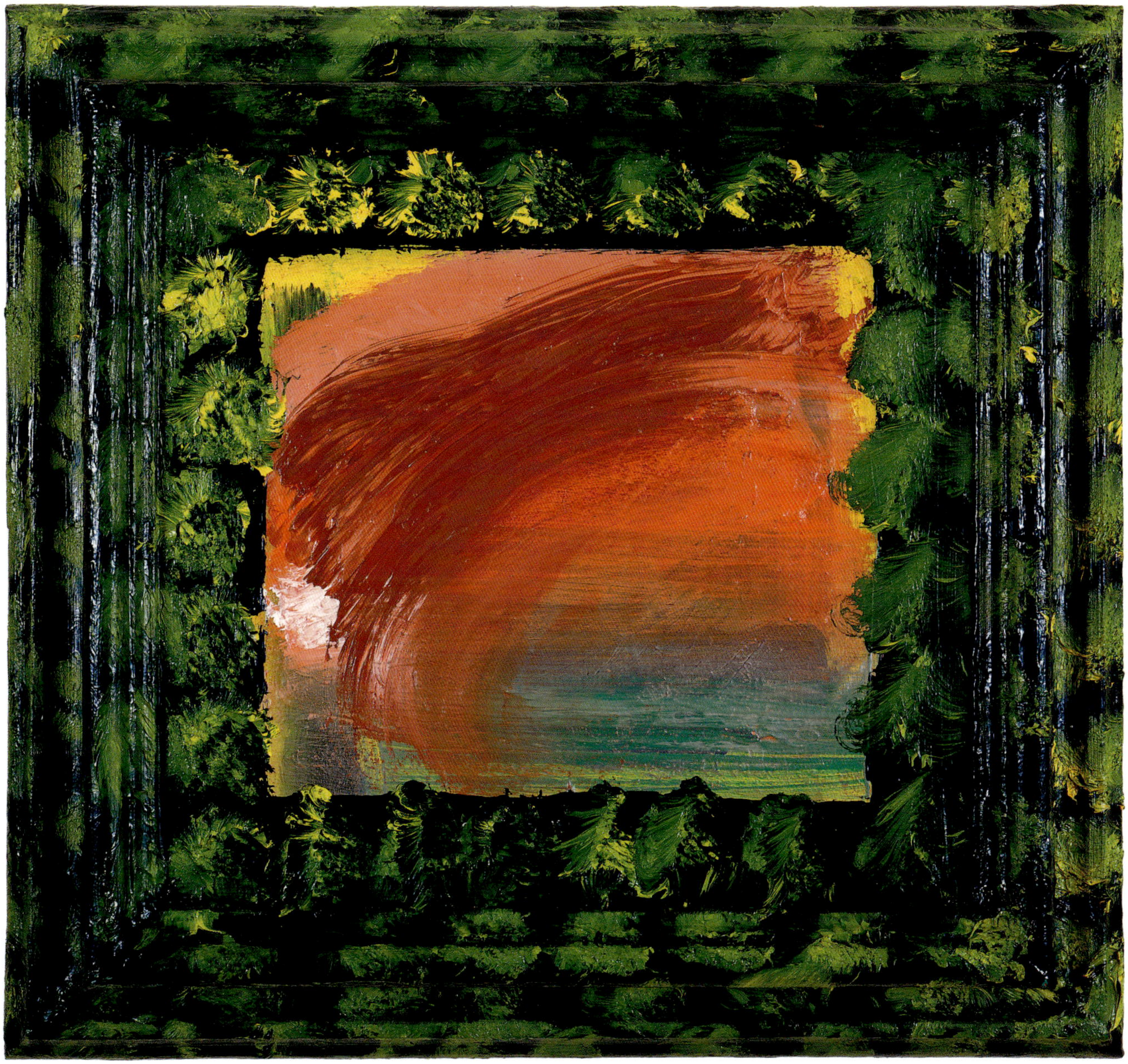

SMALL VIEW IN VENICE
1984 – 86

interpretation, but recognition, because their ambition is to look something like feelings that most people have known. Yet their titles also raise expectations which the images themselves defeat. *Jealousy* and *Passion* have a Seven Deadly Sins tone to them, suggesting the theologically condemnatory images of the Middle Ages. They invoke allegorical visions of man ensnared by the attributes of his vices, coiled round with serpents or burning in flames. But Hodgkin's art is not an art that seeks to pass judgment, and the titles of these two pictures are also joking and self-deprecatory, acknowledgments of the impossibility of absolutely encapsulating their themes.

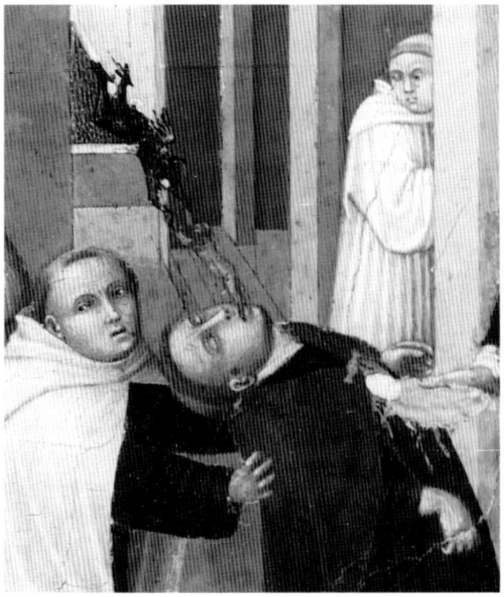

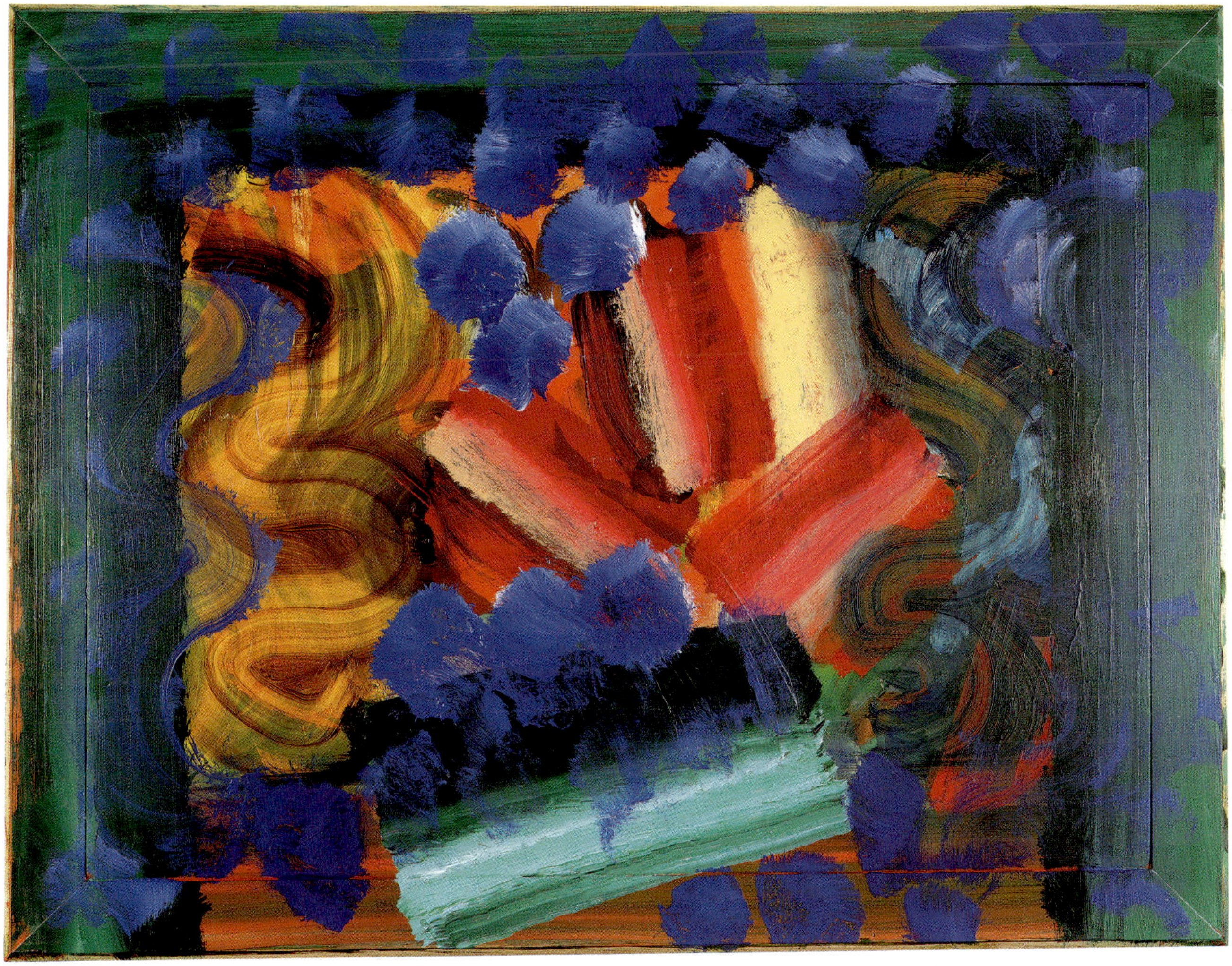

SAD FLOWERS
1979 – 85

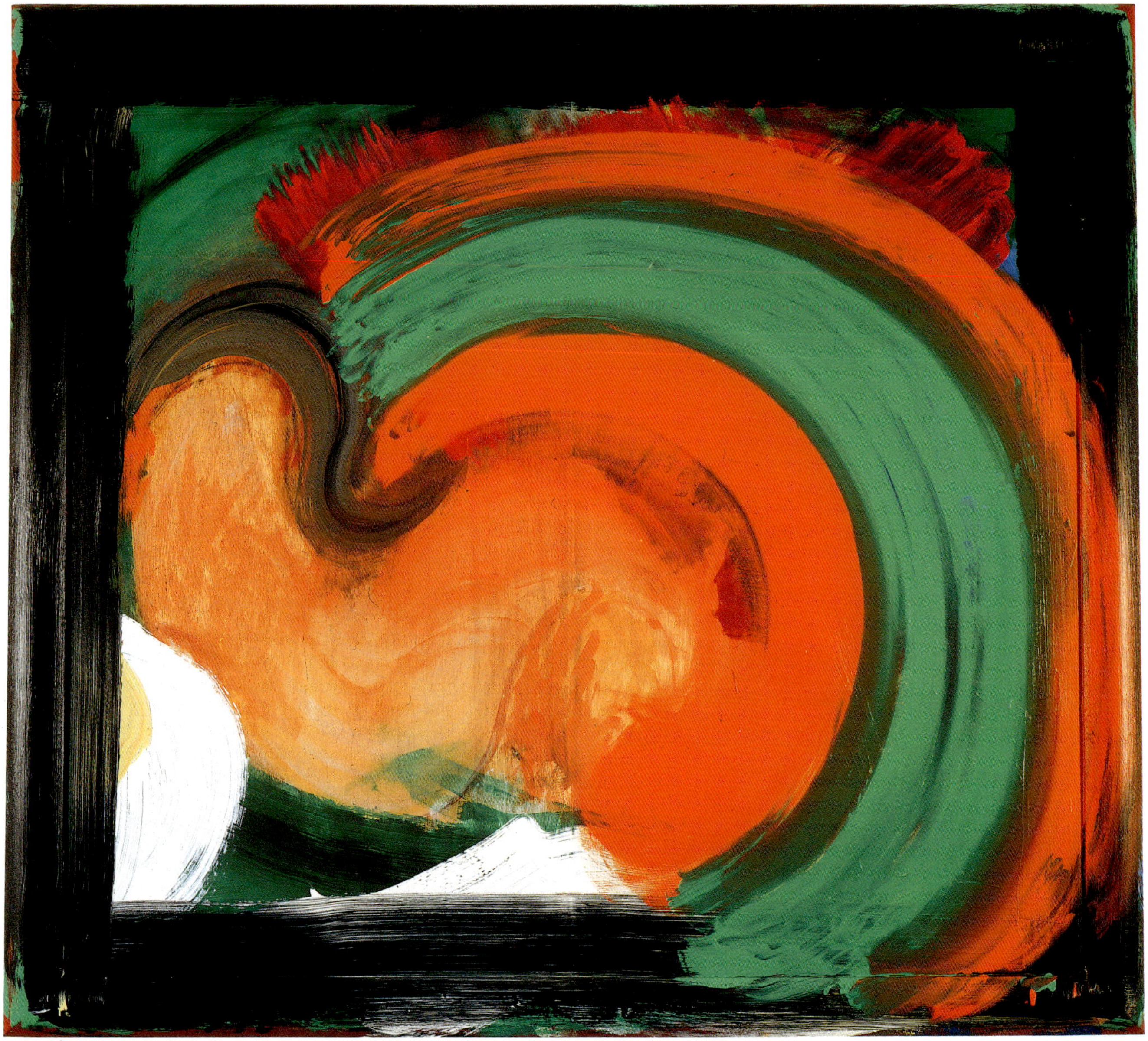

LOVERS
1984 – 92

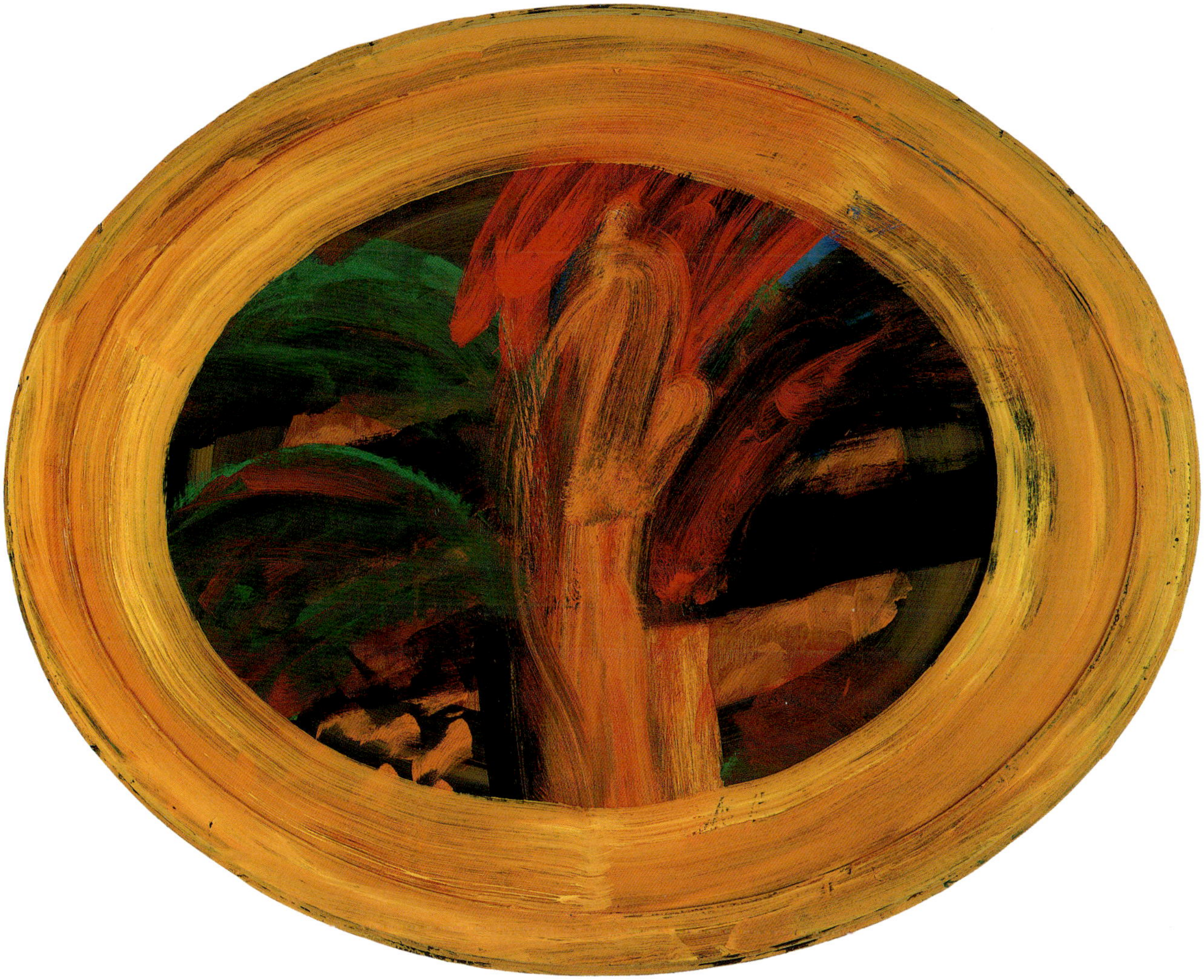

AFTERNOON FLOWERS
1989 – 95

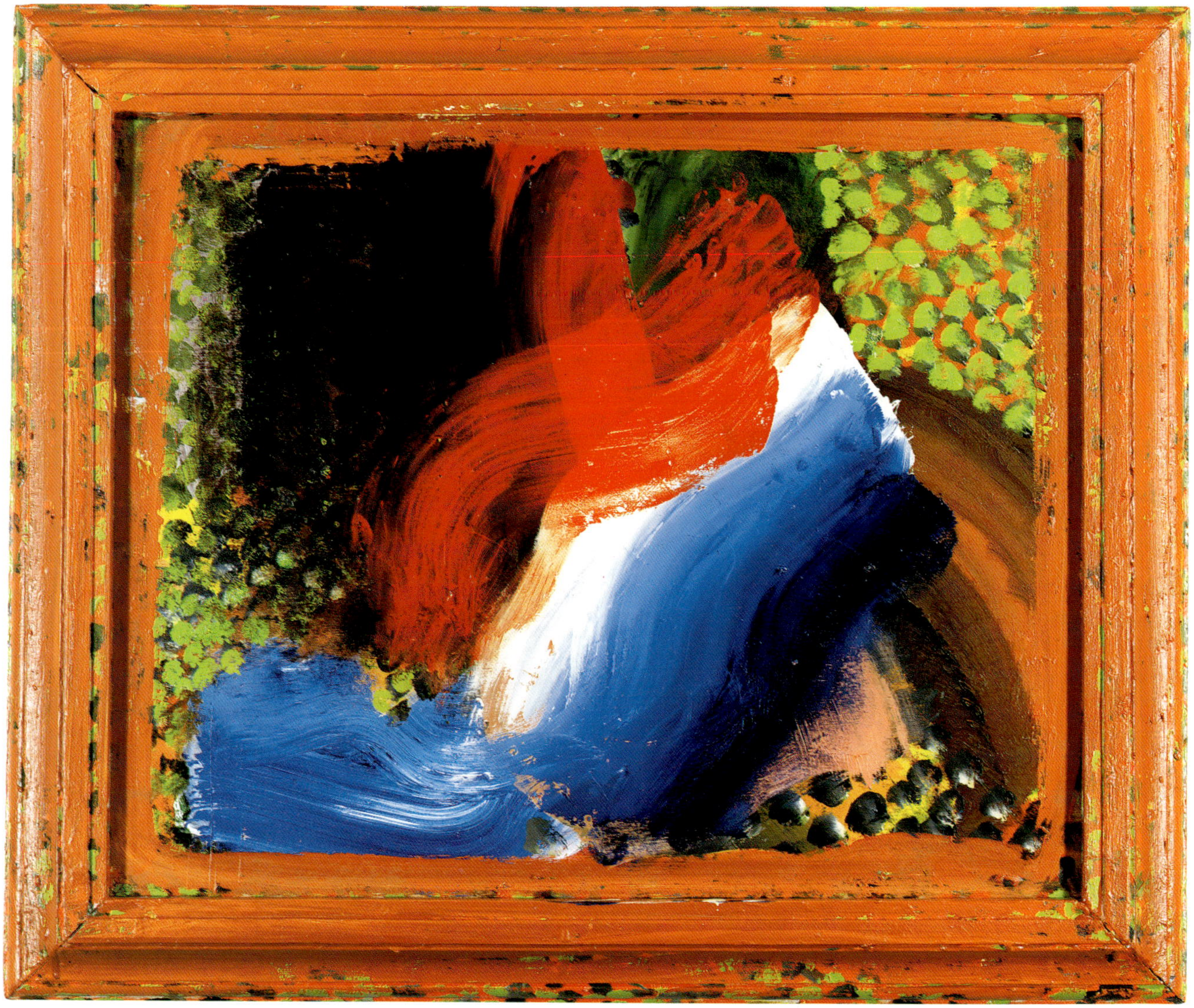

DISCARDED CLOTHES
1985 – 90

4
ABSENCE

Discarded Clothes (1985–90) is a picture about absence, a picture that talks of the human presence that it does not contain. It consists of swathes of bright paint that have the quality of abandoned garments, haphazardly piled, left by someone who has exited from the picture. The identity of the person remains concealed. The painting is about remembering somebody in their absence, almost fetishistically, through the details of things that they have left behind, things that once touched them or were part of them.

Pictures are themselves, metaphorically, discarded clothes. They are objects that are traces of the painter's sensibility, things left behind by him but which speak only partially of his vivid physical and mental and emotional life. An artist cannot put himself or anyone else into his painting. All he can put into his painting is paint. Every picture is, in the most primitive and powerful sense, about the absence of the person who painted it. It is about the fact that the hands which once formed this object are no longer there, retouching, adding, modifying. It is about its own independence from its maker.

Discarded Clothes acknowledges the inevitable imperfection of every representational picture: its inability to be more than a painted surrogate for a fraction of the life of the person who brought it into being. But defeat can also contain the possibility of success, because these ambiguities and deliberate omissions are the source of another kind of truth to reality. They suggest that our definitions of ourselves, the identities we invent to negotiate a way through life, are as imperfect and partial a reflection of the truth as paintings. They suggest that our identities are also works of art. Hodgkin's bright puzzles have the character of an insinuation. They remind us how little any of us know, about ourselves or others.

Red Bermudas (1978–80) finds comedy in the patchiness of human memory, and takes a wry pleasure in its own ludicrousness as a 'representational picture of an emotional situation'. The red bermuda shorts of the title have been transformed into a pair of bold, columnar swipes of red paint at the bottom of the picture. An article of clothing has become a painter's vivid cipher for a thing. The picture confronts the oddity of certain memories, the way the mind often recalls moments in life by distilling what really happened – what someone said, what they looked like, what it seemed to mean at the time – to apparently illogical details. The memory of a dead friend might merge, for no apparent reason, with the memory of the way a certain building cast a certain shadow on the day he died. The memory of falling in love with someone might be accompanied by the memory of a cigarette stubbed out suddenly in an ashtray. The strangeness of the image, the insistent blatancy of those red bars of paint in this enigmatic landscape of pictorial artifice, with its hints of potential forestry and sea, is both arresting and witty. *Red Bermudas* is a comical epiphany, a painting about the absurd, mysterious character of recollection.

The attempt to give painted objects the texture of mental phenomena frequently results in compelling weirdness. The appearance of *Day Dreams* (1977–80) runs counter P. 54 to its title. It is a painting of dreaminess turning day into night. The image is framed (perhaps with a sidelong glance at Matisse's *French Window at Collioure*) as a view through a window, but the view has been sabotaged by fantasy, perceptible facts dissolved into a chaos of nocturnal forms, smudged, blurred, layered on a field of spreading darkness. *Still Life in a Restaurant* (1976–79) defines recollection as a dredging up P. 55 of remembered fragments from the black pool of the past. Fudged patterns, hazy memories (of the patterns of a tablecloth, perhaps, or other details of interior decor, but only barely readable as such) struggle into visibility while darkness encroaches on all sides.

In a French Restaurant (1977–79) plays ironically on the contrast between the P. 56 hesitant evocativeness of Hodgkin's own language and the unequivocal, semaphoric

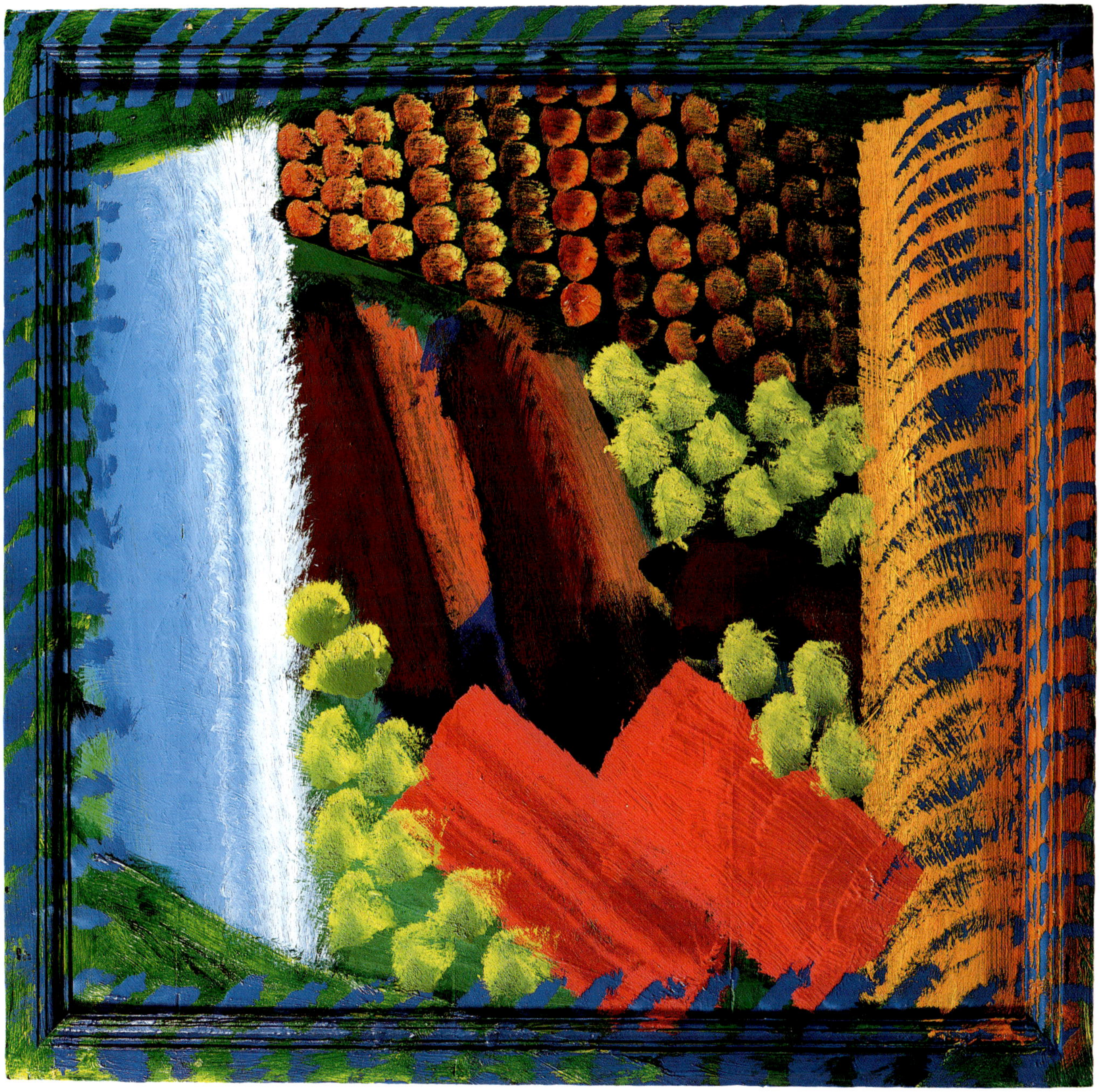

RED BERMUDAS
1978 – 80

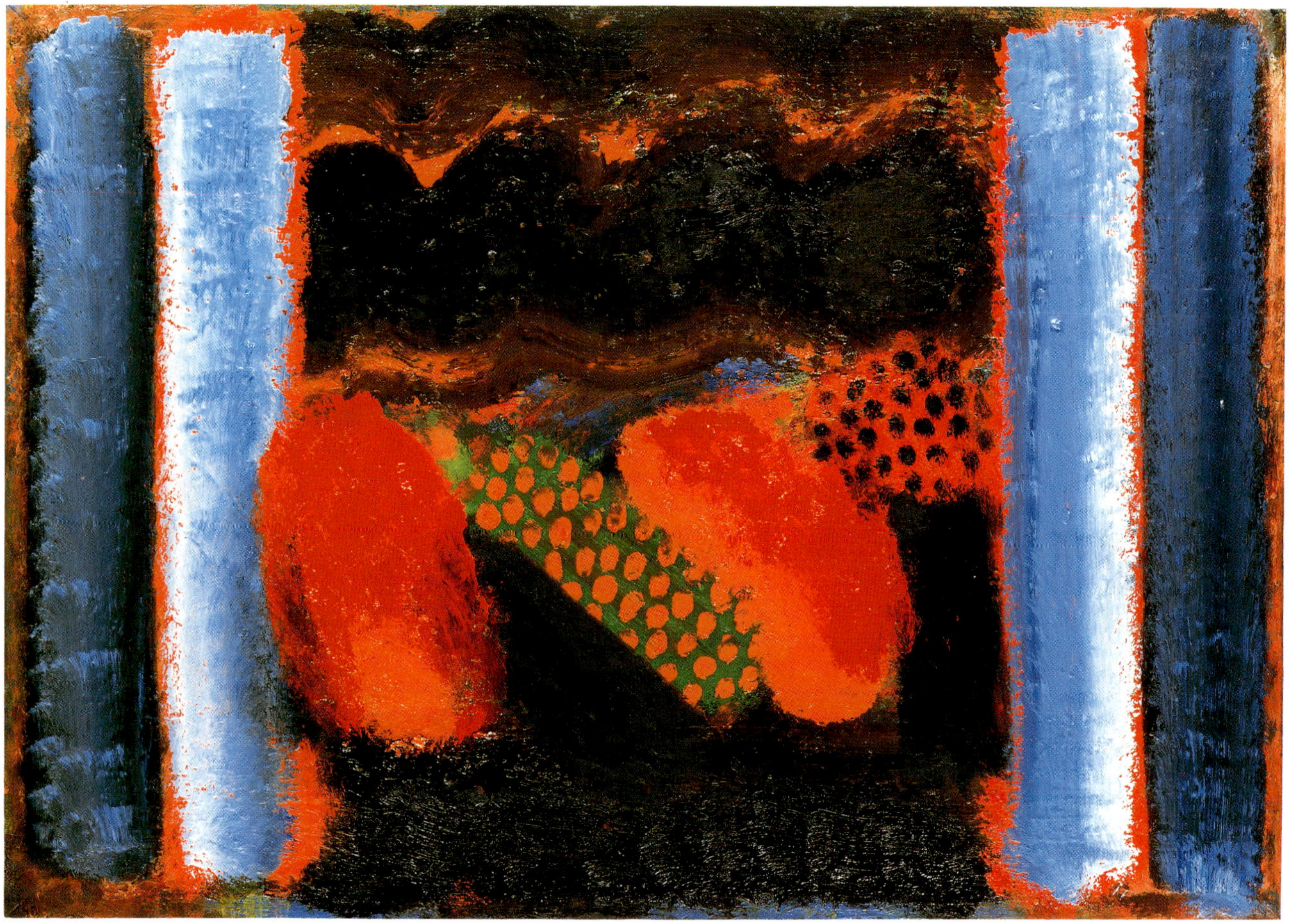

DAY DREAMS
1977 – 80

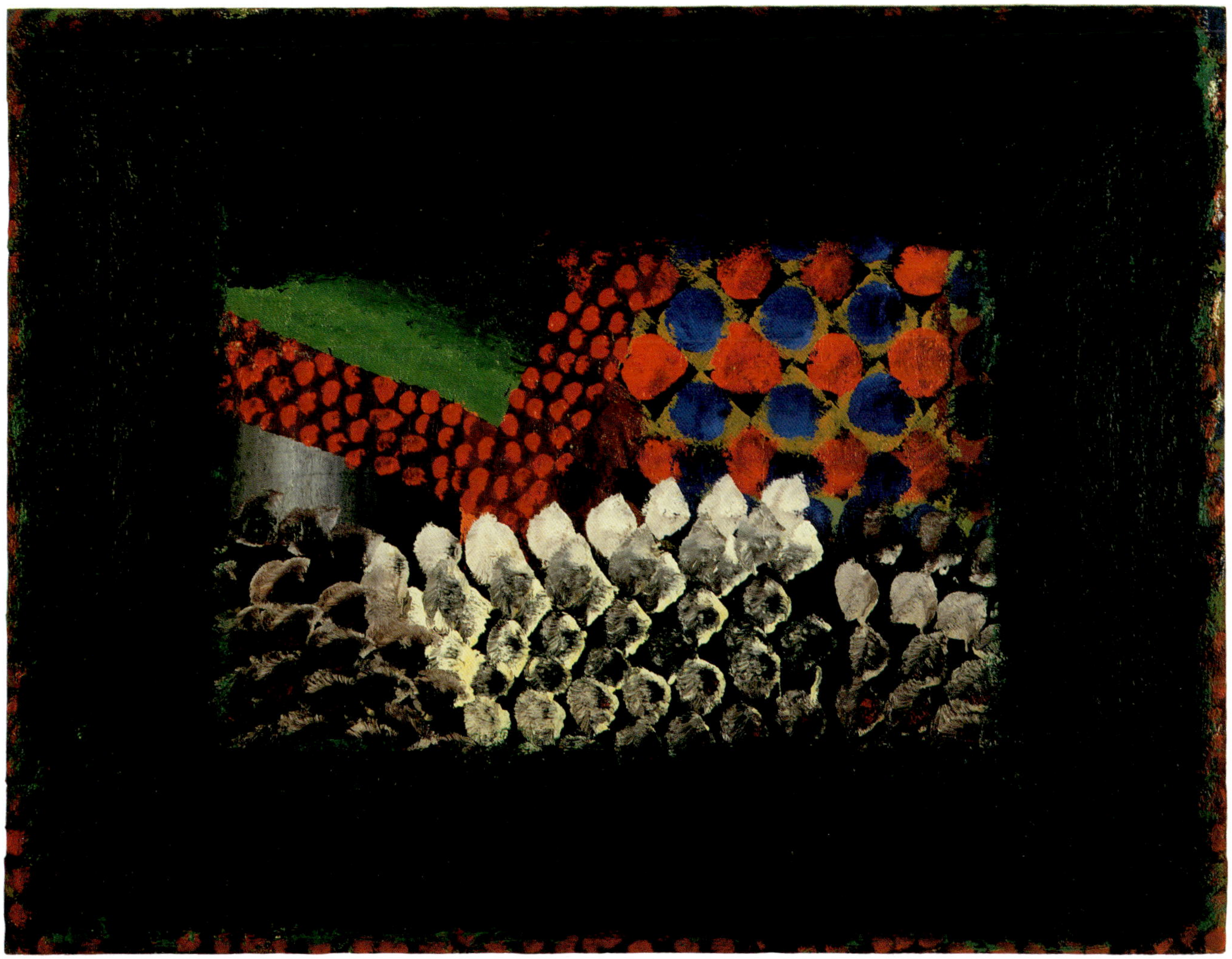

STILL LIFE IN A RESTAURANT
1976 – 79

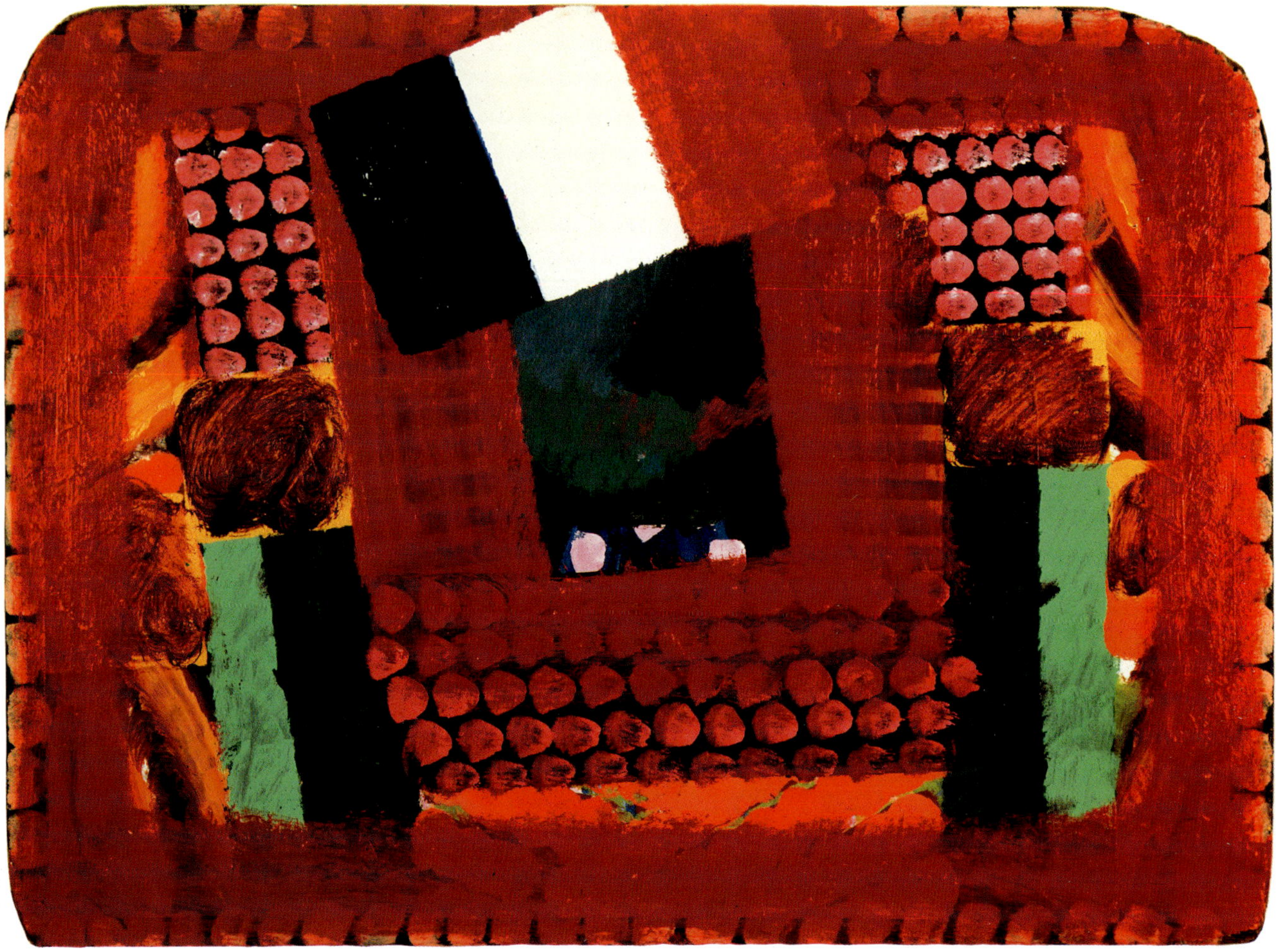

IN A FRENCH RESTAURANT
1977 – 79

clarity of conventional visual signs – in this case the French flag, painted into the top edge of the picture with deliberate, banal straightforwardness. It looks like a postage stamp stuck, imperfectly, on to a palimpsest, a curious intrusion into a painting whose puzzling depths, spatial ambiguities and vaguely figurative gloamings suggest a world of private emotional complexity charged with private feeling. But the flag may be there to make a point. It signals the inadequacy of simple visual conventions as representations of the real and stands in for the kinds of oversimplification which the painting itself refuses to countenance. Flags pretend to represent whole nations, but the picture serves

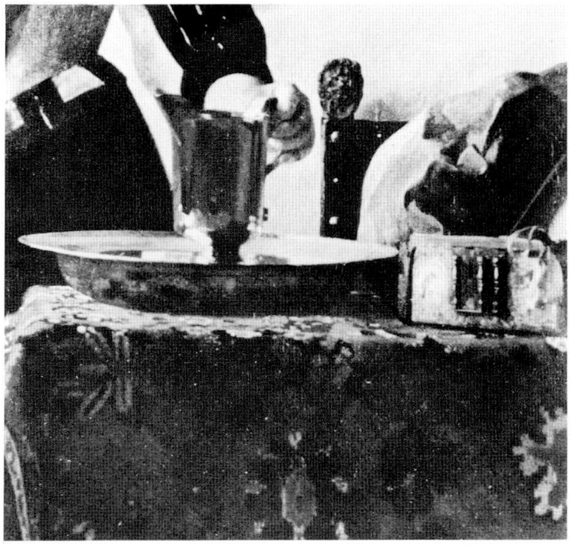

as a reminder that all of France cannot be reduced to a tricoloured piece of cloth. It is hard enough, the painting insists, to paint a single moment in a single life.

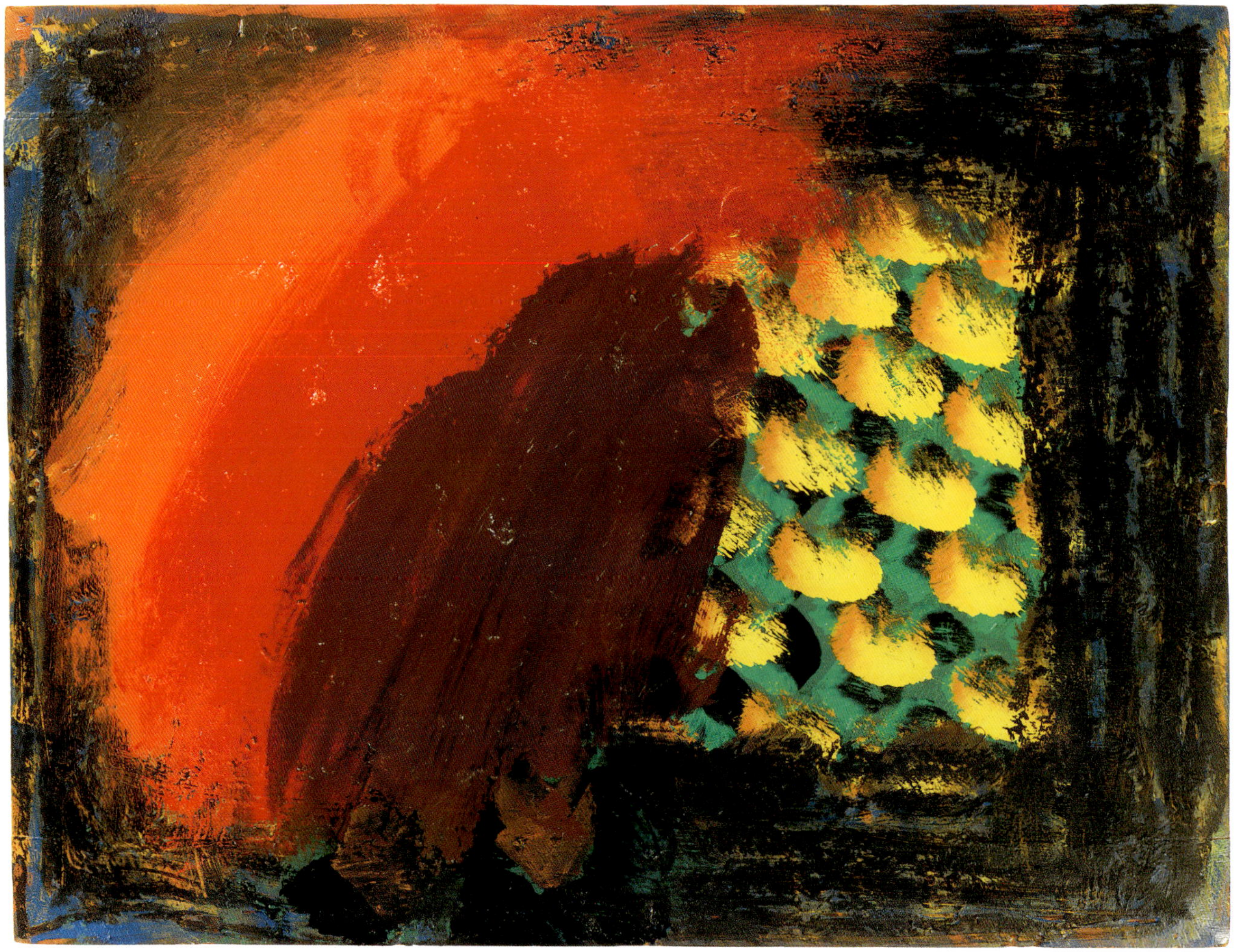

KATHY AT THE RITZ
1991 – 93

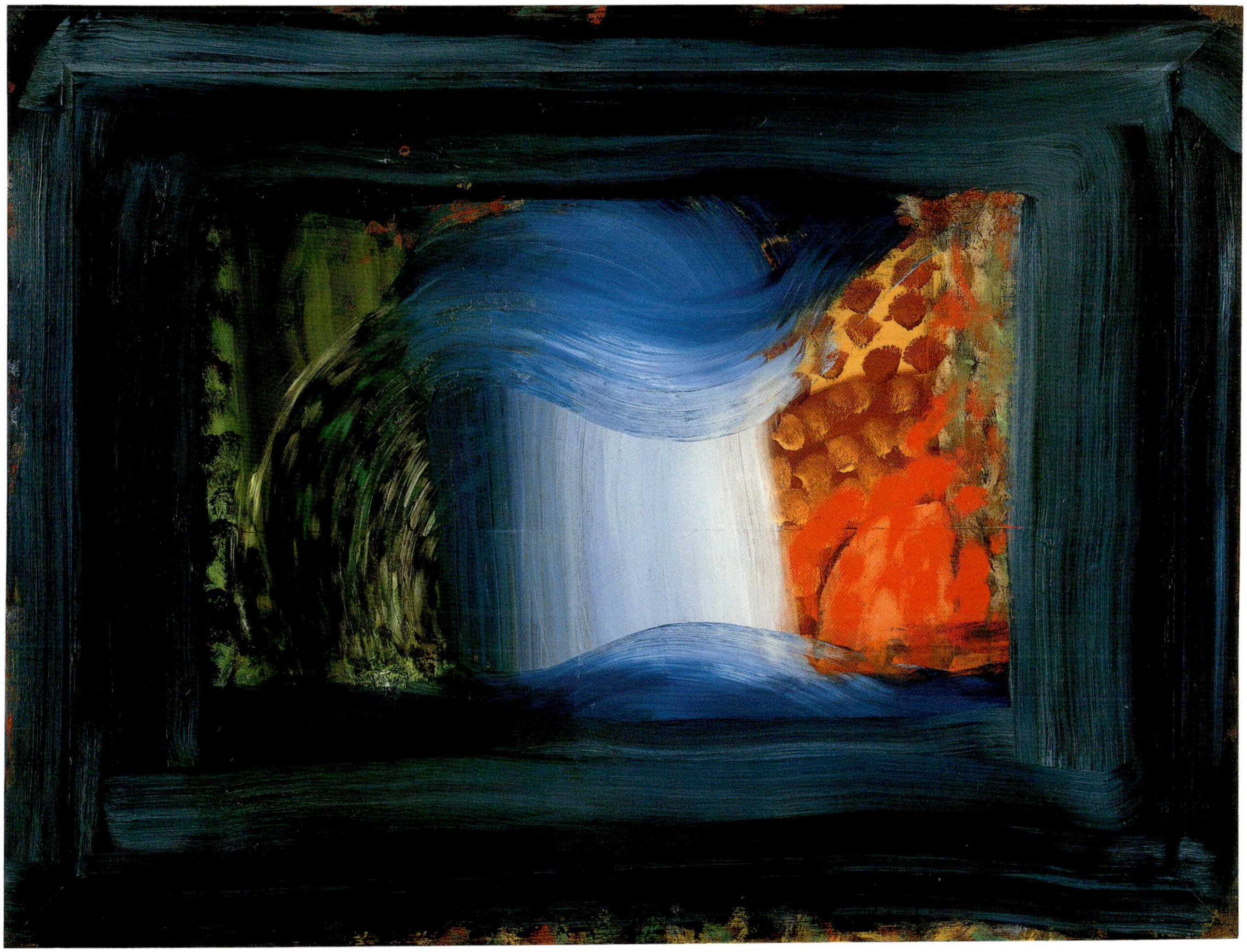

MEMORIES OF MAX
1991 – 95

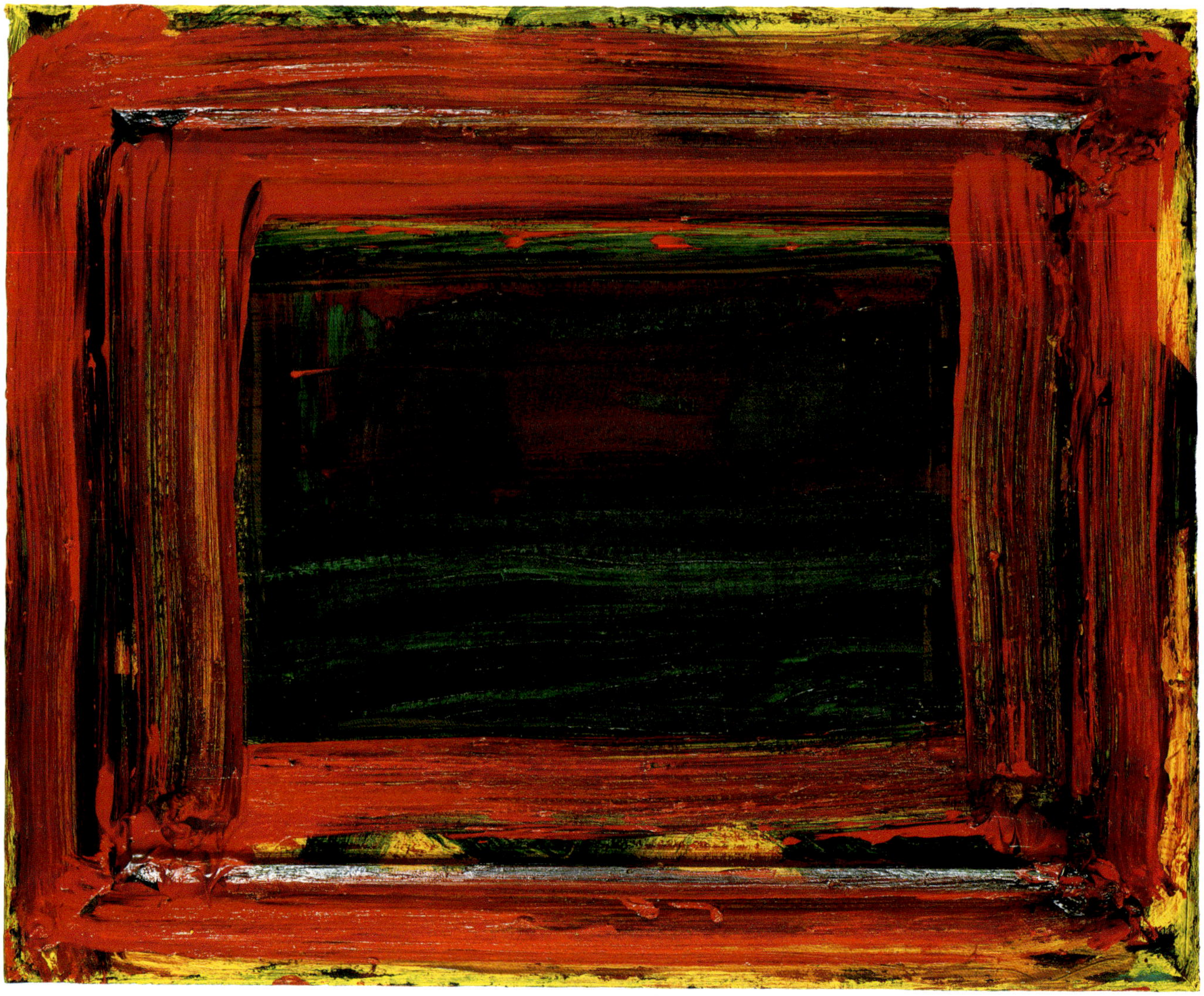

VENICE EVENING
1984 – 85

5
IN VENICE

To represent is, literally, to *re*-present. It is to attempt to reincarnate a moment, something seen and felt, that is already in the past. It is to attempt to bring back something that is irretrievably gone. A large part of the artist's fight has been to find ways of expressing this in paint, of negotiating a compromise between his ambition to resuscitate the past and his knowledge of the ultimate impossibility of such a project. He has had to create a pictorial language capable of balancing on that particular knife edge, a language that would enable him to create pictures that declare their dual status both as painted memories and as images of the imperfect nature of all remembrance.

Venice Evening (1984–85) is a picture suspended between recollection and loss. It can be taken entirely literally, as an impressionistic rendering of meteorological fact: a picture of darkness made visible, of dusk falling in the city of mist and wetness on some gloomy winter afternoon. But metaphorically, *Venice Evening* mocks itself, declares itself to be a mere painted substitute for an experience that can never be recaptured. Of course a moment lived can never be turned into a thing, and this small tablet of painted wood bears sad witness to that. It is a picture that opens on to a void, a picture with an empty centre. But it also extracts poignancy from its own unshielded inadequacy. It suggests the violence that art necessarily does to experience by remaking it *as* art, but conjures pathos from that. The memory that cannot be recaptured, that evades the painter's necessarily clumsy attempts at objectification as surely as all memories defy the attempt to relive them, becomes a source not just of longing but also of pain. *Venice Evening* is a picture that looks like a wound. It is a dark, bodily prospect, framed in blood.

Hodgkin's Venice is not really a place, but rather a set of ideas, attitudes and feelings. The Venetian paintings amount to an anatomy of melancholy, a painter's way of talking about the sad inevitable passage of time and the changeability of all things. Their Venice recalls, in some respects, Turner's Venice, which is also a city remade as a vision, a place where the solidity of objects, the fixity of things, comes perpetually under threat. Turner's Venice is a place of explosive light and colour, of vapours and spray and broken watery reflections. It is a place of elemental flux. So, in a sense, is Hodgkin's, although his Venetian paintings are not ruled by quite the same violent, grandly cosmic forces of chaos as those of Turner. His Venice is a place where things are seen, dimly,

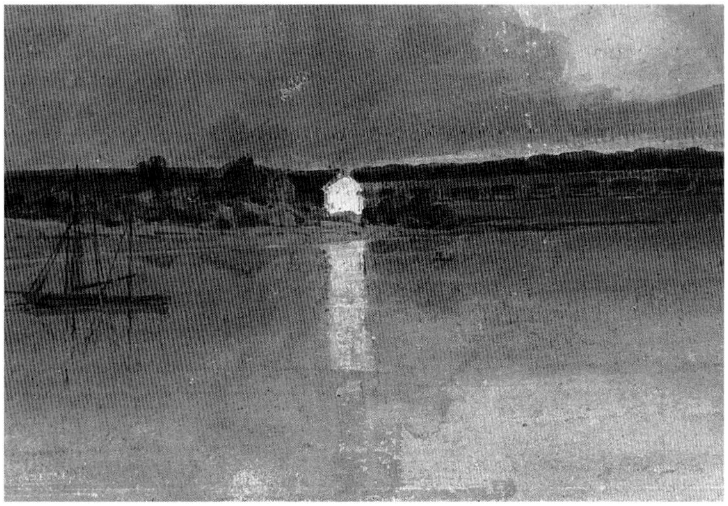

through veils of dense obscuring atmosphere, where objects metamorphose into barely perceptible apparitions.

House near Venice (1984–88), which is faintly reminiscent of Girtin's famous watercolour, *The White House, Chelsea*, is a painting of a building and its reflection in water. It is a painting of something looming out of obscurity, emerging from the loose fluid veils and stains of paint that are so often Hodgkin's shorthand for weather, in his Venetian paintings and elsewhere. It is a painting of a thing that has assumed the clarity of things seen in dreams or suddenly remembered across a gap of years, sharply detailed while all around has become obscure.

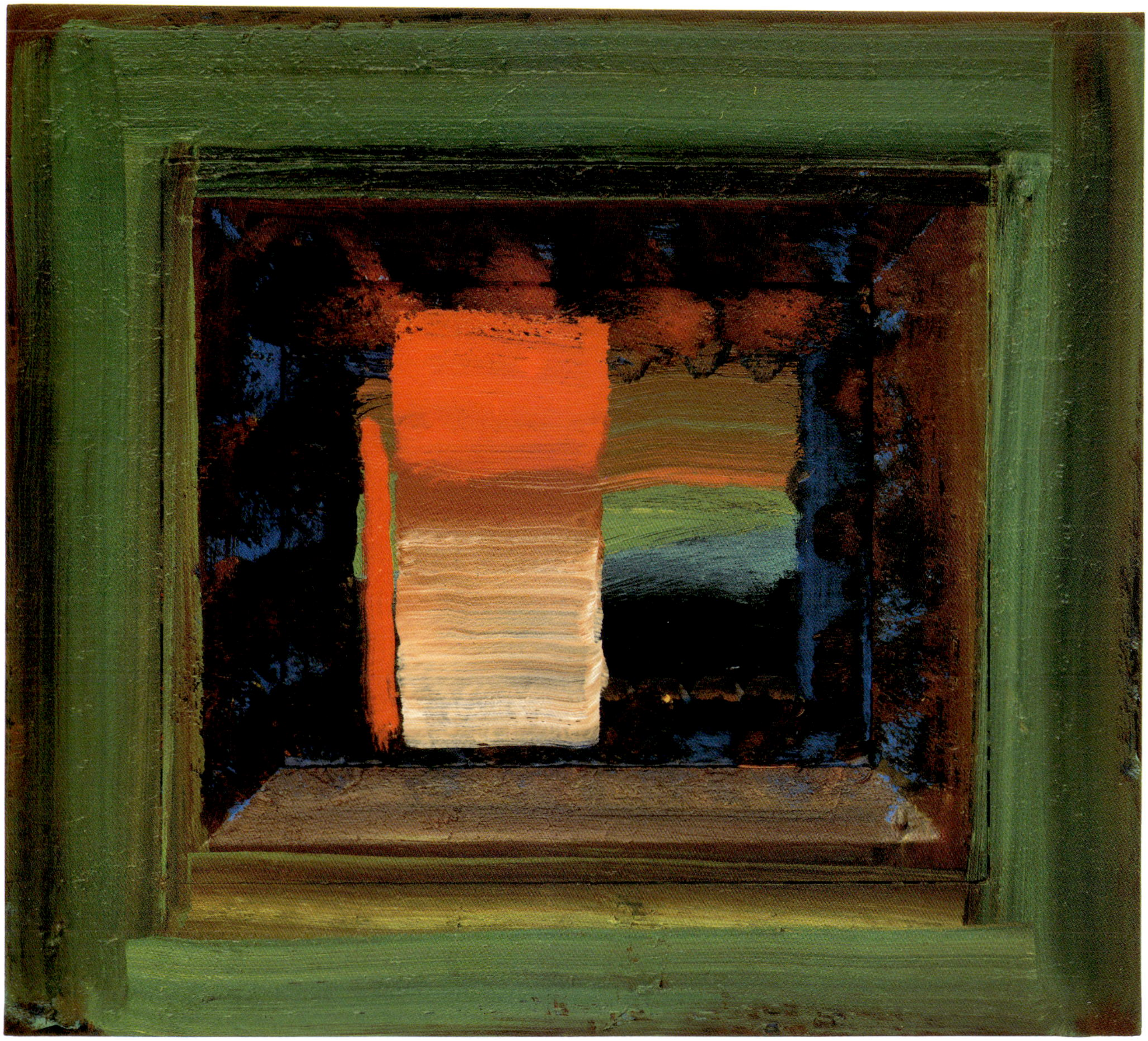

HOUSE NEAR VENICE
1984 – 88

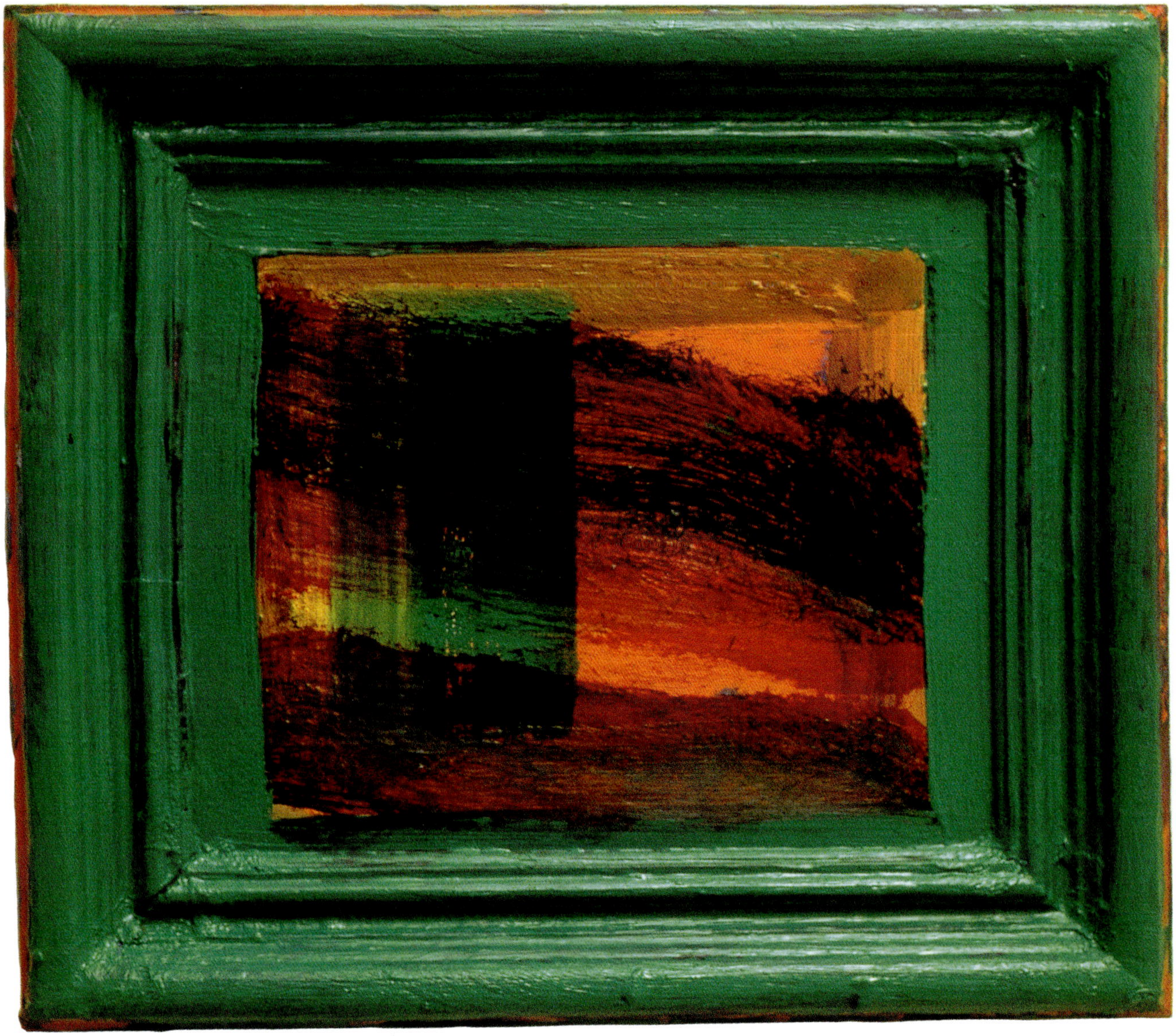

VENICE / SHADOWS
1984 – 88

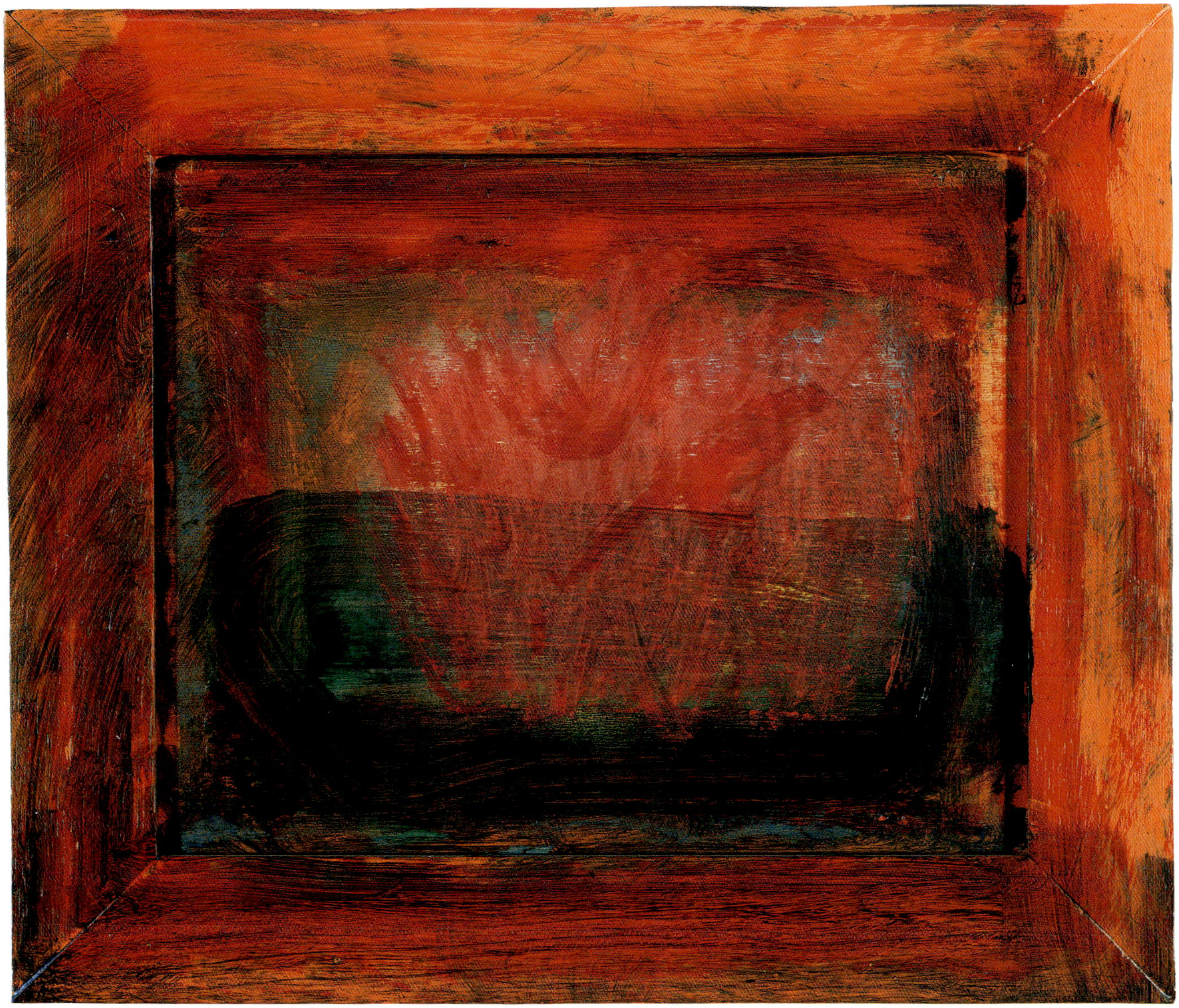

FIRE IN VENICE
1986 – 89

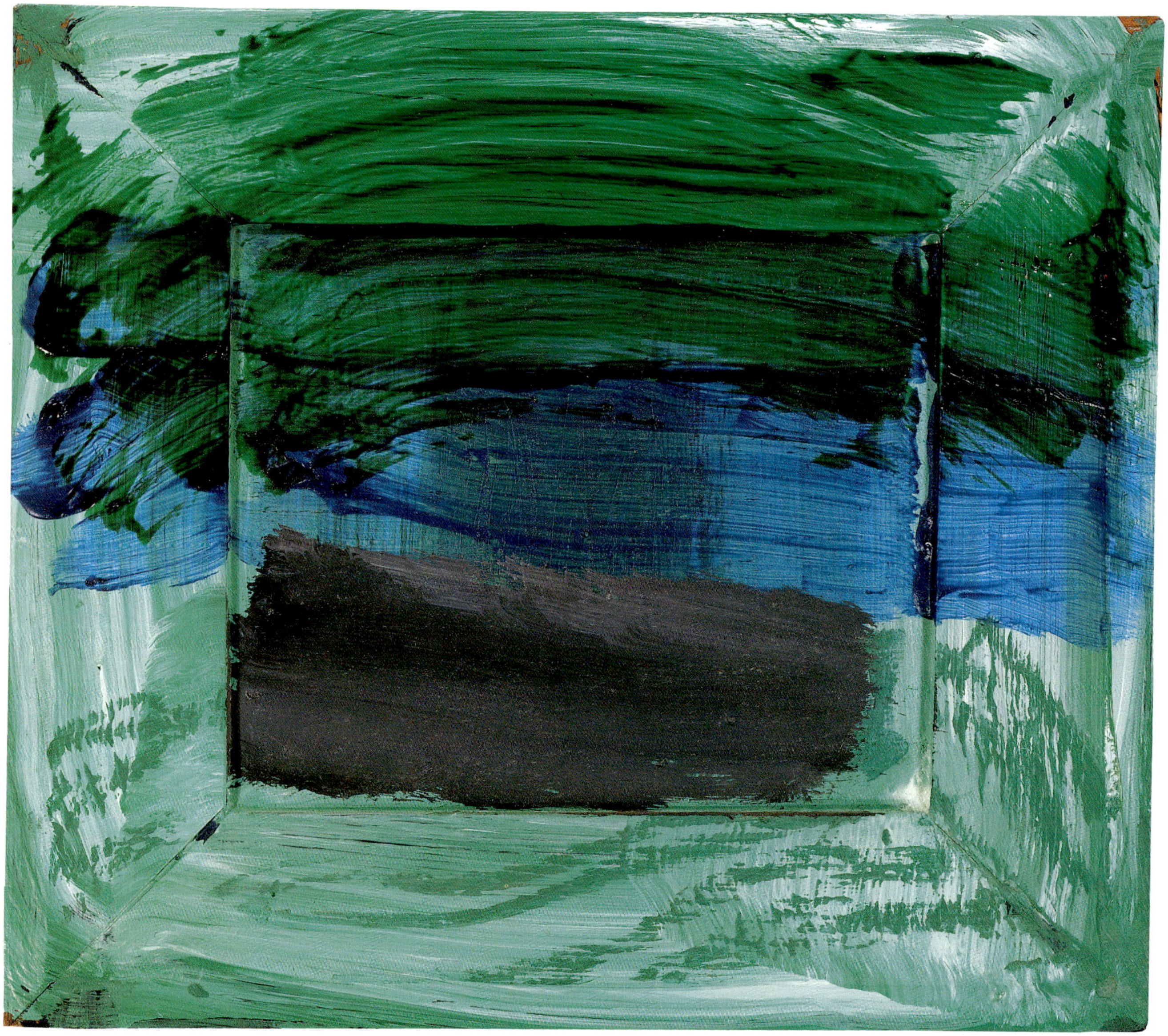

VENICE GREY WATER
1988 – 89

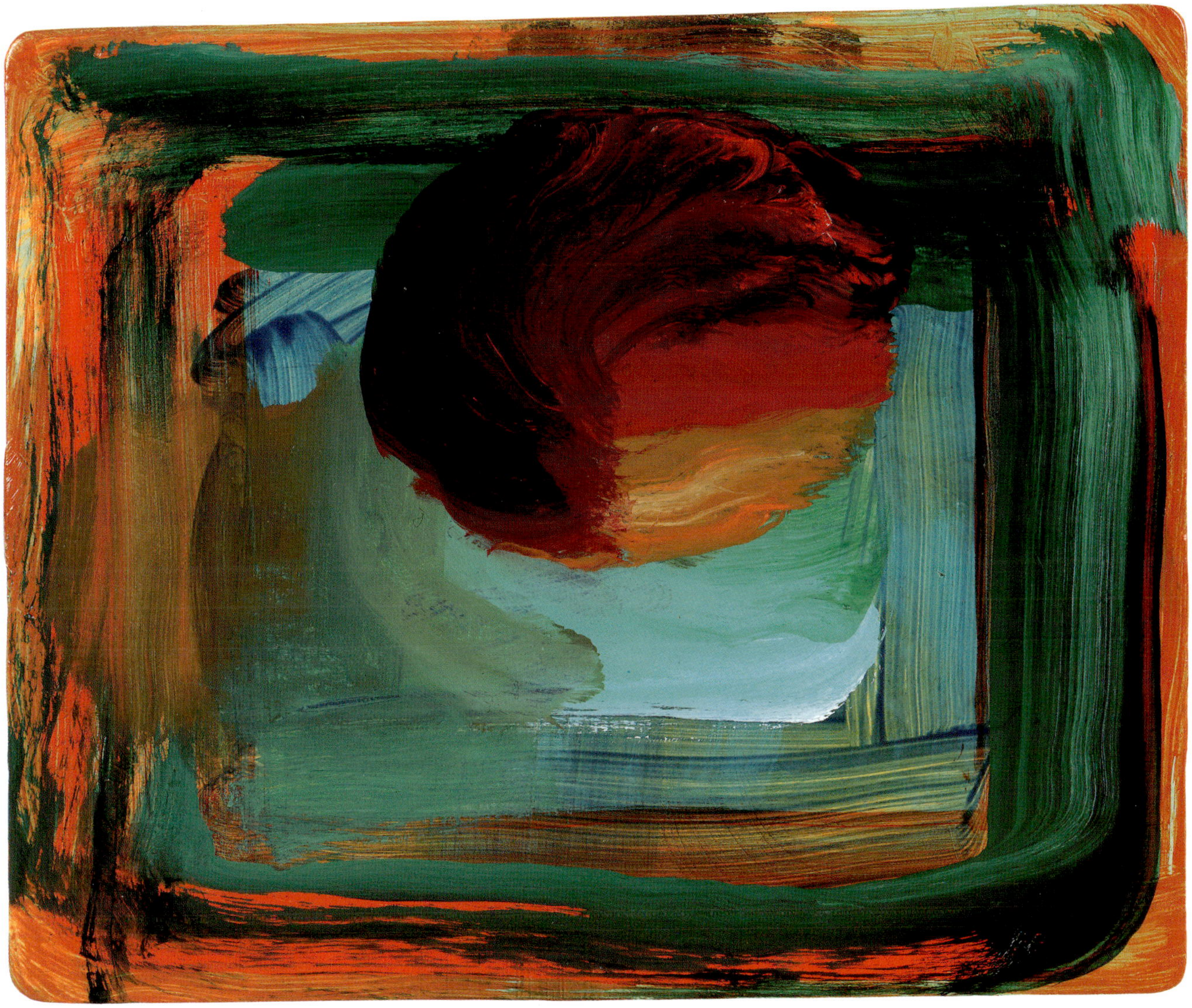

VENICE SUNSET
1989

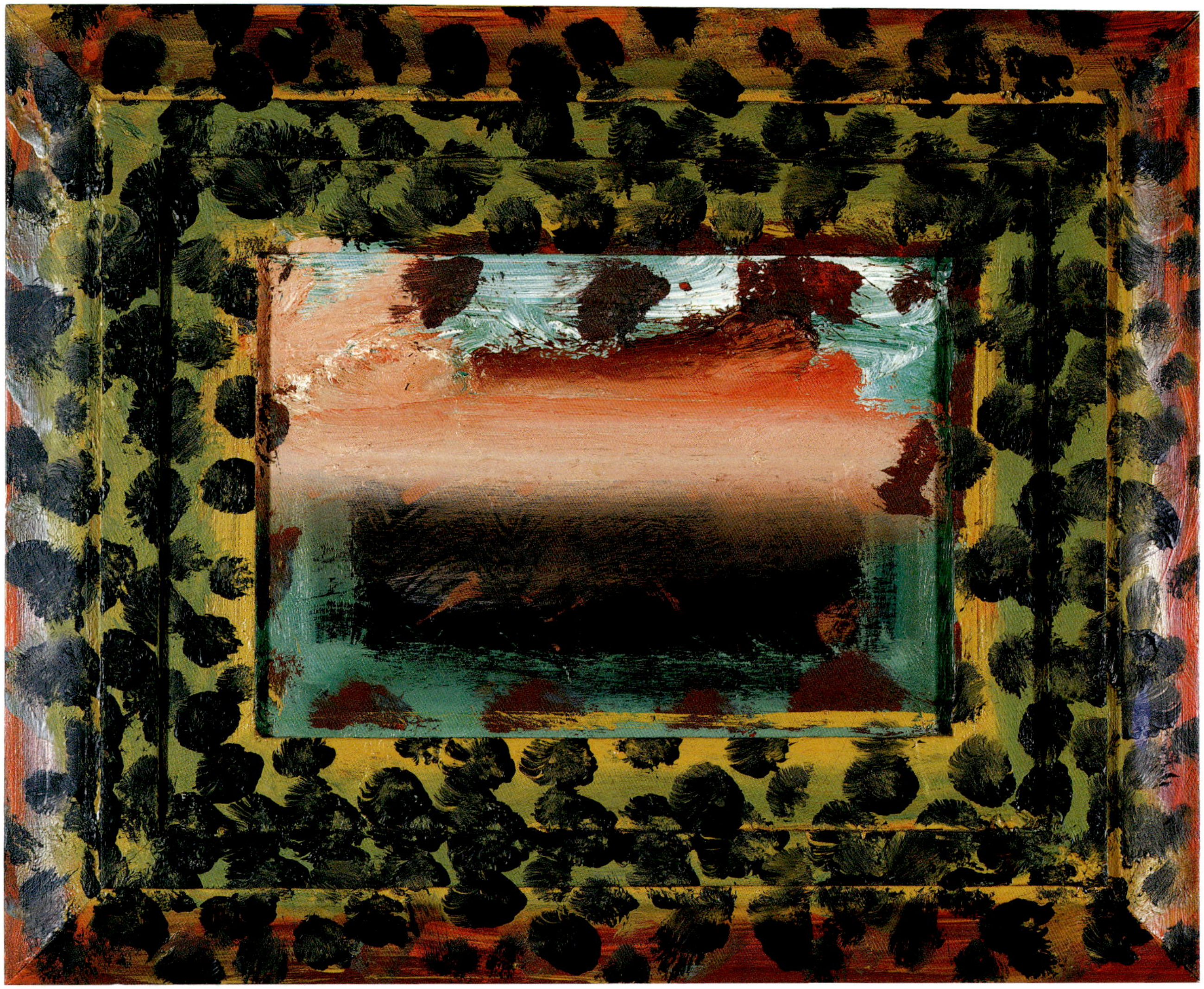

VIEW FROM VENICE
1984 – 85

This Venice is an unstable, watery place, where things come into view briefly, only to be lost again from sight; where things seem ghostly, barely apprehended; where they take on the fugitive quality of moving reflections seen in unstill water, or the quality of P. 64 shadows. *Venice/Shadows* (1984–88) is a painting of opaque, shadowy mystery, an enigmatic red haze in which you see, floating (it could be a building or the shadow of a building), a single lozenge of green translucent paint. Adrian Stokes wrote a short book about Venice in the 1940s, some passages in which seem to anticipate the feeling in Hodgkin's paintings of the city. 'It is one thing to walk past a building,' Stokes wrote, 'another to glide past, to slip slowly in a continuous movement. The hesitancy of water reveals architectural immobility... Water has no lid. An oar fathoms it, it opens just so much, closes, heals from beneath.'[11]

Hodgkin, so much of whose art is constructed around the tension between what is solid and what is fugitive, reinvents Venice as an image of his own preoccupations. His pictures of the city are often really just pictures of water, pictures of hesitancy alone – P. 65 although *Fire in Venice* (1986–89) provides an incandescent counter to the aqueousness of many of the other paintings, an image of the world swallowed up by flames. Water in the Venice pictures seems to become more than itself, to take on something of the texture of thought, mobile, easily disturbed, unpredictable, alternately clear and clouded. P. 66 *Venice Grey Water* (1988–89) is the most watery and the most distilled of all the paintings. It is a small, small, liquid image of something that is always changing, from blue to green to grey to dark blue, an image that works its effects through layerings and different levels of transparency and opacity. Venice has become a pretext. Topography is displaced by metaphor.

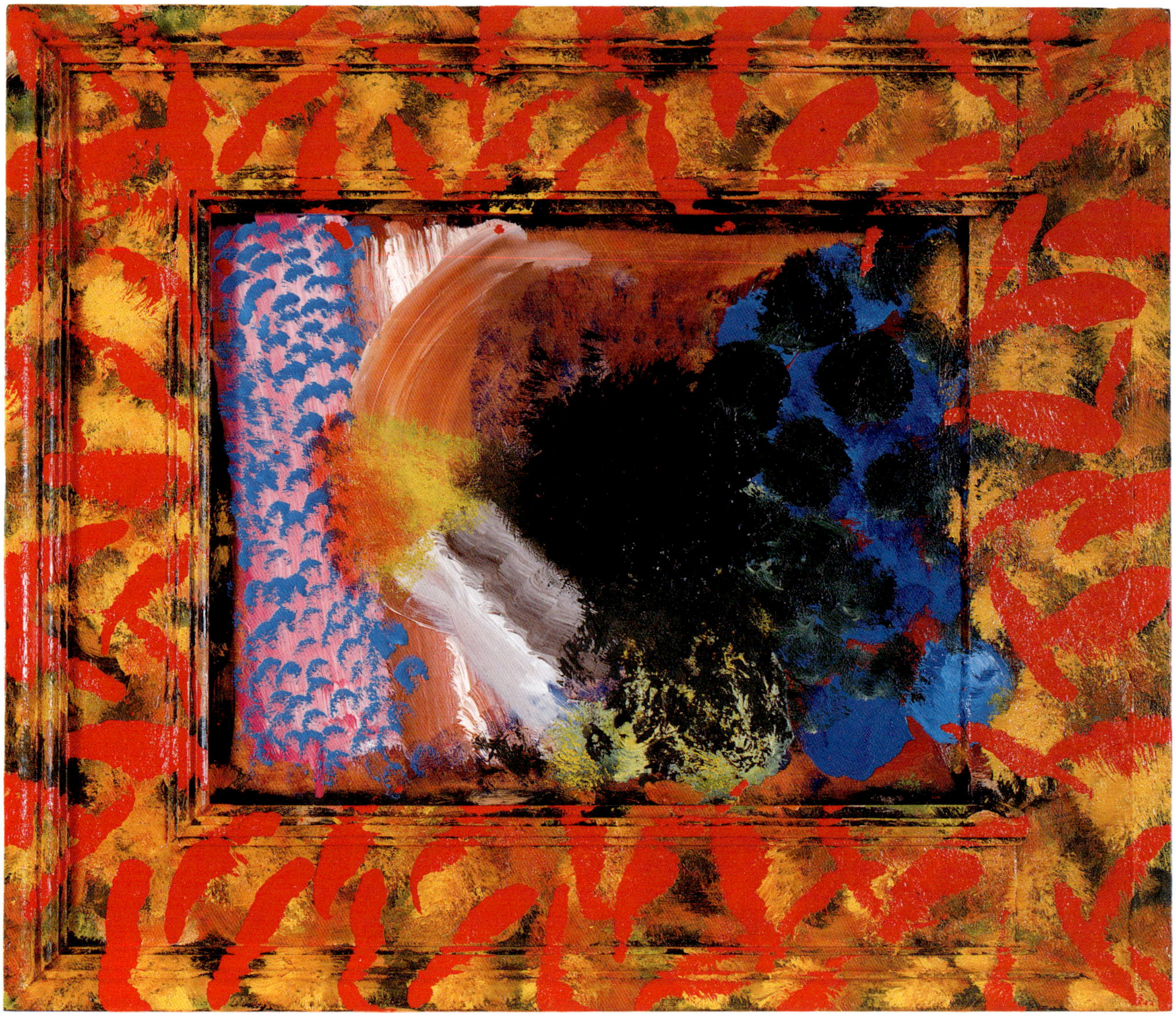

COUNTING THE DAYS
1979 – 82

6
TIME

Time is complicated in these painted worlds. Every one of the pictures attempts to re-incarnate past experience, to turn the infinite complexity of a particle of past time into a solid, present object, something palpably *there*, something you can see, something with fixed dimensions. Yet the paintings simultaneously declare a pained knowledge that the P. 60 single, static image can never aspire to represent the way things are or once were. *Venice Evening* may be Hodgkin's most literal statement of that knowledge, but it is implicit in all of his art. It is built into his pictorial language, those mobile blurs and smudges and swipes of paint. It is manifest in his confirmed habits of occlusion, of screening, the most P. 72 blatant example of which may occur in *Grantchester Road* (1975), where the one figure in the painting has been disconcertingly half-obscured by the sudden arrival of a black P. 73 pillar of paint. The most perverse example may be *Souvenirs* (1980–84), one of the largest of all the pictures, the theme of which is the appalling struggle of recollection. *Souvenirs* is almost insolently obscurantist, a vast field of dots concealing a hidden world of incident, barely glimpsed. But remembering is like this. The television set of memory is not easily tuned. The screen fizzes with interference.

The paintings emerge out of the tension between opposites: between what is seen and what is hidden or obscured; between what is there and what is missing. And that tension is really the expression of the painter's sad temporal consciousness, his sense that what is past can only imperfectly be made present. The pictures are full of allusions to the pictures-in-progress that they once were, most manifestly in the layers of under-painting that so often survive as fleeting visions in the finished work. Hodgkin's dating

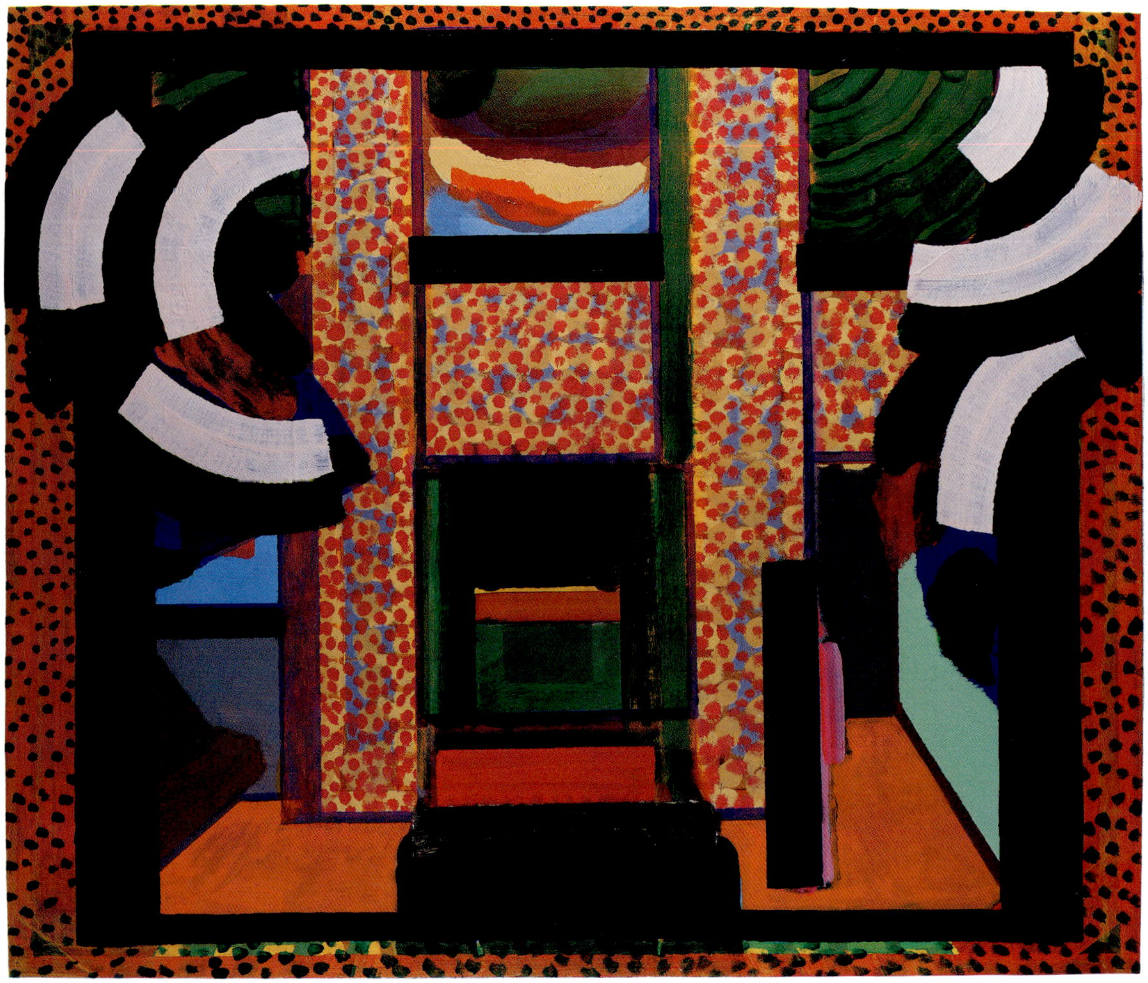

GRANTCHESTER ROAD
1975

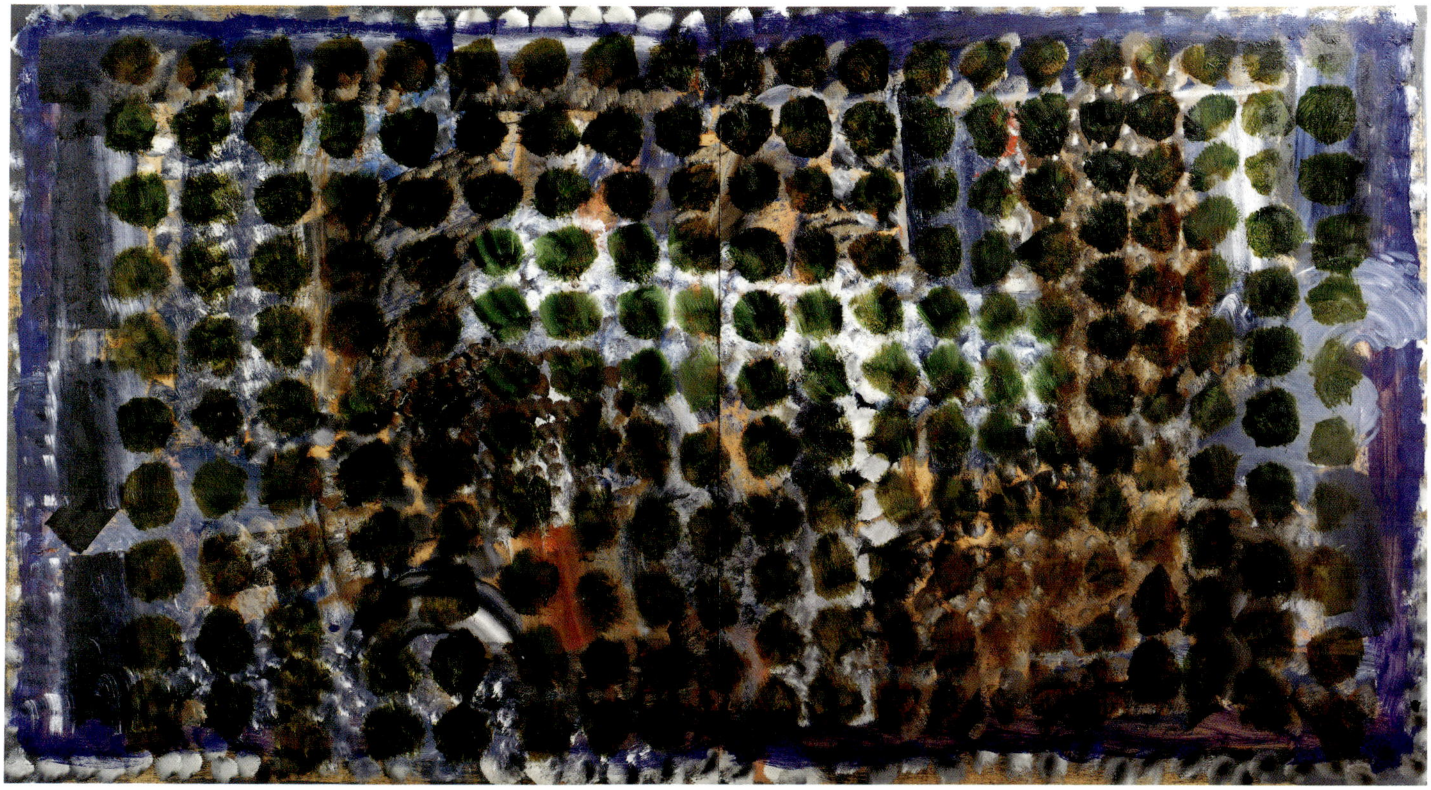

SOUVENIRS
1980 – 84

of his own works, which often indicates that a particular painting was executed over as long a period as five or six years, is informative but also superfluous. The pictures themselves bear the marks of their own histories like buried memories of dead selves.

The paintings are both framed and unframed, since the artist treats the frame as integral to the support. His pictures start as blank panels of wood within frames and he paints on both elements, so frame and image are integrated, become one and the same thing. Sculptors have always understood the importance of edges, which define precisely how form contains space; painters, often content to let others frame their pictures for them, have infrequently understood it. Picasso, who was both painter and sculptor, was a great exception. Hodgkin also knows that a painting's edge is its most vulnerable point. It is where the work of art ends and the world begins. It is where the painting completes itself or, conversely, declares its incompletion. It is where the painting, which – unlike the book, the play, the musical composition – has no given linear structure, no predetermined beginning or end, negotiates with its own limits. The edge of the painting is where the artist makes his entrances and exits. It is the mark of his competence and confidence, his control or lack of it. Paintings succeed or fail at their edges.

The habit of bracketing images within dense borders of patterned or monochrome paint – seen in *The Green Château* (1976–80), *After Dinner* (1976–77), *In Alexander* P. 76
Street (1977–79) and countless other pictures – often turns the paintings into views *through* or *into*. It is a device that lends them much of their intimacy. The density of Hodgkin's painted frames casts them in the role of buffer states, shields of colour erected to shelter the fragile, evanescent images at the heart of a painting from too close and immediate a contact with the world beyond the painting. It also turns his pictures into conduits, leading into private or secret worlds. Sometimes the artist seems to be painting moments – *Reading the Letter* (1977–80) might be an example, with its oppressive con- P. 77
gregation of forms, a dark gathering of forces charged with malevolence, with an intensity that seems the product of claustrophobia – that he might prefer to forget.

The sense of looking through and into and beyond, so powerful in Hodgkin's painting, also carries another charge. The painted world-within-a-world and the eye's journey through to it become analogues for the painter's own, temporal struggle: the

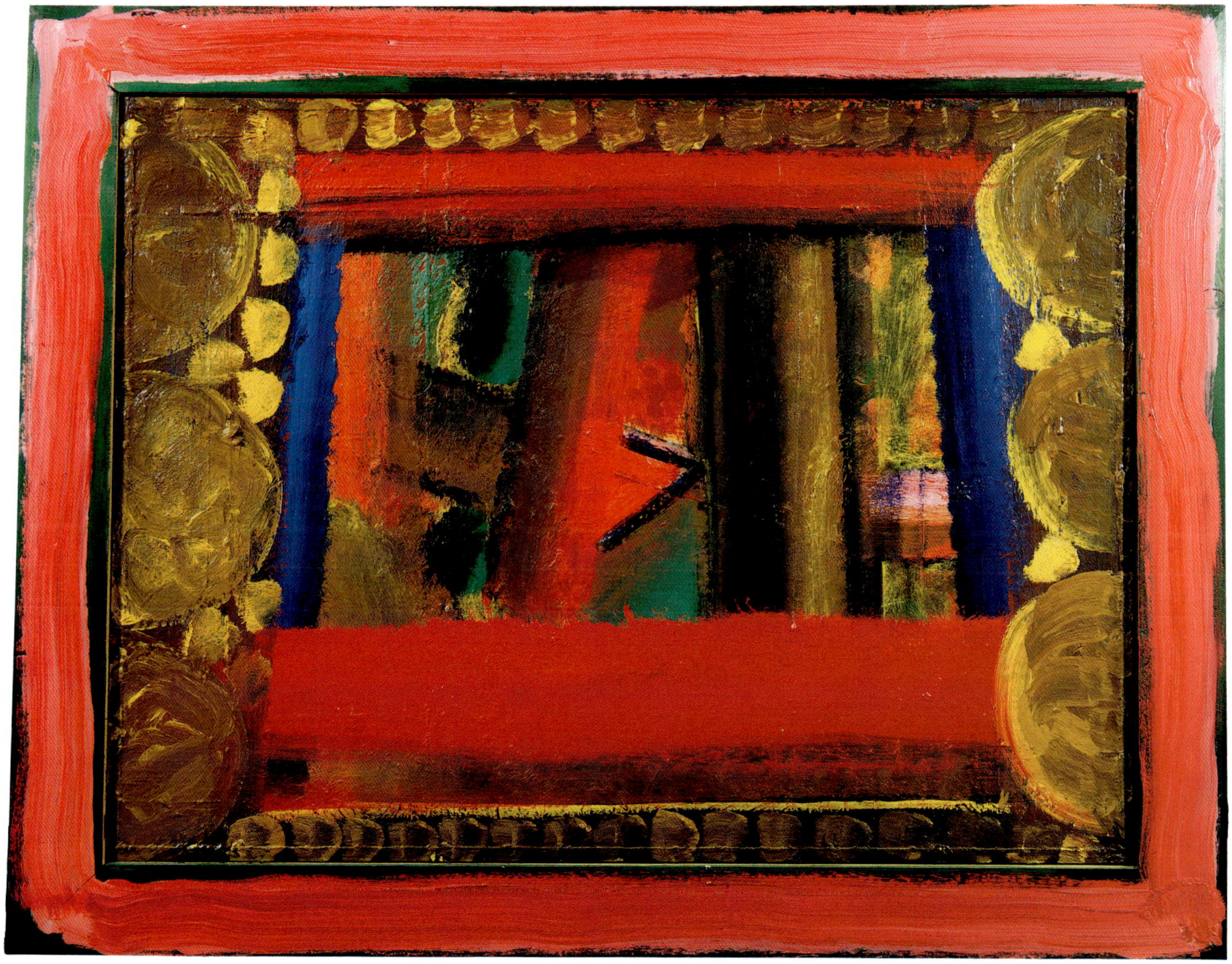

THE GREEN CHATEAU
1976 – 80

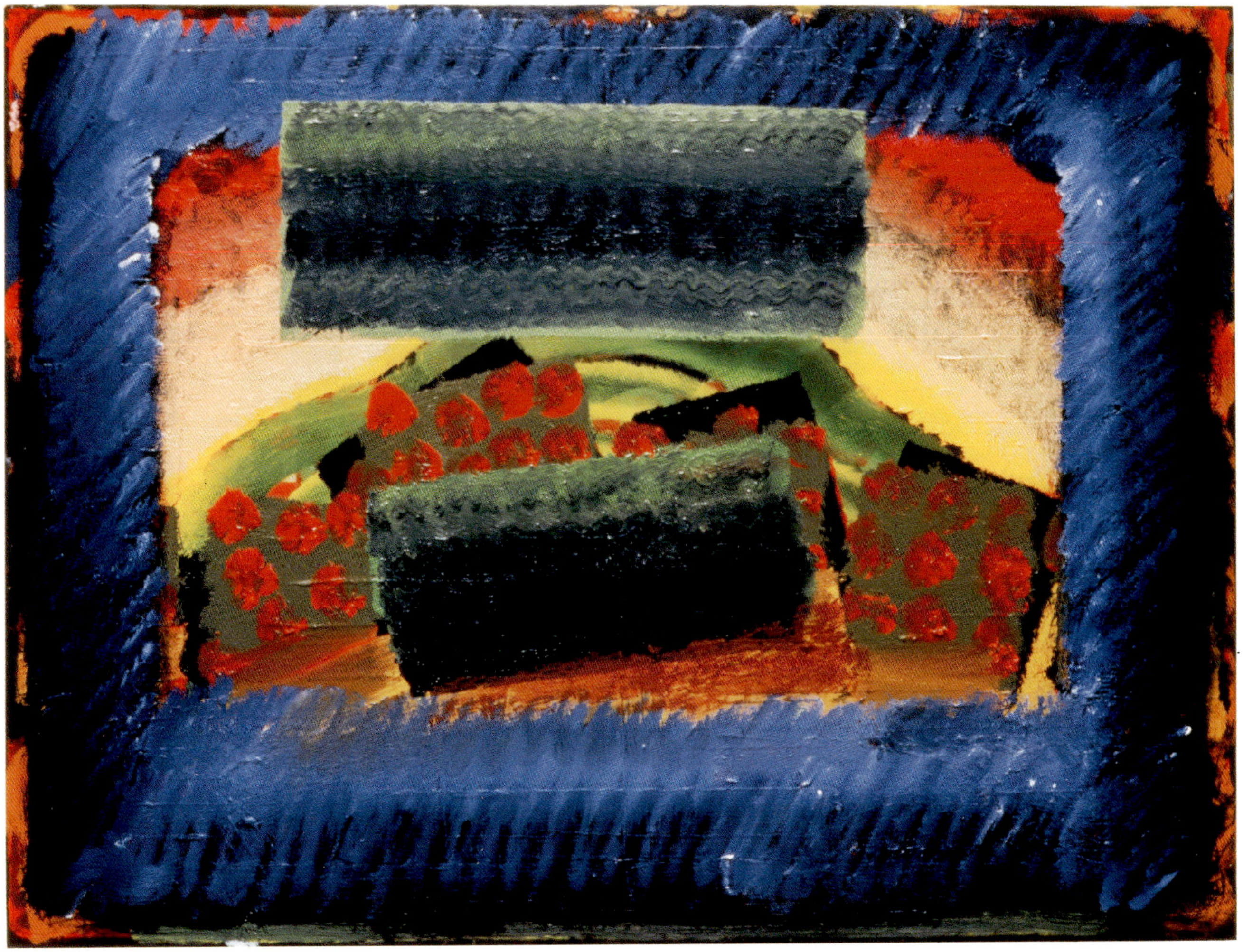

AFTER DINNER
1976 – 77

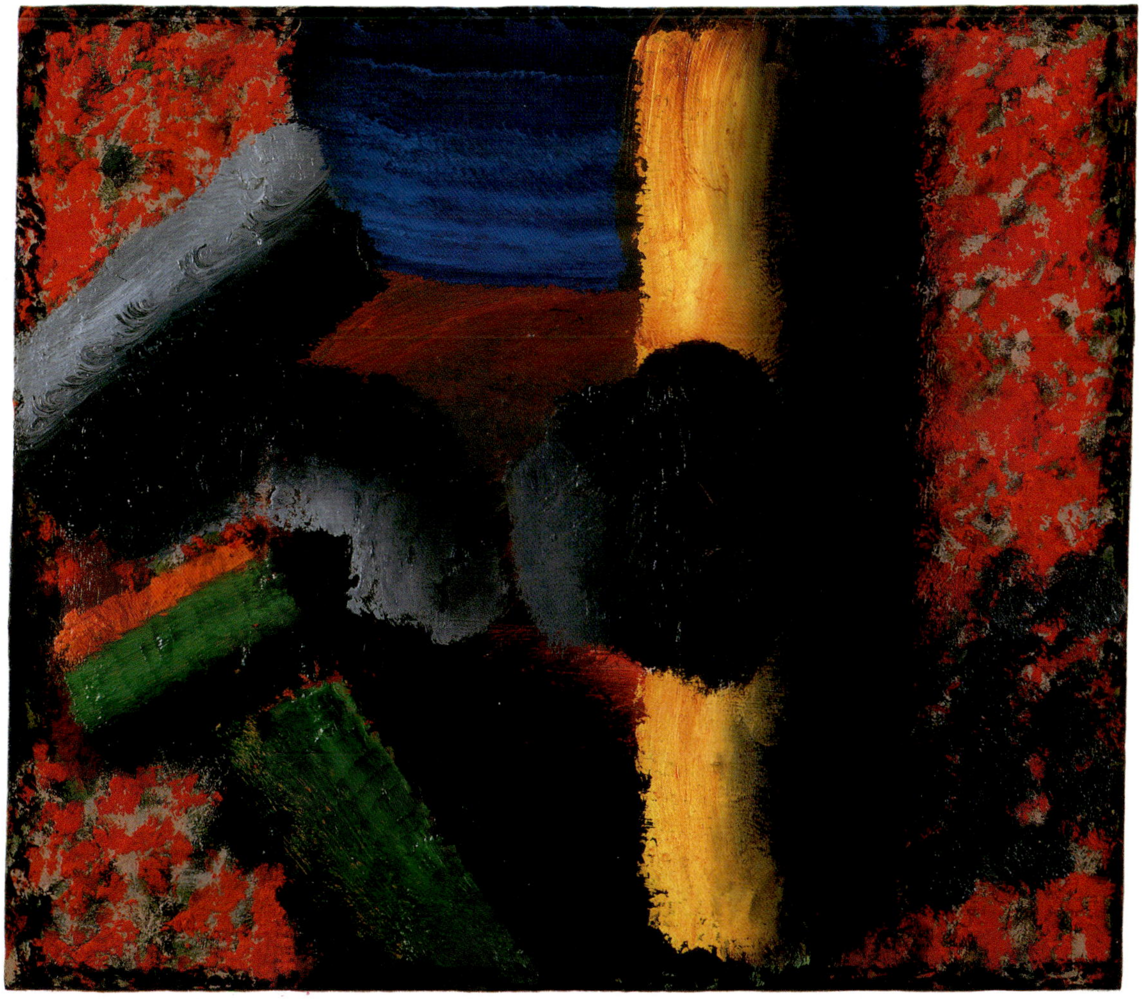

READING THE LETTER
1977 – 80

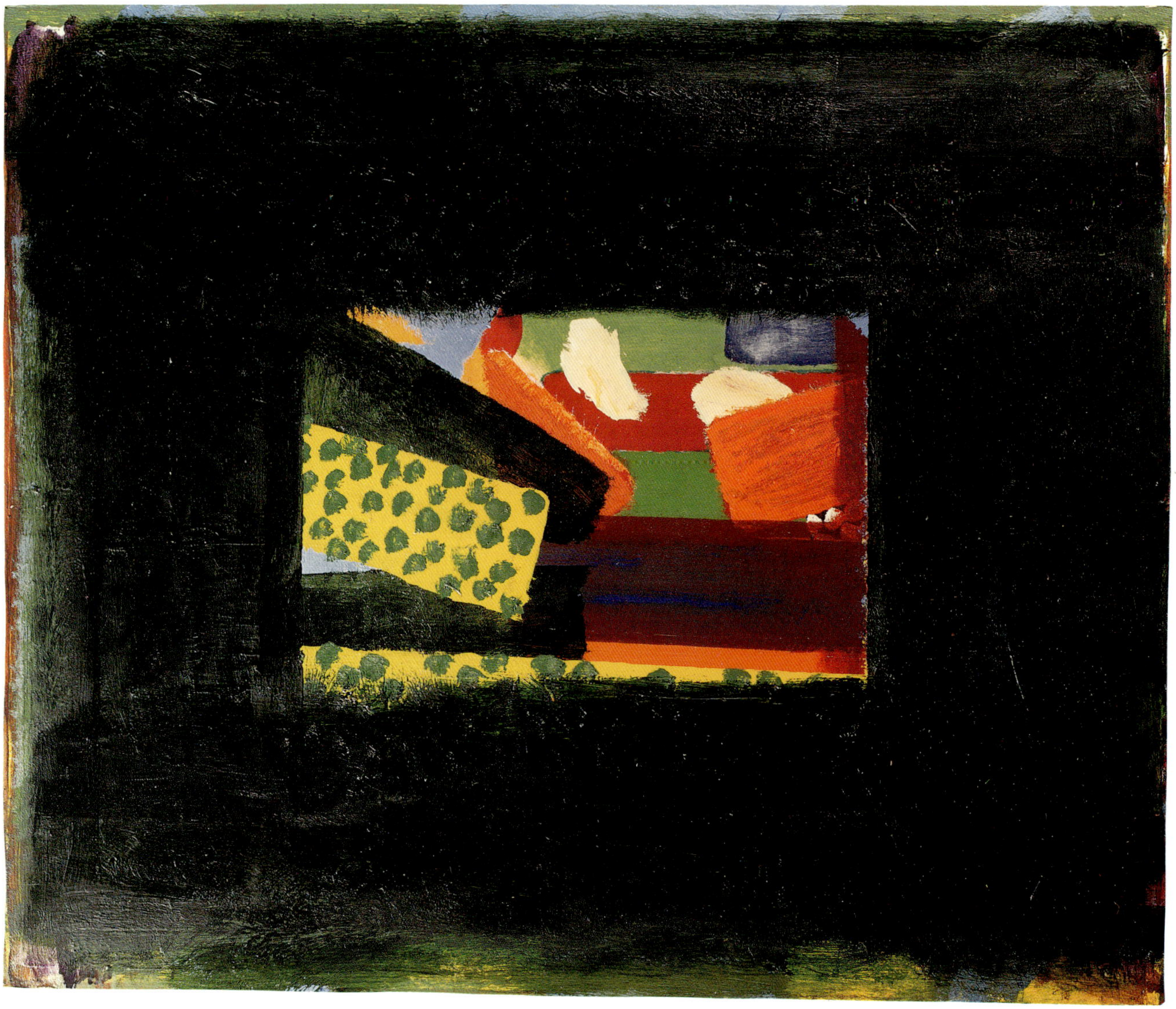

THE HOPES AT HOME
1973 – 77

viewer's struggle to get from one place to another, to make the leap from the world in front of the painting to the world within it, is a metaphor for the artist's struggle to get
P. 134 from one *time* to another. *A Small Thing but My Own* (1983–85) may be Hodgkin's most compressed and poignant memorial to that struggle. It is about exactly what its title says. It is about a small thing, but the painter's own. It is about his past, glowing and indistinct.

The tension between an image and its frame (which often obtrudes to the point where the frame becomes an obstacle to vision as well as its enabler, something that

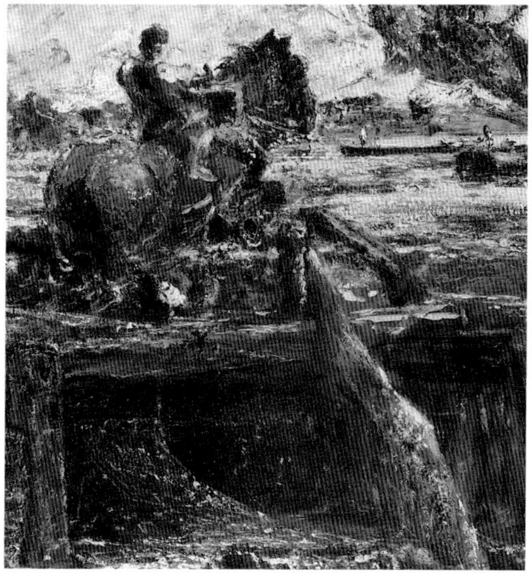

blocks as well as focuses) is another expression of the perennial tension in Hodgkin's work, between art and all that art cannot capture. *The Hopes at Home* (1973–77) addresses this with particular directness. It is a picture that is explicitly about something having been almost lost from sight altogether, its bright focused centre so fenced in by surrounding blackness that it seems threatened more than framed. The artist's abstract bars and blobs and flickers of pigment coalesce, here, into an idealized landscape, but this is a version of pastoral charged with a sense of melancholy. The past is seen as a beautiful but fragile vision, an unenterable Eden, like the garden which Lewis Carroll's outsize Alice sees through a door too small for her to walk through.

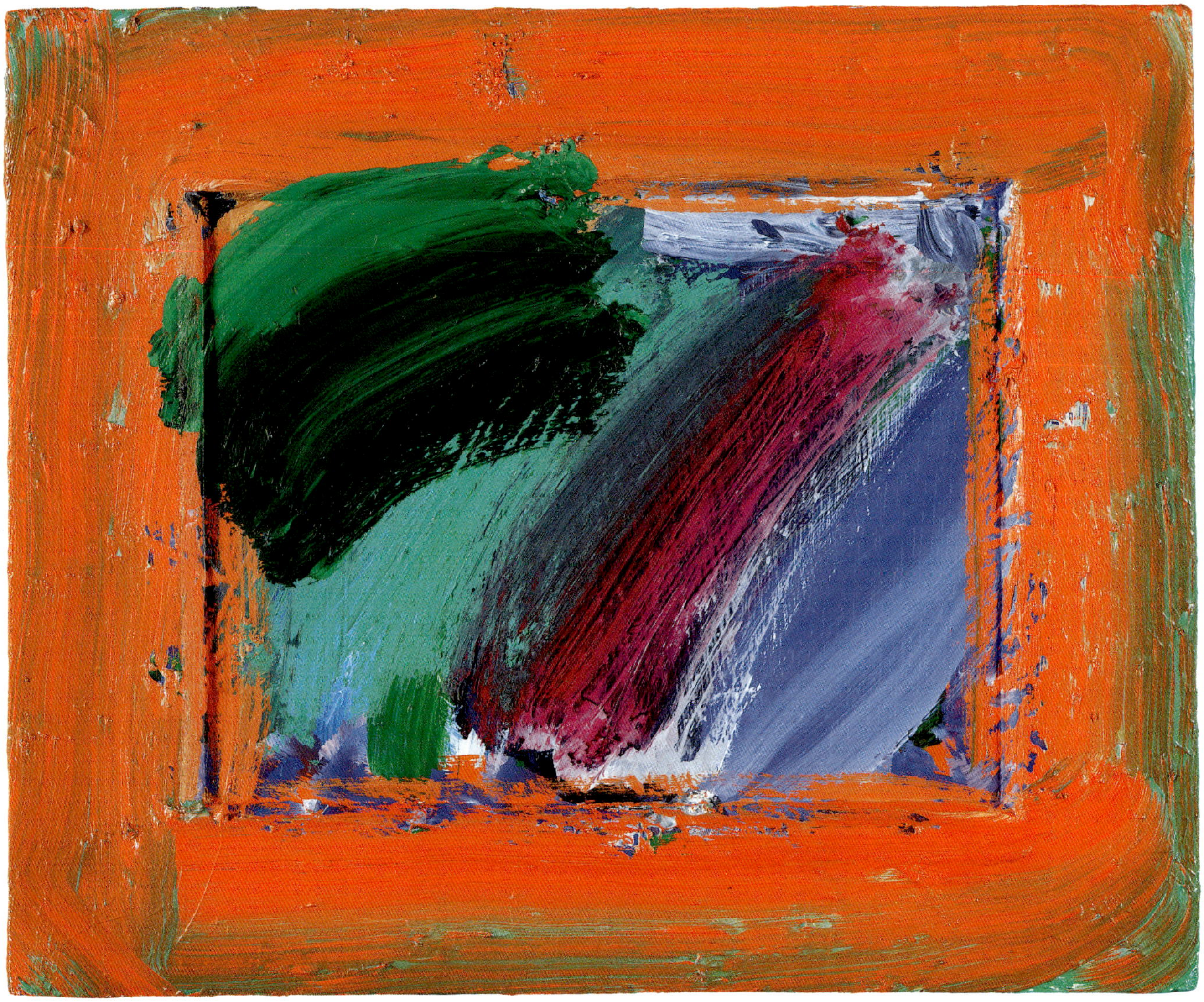

AFTER THE SHOP HAD CLOSED
1992

The blocked prospect, the prospect interrupted or threatened, speaks of memory and longing and the desire to reach a place or time that is as distant and ungraspable as a fantasy. Constable knew this too, and, although his art could hardly look less like Hodgkin's, there is nevertheless a link between them: an emotional affinity, rooted in recognition of the same truth. Constable's art is made out of the tension between foreground and distance, between the far-off, sunlit prospect and the dark, dank, vegetation-choked foreground that so often, in his works, obstructs passage to distant places of glory. His art is about the desire for an impossible escape from here to there and, by implication, from the confused morass of the present into the paradise of the imagined past (or the unattainable future: memory and anticipation are linked, in Constable's world as in Hodgkin's).

The painter uses pictorial space, and the relationship of prospect to what frames it, to talk about time.

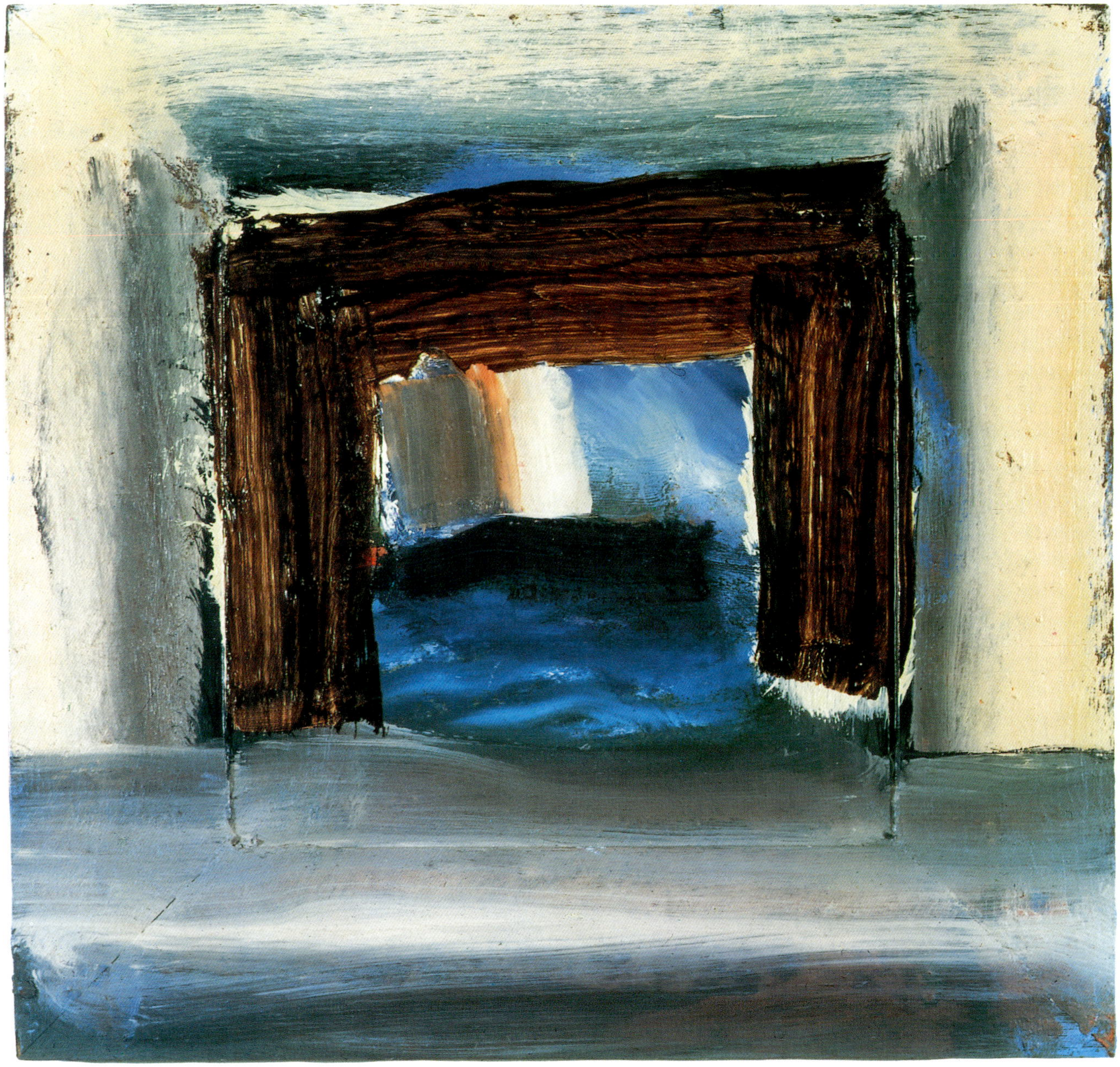

AFTER COROT
1979 – 82

7
A PAINTER OF MODERN LIFE

Howard Hodgkin is a modern painter, but in an old-fashioned sense. In the mid-nineteenth century, Baudelaire recognized a new kind of artist, 'the painter of modern life'. Such a painter understood that 'modernity is the transitory, the fugitive, the contingent'. Hodgkin stands squarely within the tradition of modern painting that Baudelaire defined in those words. *After Corot* (1979–82), a tiny seascape framed as if through an archway, a miniaturized blur of blue water and sky, as frail and evanescent as a memory, is a picture which spells this out with particular clarity. It is a homage not just to the oil sketches of a particular nineteenth-century French painter, but to an entire romantic and post-romantic tradition of representational painting dedicated to catching the fugitive, transitory moment of existence.

Hodgkin's paintings are shot through with a sense of the transience of things, with a sense of time's unforgiving march from moment to moment and of the way in which time ineluctably shatters every life into a thousand separate shards of experience. No pattern, no cosmic order of events is suggested. The time of the pictures is, it might be said, the time of nineteenth-century painting – the time of the moment, the fleeting instant – accelerated to a point where imagery itself, the perceptible object, has been all but obliterated.

Baudelaire's prophetic essay about a painting of modern life rooted in a sense of the transitory and the contingent would be apparently fulfilled, within a few years of his writing it, by the Impressionists. Here was the ultimate painting of instantaneity – or at least that was what was claimed for Impressionism in the rhetoric of its theorists. No art, it was once thought, could ever be more of the moment than Impressionism, a creed as much as a school of painting, whose primary article of faith was truth to the perception of a single instant, the unrepeatable conjunction of light and shade, the wind fluttering the leaves on a tree in just *this* particular way, which it was the painter's job to replicate on canvas. But the Impressionist canvas was, in truth, an extremely artificial re-creation of that momentary experience: the moment itself was of such short duration, compared to the time necessary to complete the painting, that the painter was always in the position of reinventing the 'truth', in all the instantaneous freshness of its apprehension, long after its passage into the vault of the past.

The instantaneity of Impressionism proved to be less definitive an expression of Baudelaire's sense of the transitory, perhaps, than its practitioners had hoped. Other, yet more instantaneous ways of painting the instant would be found – notably by the Cubists, whose images indicated (among other things) the fraudulence of any static image's claim to be representing the momentary quality of experience. Cubism made the image speak simultaneously of many experienced moments and perspectives. It declared that experience is too broken, too subtly fractured by the ways in which people move through time and space, to be reassembled by the painter. Its shattered bones cannot be set. Cubism bequeathed, to the modern painter alive to its significance, a notion of time (and therefore of life) that is forever and unmendably broken.

Venetian Glass (1984–87) is one of Hodgkin's tiniest pictures, and one of his most P. 86
apparently literal. It looks like exactly what its title suggests: a tiny piece of glass, housed in a dense frame of painted blue. The brilliancy of its colours, red and blue and green, makes this a painting that seems to aspire to the condition of stained glass. The obdurately opaque material of oil paint here seems translucent, radiantly backlit. Yet the painting's simplicity, its economy of means, its self-evident literalism, are deceptive. It is a painting that speaks of more than its apparent subject. And it is a painting that speaks as directly as any other in his oeuvre of the artist's besetting concerns. A framed piece of glass is remade into a metaphor, an image that transcends its overt content. It is a picture of something damaged but potentially loved, something broken that can also be cared for, looked after.

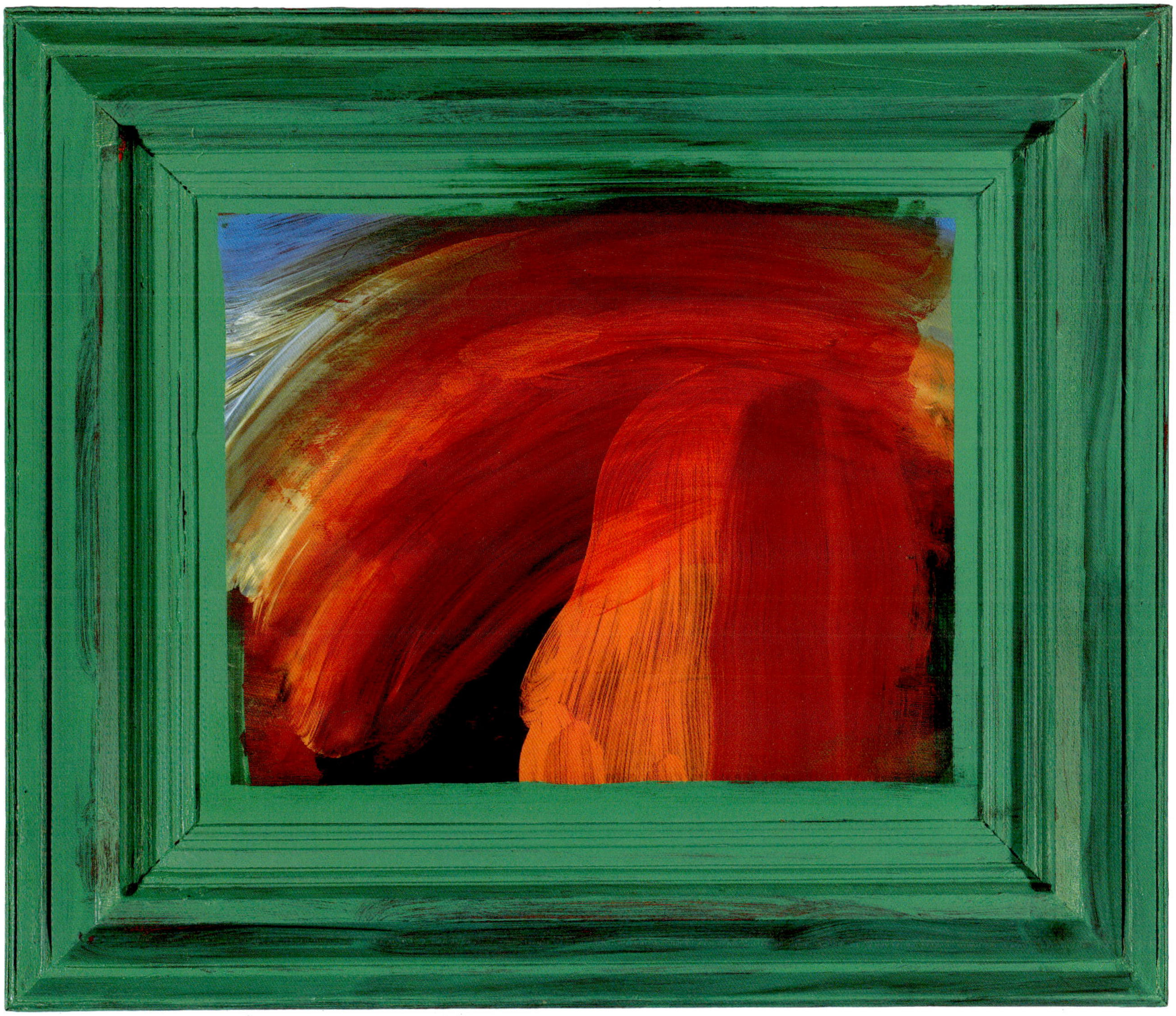

AFTER DEGAS
1993

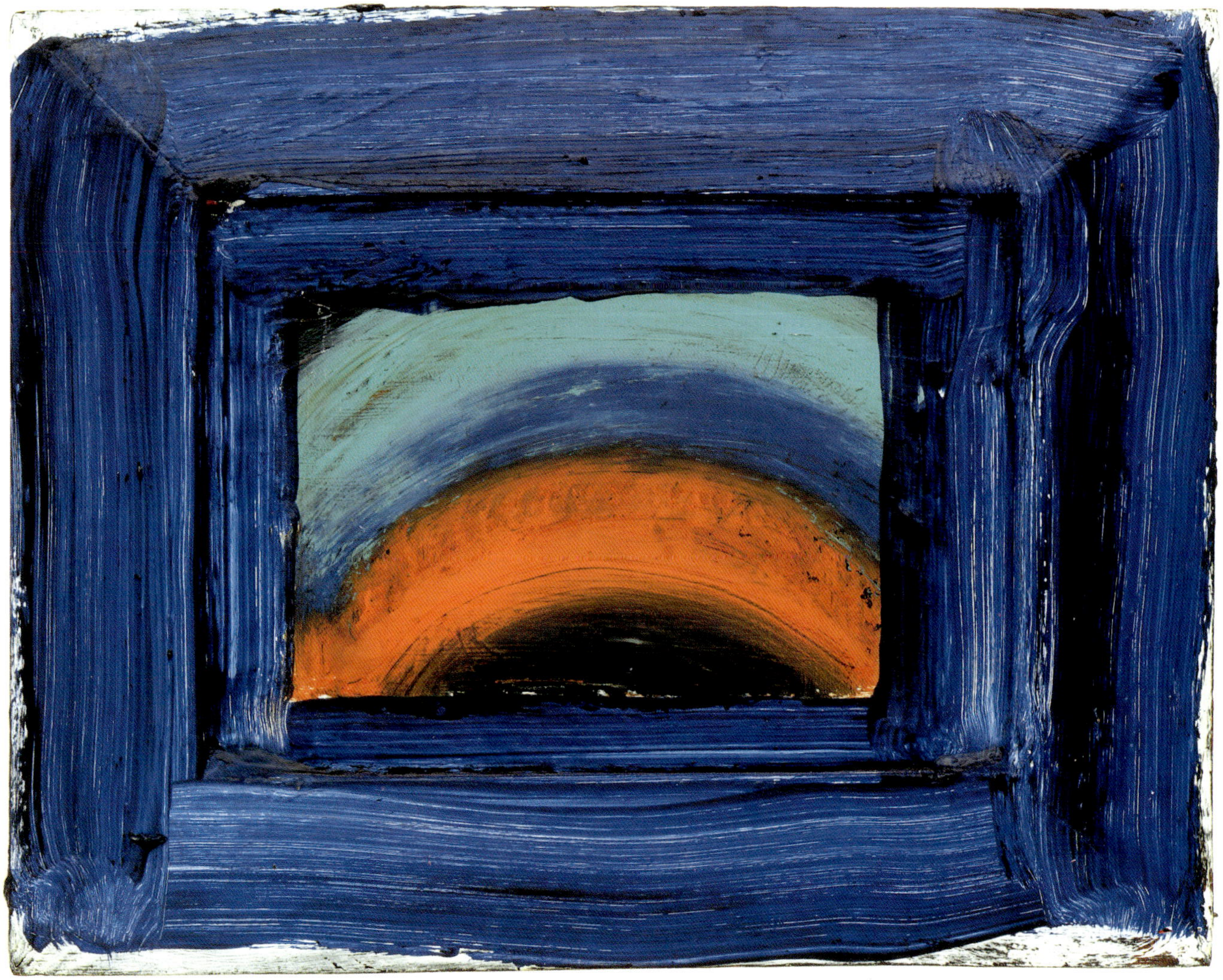

VENETIAN GLASS
1984 – 87

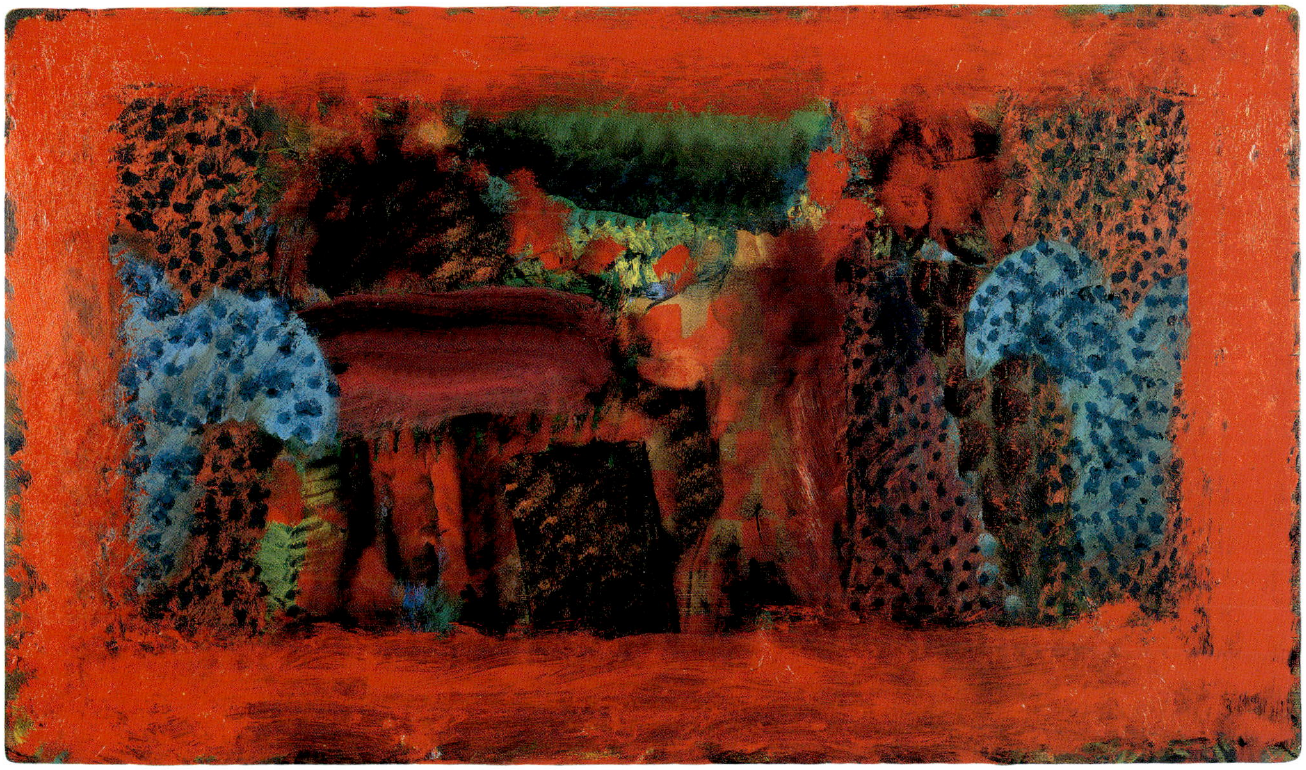

INTERIOR AT OAKWOOD COURT
1978 – 83

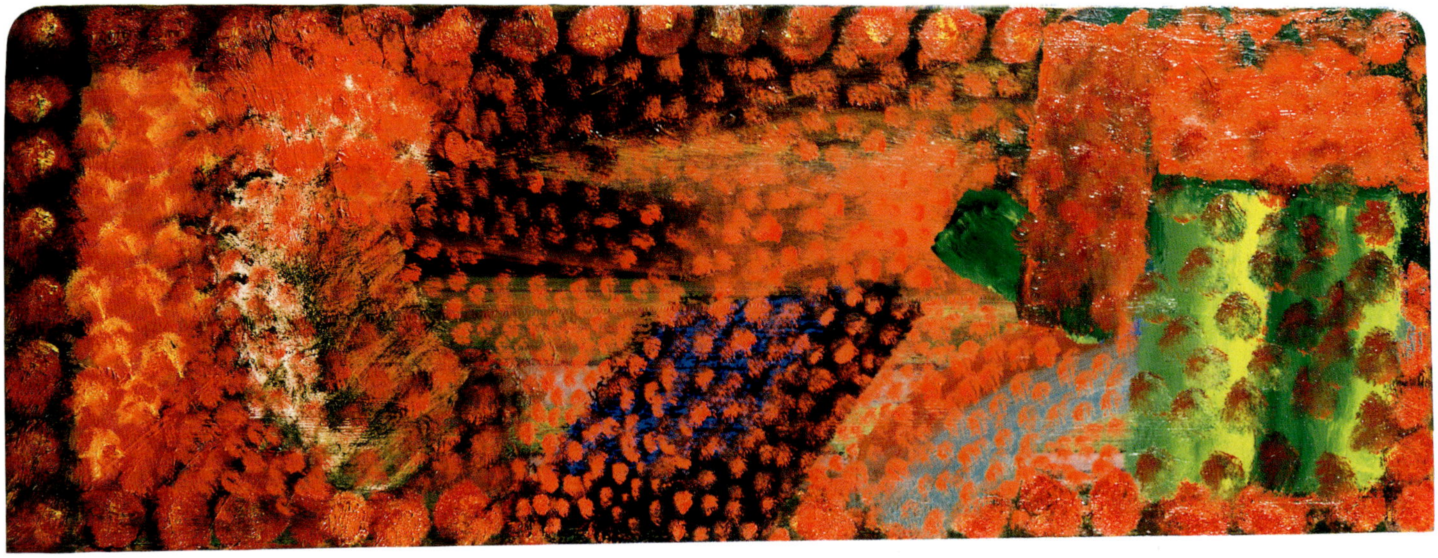

TEA
1977 – 80

The paintings are rich in metaphorical suggestion, but metaphor, in this art, never becomes its big brother, symbolism. Symbolism is self-important, grandiose, all-explaining, and the works never pretend to that kind of overbearing consequence. They are about moments, perceptions, sudden visions or insights. Hodgkin's sense of time – defined in his art as a fast-running river of events from which the occasional lived moment surfaces with the clarity and distinctness of a dark rock rising above water – is intimately related to this quality of modesty in his painting. It is a quality of *un-self-importance*, but it is also defiant, in its own way. When the artist paints a subject
P. 87 such as *Interior at Oakwood Court* (1978–83), a glowing thicket of forms mingling and mixing, evoking social (and perhaps sexual) contact; or when he paints *Tea* (1977–80), a blooming constellation of pictorial incident, hanging a thousand dabs of paint in the air like a thousand barely heard remarks in an indistinct conversation; or when he paints
P. 70 *Counting the Days* (1979–82), a picture that surrounds a patch of blackness with rich pattern and bright liquid colour like the forms traced by the imagination around the absence of someone awaited, he insists on the inconsequence of his subjects, and on his art's rootedness in real fragments of real time. The paintings are not concerned with other, more cosmically explanatory or preacherish or millennial conceptions of time. They argue that the moment is all we have.

The metaphorical reach of the paintings signals their intention to speak of more than the memories that are their inspiration. The memories themselves are unimportant, in the end, and the art acknowledges this by making it often impossible to figure out their specifics from what it presents to the eye. What survives is a sense of them, a glimmering of their significance that might (the painter hopes) strike a chord of recognition in those who look at them. Hodgkin's pictures suggest that he is under no illusions about the power of painting. These are not pictures that will explain the world, let alone change it. But the instant, the chance experience, the sudden glimpse of something (anything, just a piece of broken glass, even), can become a work of art that talks, modestly, about larger things than the life of just one person. And when the paintings achieve that un-self-important kind of grandeur, they recall the art of other painters of the instant. The recollection has less to do with the formal qualities of art (what art looks like), than with its functions and ambitions (what art does).

The pictures may recall the art of Degas, who, in his many paintings of dancers rehearsing, created images not merely of young Parisian ballerinas wearily grounded after their exertions, but paintings of how hard it is to cheat reality; paintings of the physical cost of the attempt to defeat gravity (to fly, which is what the classical dancer is doomed to attempt, again and again); paintings of truth at odds with aspiration. They

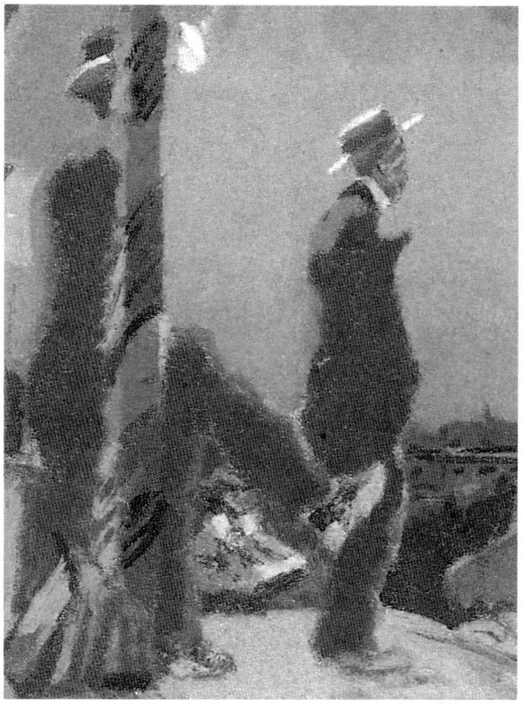

may recall the art of Sickert, finding ineffable melancholy but also courage and even a faith in life in a late afternoon performance of fairground entertainers. Painting *Brighton Pierrots* cavorting at dusk before rows of empty deck chairs, Sickert distilled the sadness and bravery of the world to the uneven contours of a performer's be-trousered leg profiled against a scarlet sky. Hodgkin distils the poignancy and fragility of life to a piece of broken Venetian glass in a frame.

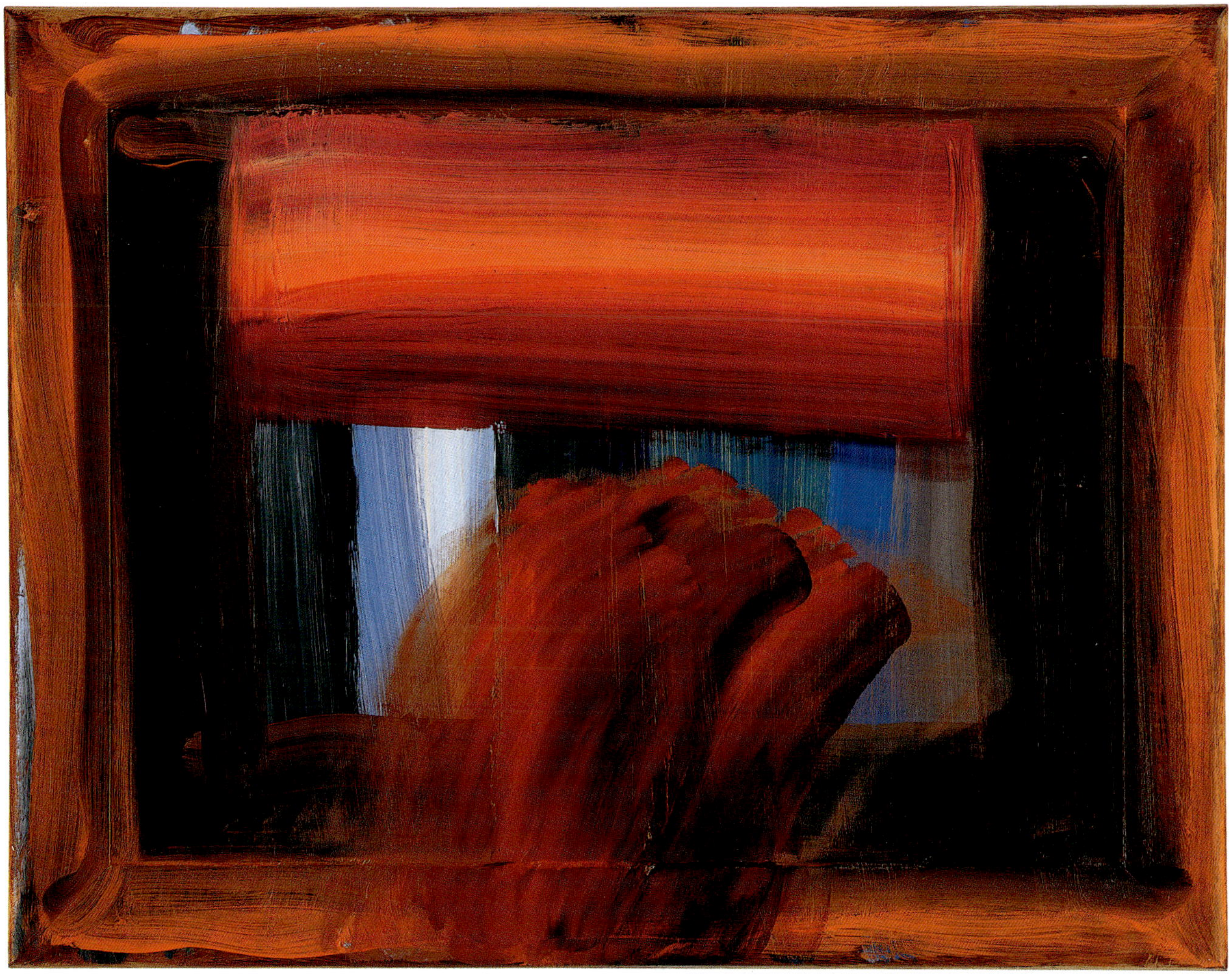

IN PARIS WITH YOU
1995 – 96

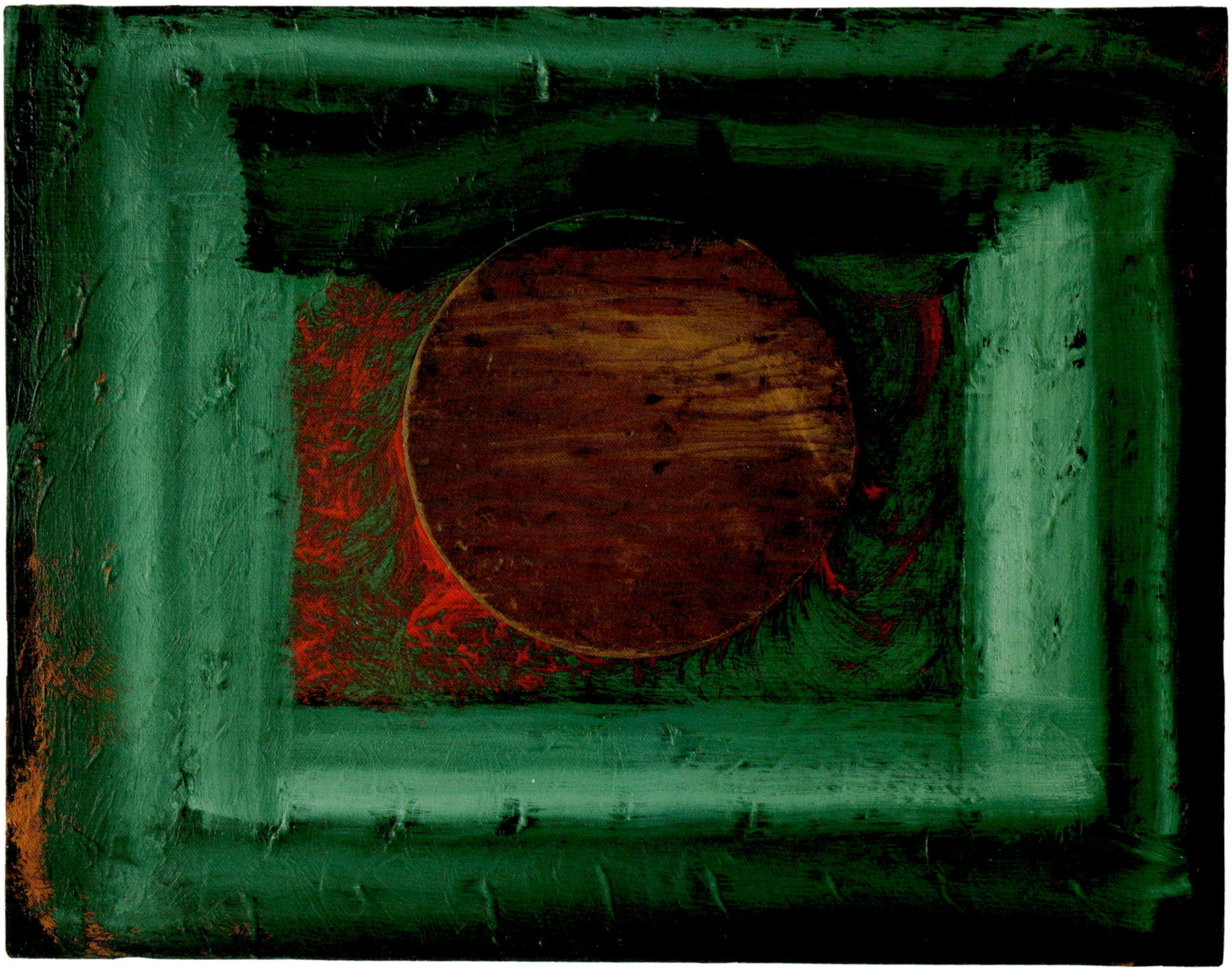

THE MOON
1978 – 80

8
TRANSFIGURATION

> His paintings are not windows onto an external nature. They are not windows through which light passes, but mirrors that return light, and with it a transformed nature.[13]
>
> John Elderfield on Matisse

The paintings speak of transfiguration as well as perdition, of exuberance as well as sadness. They celebrate the transforming role of remembrance, which is always an alteration of the facts. Every painting is a surrogate for past experience. But it also aims to outlive it, to transcend it. Each picture is not, strictly speaking, a representation. It is, rather, an *instead of*, a thing with the power to supplant and exceed the experience that prompted it; a thing, too, that must become independent of its maker, must in the end come untethered from his life and feelings.

When Hodgkin paints *The Moon* (1978–80) – one of the most Cubist in spirit of all his pictures – he emphasizes the artifice of art by engineering a near absolute separation of form and colour, the object and the veil of atmosphere through which it is perceived. Where is Hodgkin's moon, exactly? It is not quite in that disc of unprimed, unpainted wood at the painting's centre (the seat of an old stool, incidentally, glued to the support); nor is it in the spreading zones of emerald green that frame that mute brown circle. It is in both places at the same time. This is a painting about how memories are made up of discrete elements that can never quite be made to cohere. Yet as a painting of that process, the process of remembering (or trying to remember) something beautiful once seen – as a picture of *that*, it is entirely coherent. It is a picture, too, that wins from the brokenness of experience a new form of totality, the totality of a painting, a work of art that not only stands for the moon but that replaces it, stands *in* for it.

Rain (1984–89) is one of Hodgkin's largest paintings. But it does not look large. It possesses the brilliant density of a miniature. It is a painter's response to a self-imposed challenge: how to invest a painting of an utterly inconsequential event (it is always raining, somewhere) with a charge of remembered feeling that will raise it above the mundanity of its subject matter; how, in short, to turn raw experience into art. The closest precedents for this picture, as for *The Moon*, may lie in the Synthetic Cubism of Braque and Picasso, those tremendously urgent, crowded pictures of inconsequence made consequential; those pictures of ordinary life's actual complicatedness – phrased in the visual language of collage, a disparate yoking together of impressions – and the difficulty of encapsulating it. *Rain* strikes a similar bargain with uncertainty, presenting a flurry of forms merging beneath leaden grey clouds. But it is a painting that also has the quality of an epiphany, or waking dream, a picture that conjures a certain kind of rare moment in life. One of those moments, perhaps just *after* it has been raining, when the world seems touched with freshness and optimism, when its colours seem brighter than usual, newly vivid, glossed by wetness. One of those moments when life seems worth living, after all. In *Rain*, the artist remakes meteorology as metaphor and extracts an image of unexpected hope, even transcendence of a kind, from a wet afternoon in the countryside.

Art has always been a form of redemption, a transfiguration of the commonplace, and the very act of turning something into an image – whether it be a bison traced on the wall of a cave or a milk jug painted by Chardin – alters and aggrandizes it. Art is transubstantiation, and the eucharistic ritual of the Mass, where wine becomes blood and bread flesh, has a lot in common with the primitive and ritualistic activity we call painting. This is one reason why painting and religion have always had such a close and uneasy relationship with one another. To be a painter is to arrogate to oneself the powers of divinity. It is to remake the world. Painting transforms the mundane, both metaphorically and materially. Painting is itself *made* out of ordinary things that have been transfigured, the base matter of earth or oil or ground-up stone. Every painter is a shaman of sorts.

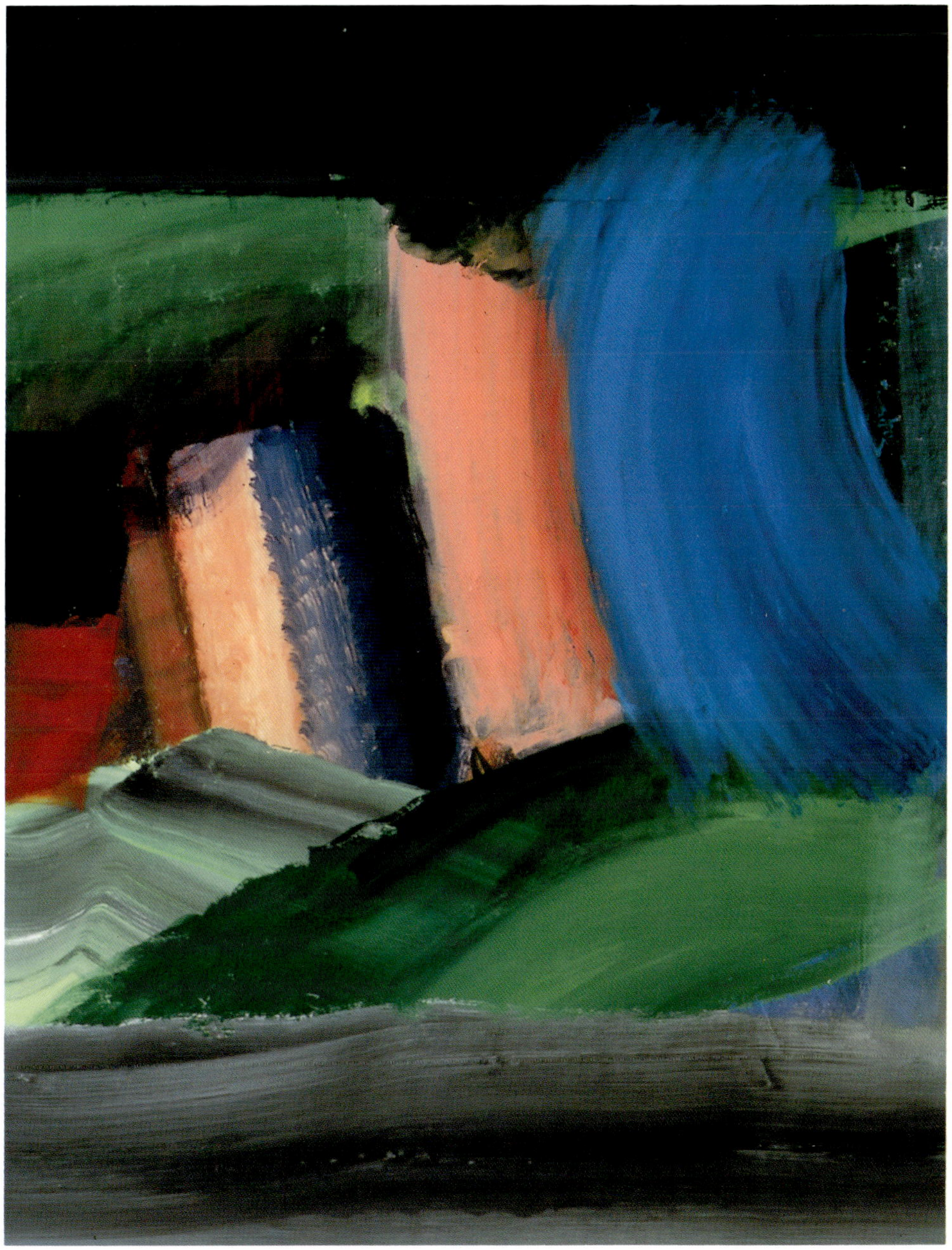

RAIN (DETAIL)
1984 – 89

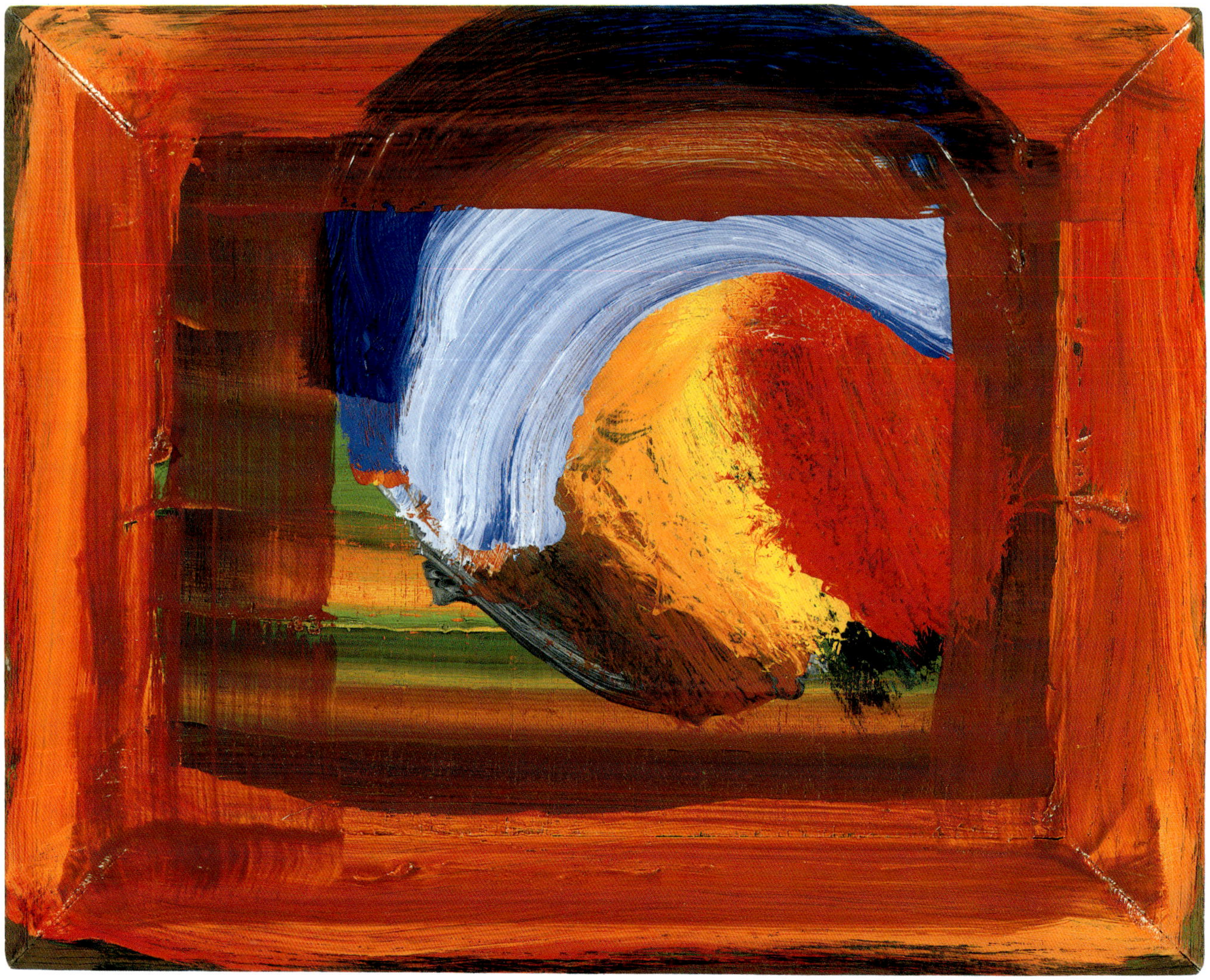

FRUIT
1988 – 89

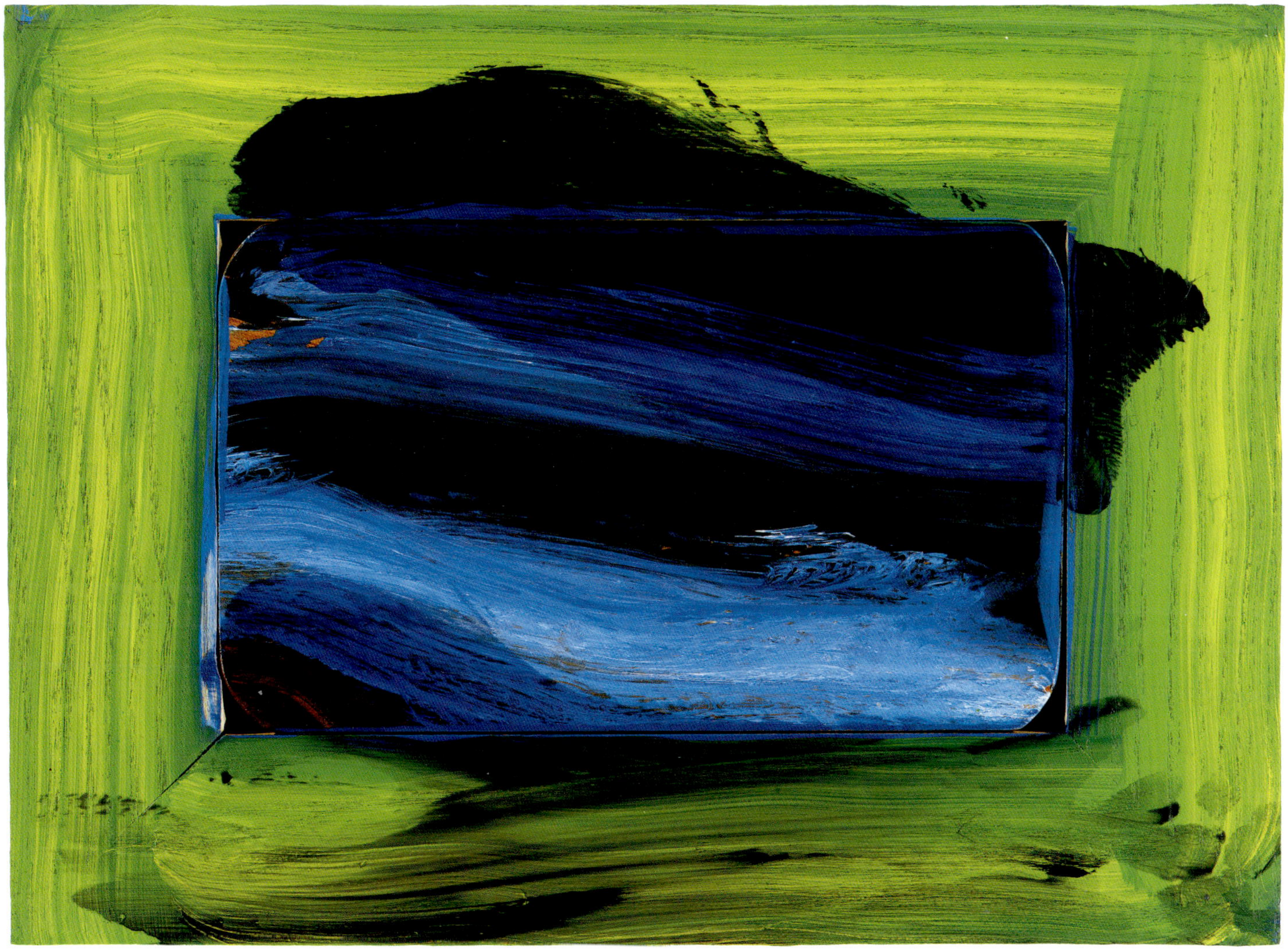

FISHERMAN'S COVE
1993

Hodgkin's art quietly reaffirms the primitive, occult power of painting. The artist can make up his own, parallel world, can make it brighter and better and more radiant than the real thing. When Hodgkin paints *Rainbow* (1983–85), he attempts, with a form of necessary hubris, not to represent nature but to outdo nature. Nature is reordered, distilled to a lucid arrangement of curved strokes of brightly coloured paint. *Rainbow* is a picture that aims undisguisedly at beauty, that wants to ravish the eye and that asserts art's power to re-create the world in other and more radiant terms. The artist can paint the rainbow without the rain. P. 100

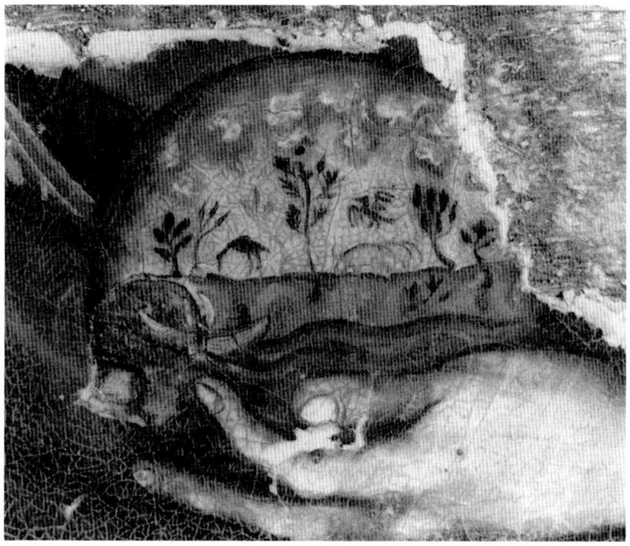

In 1890, Maurice Denis counselled painters to 'Remember that a picture – before it is a battle horse, a nude woman, or an anecdote – is in essence a plane surface covered with colours put together in a certain order'.[14] Hodgkin's paintings always insist on this truth. Immense pleasure is taken in the nature of oil paint, in the codes and conventions of pictorial gesture, in the blatant unreality of art. *In the Bay of Naples* (1980–82) is a tremendously sensual painting, almost a bravura demonstration of the things that the painter can make paint do: dots and blobs of red and blue and green paint bob and twinkle on a dark ground, like lights seen out at sea; a vertical bar of pink and blue paint evokes something quite different, more architectural, more solid; a liquid, serpentine

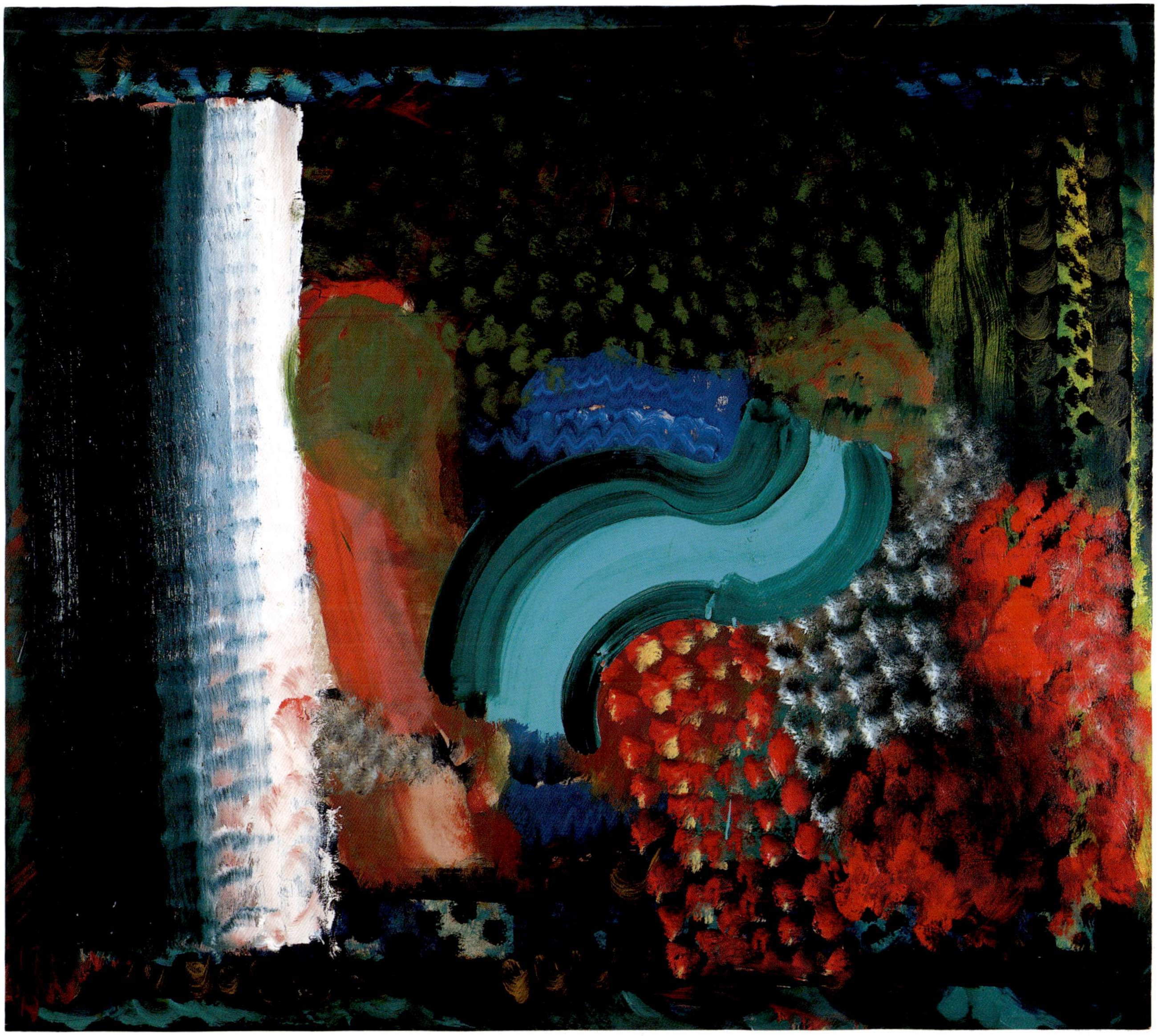

IN THE BAY OF NAPLES
1980 – 82

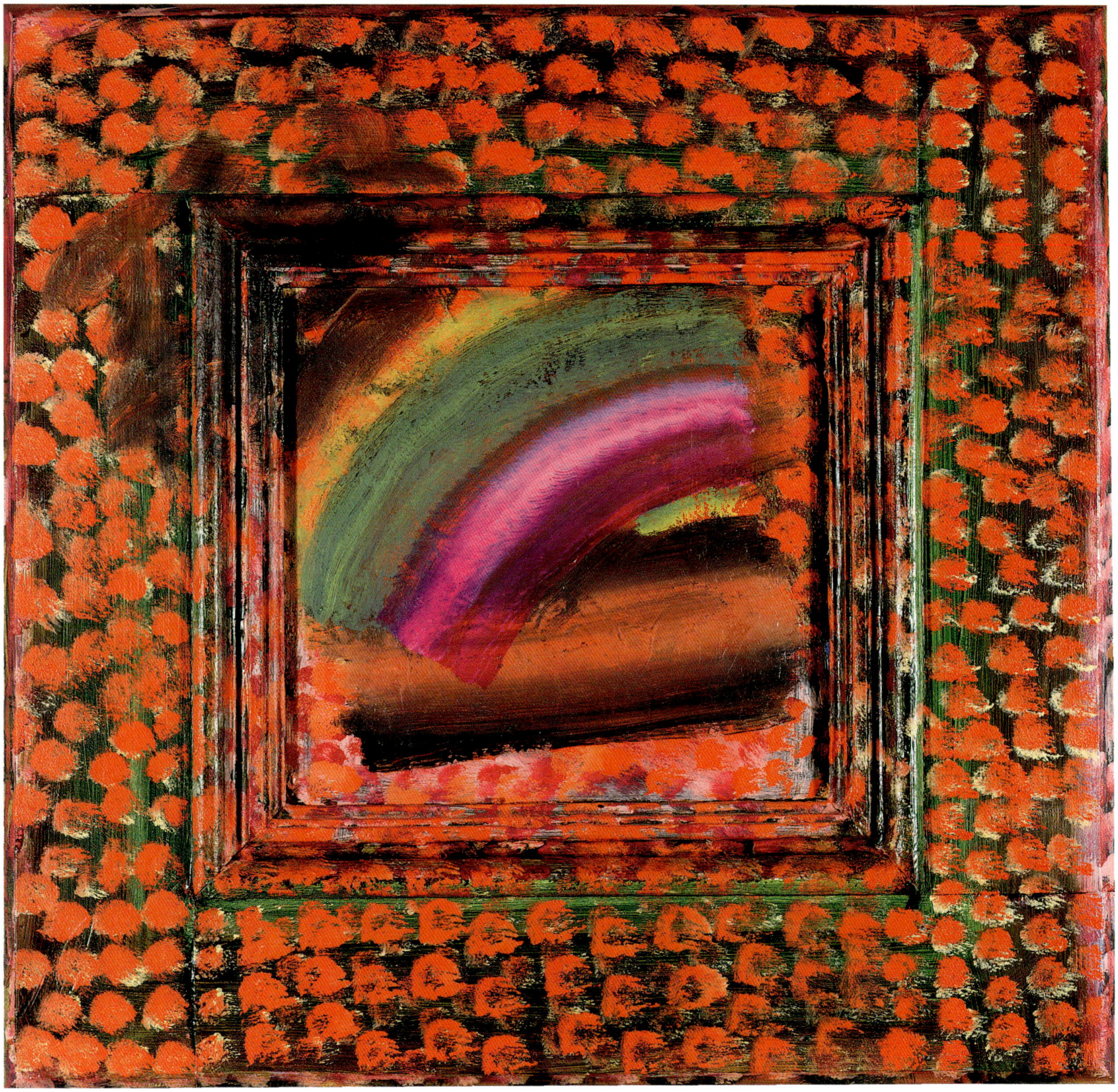

RAINBOW
1983 – 85

swathe of turquoise and dark blue and green paint at the painting's centre, summarily applied in a few strokes of the brush, is a wave transmuted, boldly, simply, into one of Hodgkin's many pictorial signs for water. This is not so much a landscape painting as a landscape of paint, a world of pleasure to be entered into. A painting can be, not just the world transfigured, but another world altogether. An instant elsewhere.

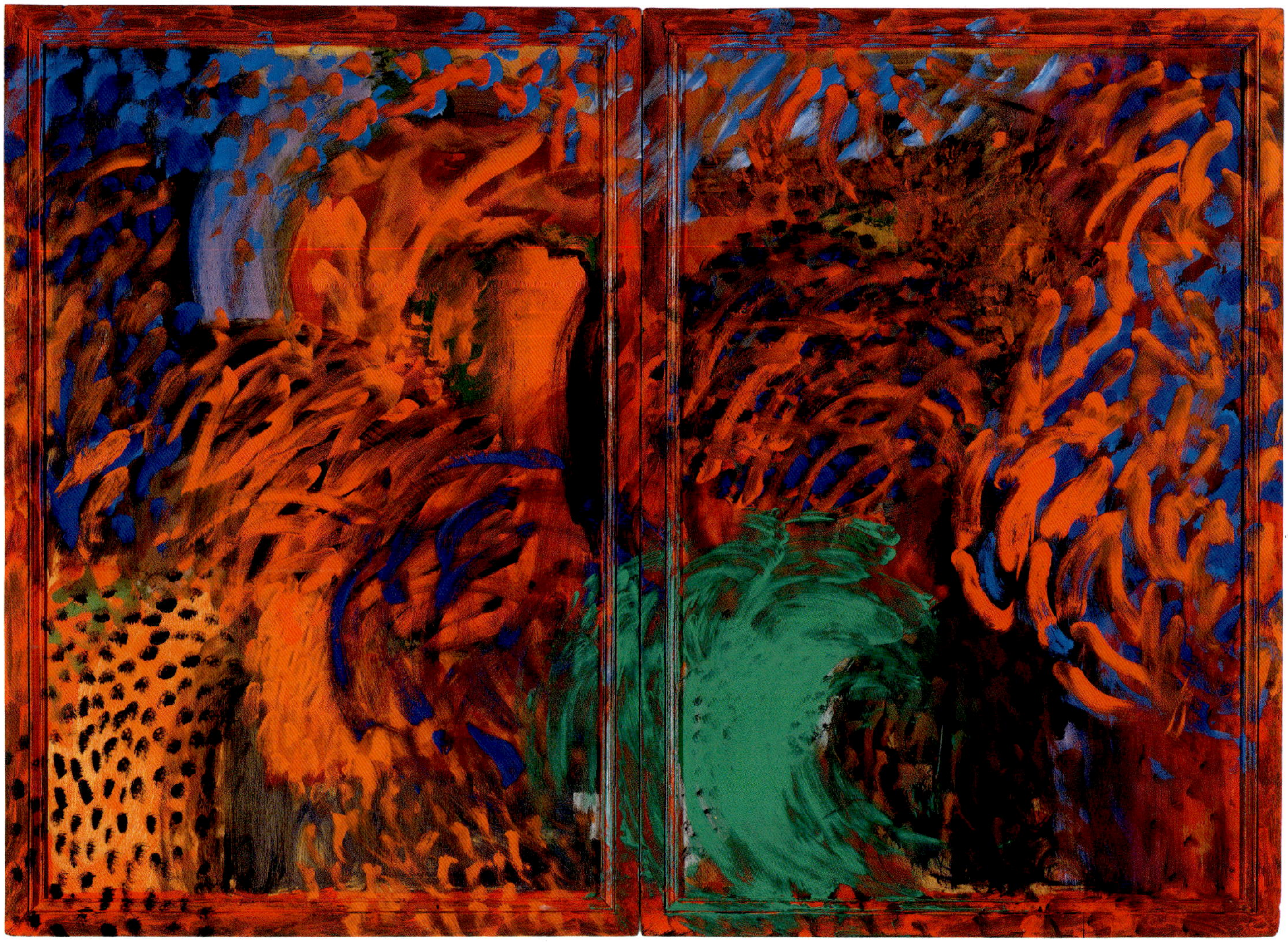

WHEN DID WE GO TO MOROCCO?
1988 – 93

9
ELSEWHERE

Travel is a recurrent theme. The titles of many of the paintings are not just oblique clues
to their subjects, but they also add up to a kind of haphazard itinerary, the diary of a life
PP. 45, 148 seen as a journey: *Small View in Venice* (1984–86), *Waking up in Naples* (1980–84),
PP. 106, 56 *Egyptian Night* (1983–85), *In a French Restaurant*, *The Terrace, Delhi*, *When Did We
P. 102 *Go to Morocco?* (1988–93). The idea of travel is implicit in all of the paintings, which
have the fragmentary, opaque or poignant quality of souvenirs brought back from
abroad.

To travel is to see different things and it is also to see things differently. When we travel to a foreign place, our habits and routines are disturbed and our experience of the world takes on an unfamiliar texture. We notice things that back home we often take for granted: the colours of a landscape, the forms of its vegetation, new sounds and smells; the architecture, how coffee is served, designs on cigarette packets, the way people dress and the sort of litter they leave on the street; the heat or the light, the size of raindrops and the sound they make when they land. Travelling, we study the world more inquisitively and alertly than usual. We look at it as intently as if it were art.

The frequent references to travel in Hodgkin's art, the countless allusions to places that are foreign and alien and unfamiliar, record the painter's movements, but only imprecisely. They also amount to a statement of ambition for the paintings themselves. They say that to look at a picture should itself be to travel, to be transported, to be taken somewhere else. Every painting is its own self-sufficient world, to be experienced as we would experience a foreign place travelled to for the first time: radiant, uncanny, alien, seen more urgently and more freshly than the places we know too well. This may partly explain Hodgkin's preference for colours that are clear and fresh and unclouded, colours as seen by someone who approaches the world with the attitude of one travelling, who sees it unveiled and undimmed.

In Tangier (1987–90) exuberantly demonstrates the transporting capacities of painting, its provision of an alternate world of artifice. In painting, things can be distilled to their essences, rendered down to glorious code: six swipes of green for a palm tree, two bars of red and one of yellow for a sunset, a curve of subtle, half-hidden blue for a glimpse of sea. Similarly, *Egyptian Night* is not really a painting about Egypt but a painting about how painting can take you somewhere else, suddenly and simply. Egypt, here, is simply a metaphor for the potential for exoticism that lies within art, its oddity and vividness. The picture can be made out as a representation – in fact it is fairly literal: a pyramid, its two visible sides differently lit and differently coloured – but it far exceeds its representational brief. Hodgkin's sky of cerulean blue is illuminated by a thousand blurred, falling stars, surreally coloured, multitudinous blobs of red paint tumbling thickly like the shaken flakes in a toy snowstorm.

Both pictures evoke the sudden impact the strangeness of a place can have on the mind and the eye. But the paintings also *replace* those experiences thoroughly and ruthlessly and revel in their own abrupt artifice. Adrian Stokes, in Venice, saw 'the undulating floor of St Mark's' as 'water with all its colours eternally healed'.[15] Art can compensate for the transience of things. Art can fix experience, can make of it something solid, true, lasting. Works of art might be inevitably sad memorials but they are also monuments.

Hodgkin's uses of his pictorial language are not fixed, because his first allegiance is to each separate picture rather than anything like a consistency of style or the dogged pursuit of a particular representational method. This may partly explain why the paintings hang so uneasily next to one another (and next to paintings by other artists). Their singular, sore-thumb quality is one by-product of the painter's determination to make each object a separate world, subject to its own rules, rather than just another autograph work, another Hodgkin.

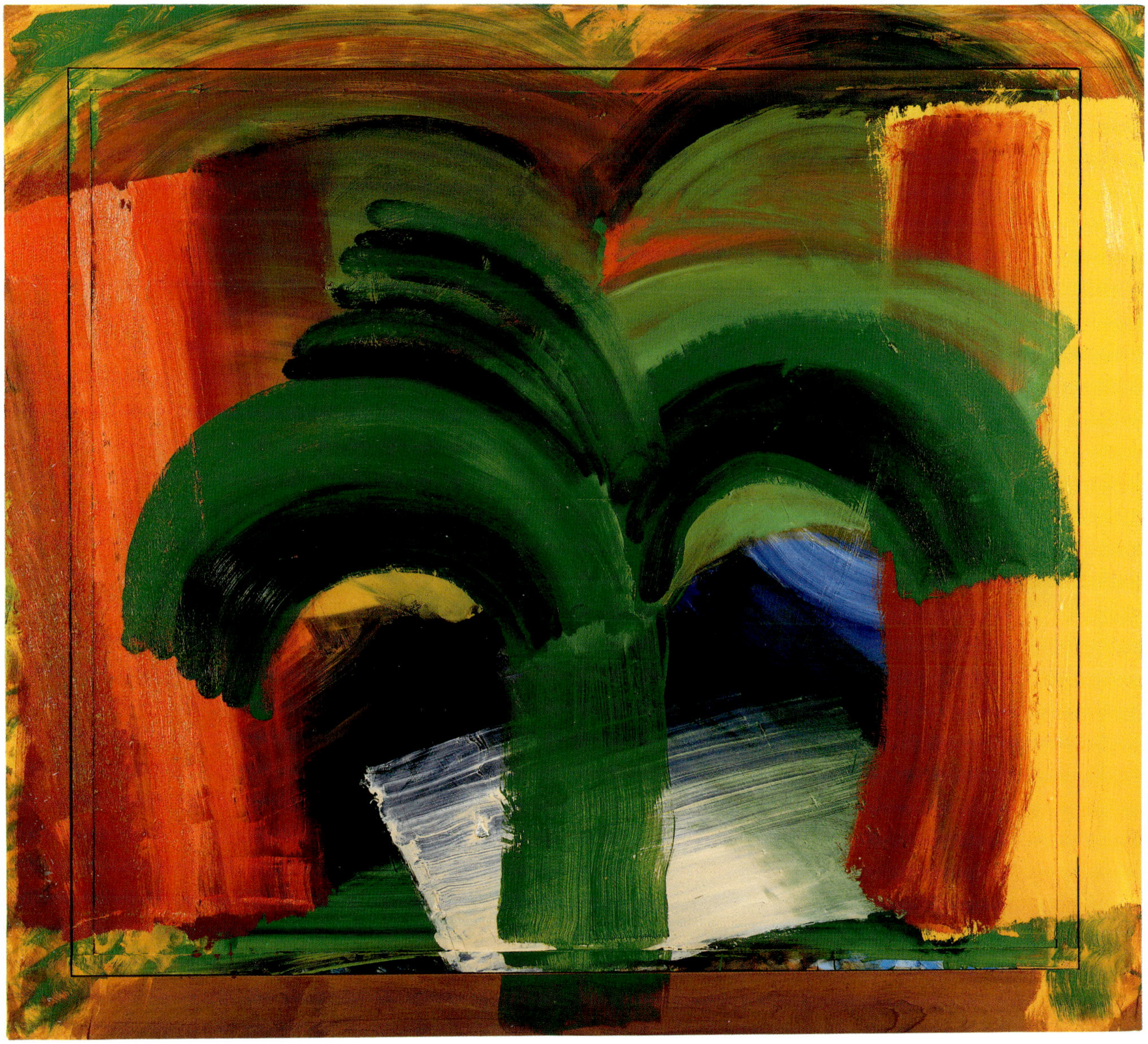

IN TANGIER
1987 – 90

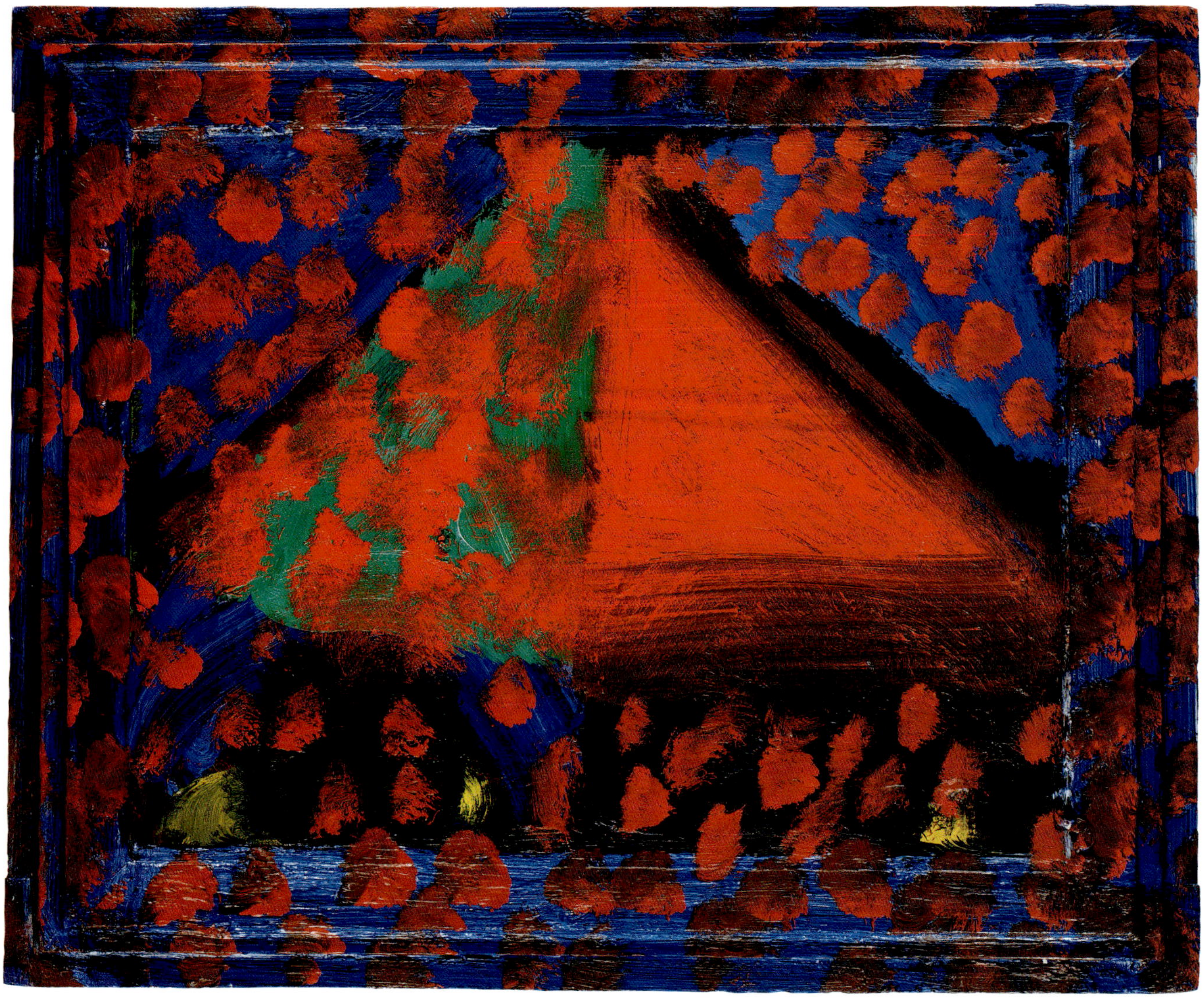

EGYPTIAN NIGHT
1983 – 85

The blob of splotched paint can be read as figure, as meteorological incident, as leaf or tree or decorative pattern or (simply) as blob; the smooth sweep of paint can be read as figure or rainbow or wave or as the spreading fronds of a palm tree. This art rebukes or refutes the art of more programmatic, systematic painters which it occasionally, distantly echoes, through the wilfully varied deployment of its devices and through the wilful, self-evident artifice of its effects. *In Central Park* (1983–86), an P. 108 autumnal painting that might suggest a canopy of leaves seen from beneath, a haphazard pattern of foliage shot through with sunlight, is like an Impressionist painting gone wild. The dabbed marks of Impressionist painting (or Pointillist painting, which was Impressionism given even more of a pseudo-scientific rationale) have, here, become almost entirely detached from their supposed referents. Here, the mark phrases itself unambiguously as an analogue, a surrogate for things. Before paint is anything else, it is paint.

The places that are made in painting are always fantasies. They are like descriptions of places in books or on the backs of postcards in that they are mediated, inevitably, by the temperament of someone else. They are places experienced at one remove. The fantasy is pleasurable, but the consciousness that it *is* a fantasy remains. Painting can take you to places that you could never, in reality, visit. Painting can take you to the moon. *Dark Moon* (1983–84), a small circle of painted wood, 31.4 centi- P. 107 metres (12⅜ inches) in diameter, explores the gap between reality and painting, between fact and aspiration. The moon can be reached for, but what you actually get never turns out to be the bright dreamed-of circle of pure white, glowing in the sky. What you get is clouded, opaque, muddied by the consciousness of failure or by unhappiness or the rejection of others. The other worlds created in painting can talk of what happens in this one, of real predicaments and dilemmas and disappointments.

Hodgkin's places are mostly, for an Englishman, exotic places. India, Africa and the Mediterranean are associated with un-English heat and colour, un-English radiance. They are places that are definitively elsewhere. But their elsewhereness is more than a matter of topography. It is, the paintings inspired by the places suggest, a matter of temperament and of aesthetics and perhaps also a matter of self-definition. *Goodbye* P. 109

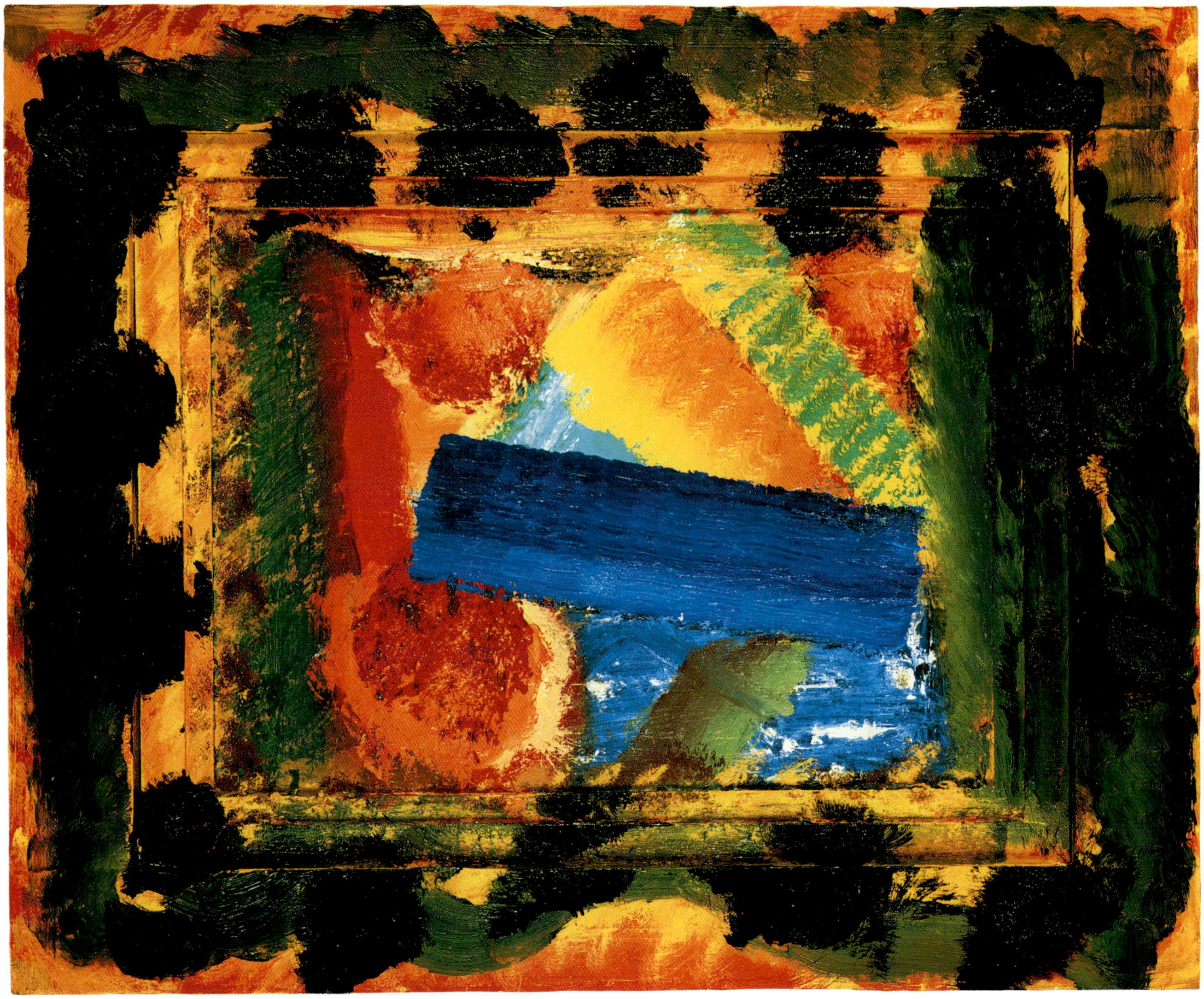

GOODBYE TO THE BAY OF NAPLES
1980 – 82

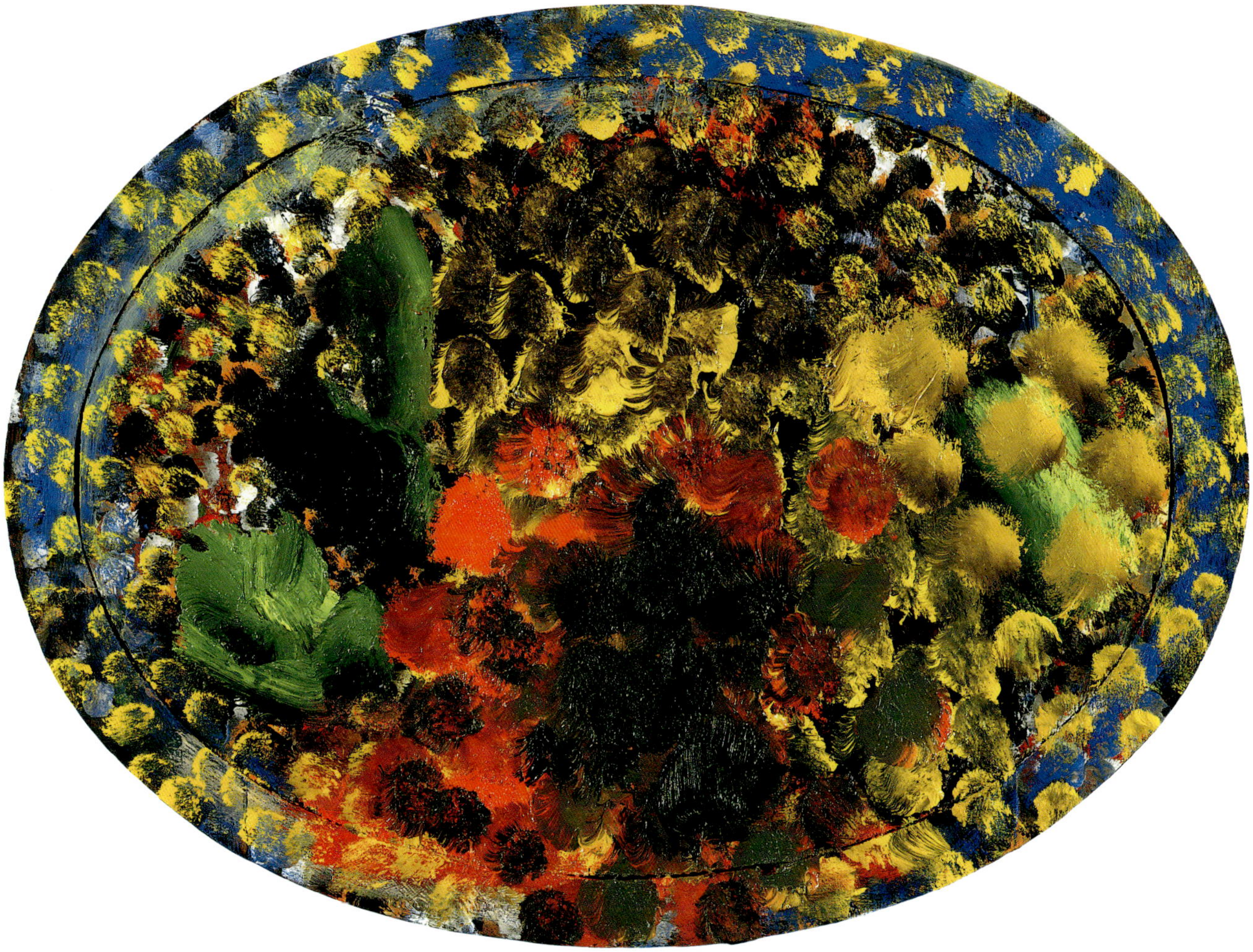

IN CENTRAL PARK
1983 – 86

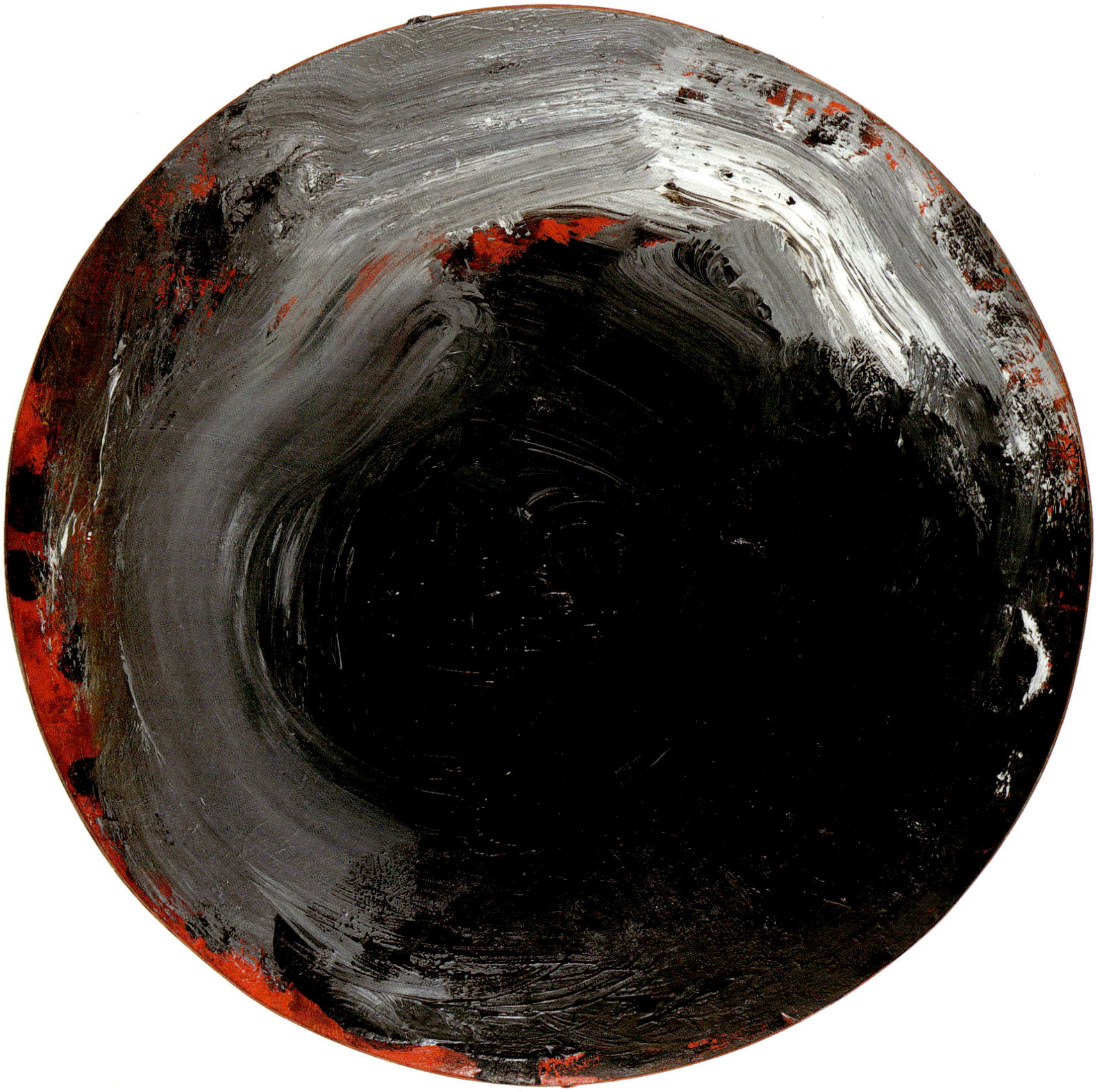

DARK MOON
1983 – 84

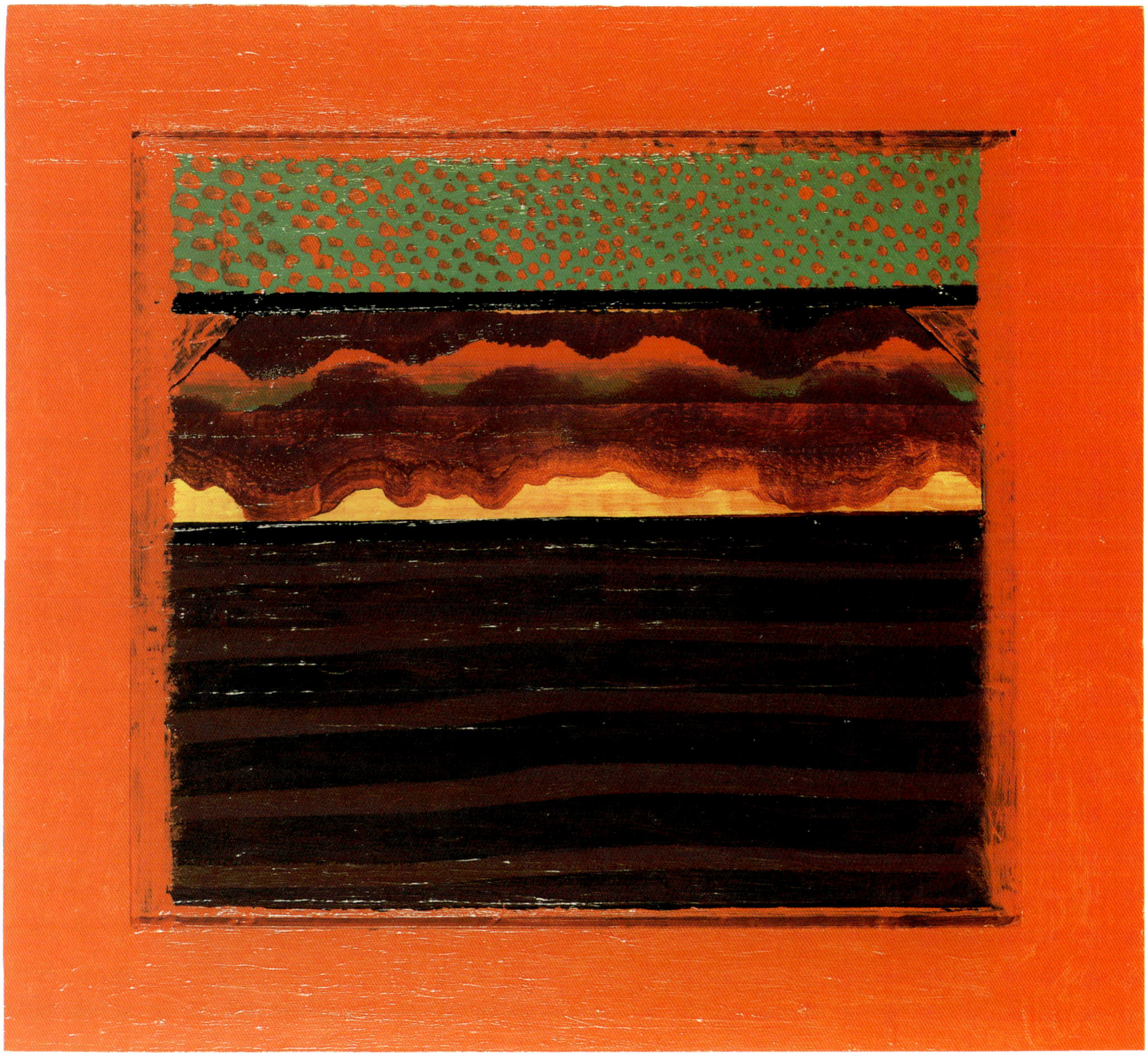

BOMBAY SUNSET
1972 – 73

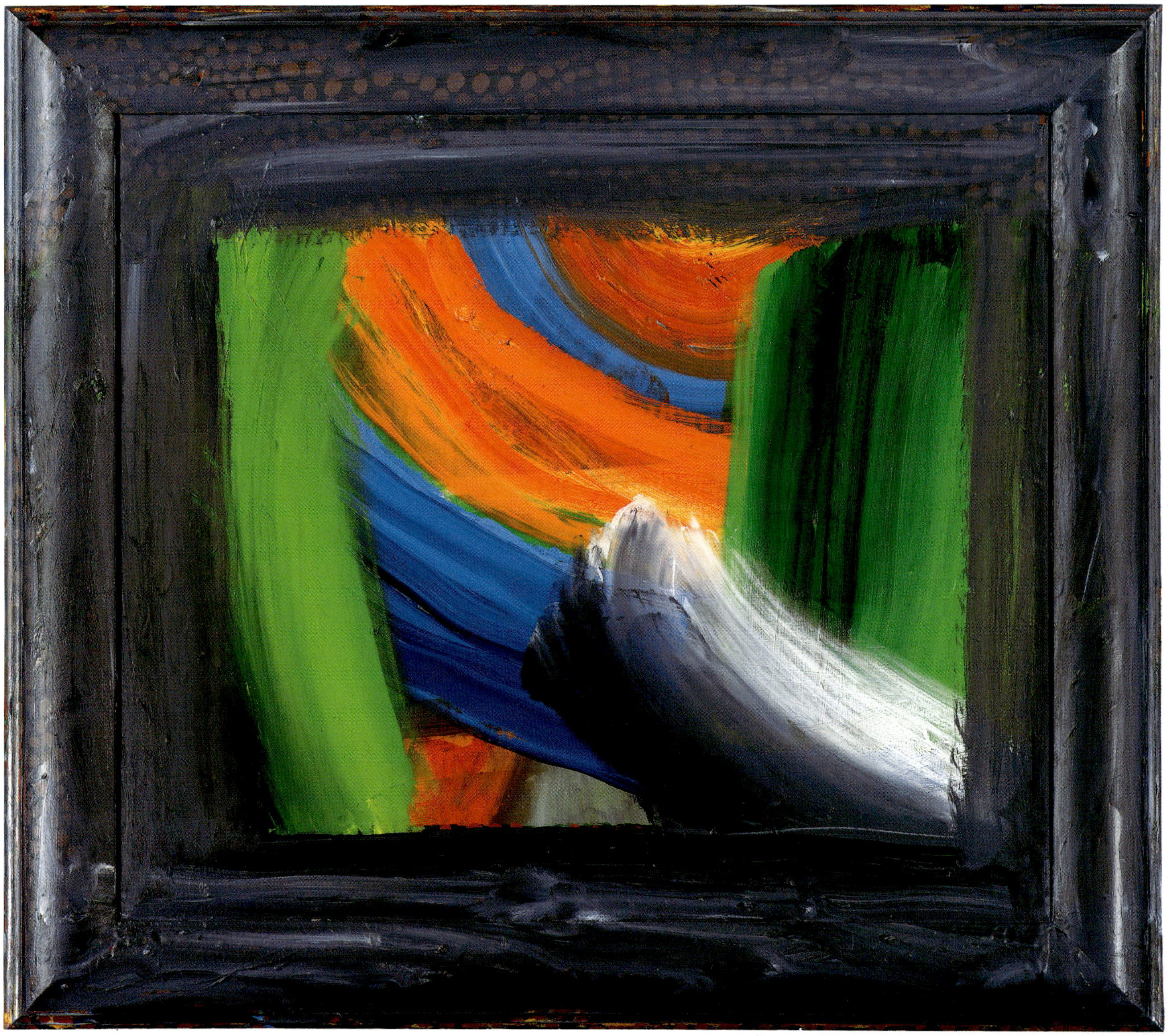

THE LAST TIME I SAW PARIS
1988 – 91

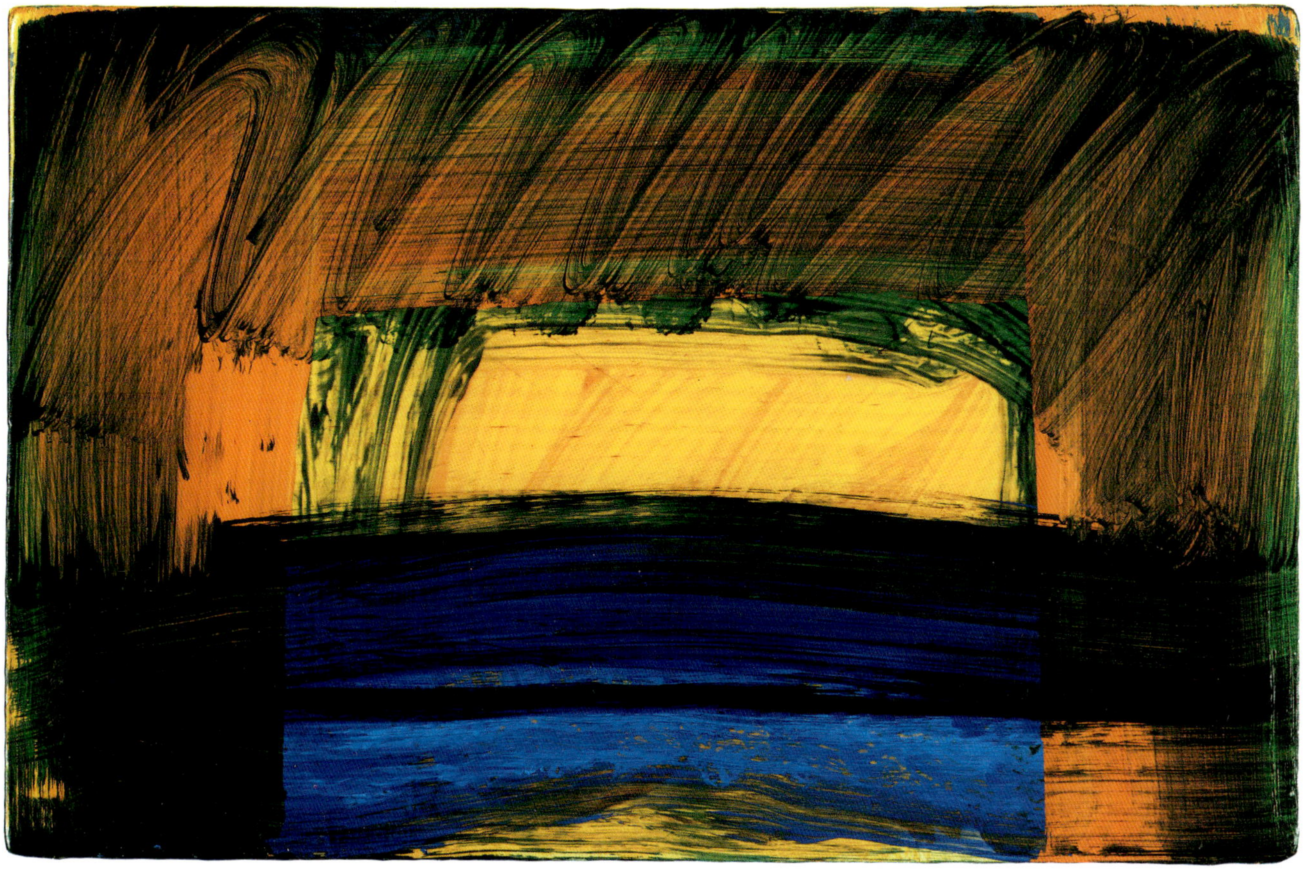

KERALA
1992

to the Bay of Naples (1980–82), or *Bombay Sunset* (1972–73), or *Kerala* (1992) are assertively, aggressively un-English in the sun-struck brilliance, the sudden vibrancy of their colours. They might not be directly representational pictures of the places suggested by their titles – although *Bombay Sunset*, painted, as Bruce Chatwin once wrote, 'in the colours of mud, blood, and bile',[16] may contain a sense of discovery of the violent colours of the Indian landscape – but they are definitely pictures of places that look and feel nothing like Britain. They may be paintings about not wanting to be British, or at least about not wanting to be British in a certain way. PP. 111, 113

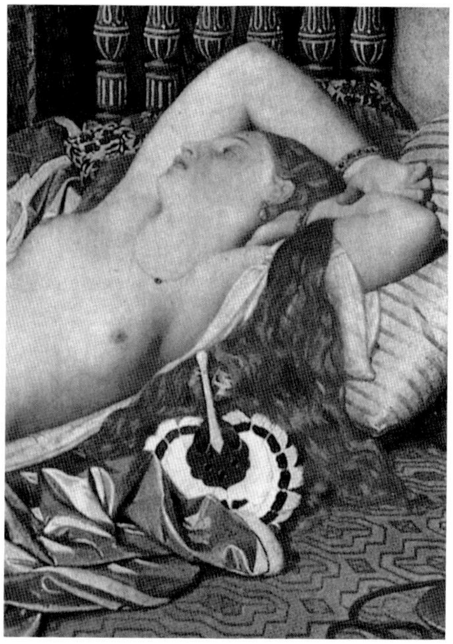

Paul Fussell has written an account of British anti-Britishness in the years between the two world wars, *Abroad: British Literary Traveling Between the Wars*. In it, he describes the malaise of writers sick of their own nation and enthused with the notion of foreignness, which may not be entirely irrelevant to Hodgkin's painting and the discontents of which it speaks. He quotes the writer C.W. Tomlinson, who argued that 'every travel agency constituted evidence of secret disaffection, just as every travel poster was really an implicit satire on the local scene. "No wonder it pays", (Tomlinson) says, "to decorate the walls of the capital with romantic but seditious pictures of palms, midnight suns, coasts of illusion and ships outward bound. Nothing could so plainly indicate our revolt from the affairs we must somehow pretend to venerate."'[17] And he lists the adjectives applied to the British scene by Tomlinson's contemporary, George Orwell: 'dingy... fly-blown...discolored...musty...grey...dead...damp...joyless'.[18]

Hodgkin's dissent from his own Britishness is no less pointed. His work dissents from a British tradition of artistic amateurism, incompetence and dullness. It dissents from a British tradition of a thousand dark and lifeless fifth-rate portraits, a tradition of coffee-coloured landscape paintings and of murky conversation pictures by the score, a tradition ruled by dun and brown and ochre and kipper-coloured art. It dissents from a tradition of dutifully colourless painting (although it also allows for one or two exceptions, notably Constable and Turner). Hodgkin's own seditious pictures of palms and midnight suns are both embrace and refusal.

Topography can be a form of polemic, and the places a painter paints can be his way of marking out his own territory. That territory is not really India or Africa or the Mediterranean, since places in art are always just constructs, pretexts for painting pictures (the Orient of Delacroix or Ingres or Matisse never existed, except in art). It is, rather, the territory of his painting, the terrain of the pictures themselves, that is being defined. And it is their freedom to be other worlds, their horizons not limited by certain safe, polite, well-mannered British attitudes to colour, feeling and expression, that is being fought for.

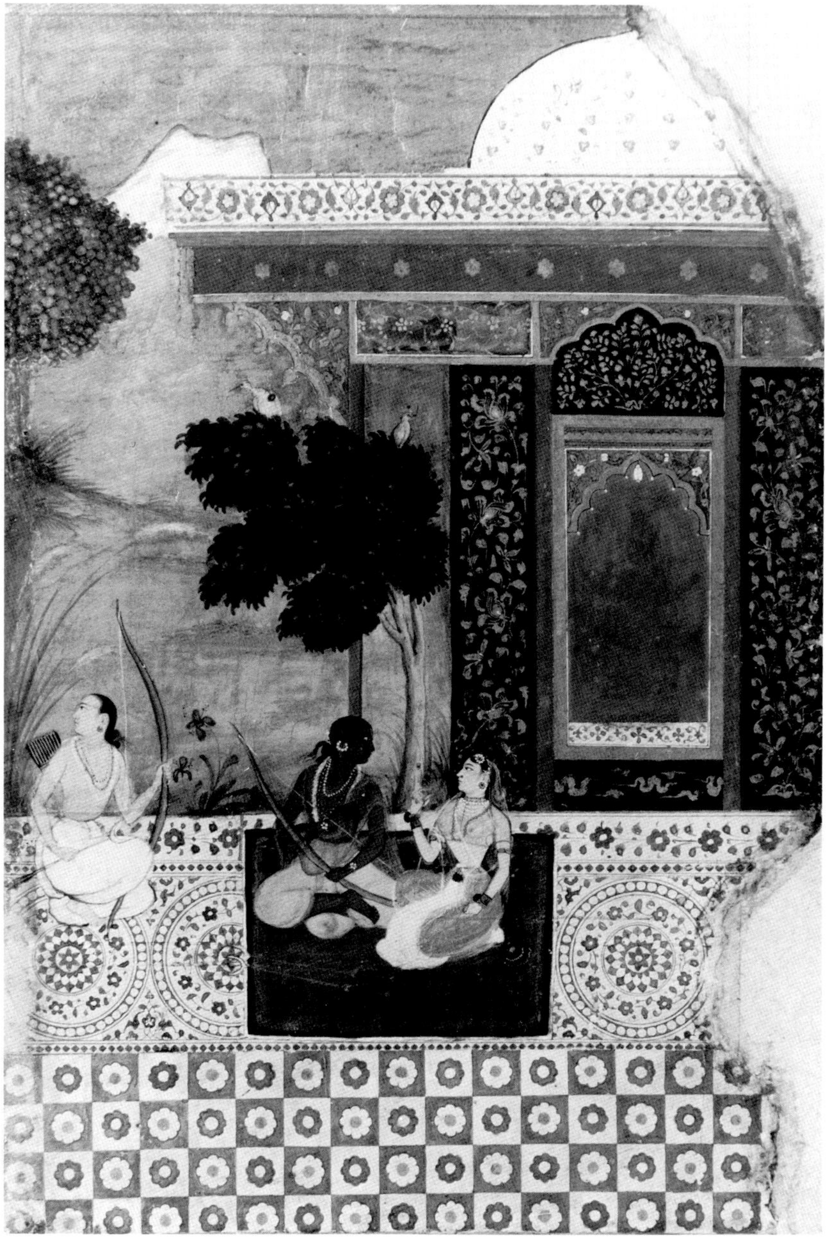

10
INDIAN ART

The painter's frequent travels to India and his extensive collection of pictures painted in the Indian subcontinent have led to a certain misconception about the relationship between his art and Indian art. The standard explanation advanced for his love of Indian art is superficially convincing. Here is a Western European artist, working within the Intimist tradition of Bonnard and Vuillard, who admires Indian art for its brilliant, miniaturist qualities. Here is an artist who finds, in the art of the Indian subcontinent, parallels to his own preference for bright, unsaturated colours and a visual language of eloquent compression.

But this is to disregard the true qualities of most of the Indian art that Hodgkin owns. Many of the Indian pictures in his collection are not painted to the scale of the miniature, the page in a book, but are large, long, panoramic images. One of the more striking features of his collection as a whole is the predominance of low-toned, essentially linear paintings and drawings, especially from the Kota school. His interest in Indian painting may be hard to account for because it does not fit the standard genealogical model of influence: the notion that artists who collect art are always in search of their ancestors; the idea that x must like y's work because he finds in it a striking prediction of his own. But collecting, for an artist, can play another role. It can provide an escape from the self and its preoccupations.

In most respects Hodgkin's Indian paintings run directly counter to the tendencies of his own art. The narrative clarity with which an eighteenth-century painter working in Rajasthan tells the story of a day's hunting, or the descriptive complexities of a mid-seventeenth-century painting of a marriage procession by an artist from the Punjab hills, are not to be found in Hodgkin's own painting. His art sets itself against such forms of descriptive minuteness.

But the collector and the artist are not two entirely different people, and influence need not express itself through a congruence of styles, indeed through anything even approaching mimicry. Hodgkin owns very few overtly religious or allegorical Indian pictures, and has a large number of essentially secular depictions of real places in which people are engaged in the commonplace activities of court and ordinary social life. His art itself speaks determinedly (if very differently) of mundane existence, of shared

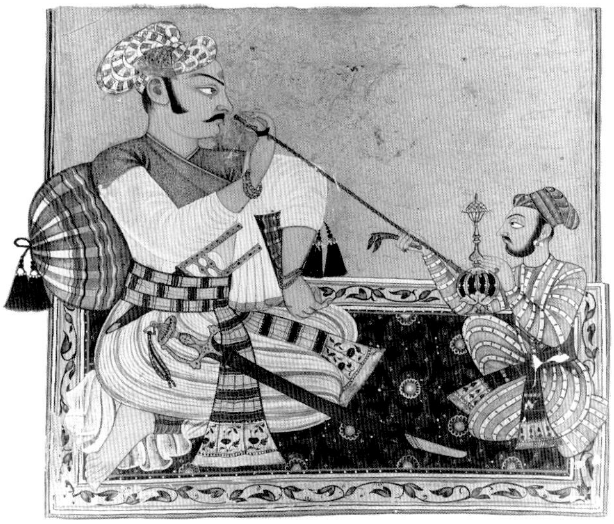

experiences and social occasions. And it speaks, as his Indian art sometimes does, of moments of intense emotion suddenly frozen, shielded within areas of painting that are essentially conventional forms, richly patterned enclosures. To see the two lovers who gaze so intensely at each other, rapt in a field of high artifice, in his Mogul painting of *Rama, Lakshman and Sita in Panchavati* (*c.* 1595–1600) is perhaps to sense something of this deeper, unpredictable affinity between the art of the collector and the art he collects. When Hodgkin succeeds, in his own painting, he engineers a tension between the conventions of pictorial form and the pressures of lived, felt reality which is precisely analogous to the effect of this sixteenth-century picture. He conveys an intense emotion, suspended within the artificial world that is a painting. Hodgkin uses his own, self-created vocabulary of feather-edged bars, blobs and bands and stripes of colour to create an image meant to exceed the formal nature of its devices, an image that conveys a feeling, an image that lives in the subtle play between its forms and the sudden shaft of reality that it seeks to communicate.

But the strongest link between his art and the Indian art that he has collected may be still harder to pin down precisely. It is an affinity that is really a shared faith in painting simply and confidently to create its own world. Indian art is fantastically daring and assured in the way in which it uses different mimetic registers within a single image.

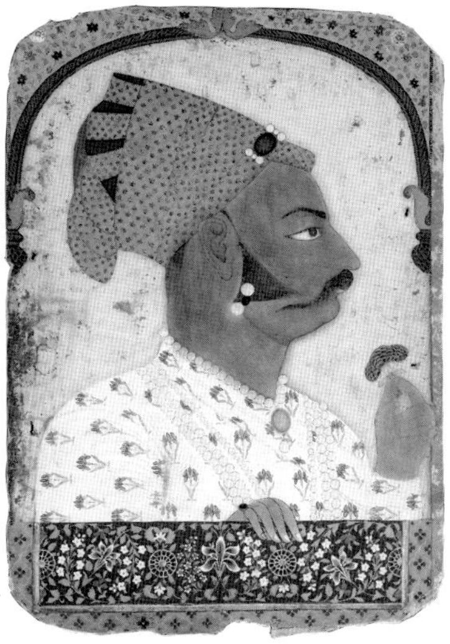

A seventeenth-century Mogul painting of an elephant and its rider may, for instance, demonstrate three or four or more different painted codes for likeness. These might range from absolutely flat pattern for the decorated cloth on the elephant's back to the diaphanous, translucent tones used for the fabric worn by its rider; or from the smooth, linear idealization of the elephant's anatomy to the highly realized painting of the rider's flesh. Such radical slippages in and out of focus, towards and away from idealization, will not be found in Western art (or hardly ever) until the advent of Cubism. What Indian art declares, and what Hodgkin's art affirms, is art's absolute autonomy. Painted worlds need follow no rules but their own.

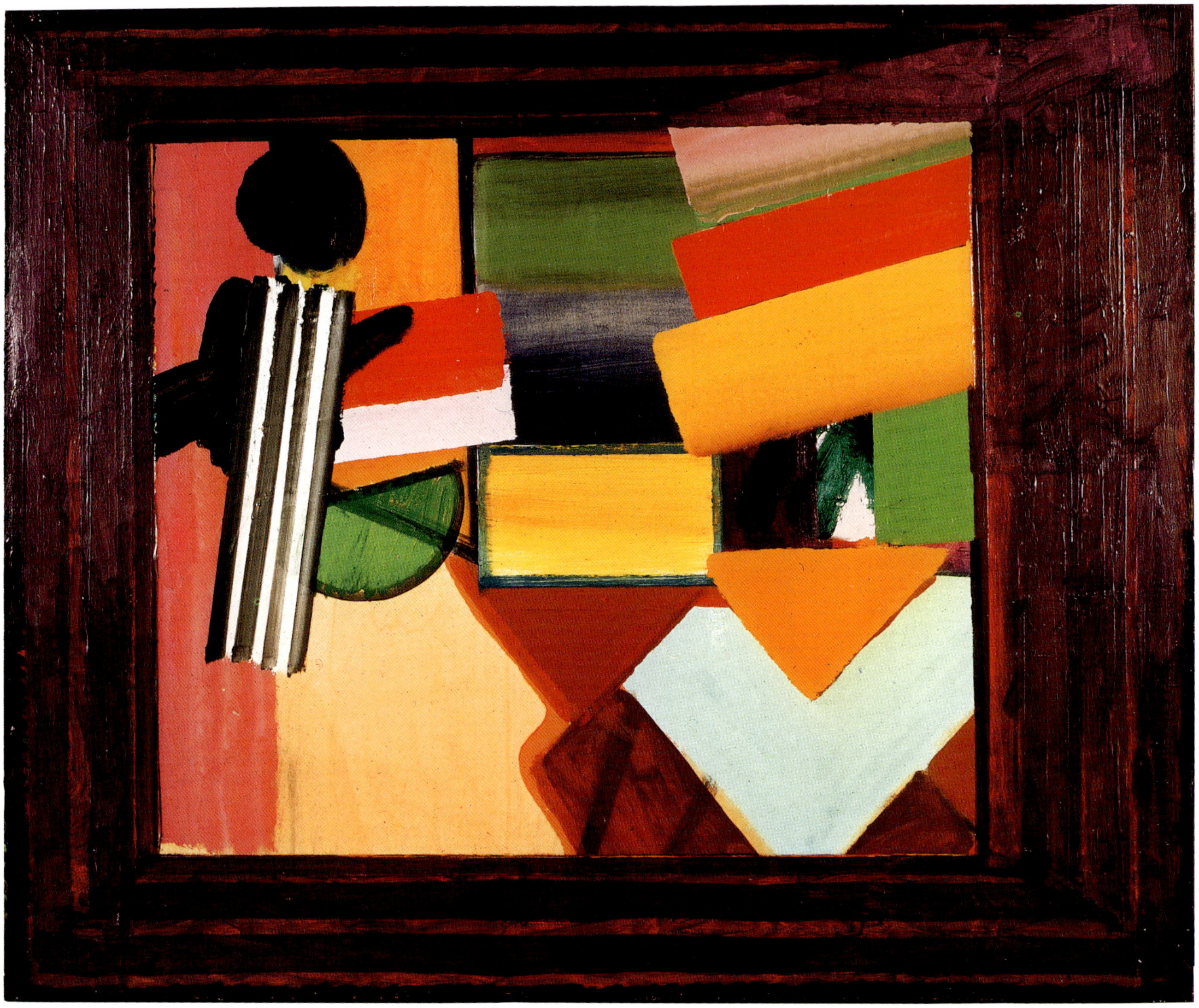

TALKING ABOUT ART
1975

11
TALKING ABOUT ART

About ten years ago a painter wrote to me and said of HH that 'he can only paint one picture but it's a good one'. I quoted this to him in the hopes of getting a powerful rebuttal. Sure enough, H quite rightly said that the remark was idiotic, in that all his pictures are different in essence and, inevitably, in that they all start from different and unique emotional situations and go their different ways for that reason. If he or anyone else wanted to paint, or finish with, 'the same picture', the procedures he actually employs would be senseless.[19]

John Russell

All artists have their habits and preferences, and sometimes these acquire the character of rhetorical devices. But Hodgkin is not a programmatic painter. He does not paint according to rules or systems. Compasses and rulers and masking tape are not part of the paraphernalia of his studio. He is not the artist as conceptual overseer. His paintings are his own, and they are handmade. He has not sought to armour his work in theory, and he has never staked his career on the sorts of technical or ideological innovation which, according to those who continue to uphold the evolutionary myth of modernism, keep the modern artist marching bravely along the path of radicalism.

Hodgkin has only ever painted one picture that could be described as something like a manifesto for his art. But it is actually (and characteristically) more of an anti-manifesto, a declaration of dissent from the notion that the modern artist needs a theory or a programme to paint by. In 1904, Paul Cézanne famously advised Emile Bernard to 'Treat nature in terms of the cylinder, the sphere, the cone'.[20] Hodgkin has P. 123 painted his own, tongue-in-cheek response to Cézanne's didactic remark, *The Cylinder, the Sphere, the Cone* (1978–84). The picture is a heavily ironic refutation of systematic painting, a deliberately botched exercise, a work of art that conspicuously fails to simplify the world to a platonically idealized geometry of form. This cone is a fuzzy-edged sailing-ship adrift on a sea of mottled red and yellow. This cylinder is an inflamed, wilting phallus. This sphere is a messy void of flesh-coloured paint stained with red and white blotches. *The Cylinder, the Sphere, the Cone* is a painting that prefers complication to simplicity, and that pictures a world at once muddied and opaque and marked by inconsistency.

Hodgkin was born in 1932, which means that he has lived through (among other art movements) Surrealism, Abstract Expressionism, Colour Field Painting, Minimalism, Pop and Conceptualism. No artists are untouched by their own times, but direct links between Hodgkin's art and the art of his contemporaries seem particularly hard to establish. He belongs to no particular twentieth-century school or movement, and the sorts of ancestries that can be constructed for him (one or two attempts to do so have been made earlier) tend necessarily to a certain vagueness. They are ancestries of intention, of feeling, rather than ancestries of style. Hodgkin's oeuvre itself is somewhat resistant to generalization, since his approach to painting runs so resolutely counter to that of the serialist painter, or of the painter whose work conforms to the ideology of a particular school. His pictures aim at precision, at truth to their own, individual subjects, and, although certain themes and preoccupations might be said to run through much of his work, it would be a mistake to emphasize them too strongly.

The paintings have their own, unmistakable character, but that is not remotely to say that they all conform to type, that they are all examples of *the same sort of thing*. They are not. The portraits demonstrate the variability of the work as a whole. Painting the food writer *Paul Levy* (1976–80), Hodgkin reduces the subject to a pasty smear of P. 124 pink with smudged eyes and mouth, surrounded by thick blobs and blotches of paint the colour of confectioner's custard. Painting David Hockney in *D.H. in Hollywood* P. 125 (1980–84), he turns his subject into a proud erect phallus, a red upstanding penis in the middle of the painting, above a line of blue blobs that reads as the Hockney swimming pool. Hockney-as-phallus is encircled by a double band of orange blobs, ambiguous marks that have something of the theatre about them. They could be footlights, or perhaps Hockney's dazzled entourage, a poolside party of congratulatory admirers. The

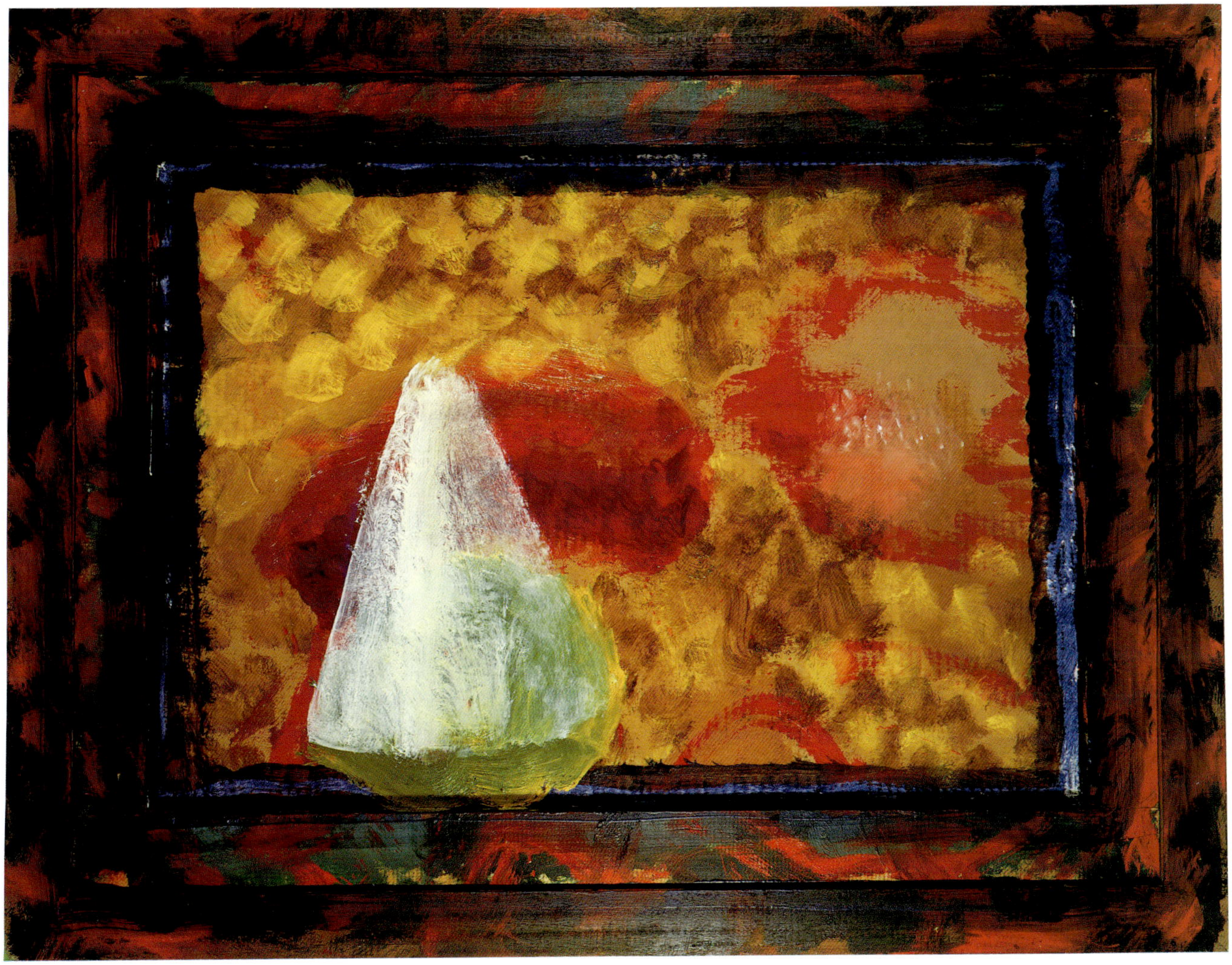

THE CYLINDER, THE SPHERE, THE CONE
1978 – 84

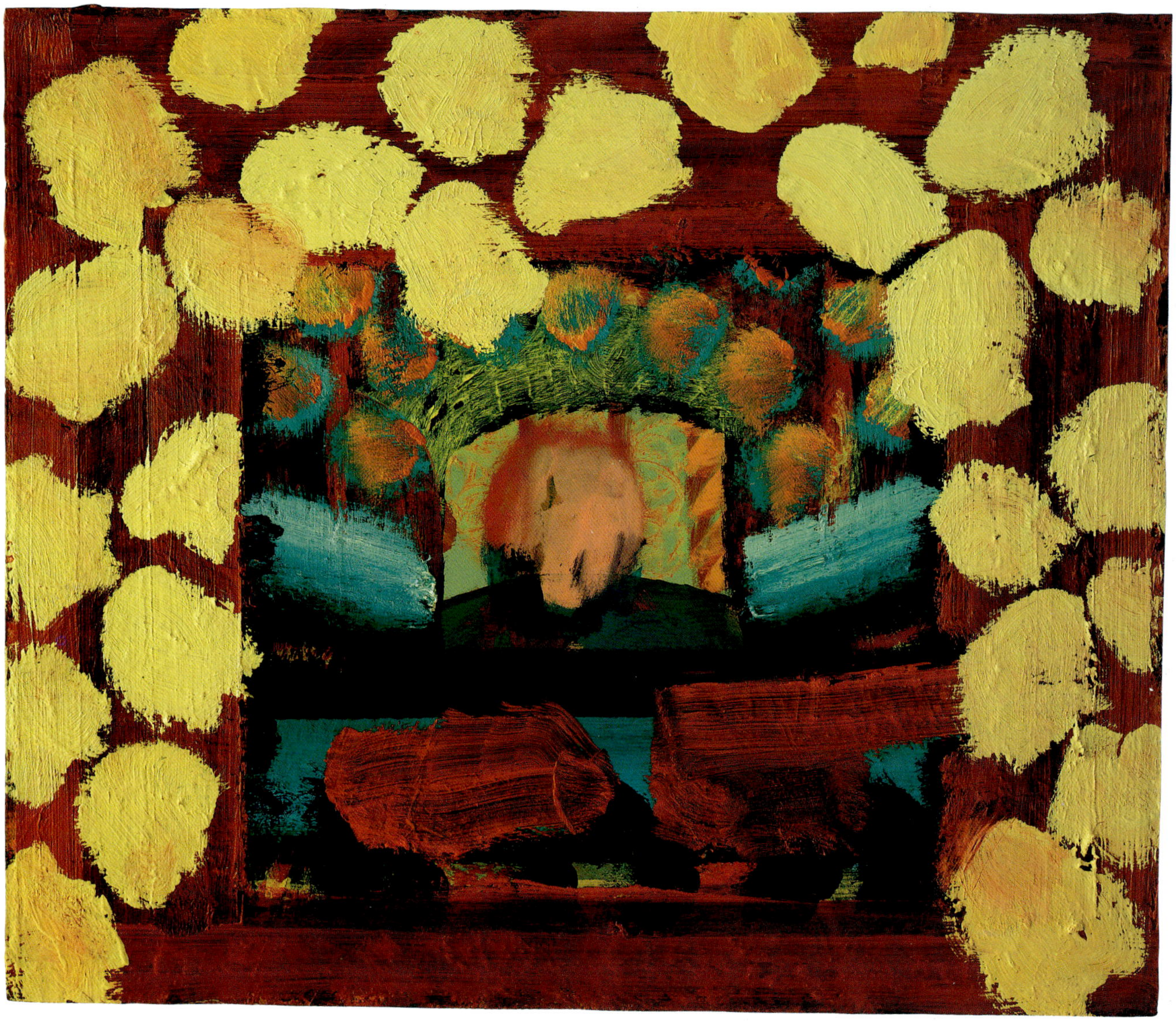

PAUL LEVY
1976 – 80

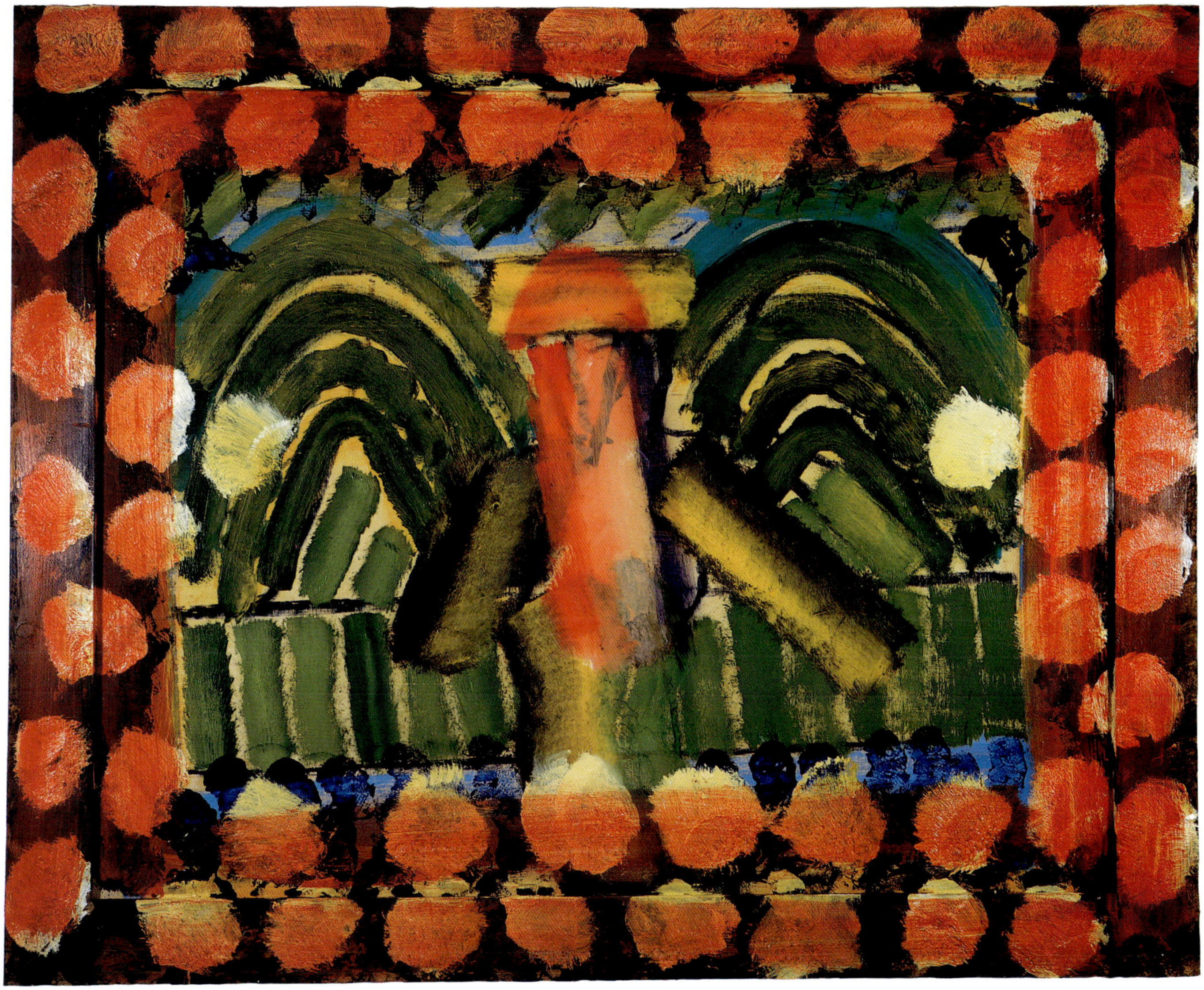

D.H. IN HOLLYWOOD
1980 – 84

two portraits use the same, almost clumsy, simplified language of form that is Hodgkin's style, but they use it to talk about quite different things. One is a gently mocking, affectionate monument to gluttony, its pleasures and consequences, the other an image of social and sexual pleasure, of conviviality as a form of exuberant performance.

Hodgkin's painting speaks of many things in many different voices, and it continues to do so. One of the most remarkable features of his art is that it has shown no signs of easing down. There has been no gentle subsidence. His decision to follow the pitted track of his own concerns might make him seem, somehow, irrelevant to Art History (that grand and somewhat meaningless abstraction), but that is no bad thing.

One of the great received ideas of the twentieth century was the notion, enshrined in most modern institutions of art, most museums and art schools, that it is the sacred duty of every artist to be radical in some way, whether it be political or philosophical or merely technical. Artists anxious to discover every unmapped corner of radical thought and gesture have made art out of everything that art was once supposed not to be made out of. But the culture of radicalism is subject to the law of diminishing returns. As, gradually, the field of potential innovation has shrunk, so genuinely radical gestures have become harder and harder to achieve. The result of all this begins to look distinctly peculiar: vast quantities of art that looks radical but cannot actually be radical because its language has been depleted by over-use; academic radicalism; conformist radicalism.

The legacy of radical avant-gardism is, in one sense, a broken visual culture. The twentieth century saw the fracturing of the older traditions of painting and sculpture into minute shards of innovation. It was done in the name of modernity and self-renewal, but its consequences may have been less liberating than the rhetoric of radicalism once made out. Most of those tiny fragments, because their iconoclastic charge derived so often from such a small, single alteration to the texture or content of a work of art, have proved deeply resistant to subsequent development or enrichment. It is the ideas that they once represented, the challenges that they laid down to the tradition of painting, that made them seem worthwhile. Perhaps never, in the history of painting and sculpture, have so many different artists found themselves in cul-de-sacs of their own devising.

Hodgkin's decision to persist so obdurately in attempting to paint pictures about human emotions and predicaments does not make him a conservative artist. It makes him a painter who is constantly challenging and testing the expressive limits of his art, rather than an endless refiner and modifier of a once-radical formula, another of late modernism's squeezers of water from stones.

Good taste is the last resort, the consolation prize, of the played-out, once radical artist. It is all he has left: the meaninglessly beautiful disposition, rearrangement, repetition, of forms and formulas that have lost their expressive potential. Hodgkin's art can

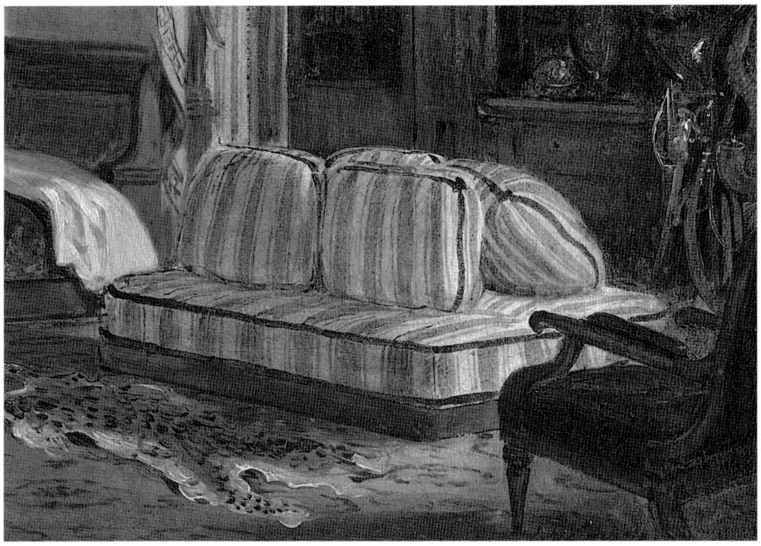

be beautiful, but it is by no means always beautiful, because it is driven by feelings and the need to express them. It is often tasteless, or at least blatant in ways that people who prefer their pictures to be emptily tasteful, nicely decorative, prefer to overlook. The urgency of the paintings is often the urgency of sexual desire, sexual longing.

Some members of the painter's audience have been more alert to this than others. A few years ago a couple was overheard admiring one of Hodgkin's most erotically direct pictures. The woman said that she loved its colour scheme and compared it to that of old japoniste lacquer chests. The man replied. '*That*', he said, pointing to the painting in question, 'is a picture about fucking – so don't talk to me about fucking antiques.'

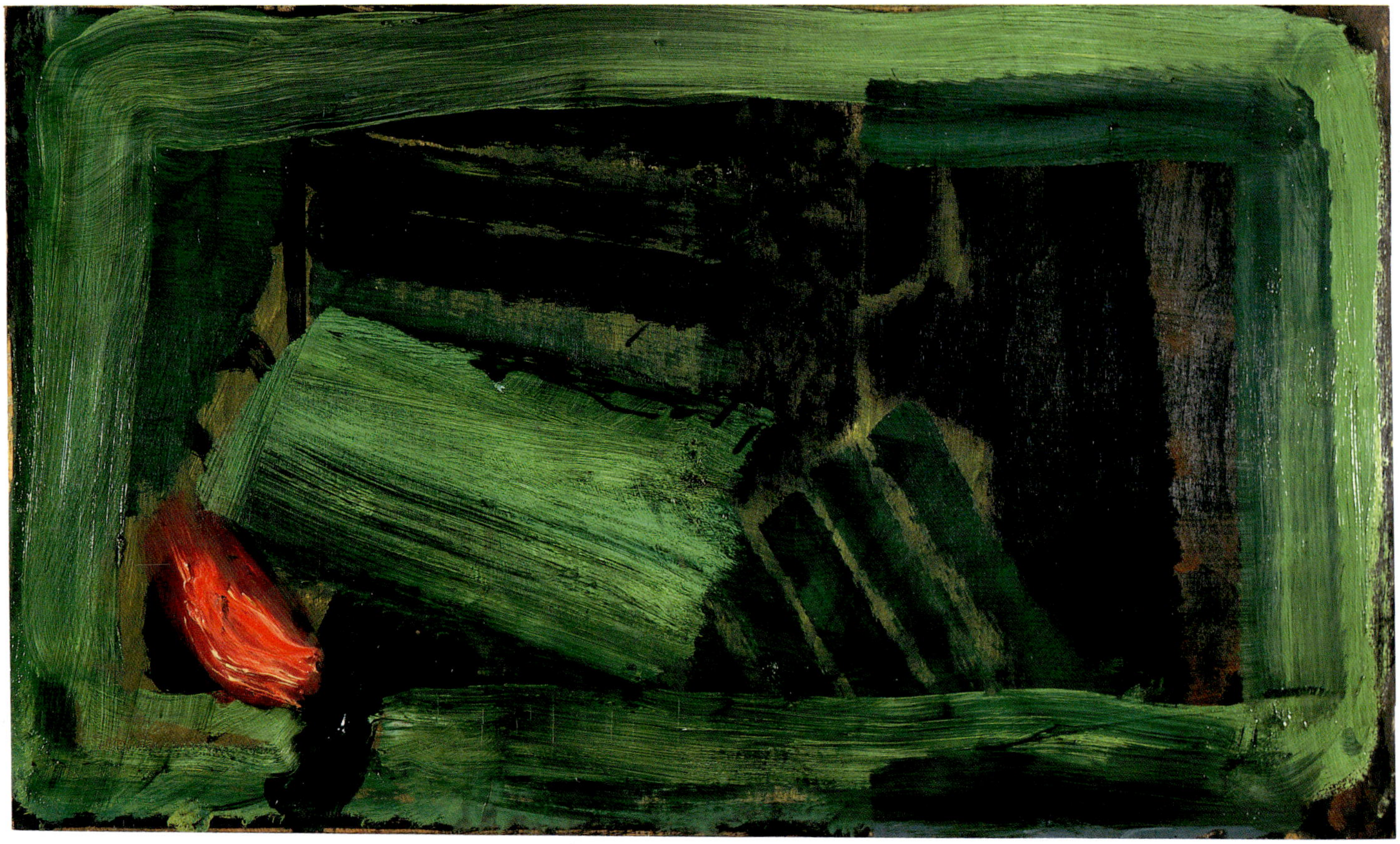

CLEAN SHEETS
1982 – 84

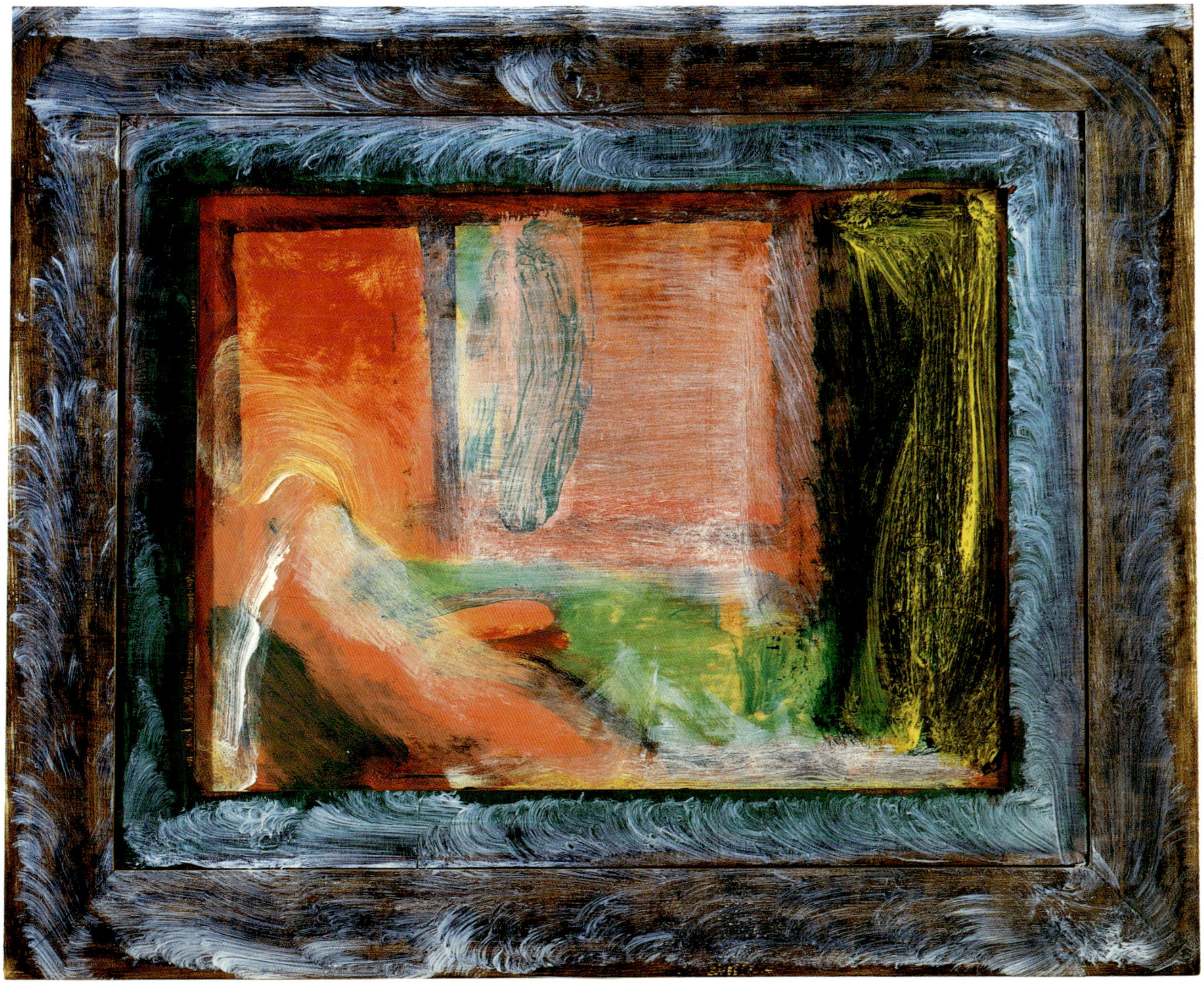

NONE BUT THE BRAVE DESERVES THE FAIR
1981 – 84

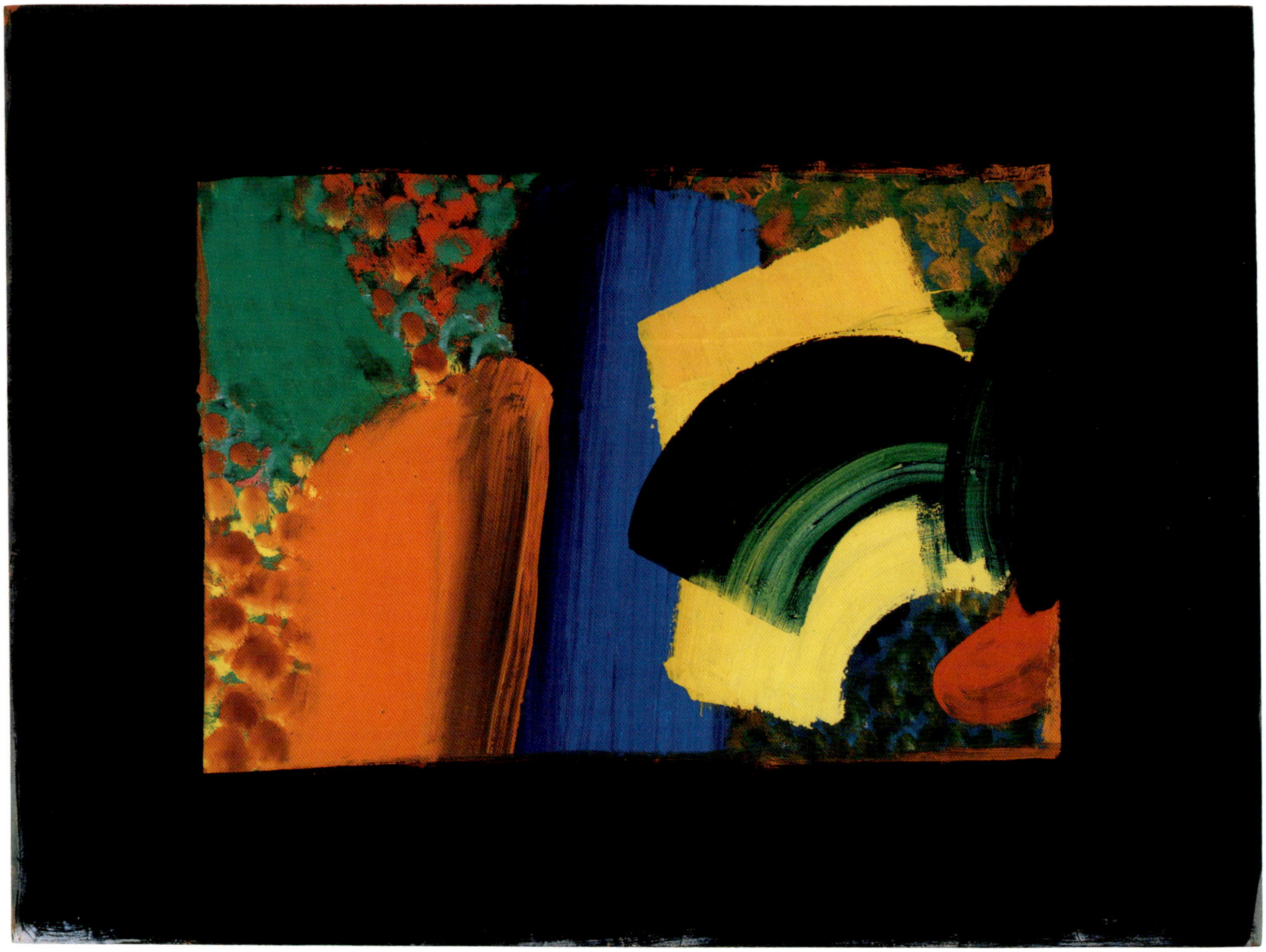

PATRICK CAULFIELD IN ITALY
1987 – 92

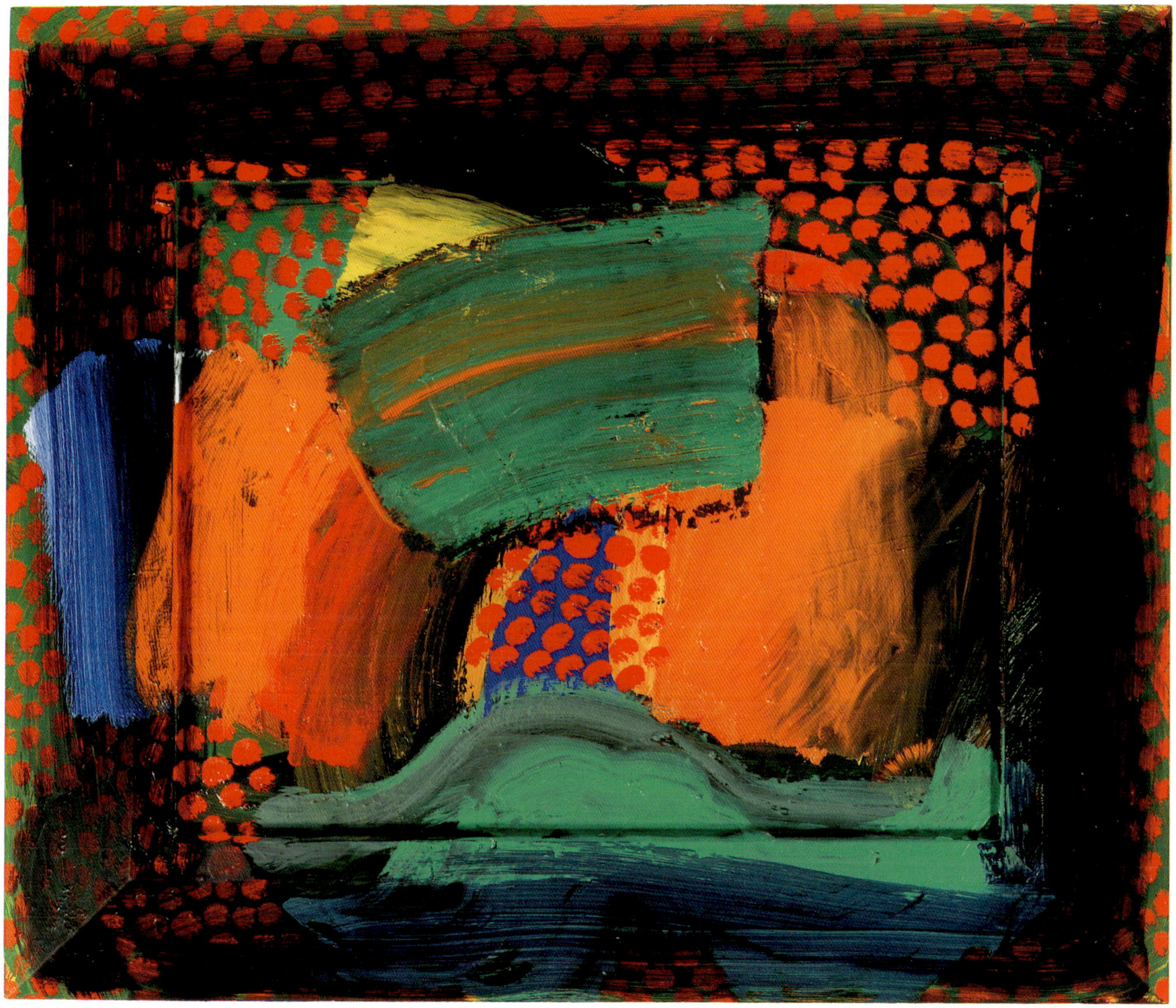

PATRICK IN ITALY
1991 – 93

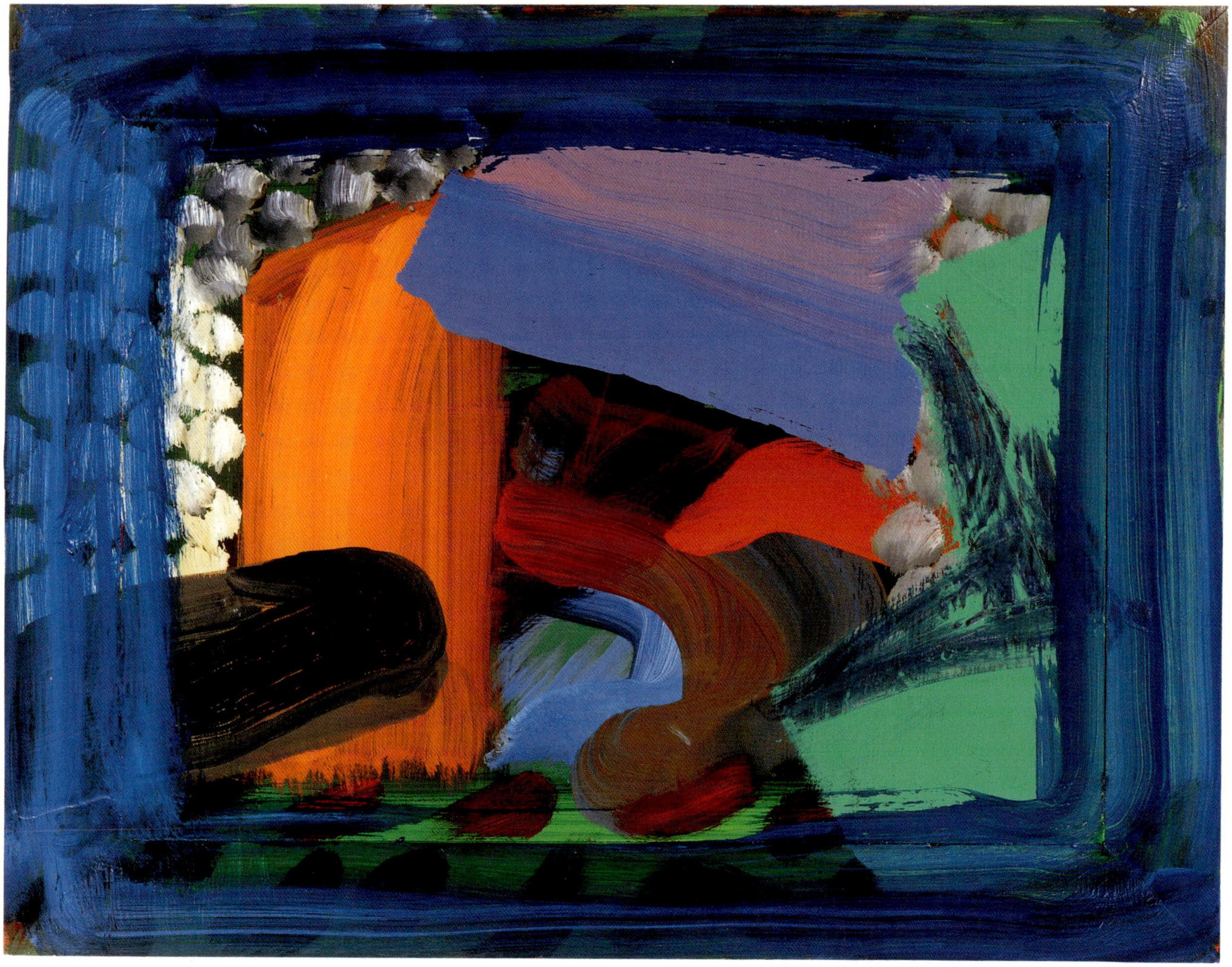

AFTER VISITING DAVID HOCKNEY
1991 – 92

P. 148 There are, in fact, a lot of pictures about fucking. *Waking up in Naples* is a picture about nudity, about remembered pleasure in someone else's body. It is, too, a painting that flaunts its own nudity, a painting in a state of undress. The body, here, is represented as a patch of unprimed wood, marked by an absence of paint. *In a Hot Country* (1979–82) is a picture that is also a dream of sexual consummation, a picture in which Hodgkin's device of the heavily framed image becomes charged with sexual, physical intimacy. The inside of the painting is the inside of a body. A body penetrated: the pink arrow at the centre of the painting is the most blatant piece of painter's code in Hodgkin's art.

P. 129 There are also several pictures about not fucking. *None but the Brave Deserves the Fair* (1981–84) is an image that suggests lonely waiting for an absent partner, while in
P. 128 *Clean Sheets* (1982–84) the human form is reduced to a single phallic smear of red, alone in a spreading wasteland of green, a bed that has become a dark unpeopled forest. It is a picture about solitude and frustration, about wanting to be touched. It is a picture about sex, but also a picture about the condition of being alive. A picture of life (as it always is, to a certain degree) as a solitary activity.

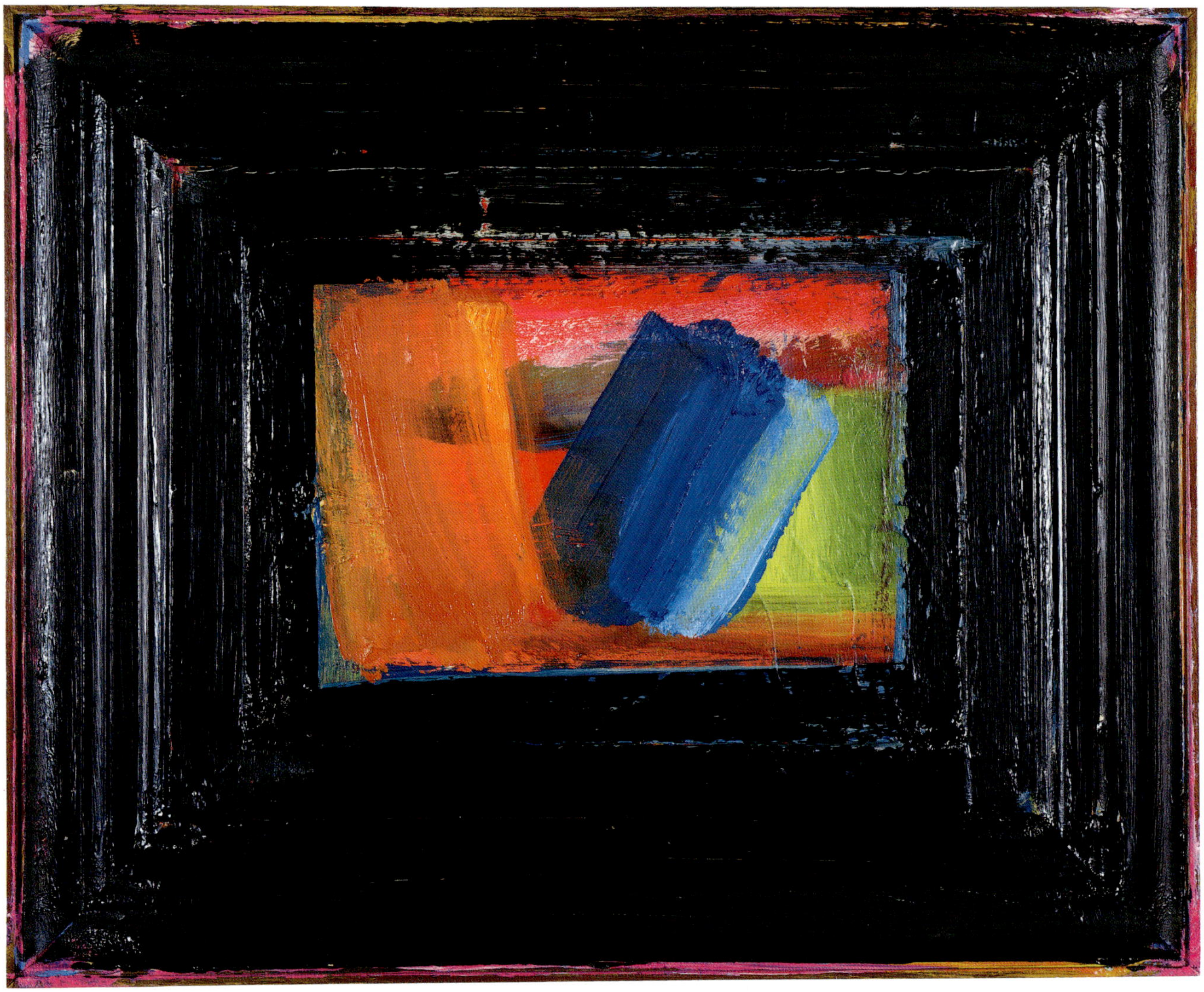

A SMALL THING BUT MY OWN
1983 – 85

12
SMALL

The minuscule... opens up an entire world... Miniature is one of the refuges of greatness.[21]
Gaston Bachelard

Hodgkin's paintings are not uniformly small, although they have acquired the reputation of being so. But perhaps it is true that his art aspires more to the condition of small than to the condition of big. If small represents a certain lack of self-importance; if it represents a desire for compression and urgency and immediacy; if it represents a willingness to improvise, to hint rather than assert – then these are characteristics shared by nearly all of the paintings, of whatever actual physical size. *Rain* and *Souvenirs* are large paintings, but their effects run counter to those often generated by largeness of scale. They speak confidentially. They speak, as all the paintings might be said to do, conversationally.

Small paintings are generally more intimate than large paintings, partly for the simple, practical reason that it is difficult for more than one person at a time to look at a small painting. Where small becomes big, where the scale of the intimate gives way to the scale of the declamatory, is a vexed question, to which the paintings themselves occasionally suggest an answer: somewhere, presumably, between the scale of *Small*
P. 139 *Rain* (1990, 86.4 × 95 cm) and that of *Rain* (163.8 × 179 cm); or, less wildly divergent,
P. 140 somewhere between the scale of *A Small Henry Moore at the Bottom of the Garden*
P. 141 (1975–77, 52.7 × 53.4 cm) and *A Henry Moore at the Bottom of the Garden* (1975–77, 102.9 × 102.9 cm). But such paintings might also be said to conflate large and small, to blur the boundaries between one scale and another.

To paint a large painting is often to sacrifice some of the density, the radiance, the saturation of colour of the small-scale picture. But these differently scaled pictures of the same subjects declare that this need not necessarily be so. The marks are scaled up, from small painting to large, so that they exist in corresponding proportion to the scale of the entire image. This speaks, among other things, of an ambition to preserve the vitality, the loadedness, of each separate pictorial gesture, to maintain its insistent material presence within the whole image against the possibility of dilution by the expansion of scale. To make an image larger is often to make it seem more drawn, more linear than before, and to focus the attention more on overall design than on the minutiae of individual marks, which become diminished and too subservient, as a consequence, to

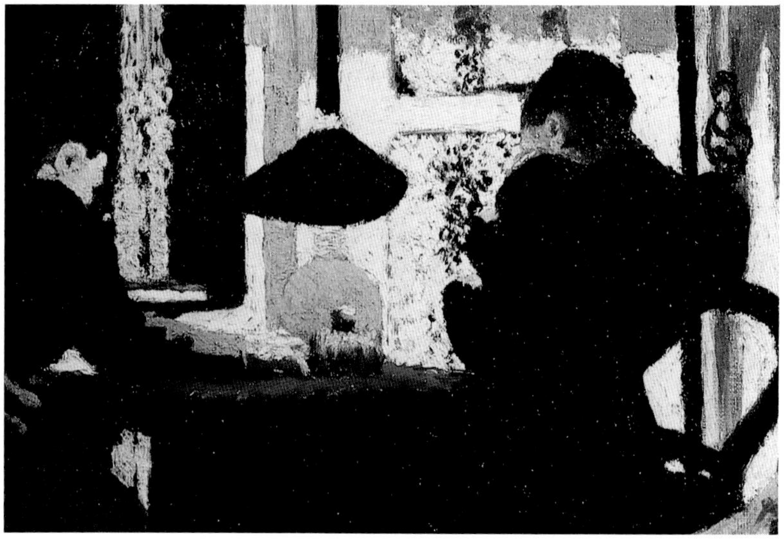

the general pictorial scheme. But these paintings fight that, assert the painterliness of painting across the range of their different scales. They have to, in order to be eloquent. Hodgkin's paintings depend on his making the qualities of paint felt – its opacity and translucency, its thickness and thinness, its colour, its juice or its aridity – in order to work their effects and convey their meanings.

Reproductions are usually uninformative about painting, pale and shrunken ghosts of things which by definition cannot be reproduced. But one measure of the intentions that lie behind *Rain* may, in fact, be gleaned from looking at it in reproduction. It looks as though it must be a very small picture, when in fact it is not. Seeing it

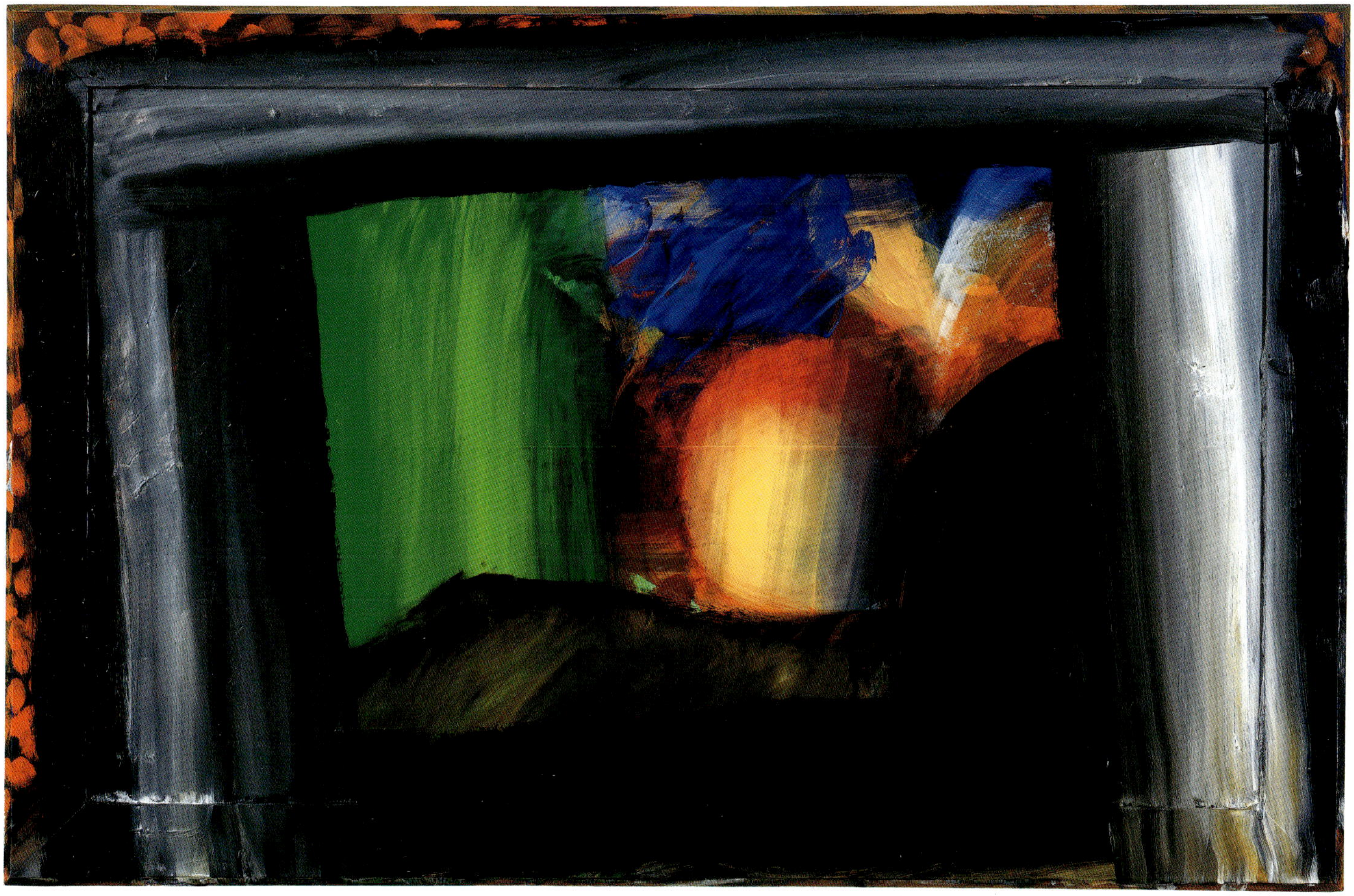

SNAPSHOT
1984 – 93

in reality is disconcerting. It is a large painting that has the immediacy of something very small, jewelled and glowing, and this combined with its scale has the effect of making you feel as if you yourself have been shrunk to the size where you can be dwarfed by a miniature. It achieves a different form of immediacy, however, from that of the truly miniature *Small Rain*, where the diminished scale of the image, and the need to peer into its blue gloaming of inchoate form and space, give the image a sense of pastness, of overt reminiscence, something that is most definitely a picture of something. But the expanded scale of *Rain*, and the corresponding expansiveness of its effects – those great swathes of gunmetal grey, that large solid smudge of cerulean blue – make it seem less like the image of an experience of weather and more like weather itself, spreading and over-mastering. Art is always artificial, and the effect is just that, an effect, enabled by the size of the image. These two paintings use size to suggest two of his different uses for art. *Small Rain* is a commemoration, its conjuring of meteorological effect dim and shielded. *Rain* makes weather present, brings light emerging from cloudy darkness into the room. It is a celebration.

The two versions of *A Henry Moore at the Bottom of the Garden* are not just PP. 140, 141 demonstrations of an artist's sense of scale, of his knowledge that certain marks, if simply transplanted without adjustment into an image of greater size, might become as anonymous as the stitches in a sampler. They look like ironic comments on the attempts of an earlier British artist, Henry Moore, to command outdoor space with monumental sculpture. And perhaps they remark a failure, these images of a vaguely phallic Moore biomorph – remade as a fuzzy blob in one painting, as a bold but tiny dark curve in another, stranded in both in an intricate field of pictorial artifice – glimpsed dimly down a garden vista. They are pictures of nature's riotous, spreading indifference to (and diminishment of) a work of art that wanted to be more than a thing but ended up as just another object, a lump at the bottom of the garden, as inconsequential as a compost heap.

Hodgkin's paintings are resolutely anti-monumental, even when they are painted to a large scale. They do not lecture or preach. They do not remonstrate nor, as monuments do, reprove the living with the example of the illustrious dead. They make no

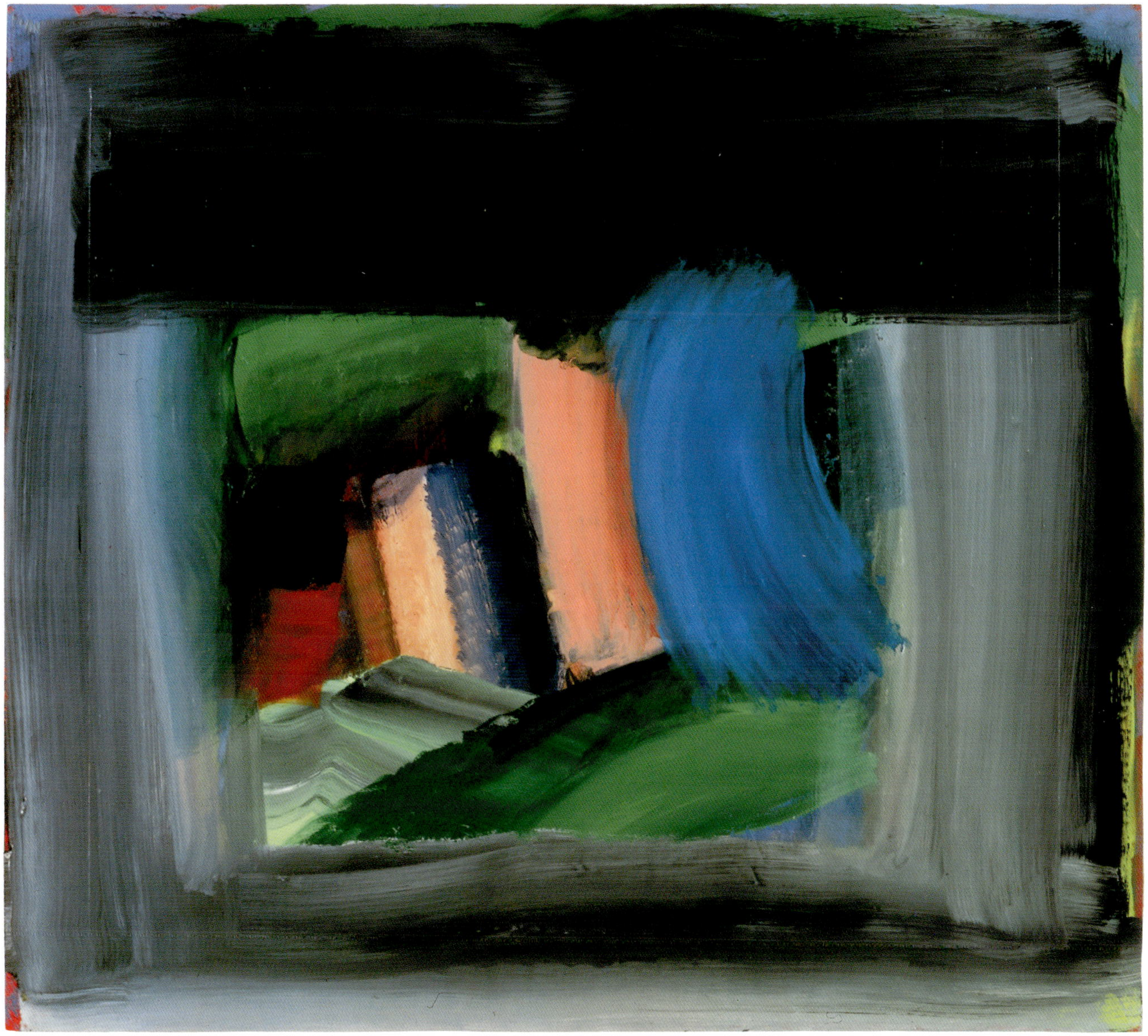

RAIN
1984 – 89

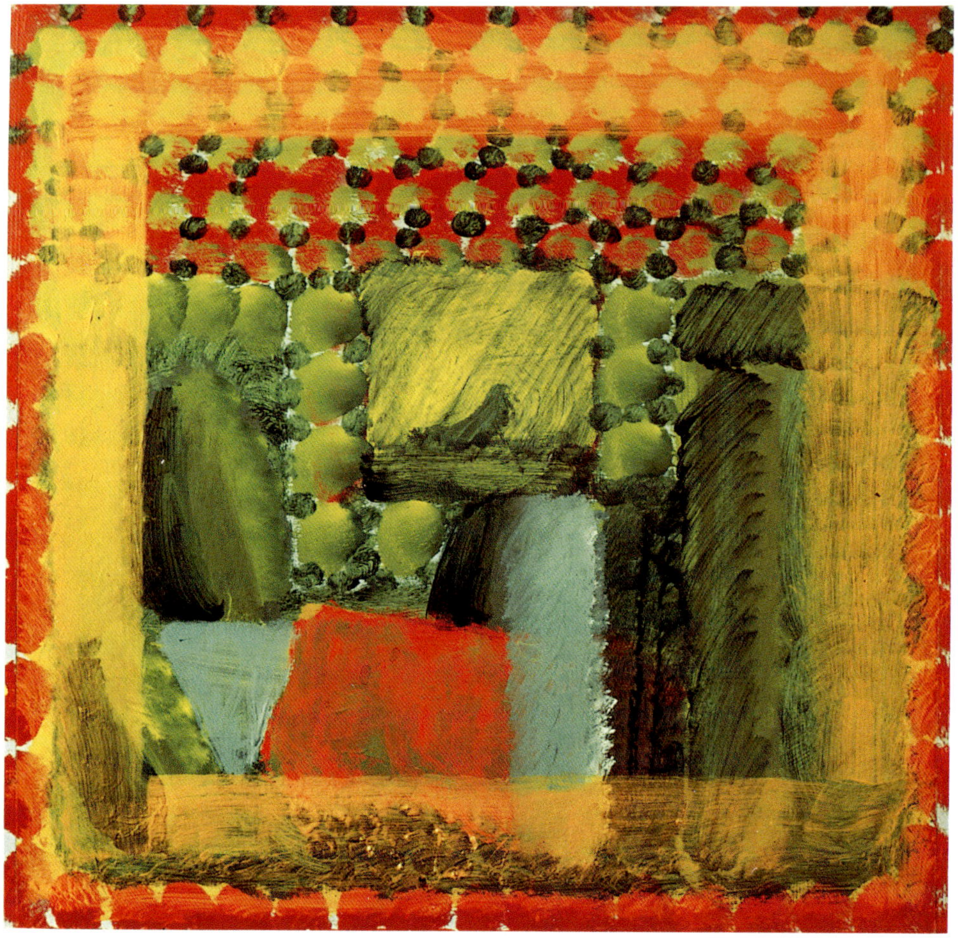

A SMALL HENRY MOORE AT THE BOTTOM OF THE GARDEN
1975 – 77

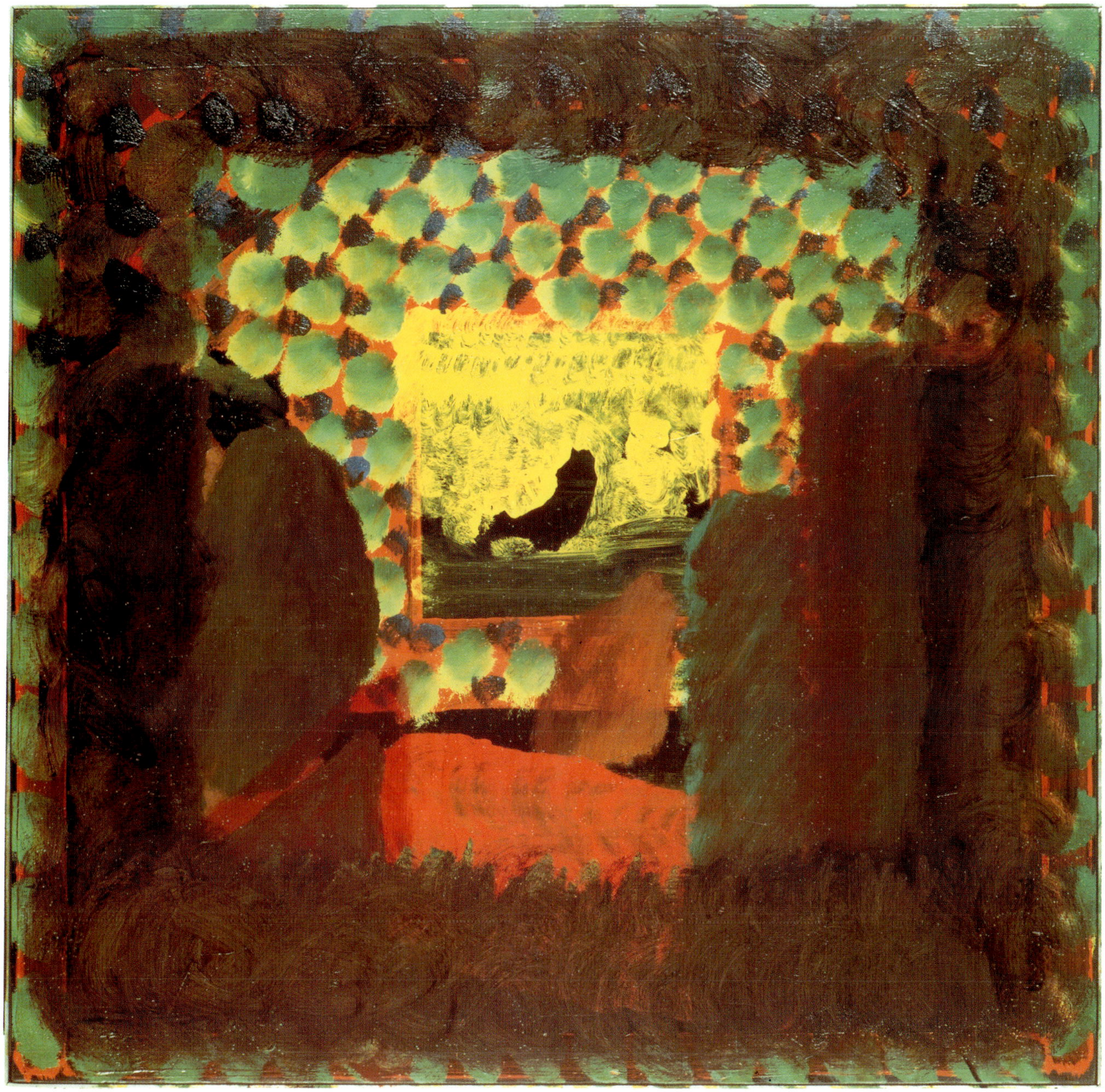

A HENRY MOORE AT THE BOTTOM OF THE GARDEN
1975 – 77

grand, sweeping assertions. They bear the same relationship to self-consciously monumental art as the diary does to the manifesto.

Snapshot (1984–93) is a very large picture with a private erotic quality more often P. 137 associated with very small pictures. That brown slope of paint in a field of green framed by borders of black and grey might suggest a human form; that disc of mixed colour at the picture's heart could be a sun or an electric light translated into a painter's code for such things; that curtain of green could be landscape or, simply, curtains. It is painted on the monumental scale of the history painting, of the grand narrative art of the past, which, since the picture offers no obvious moral and tells no clear story, intensifies its own mysteriousness. The scale of public art has been adapted to the expression of private feeling. *Snapshot* is one of Hodgkin's largest pictures, but it is also a picture that subverts the idea of large.

Many of the pictures offer an implicit rebuke to the habitual large scale, the creeping gigantism that has become the lingua franca of international contemporary art, and to spend time with them is to realize just how many other modern painters have misunderstood scale, have failed to realize that to work big all the time is like talking forever with your voice raised. After a while, what was intended as emphasis turns into its opposite, a perpetual dull bombast. Large art often says less about its overt subject matter than it does about the anxiety, ambition and insecurity of its maker. Conversely, small art, art that makes few claims to Consequence or Importance or Relevance (that dangerous trinity of contemporary art criticism), often seems freer to be eloquent, and to be moving.

Hodgkin's paintings do not just explore the limits of large and small, the threshold that separates the two. They also unpack the baggage of expectation we bring to a painting depending on its size, and they challenge our readiness to judge a picture on the basis of how big it is (and to value it accordingly: large paintings have always been more expensive than little ones, which says something about the perennial human desire to quantify the unquantifiable). They refute a received idea inherited from the traditional academic division of art into a hierarchy of genres, according to which large paintings were supposed to treat large subjects (grand biblical or mythological narratives, stories of great theological or moral import), small pictures small ones (landscapes, still lifes). The value judgments that lay behind that old academic taxonomy of painting did, oddly, survive into the late twentieth century, not otherwise noted for its respect for academic traditions. And they may, paradoxically, have been given renewed strength and vigour by the work of a group of artists who were resolutely opposed to academicism: the great painters of the postwar New York School, notably Rothko, Newman and Pollock, whose most damaging legacy to subsequent generations of artists may prove to be the notion that paintings, in order to be significant, have to be huge.

The painters of the New York School can hardly be blamed for the cult of hugeness for hugeness's sake, and they were not, other than indirectly, responsible for it. Their paintings required a certain scale to work their effects: the effects of transcendental suggestion and of the vastness of cosmic forces; a sublime disorientation of the senses which they understood could only be achieved through the creation of images larger than the human optical field, images too large to be taken in at a glance. Their paintings were necessarily large. Hodgkin's paintings are, more often than not, necessarily not large. He may have done more than any other painter working of his time to reclaim and re-explore the territory of the small picture and to reveal its own special powers and capacities.

P. 145 It is possible to imagine a painting like *Indian Sky* (1988–89) enormously expanded in scale. But it is equally important to understand that to change its scale (54.1 × 70.2 cm) would be entirely to change its nature, its effect and its meaning. Painted to the size of a mural, it would run the risk of becoming a piece of stage scenery (as many large paintings do, despite the best intentions of their makers), another contribution to that tradition of sublime Northern Romantic landscape painting that might be said to run from Turner to Rothko – the primary intention of this painting would be to stun the senses with a vision of the radiant Void, an image of ineffable Nature herself. But it is not painted to the size of a mural. It is painted to the size of an easel painting. Its scale is domestic, like the scale of chairs or tables. It is a thing that relates easily and evidently to the scale of the human body. It is roughly four handsbreadths high and

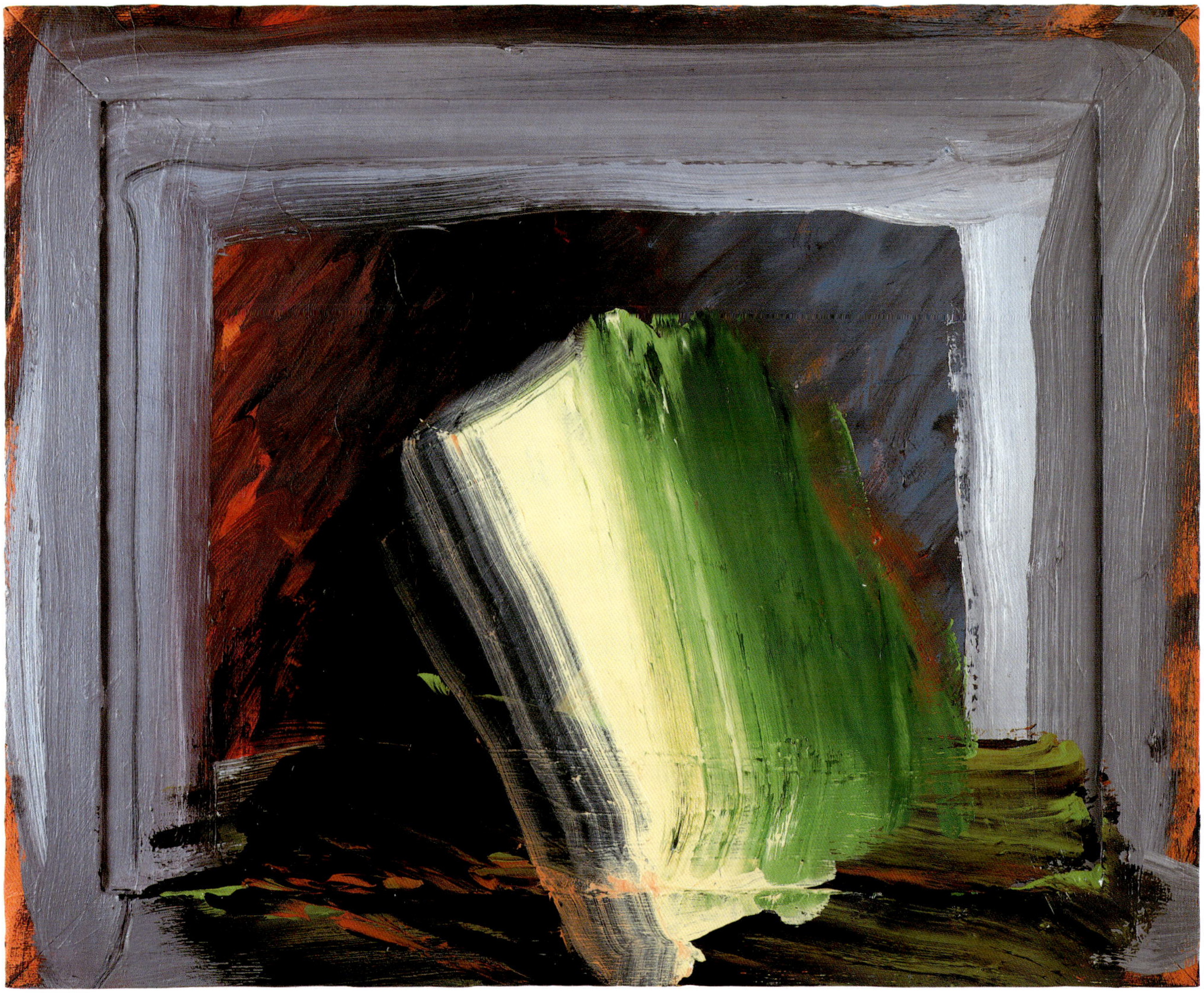

LIKE AN OPEN BOOK
1989 – 90

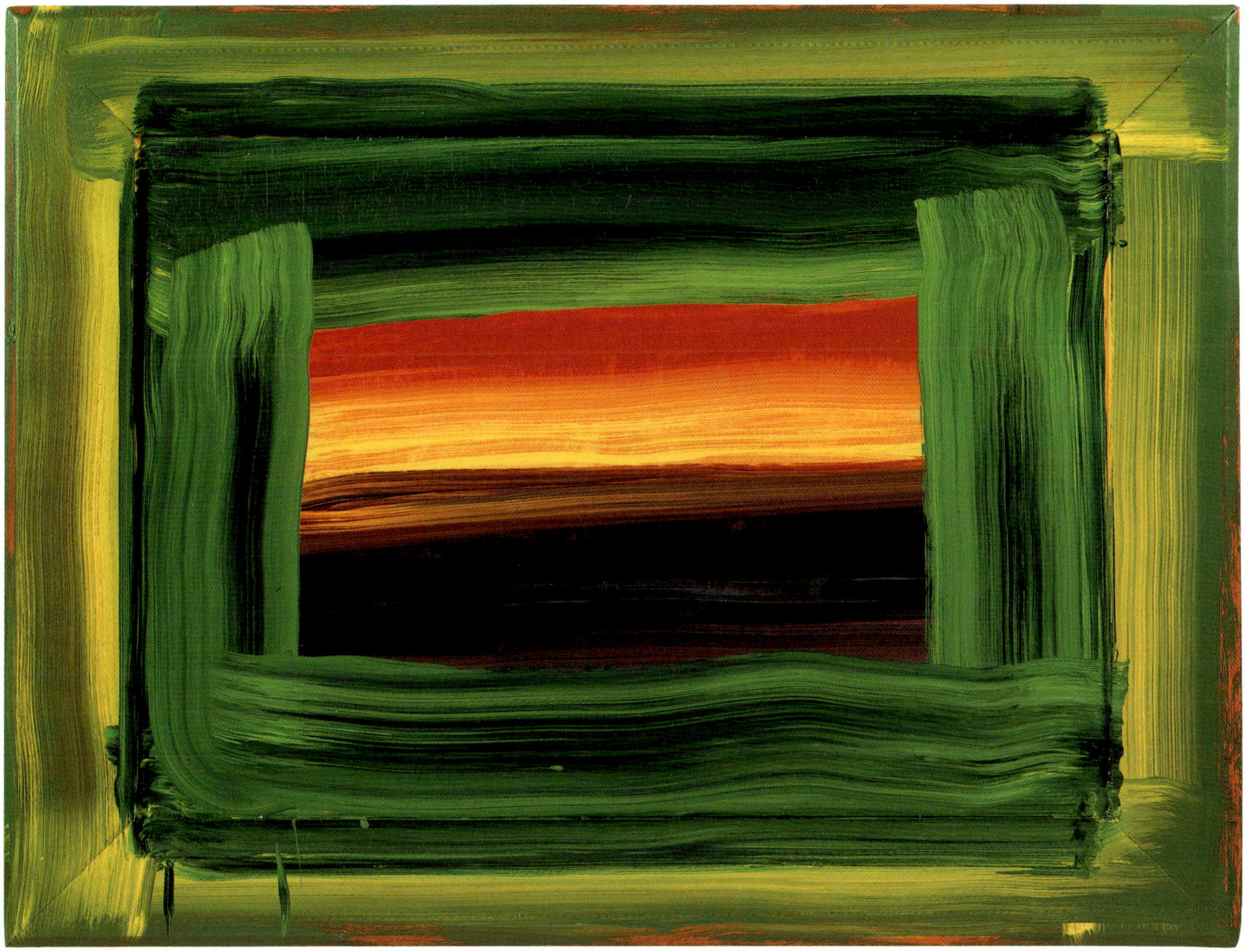

INDIAN SKY
1988 – 89

six across. The result is that *Indian Sky*, while suggesting, in its bands of bright and sombre dragged paint, the lights and darks of a sunset as it fades to night, is also emphatic about its nature as a *picture*. It does not attempt anything like a theatrical re-enactment of natural vastness (as, say, a Pollock might, on its own terms). Its tone is not heroic, but elegiac. And its qualities, as elegy, depend on its scale. Its scale is one of the ways in which it admits its own frailty, its nature as artifice, a small gesture of resistance (which is perhaps, after all, not so small) against the ease with which we forget or take for granted moments of beauty. Its scale enables much of its poignancy, allowing these narrow bands of bright colour, framed within thick fringes of green and yellow, to glow like a memory kept alive against all odds.

The titles have occasionally hinted, themselves, at the importance of smallness. *Like an Open Book* (1989–90, 52 × 63 cm) is a painting the size of an open book, P. 144
something small enough to hold in the palm of your hand. It is an assertively enigmatic picture, a smear of yellow paint as fatty as cheese, partially overlaid by a smudge of thick green, against a background of brokenly applied red and black and blue under an arch of grey. The painting phrases itself as something to be peered at as intently as small print. Disclosure, however, is denied. The self-evidence that the painting's title promises turns out to be obscurity. The picture is really a closed book, or perhaps, rather, it is a book written in a foreign language. *Like an Open Book* is a painting that will not be read, and therefore also one that challenges the association between smallness and minute detail, because all within this small image is vagueness and flurry. But the attempt will be made none the less, since it is a painting which, like most of Hodgkin's works, turns the viewer into a reader, an interpreter, an annotator of the arcane text that is the image. Small scale, here, heightens the enigma, makes it a thing that demands investigation: a whodunnit. Pursuing enquiries, it seems that the forms that are the painting's dramatis personae, perhaps because they are uprights, read as figures. There is something carnal about their merging. The picture looks like a physical act memorialized.

The paintings often make use of, as well as confound, the expectations brought to small-scale works of art. They often exploit the associations of small, and perhaps they do so most insistently when their subjects are corporeal or erotic. There is a long history of small-scale erotic imagery: the Victorian pornographic photograph; Degas's brothel monotypes, those little dark images of bourgeois lust and its appeasement, of transitory encounters in stifling interiors; Picasso's erotically entangled artists and models; and countless other instances of the small-scale erotic image, ranging from Marcantonio Raimondi's erotic illustrations to Pietro Aretino's *Lives of the Courtesans*, to Beardsley's *Lysistrata* etchings and the erotica of Turner which so scandalized Ruskin that he had most of them burned after the artist's death.

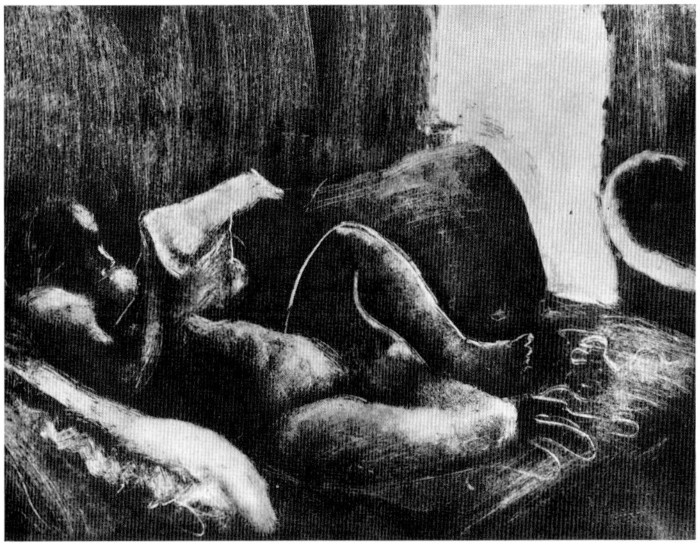

The link between erotic content and small scale is, on one level, extremely practical. Erotic images always needed to be small because they were art's equivalents of books meant to be read with one hand. But small scale also serves the close focus of erotic attention, the exclusiveness of its concern with bodies, and with flesh.

P. 45 Hodgkin's smallest paintings often carry this erotic charge. *Small View in Venice* (43.2 × 45.7 cm) is a disconcertingly abrupt experience, the pinkish wet swipes of paint at its centre so overt a code for flesh that looking at it feels like walking in on someone in the nude. The smallness of the painting, and the dense framing device that keyholes that central patch of pink so starkly, contribute to the sense of furtive discovery. *Waking up*

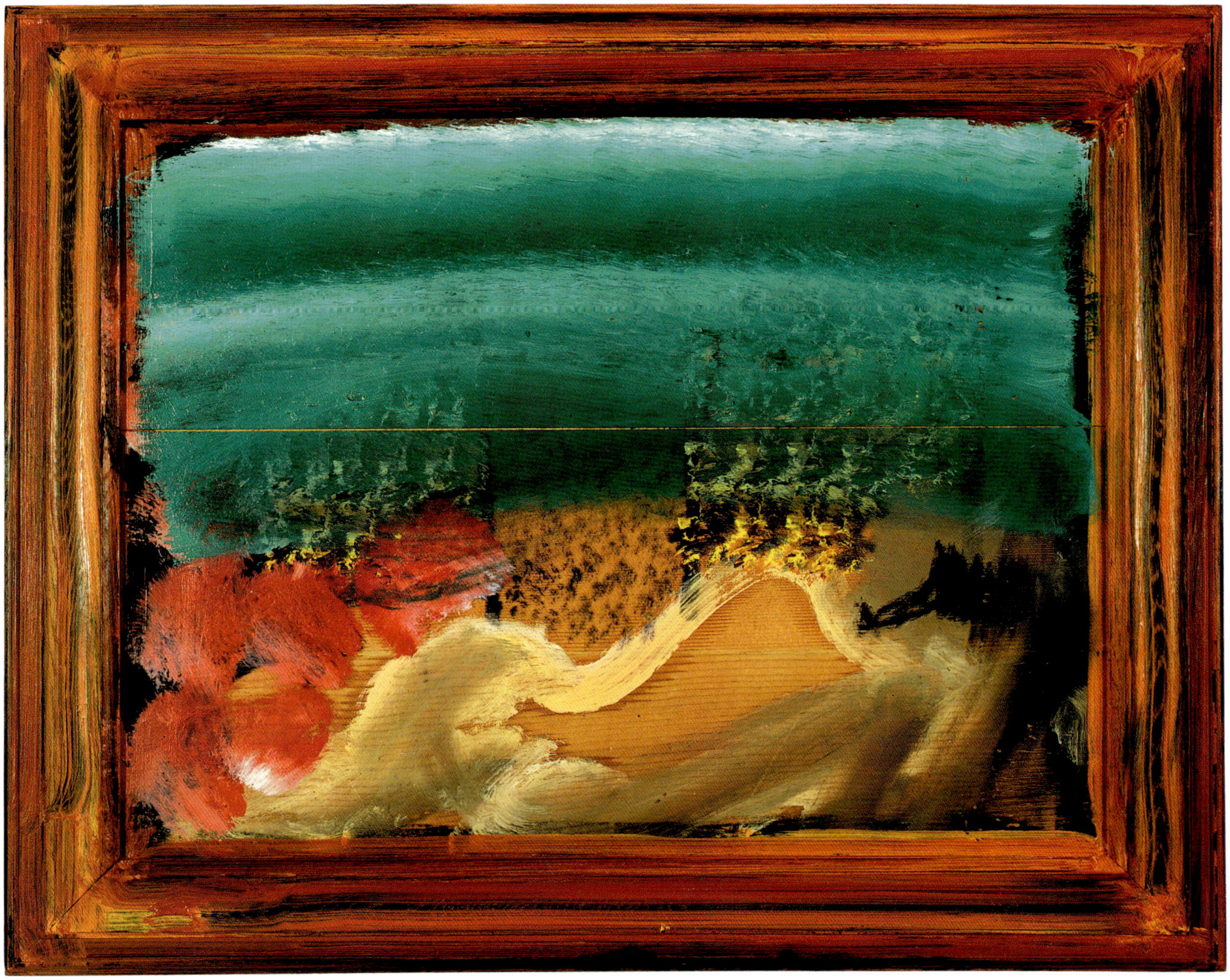

WAKING UP IN NAPLES
1980–84

in Naples (59.7 × 74.9 cm) is somewhat larger than *Small View in Venice*, but is less intensely surprising, more luxuriant. Everything else in the picture – the sea or sky, some scarlet puffs of paint that could be bedclothes – merely emphasizes that this is, in essence, a painting of a naked back, rendered audaciously by the simple expedient of leaving the wooden support bare to model it.

It is hard for large paintings to conjure quite this same, intense sense of the palpability of what they image forth, since they demand viewing at a greater distance. Small paintings draw the viewer in, encourage the discovery of those tricks that they propose as equivalents for things – bare wood for a back, say, or scribbled black lines for hair – and the result is a form of honesty. They give you their equivalents for the world, for people and objects and feelings, but they also vouchsafe you the absolute knowledge that they are only (and can only ever be) equivalents.

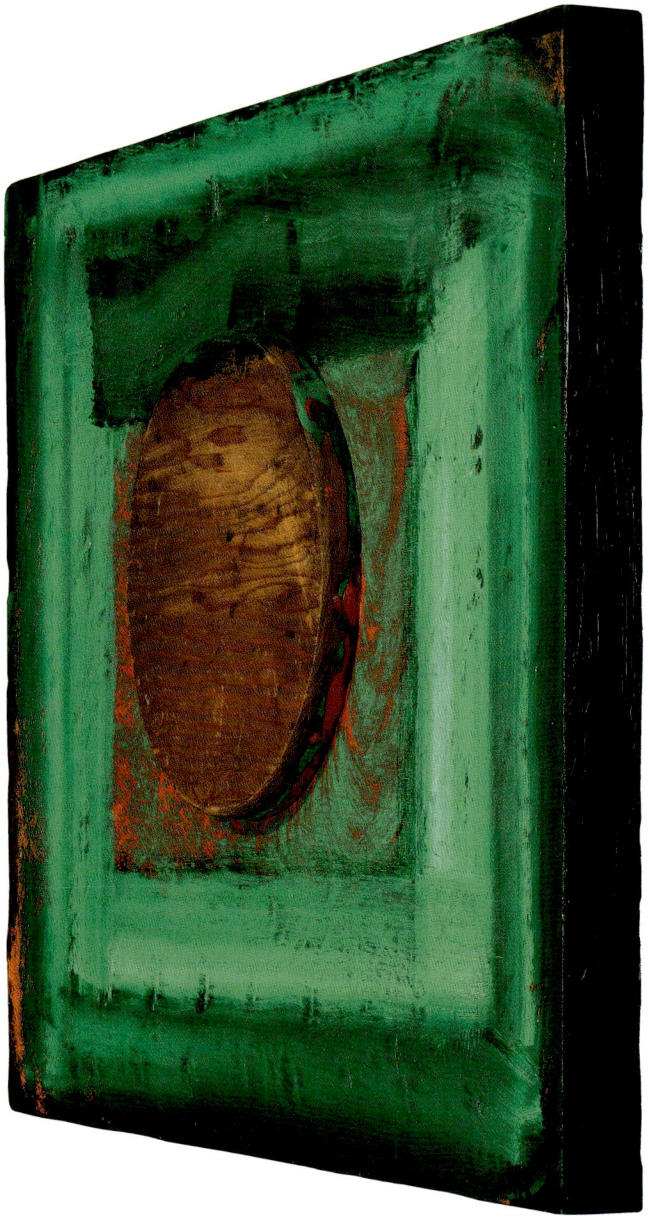

THE MOON (SIDE VIEW)
1978 – 80

13
THINGS

Small paintings make no secret of their own artifice, acknowledge the limits of their illusionism by allowing the viewer to see round it. They might be said to exist, in relation to the various other forms of visual art, at the opposite end of the spectrum to the cinema, which aspires to the complete abolition of a sense of the artifice of spectacle, and which often achieves an immediacy and a completely beguiling form of illusion that painting cannot hope to match. Large paintings, paintings painted to something approaching the scale of the panorama (the most immediate antecedent, in the visual arts, of cinema), often attempt to overcome or defy their own artificial nature by overwhelming the viewer with their scale, plunging him into a vision of things so immense that it shuts out the real world, albeit only temporarily. Pollock may have managed this trick more effectively than any other twentieth-century painter. But small paintings, which are always framed by the real world, which abut it so manifestly, are self-evidently objects, hung on a wall. They are things that might be held, felt, weighed, as well as looked at or into. Hodgkin's paintings flaunt their palpability, their nature as things like so many other things in the world: hammers, paperweights, kettles. Their thing-ness, inseparable from their eloquence, is a painter's way of anchoring his fantasy, his melancholy and his lyricism.

P. 153 *Sunset* (1990–93) is one of the saddest and most moving of all the paintings, one in which Hodgkin's characteristic device of occlusion is invested with a new and emphatic poignancy. The painting is about death, or at least it expresses a violent morbidity. The dim shining of the sun, late in the day, is reincarnated as a *memento mori*, in an image of colour – a threatened curve of modulated orange, blue, red, crimson – blotted out, blocked out, obscured by two arcs of black and grey. Those great semicircular swipes of paint are like rainbows from which the colour has been drained, and the subject of the painting is at once the inevitable nightly draining of colour from the world and the thoughts that it provokes. Dusk is rephrased as a metaphor for something that awaits everyone. But the painting also, if only just, holds night at bay, perpetuates the last faint gleams of a sunset, glowing frailly in the pinched gap of brightness at its centre. *Sunset* is both resignation and protest, a painting that is almost but not quite inconsolable, that knows but also staves off the inevitability of blackness, that sees but also rages against the dying of the light.

The two extremes of the picture (light, life, colour; darkness, death, absence of colour) are also implicit in its nature *as* a picture. The paintings are things that aspire to be more than things, objects that try to embody hopes and feelings, aspirations and emotions, but that are also and inevitably just objects. *Sunset* incorporates the sad paradox of painting by making it part of its actual subject. It is a picture that lives in the tension between bright illusion, distant vision (those passages of sunset colour) and sullen, insistent materiality (those passages of darkness, painted in a quite different, thicker manner, clotted with scumble). Part of the painting's sadness lies in its confession of its own, dual nature. It is a vision, something that performs the oldest function of art by proposing and creating its own world, but it is also something that is, simply, part of this world, unable to rise entirely above it.

When many painters lost faith with Albertian perspective, in the late nineteenth century, they also found a new form of pathos. They discovered the pathos that derives from art's acknowledgment of its own artifice, made more extremely and more variously in the painting to have been produced since Degas – it is there in the art of Cézanne and Matisse, Picasso and Braque – than at any time before. Hodgkin's painting belongs absolutely within this modern tradition, in which painting has always been in urgent dialogue with its own limitations and conventions, and in which one of the prime challenges that faces painters has been that of avoiding the empty, formalistic self-consciousness to which eternal self-interrogation can easily lead. Paintings about the flatness of painting, paintings about the nature of paintings as two-dimensional objects,

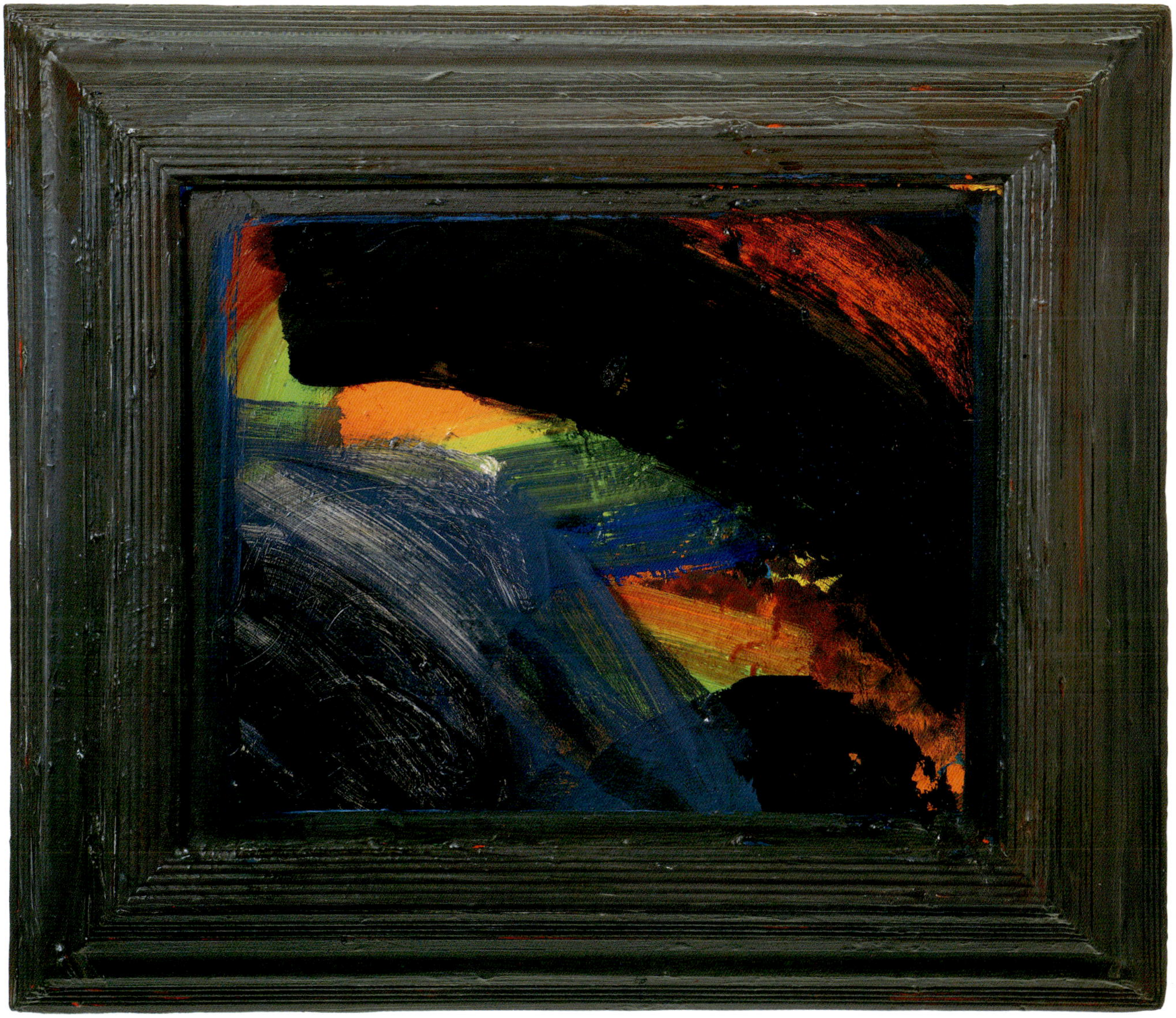

SUNSET
1990 – 93

are not in themselves engaging. The most astute twentieth-century artists have managed to harness a distinctively modern self-consciousness to an older and more vital impulse to create.

Some time around the beginning of the 1970s Hodgkin stopped painting on canvas and began, instead, to paint on wood. This may prove in retrospect to have been the single most significant alteration he has made to his *modus operandi*. Suddenly, and it would seem at exactly the same time as this physical innovation was adopted, the paintings announced their own material nature, their nature as things, with a new simplicity. Their new and blatant mundanity, their self-evident quality as objects, opened up large new areas of expressive possibility. As a result, the paintings could negotiate more subtly with the limitations of all painting; and they could talk in a whole new range of ways about the relationship between paintings and the world of which they form a part.

Before a painting has been touched with the brush, it looks like a piece of perverse, makeshift carpentry. An old, stripped frame (usually bought second-hand, sometimes found discarded) surrounds a bare, unvarnished and unprimed tablet of wood. The painting before it has been painted on looks therefore like a blank mirror, opaque wood replacing reflective glass. When the painting has been completed, the frame has been painted on so that the image and its surround are absolutely inseparable from one another. The picture is not, in the traditional Albertian sense, a window into another world. It is an image that is also simultaneously and unambiguously a thing, a painting that has achieved the self-sufficiency – and unalterability, since the paintings cannot, by definition, be re-framed – of a sculpture. Hodgkin's paintings belong only reluctantly to the genus of painting. Like the *tableaux-objets* created by Braque and Picasso in their Cubist years, which are also bordered by specially chosen or made frames conceived as integral to their compositions, they are paintings that aspire to the condition of solid things. They exist at the margin of the illusory and the real. They too are, indeed, *tableaux-objets* – literally, picture-objects.

The pictures often look battered, distressed, made out of pieces of wood affixed to one another with a kind of self-evident blatancy that makes the support, itself, an analogue for the ordinary, mundane world that art is always attempting to transfigure or transcend. The found frames, which might be old Dutch landscape frames or far P. 2 more elaborate and ornate examples (the most ornate of all is that used for *Keith and Kathy Sachs*), give the work an edge in two senses. They frame it, but they also give it something real, something inherited and solid and simply *there*, to contest and modify and order, like the found objects that Kurt Schwitters assembled into his collages, those winnings of order from the tumbled bus-ticket and sweet-wrapper chaos of the urban world. There is a similar tension in much of Hodgkin's work, which announces its status as object while simultaneously fighting it, attempting to rise above

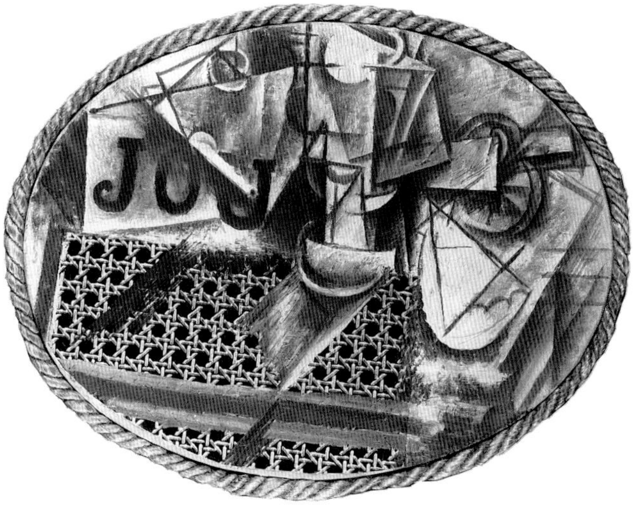

it to achieve a form of visionariness, to create a world categorically and emphatically different from this one.

PP. 92, 150 *The Moon*'s force and poignancy come from painting both resisting and affirming its material nature, from a tension between dumb fact and inflamed fantasy. The title hints at the old alliance between art and lunacy, art and the extremes of the imagination; and it also hints at the old idealistic aspirations of art, its nature as an escape from P. 157 the sublunary imperfections of the world. *Blue Palm* (1985–86) is another picture painted on a support that smacks of the amateur carpenter's workshop, a DIY enthusiast's oval made by gluing curves and oblongs of wood together, all the joins showing. But

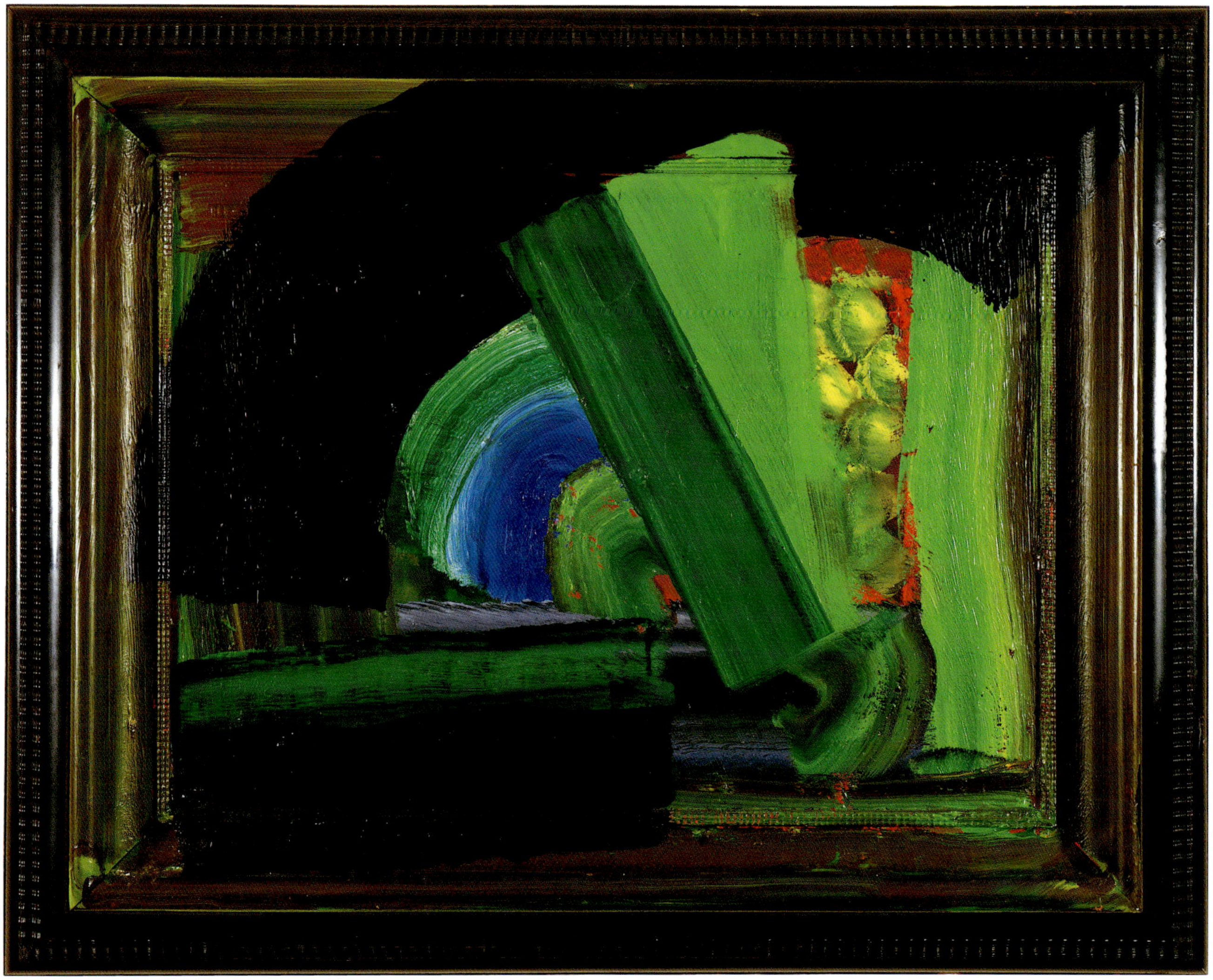

DOWN IN THE VALLEY
1985 – 88

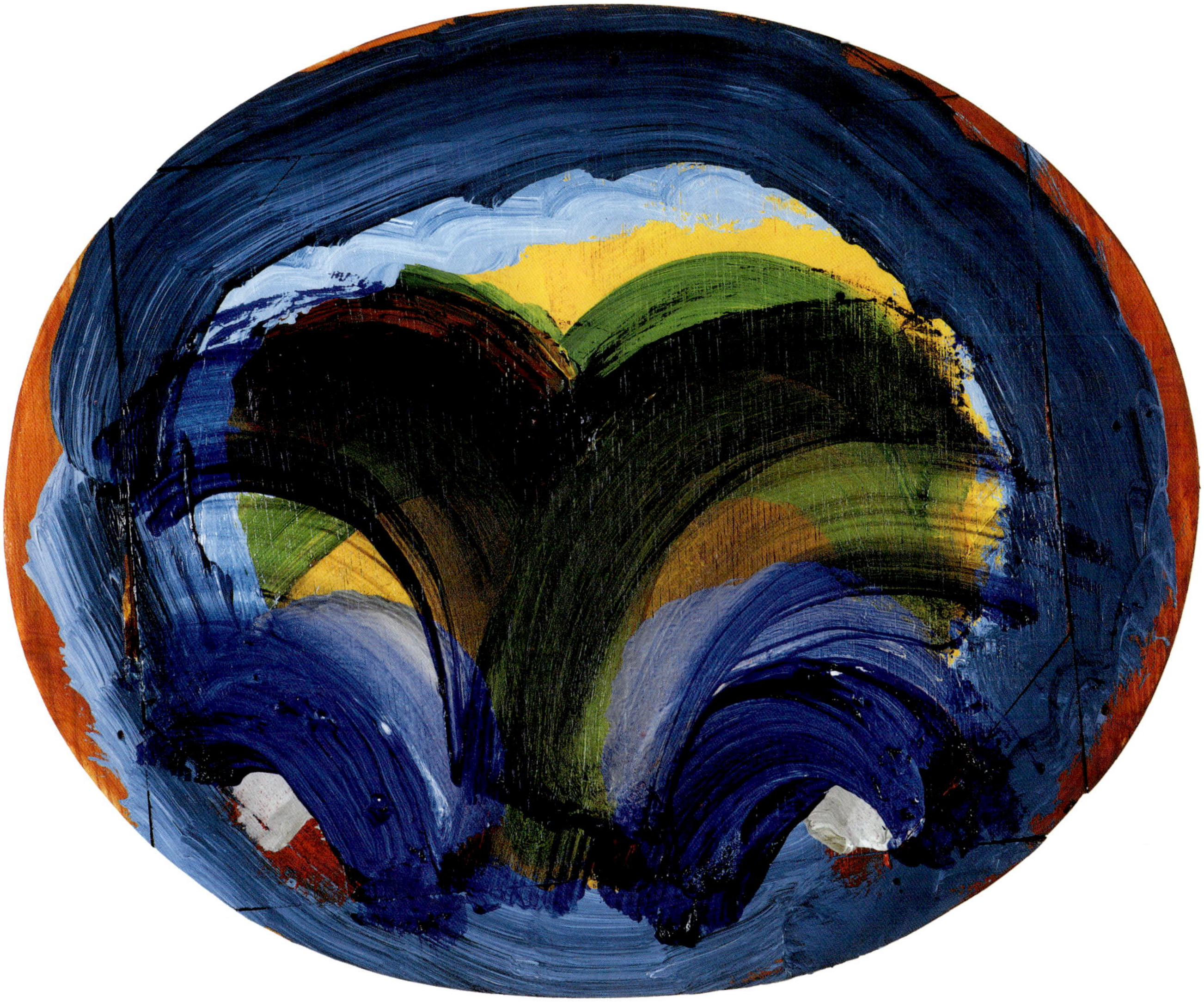

BLUE PALM
1985 – 86

the painting strikes out against its own materiality with sudden, improvisatory glory. It might *be* just a thing, an ordinary object, but it contains the dream of something that can only be dreamed of (a *blue* palm?), rendered swiftly and summarily in sweeping curves of swiftly applied paint. It is both object and not-object. Toughly fantastical, it declares art's right to reinvent an unsatisfactory world and furnish it with imagined alternatives. *Blue Palm* is a late response to Baudelaire's vision of art as responsible irresponsibility, a calculated madness capable of invigorating the

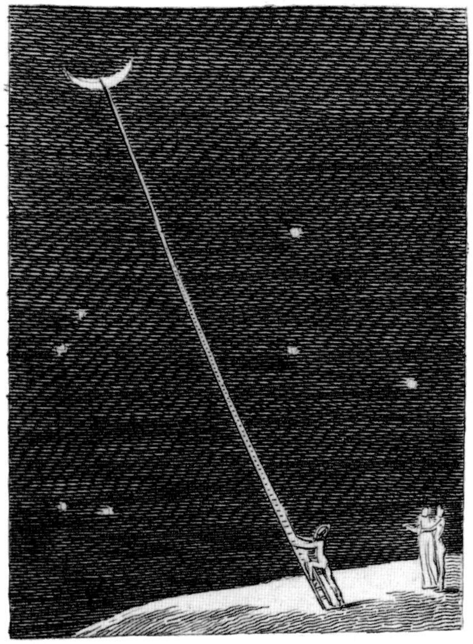

world: 'I want meadows red in tone and trees painted in blue', he wrote. 'Nature has no imagination.'[22]

Some of the paintings play more insistently on their own artifice than others. *It Can't be True* (1987–90) is a picture that contains a picture that contains a picture. Here, the characteristic device of framing one image within another has been taken to an extreme, so the painting actually frames itself three times – but it is also, at the same time, unframed, since the frame that defines its outer edge has itself been painted upon and so cannot really be counted part of the frame. It is, instead, part of the object that is

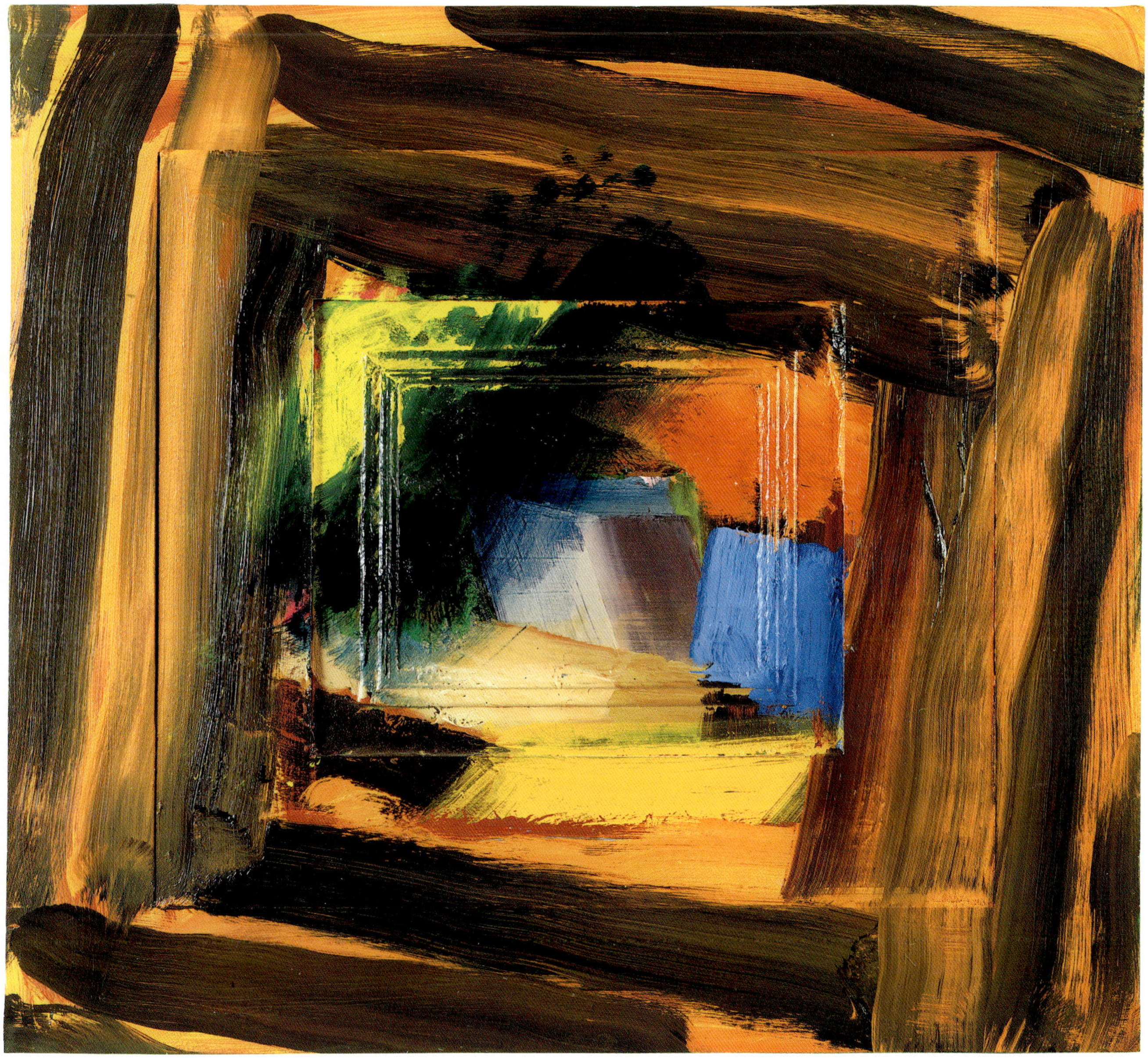

IT CAN'T BE TRUE
1987 – 90

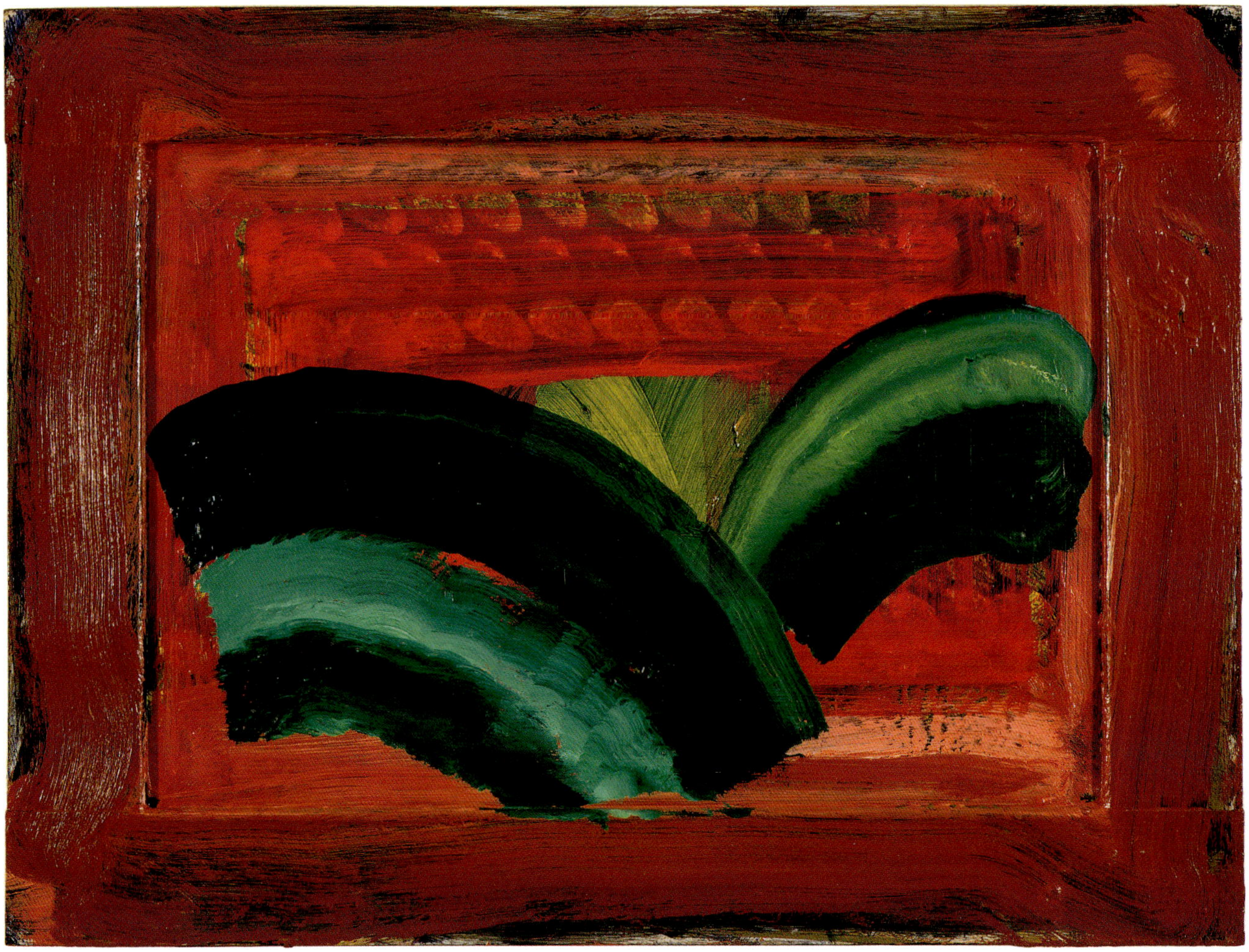

LEAVES
1987 – 88

the work of art. The effect is of a puzzle or paradox. Conventional perspective, which normally leads the eye *into* space, has been reversed. But what this picture houses, at its centre, is a flat and resistant patch of blankness eaten into but unrelieved by strokes of bright colour, red and blue and fawn; a place that offers nothing to look at and returns the eye, instead, to the periphery of the image. It is here that most of the pictorial action takes place, in large sweeping strokes of mustardy orange and brown that overlay one another. These strokes trace an empty-centred oblong that almost defines the shape of the picture, almost frames it – but also fails to, since the oblong is askew, uncompleted, and leaks off the edges of the picture. *It Can't be True* dramatizes or plays upon its own failure (or determined refusal) to provide an illusion, a picture that presents you with all the apparatus of illusionism but reveals it to be merely and only apparatus.

In the end, the picture is just a thing, surrounded by other things. This may also be P. 120 the subject of *Talking about Art* (1975), another painting that frames a painting within it, a small oblong surrounded by buzzing confusion, by planes of overlapping colour and pillars of paint which suggest the wider world that all paintings have to define themselves against and compete with. The world, perhaps, of the gallery on opening night, where paintings are treated as things to be glanced at on the way to the bar for another drink. Hodgkin's pictorial language is extremely matter-of-fact, made of marks that never begin to pretend they are anything other than marks made on a flat surface using a paintbrush. It can't be true, indeed. The paintings might seek to represent feelings, to evoke memories of people or places or things, but they are absolutely and straightforwardly honest about the imponderabilities of the enterprise that is painting, the way in which it substitutes codes for realities.

Leaves (1987–88) deliberately presents the eye with marks – rainbow curves of different greens, laid on a field of interrupted red – that are imperfectly suggestive of a larger world, in the same relation to it as a leaf fallen from a tree. It is one of a fairly large family of paintings that present themselves as blatant stand-ins for things; PP. 92, 107 others include *The Moon* and *Dark Moon*, *Rainbow*, *Artificial Flowers* (1975), *Sad* P. 47 *Flowers* (1979–85), *Tree* (1982–84) and *Small Tree near Cairo* (1973–77). *Fruit* (1988–89) makes a joke out of the arbitrariness of painted equivalents for things, giving the eye the exotic fruit of pictorial surrogacy in the form of a chaotic variegated splodge of paint that looks like a ripe peach that has landed on the painting with such force that it has exploded.

Lawrence Gowing wrote well about the insistent material quality of Hodgkin's pictures, the way in which they declare their nature as objects with such demonstrative overtness that they overcome their origins in the painter's personal experience and emerge, into the world, as armoured and self-sufficient things:

> Happening to recognise, in a mosaic of bright-spotted blue, framed in mustard yellow that is moulded with brown and linked in scarlet with a sunlit window and a sunless picture, in one of those collocations of forbidden colours that are meat and drink to the painter, a highly intelligent Senior Civil Servant, I leave her to entertain her marmalade-coloured guests. It is the totality of the mosaic that entertains us...
>
> Absorbed in the simultaneous flat-and-deep of Hodgkin's colour one no longer seeks to decode it. One dwells on it for itself.[23]

Gowing was, presumably, referring to *Small Durand Gardens* (1974), a tough and sociable picture that contains, latent within it, many of the qualities of Hodgkin's later and more accomplished art. It declares the freedom with which an experience can be converted into a painter's sign language, which in Hodgkin's art does have something of the signpainter's rough-and-readiness about it.

The same mark, the arc of paint, smooth or ridged, fluid or clotted, can be made to conjure things that are vast (a rainbow) or large (a palm tree) or tiny (a leaf). The world of the paintings is one of constantly shifting scale, where a mark can conjure enormous bulk or, equally, frail minuteness. But because the marks are always and so emphatically marks they become the flaunts of art's independence.

Much has already been written, here, about the perennial melancholy of the paintings, the knowledge they bear within them of their severance from the world, their nature as memorials to the experience of things and people and feelings that they cannot

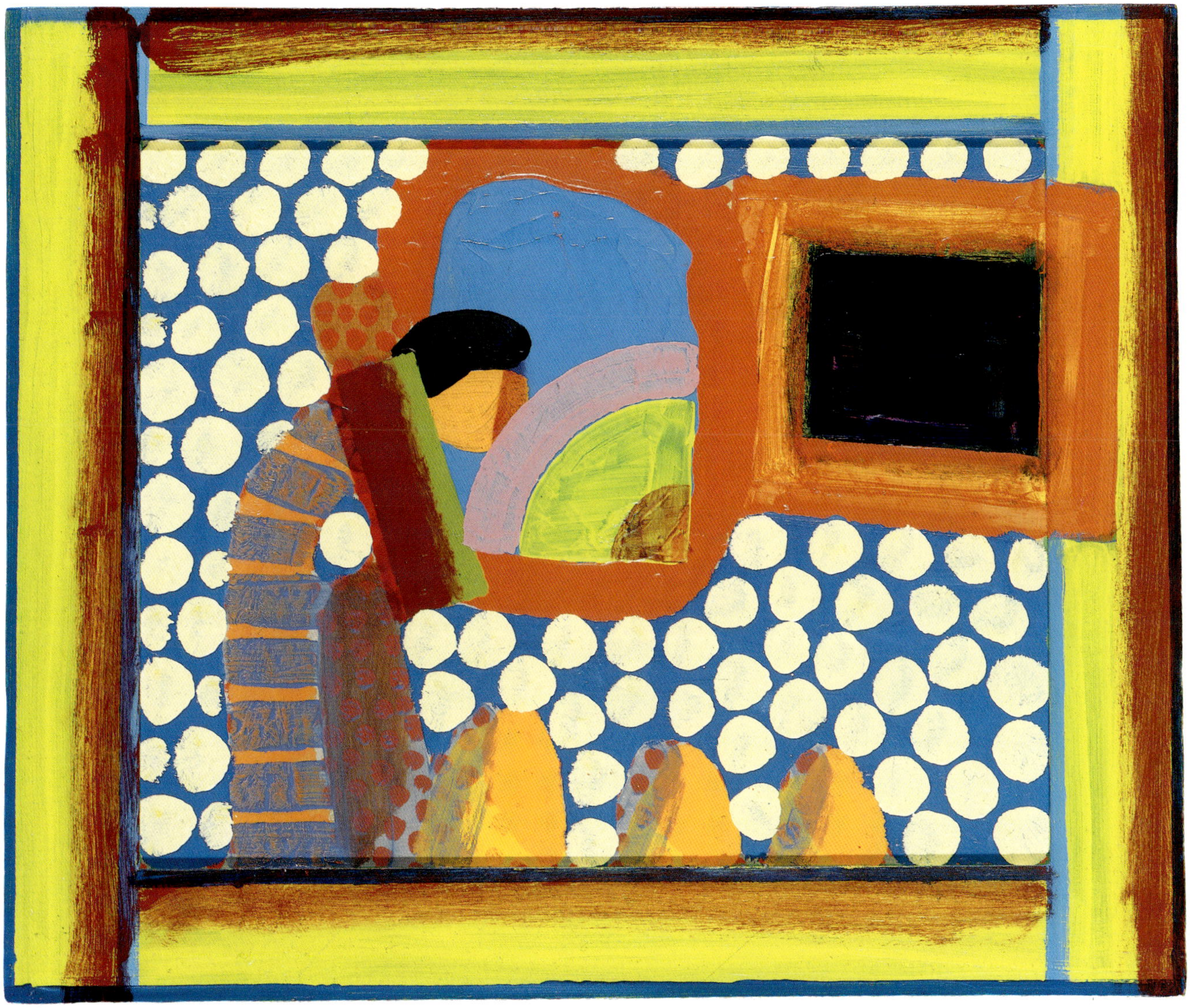

SMALL DURAND GARDENS
1974

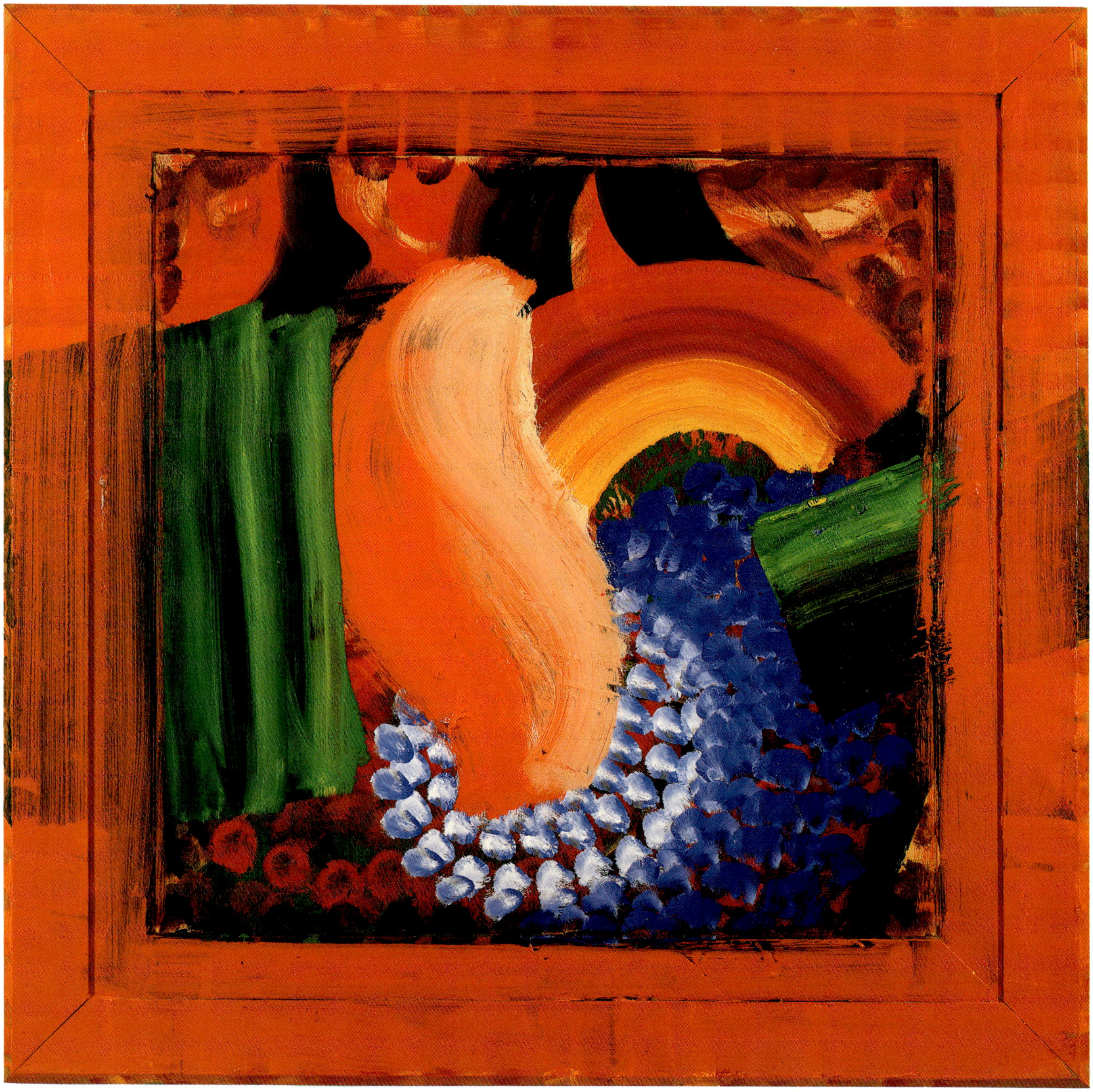

DINNER IN PALAZZO ALBRIZZI
1984 – 88

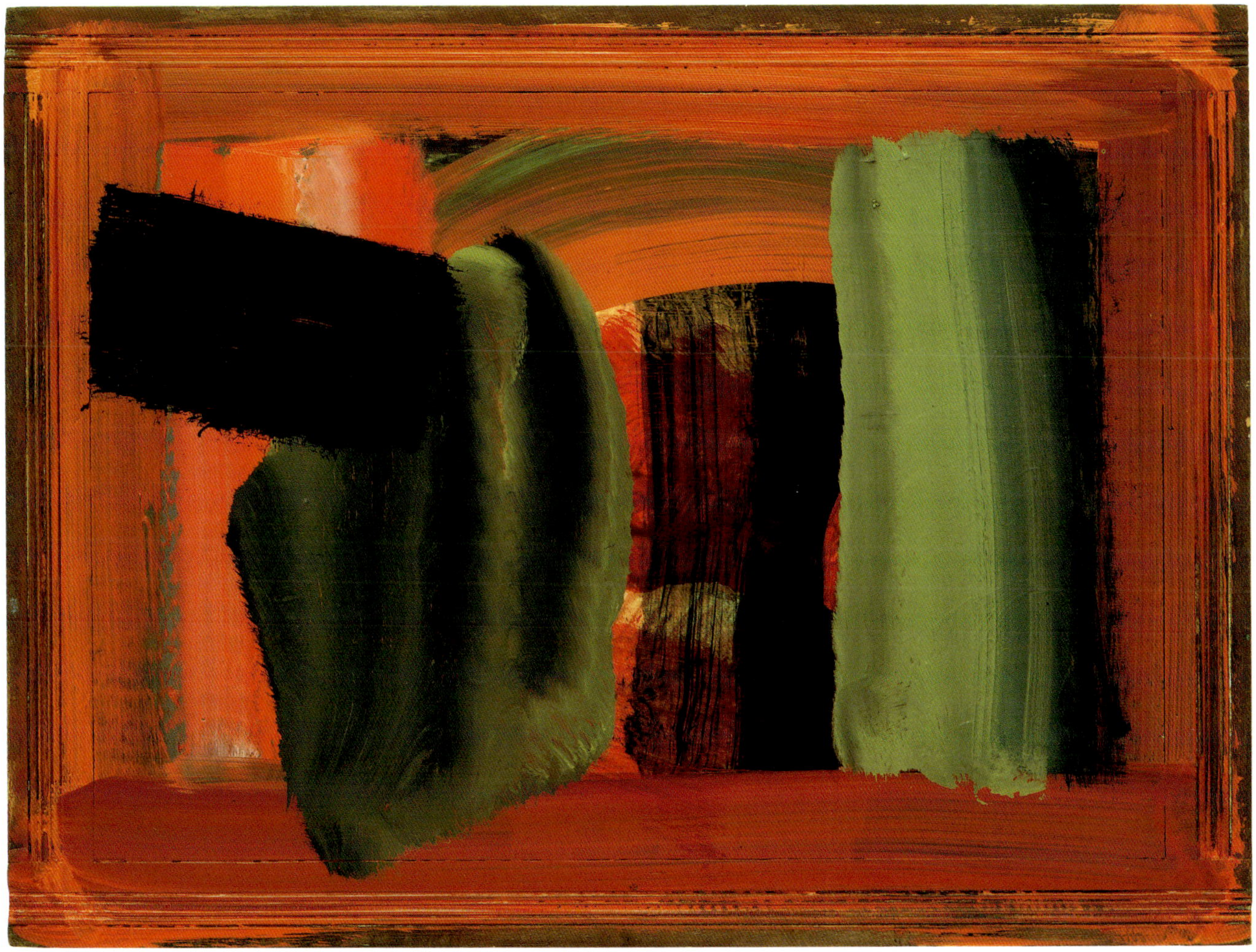

HAVEN'T WE MET?
1985 – 88

truly incarnate. This emerges with peculiar clarity in the most sociable paintings, since these are also the paintings in which their code seems strangest and most perverse. Hodgkin turns people into ghosts, translates moments of social or sexual or emotional contact into smears or swipes of paint that mingle or float in indeterminate space.

Sometimes they do so exuberantly – *Dinner in Palazzo Albrizzi* (1984–88) is an P. 164 orgy of abstracted minglings and interpenetrations, a festive collision of bright arcs and twinkling blobs and fleshy S-curves – but even the exuberance signals a loss of a kind, the fuzziness of a dream or a memory that cannot be recaptured. *After Dinner* and P. 76 *Haven't We Met?* (1985–88) are other paintings that might be said to represent this P. 165 strain in Hodgkin's art, where it most nearly approaches pure abstraction and creates a world of jostling lozenges, curious semi-opaque shapes that have an odd, subaqueous character, like seaweed moved by underwater currents.

Sometimes the paintings are more conciliatory, less baffling because more evenly balanced on the knife edge separating distinctness from indistinctness – and more content to play on the border that separates the mark seen simply as mark and the mark seen as the sign for something else, the border between painting-as-painting and painting-as-illusion. *Mr and Mrs James Kirkman* (1980–84) is a picture that holds back at the brink of abstraction, although it does so so comically and with such cartoon-like absurdity that it undermines its own figurative qualities. Mr Kirkman is lost, buried somewhere within the painting's contrived anarchy of mists and splotched veils, but Mrs Kirkman survives as a pink blob with massively outsized earrings and a green necklace painted with the thick emphasis that a little girl with an enthusiasm for fancy dress might bring to the task of painting such an object. The two portraits of Terence PP. 168, 169 McInerney (both 1981) also provide the last vestiges of the figure, the figure before it has been entirely overwhelmed by the autonomous logic of the painting. The figure of McInerney appears like a phantom loitering, at the margins of recognizability and almost obliterated by pattern, in paintings ostensibly devoted to his presence.

Keith and Kathy Sachs takes the transfiguration of subject, by contrast, to the P. 2 point of complete reinvention. There are barely any figurative vestiges here, other than in the uprightness of the two forms at its heart. It is a commissioned portrait painted on

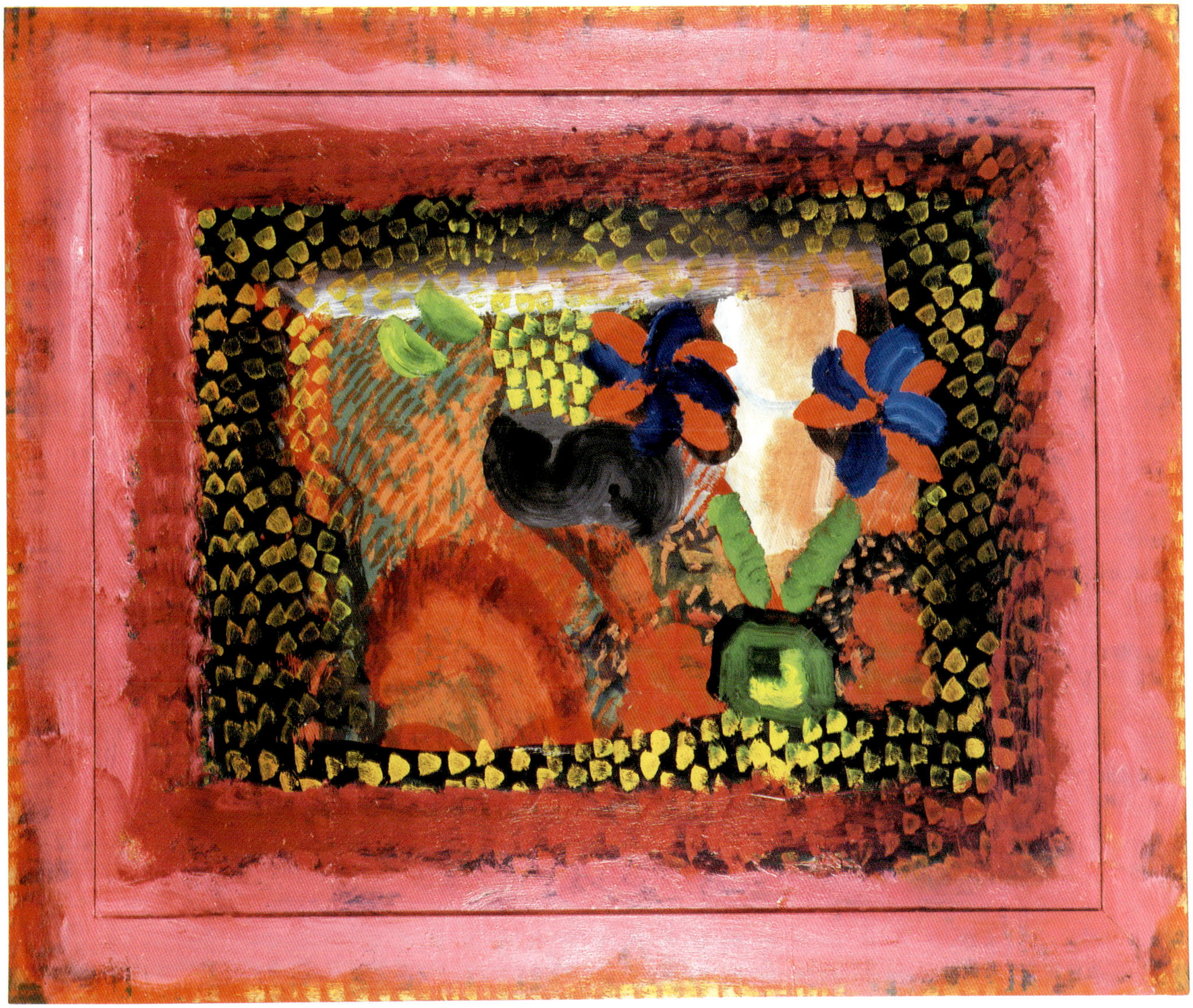

MR AND MRS JAMES KIRKMAN
1980 – 84

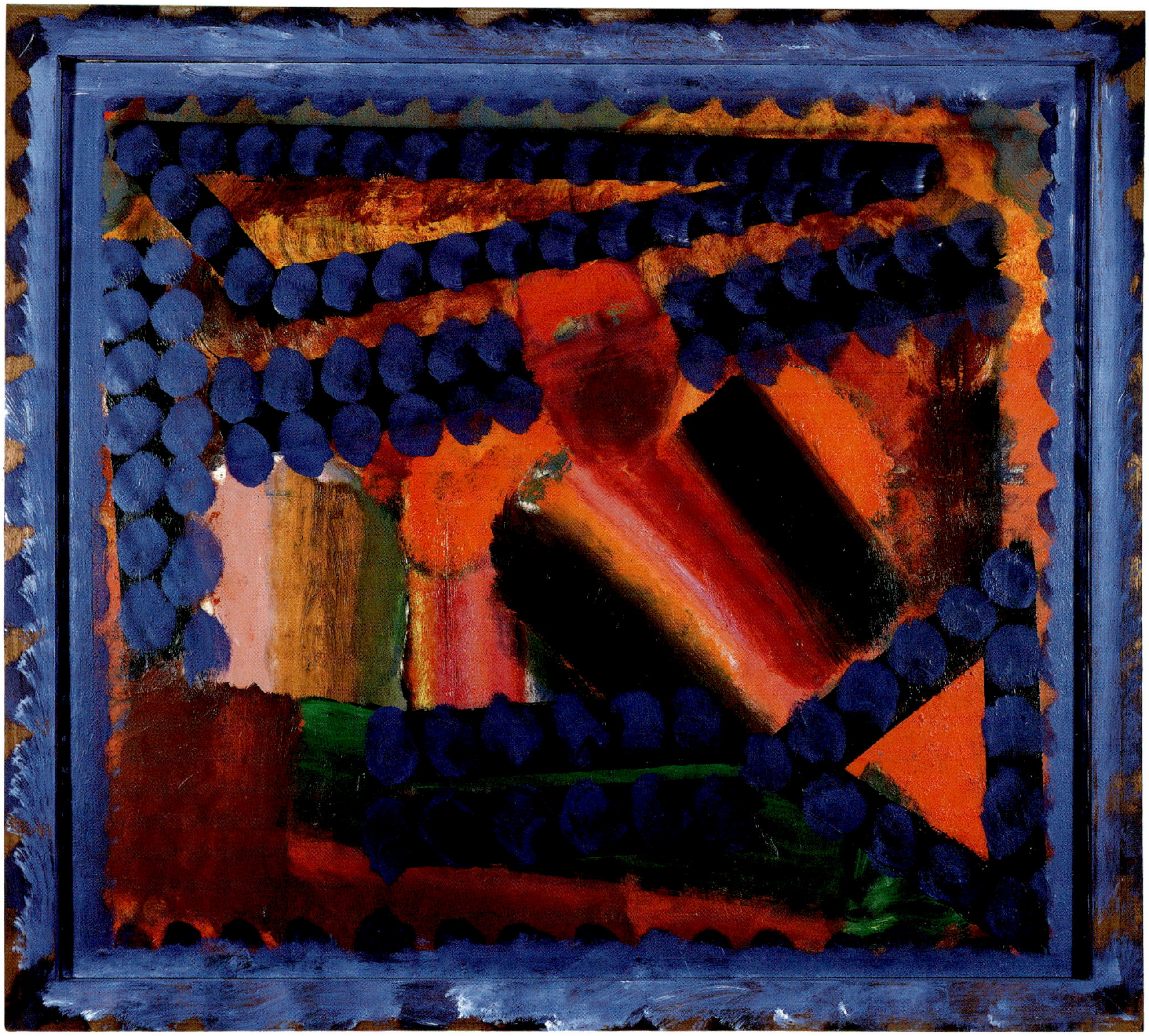

FIRST PORTRAIT OF TERENCE MCINERNEY
1981

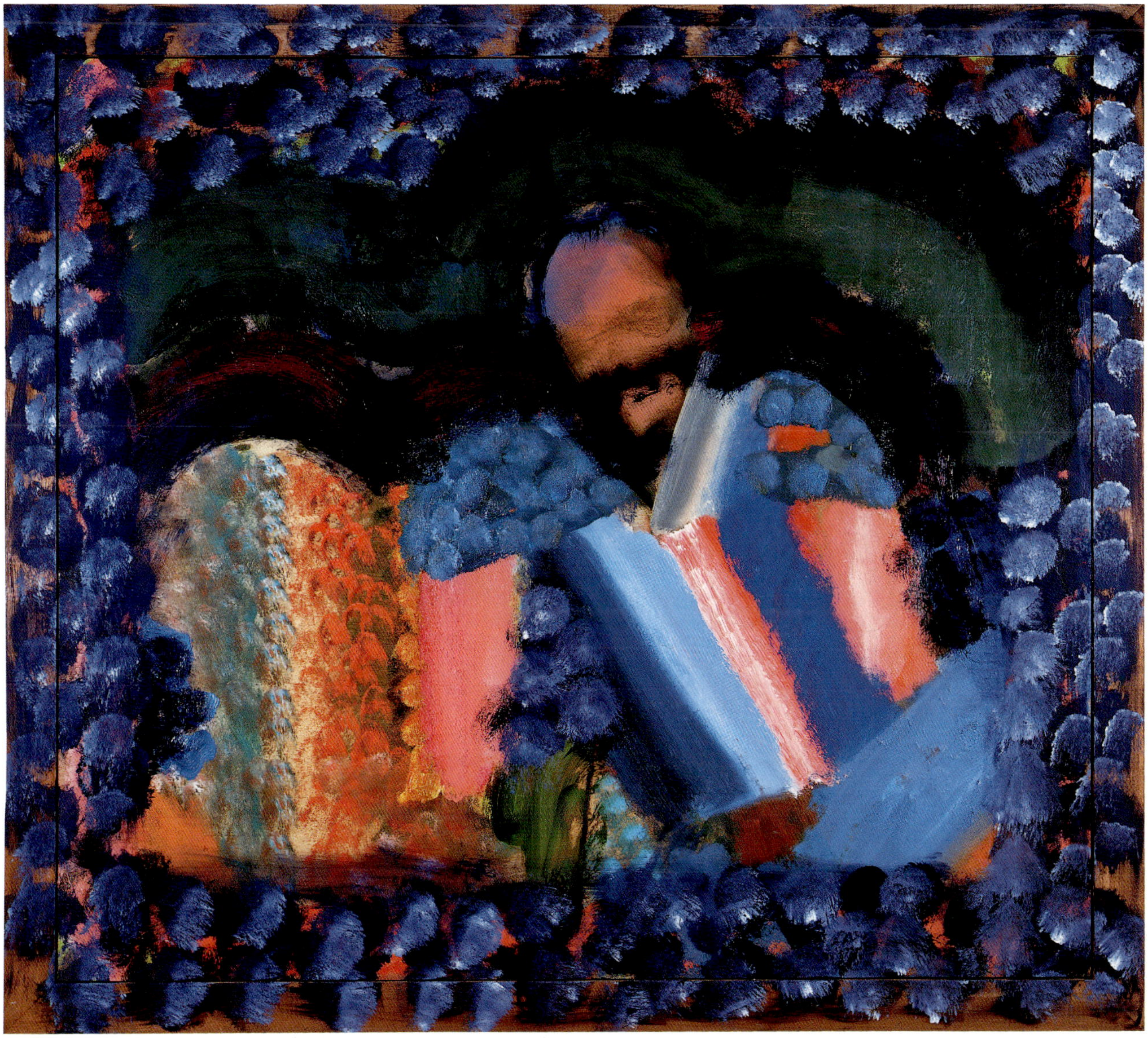

SECOND PORTRAIT OF TERENCE MCINERNEY
1981

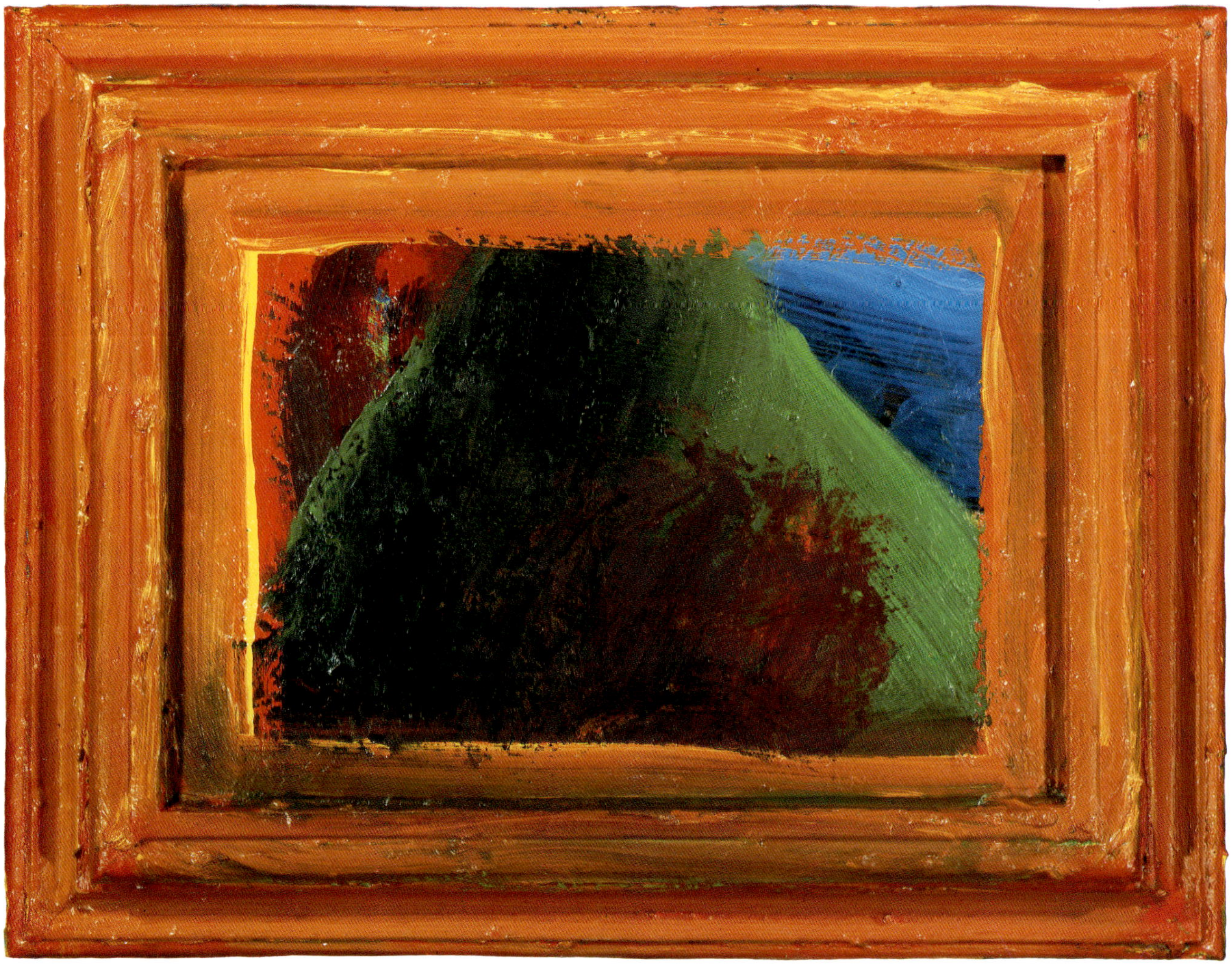

ITALIAN LANDSCAPE
1990 – 91

and within an octagonal Louis XIV frame which gives it the traditional shape of the Renaissance wedding portrait (it was a commission to celebrate a wedding anniversary). This use of an old frame recalls one of the uses that Picasso, who often liked to have his paintings placed in Renaissance surrounds, made of old frames. There is something patricidal about it. It is a device which places the picture in relation to older forms of art, in this case the traditional celebratory marital portrait, while also emphasizing the extent to which it dissents from the tradition which it occupies. The Sachs have been completely transformed into Hodgkin's ciphers for people, and the painting amounts to a declaration of freedom. If an artist decides to paint two people as a swathe of coiling green and a bent column of blue and white like toothpaste squeezed from a tube, then that is his privilege. The picture has a splendidly mad, abstracted baroque quality that depends on the contrast between the grand sweep of its forms and luxury of its colour, and the dumb thingness of the marks themselves. These shapes are plainly just paint, great rolling rivers of it flowing across a wooden surface. But they are, also, curiously persuasive analogues for the human form, leaning forms that abut and touch one another with a subtle tenderness that contains a surprising recollection of the husband and wife in Rembrandt's great painting of marital affection, *The Jewish Bride*. Painting makes its own reality, becomes its own reality.

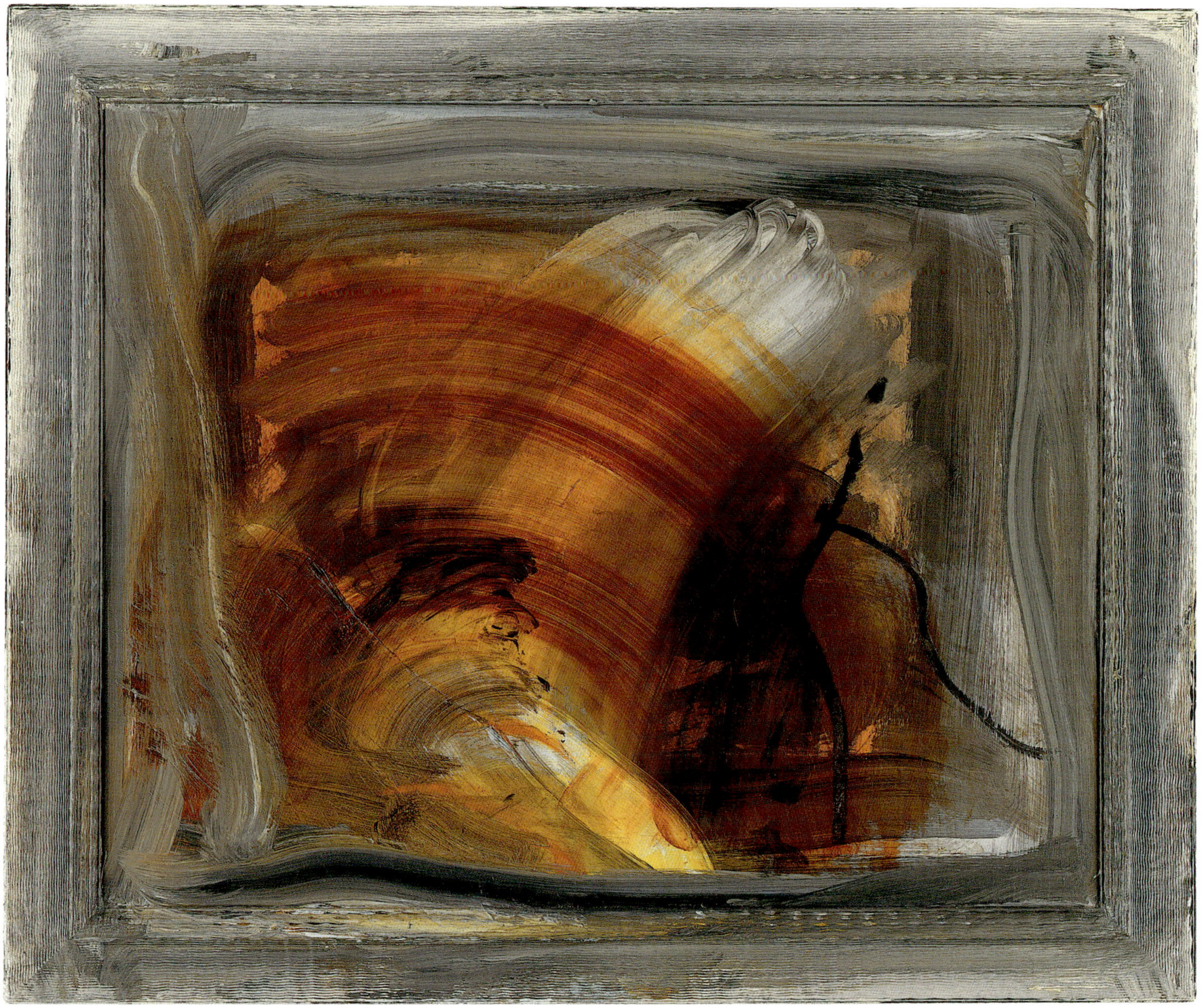

AUTUMN FOLIAGE
1998 – 99

14
'DREAMING ABOUT APPEARANCES'

The works that the painter has created since the mid-1990s announce a second turning-point in his career, comparable to that of the mid-1970s. He has 'deepened the game' in a multitude of ways, painting more freely and more fluently, and often on a much larger scale. At the same time his art has been more widely exhibited than ever before, both in Europe and America. Enthusiasm for his paintings, among art critics and historians, art collectors and the general public, has never been greater. Whether this has had any effect on the work itself is impossible to say, but it has certainly not arrested its development. Hodgkin's painting has continued to change and evolve.

The pictures have become both more open and more expansive. The marks from which they are formed are more blatant than ever. 'This is *paint*', they seem to say, so forcefully at times that one can almost hear the thud of brush on panel as one looks at them. They also continue to evoke lived experience, albeit in yet more allusive ways than before.

P. 53 To compare a picture completed in 1980, *Red Bermudas*, with one completed in 1999, *Autumn Foliage*, is to begin to see just how much has changed. It is not that the later picture is less 'finished', exactly. But it does indicate the artist's increasing technical boldness, and his readiness to exploit the eloquence and suggestiveness of certain types of mark which, at first glance, can seem almost inchoate. The viewer is not invited to focus on the discrete elements which make up the image, whereas in the case of *Red Bermudas* the temptation is almost to inventorize them, to count the swipes and number the blobs of paint, and to work out, mark by mark, what it might

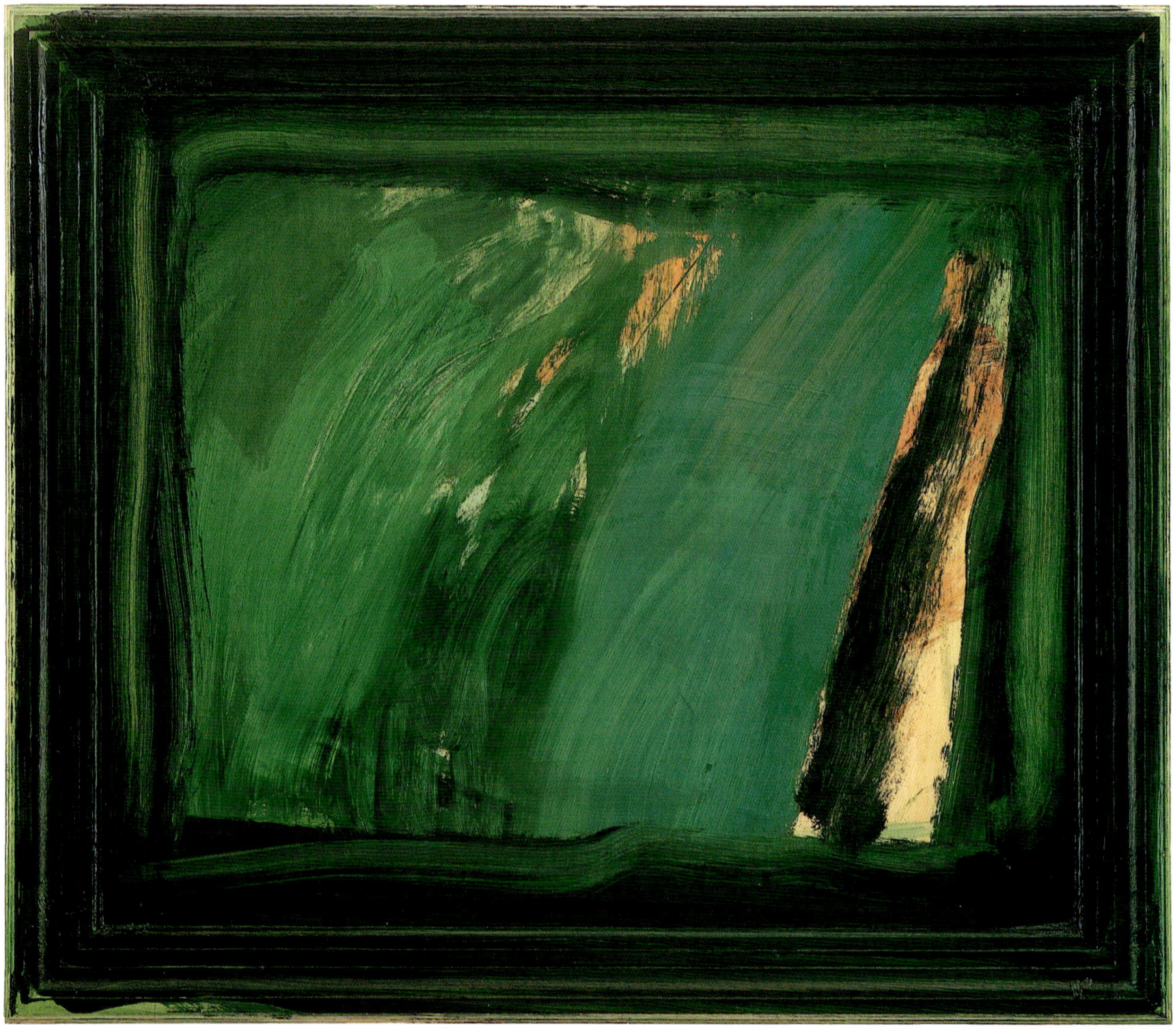

AFTER MATISSE
1995 – 99

all add up to. *Autumn Foliage* asks to be experienced as a whole, working on the eye less through an accumulation of detail than through modulations of tone and atmosphere. It is more Guardi than Canaletto. Yet it also catches its stated subject beautifully, and with an appearance of effortlessness which is characteristic of the later paintings.

P. 177 Among the pictures under consideration here the most recent, *Seurat's Bathers*, begun in 1998 and finished early in 2000, might seem to be the odd one out. But in many ways it is exemplary of the change that has taken place in the artist's work. The painting was created in response to an approach from the Director of the National Gallery in London, Neil MacGregor, who asked Hodgkin if he might like to make a work inspired by a picture in the museum, to be included in an exhibition called 'Encounters: New Art from Old'. The artist had wanted to paint a picture after Seurat's *Bathers at Asnières* (1883–84) for more than three decades, so he readily agreed.

Hodgkin has painted several other homages to artists of the past, including *After Corot*, *After Degas*, *After Morandi* and *After Matisse*. But those pictures were all based on memories of particular groups of works by the artists in question. *Seurat's Bathers* takes a single picture as its starting-point. It is painted on top of a carefully drawn transcription of Seurat's picture of men swimming and relaxing by the Seine, executed by Hodgkin's studio assistant. It is, in addition, almost identical in size to Seurat's painting.

Seurat's Bathers is unique in Hodgkin's work in that it allows the viewer to compare the artist's *donnée* with the painting that he produced from it. We obviously cannot go back in time to sit at dinner with Hodgkin in the Palazzo Albrizzi in 1984 P. 164 and compare his perceptions of that particular evening with his picture, *Dinner in Palazzo Albrizzi*. But we *can* compare the Seurat – there it is, on the wall of the National Gallery – with what he has made of it. *Seurat's Bathers* is therefore a picture that makes the artist's working processes unusually visible.

Seurat's painting seems to aspire to the timeless monumentality of a fresco by Piero della Francesca, whereas Hodgkin's reworking of it pushes it in other directions.

What was still becomes mobile; what was fixed becomes glanced; what was reserved becomes sensual, and vehement. A world where everyone and everything seems to exist, melancholically, in a perpetual state of apartness has become a world where all touch and blend, where man and land and river and city have all become part of a continuum. A reflective modern pastoral has become a kind of bacchanal, where even if the figures themselves remain still and in their pre-ordained places the paint itself is dancing. Certain elements in Seurat's painting, such as the dog, have been completely eliminated, while others have been given an altogether greater prominence. The smoke from the distant factories in Seurat's picture has become a great swipe of flesh-coloured pigment – this is the Industrial Revolution made palpable and turned into

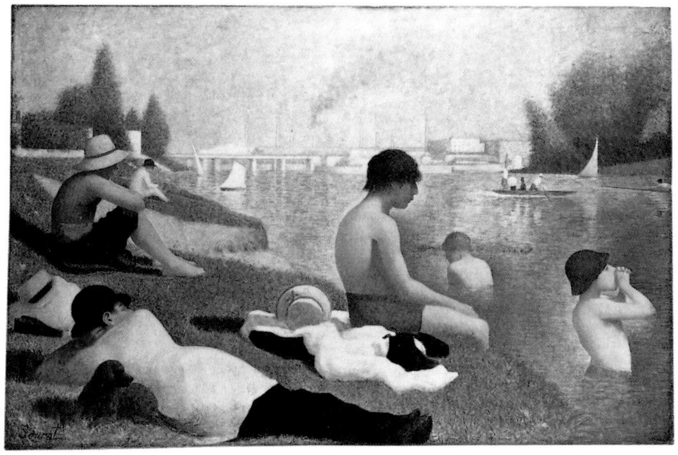

a great exhalation of human energies – while the still surface of the Seine has been churned into waves. Seurat's picture is designed to hold the viewer at arm's length, but Hodgkin's picture invites the viewer to strip off and dive in.

What originally began as a dialogue between Hodgkin and Seurat became a conversation in which other painters' voices can be heard. In creating his free variation on Seurat's work, in possessing it and making it his own, the painter has clearly borne in mind the work of nearly all the other great French painters of the early modern period. Degas and Van Gogh and Renoir; Vuillard and Bonnard and Matisse – it is almost as if each in turn has been allowed to try his hand too at reworking the *Bathers*

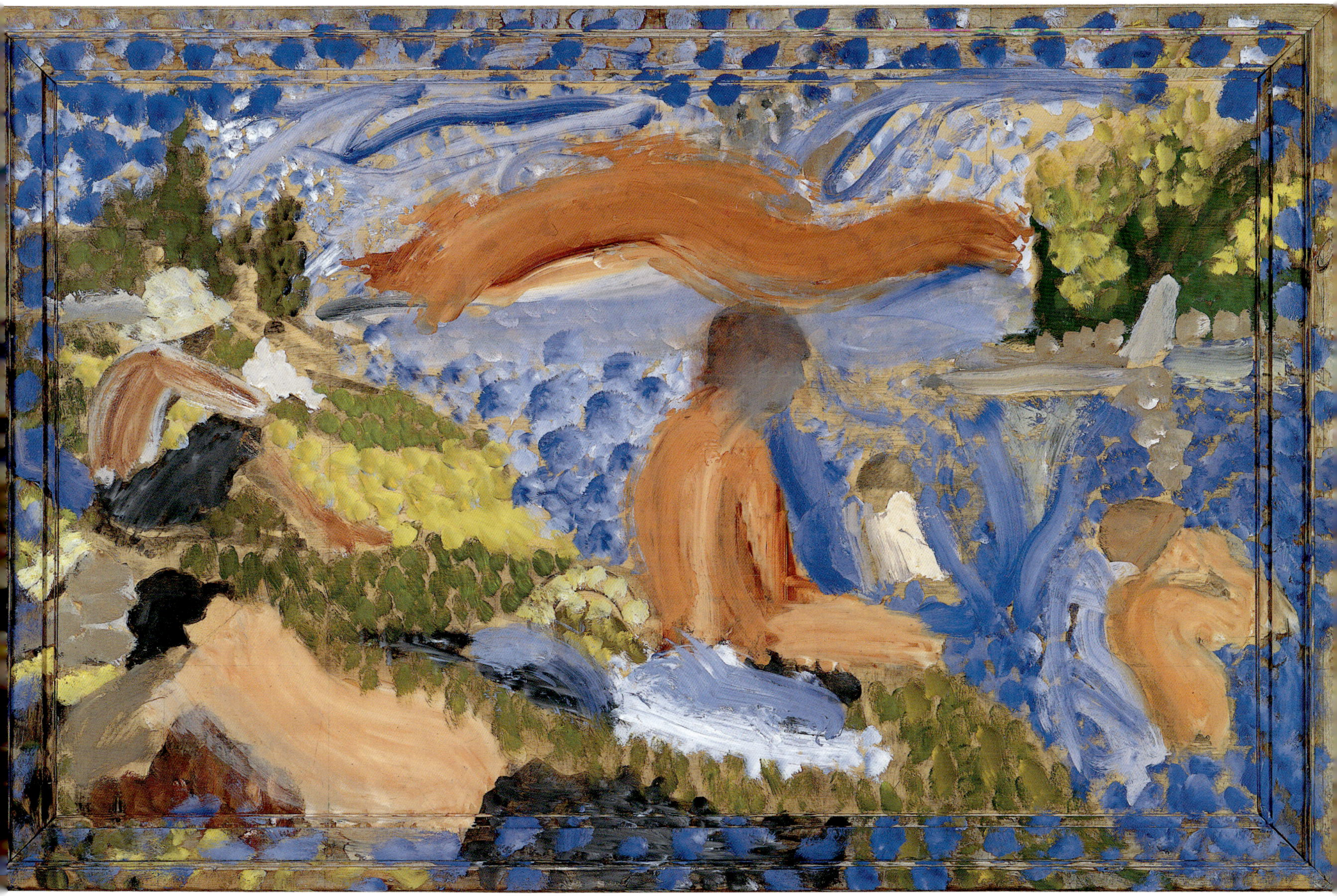

SEURAT'S BATHERS
1998 – 2000

at Asnières. The result is a riotous, exuberant work, a carnival celebration of art and life and the alchemical transformations wrought on the one by the other.

Although it is very unusual, taken in the context of the artist's oeuvre as a whole, *Seurat's Bathers* may also be seen as a kind of resume of his recent development. It is a picture in which the artist seems himself to be meditating on the nature of his own vision of things, acknowledging some of those who have helped him to arrive at it, while also measuring the distance he has travelled.

In transforming Seurat's masterpiece, Hodgkin has also created a kind of model or microcosm of the changes that he has wrought upon his *own* work since the mid-1990s. He has moved increasingly from drawing to gesture, from line to colour, from statement to suggestion – from a vision which depends on the perceived separation of man and that which he experiences to one which draws its very life and energy from a deep sense of their interconnectedness. The buzzing, pulsating world of *Seurat's Bathers* seems to express a sensibility fascinated to the point of enchantment by the mysterious nature of everyday existence. In this, it is not at all the freak or sport which some might take it to be, but the very epitome of the later pictures. Like so many of them, it calls to mind Charles Lamb's remark on the actor Munden: 'He stands wondering, amid the commonplace materials of life, like primeval man with the sun and the stars about him.'

It would be wrong to present the later pictures as something entirely new. They are not. The questions that have driven the work all along have never changed. But those questions seem to have come back with renewed force, and greater clarity. What is a self? What am I? What is the nature of human experience? How can I paint it – and how can I make, from a painting of it, a monument in defiance of time?

□ □ □

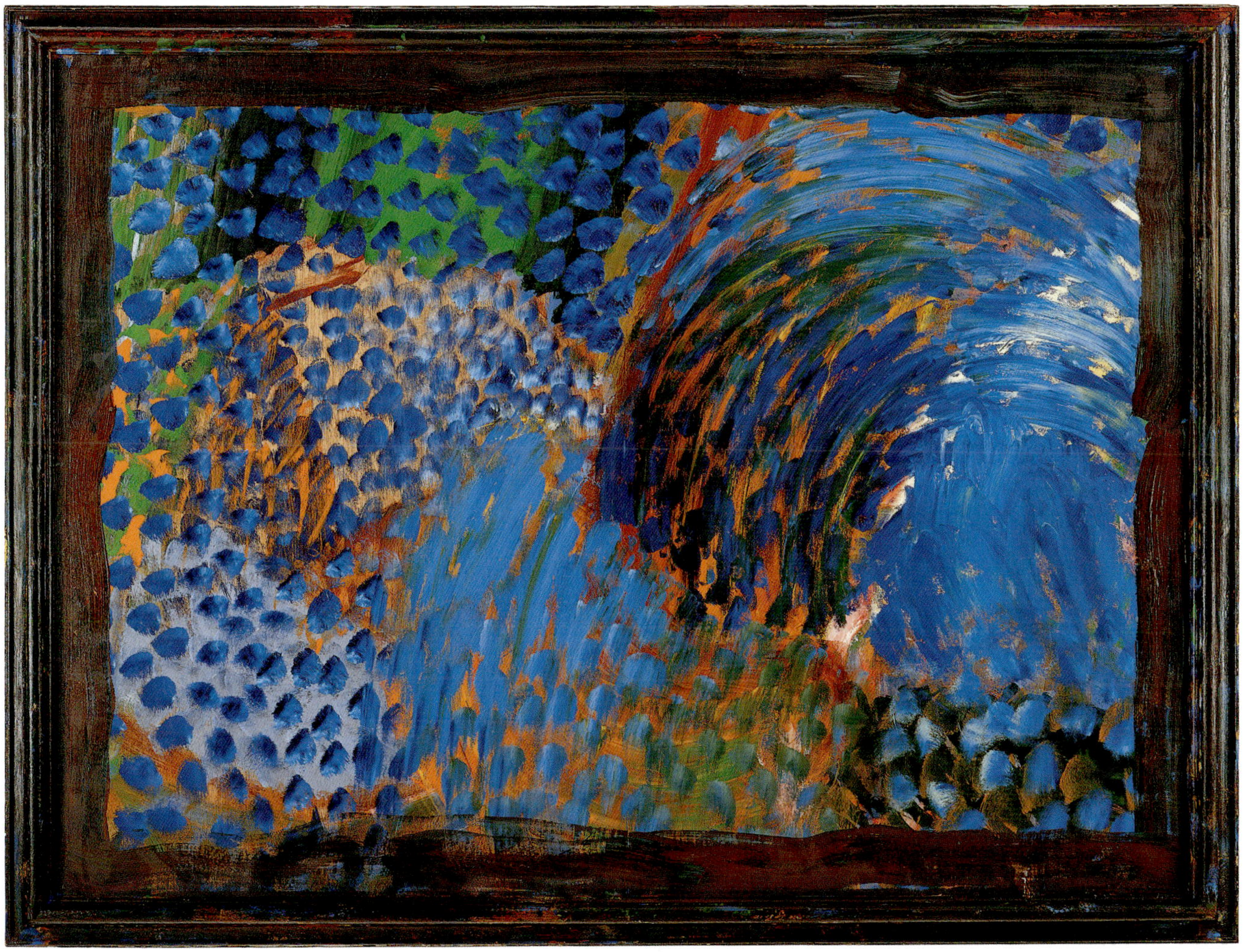

CHEZ STAMOS
1998

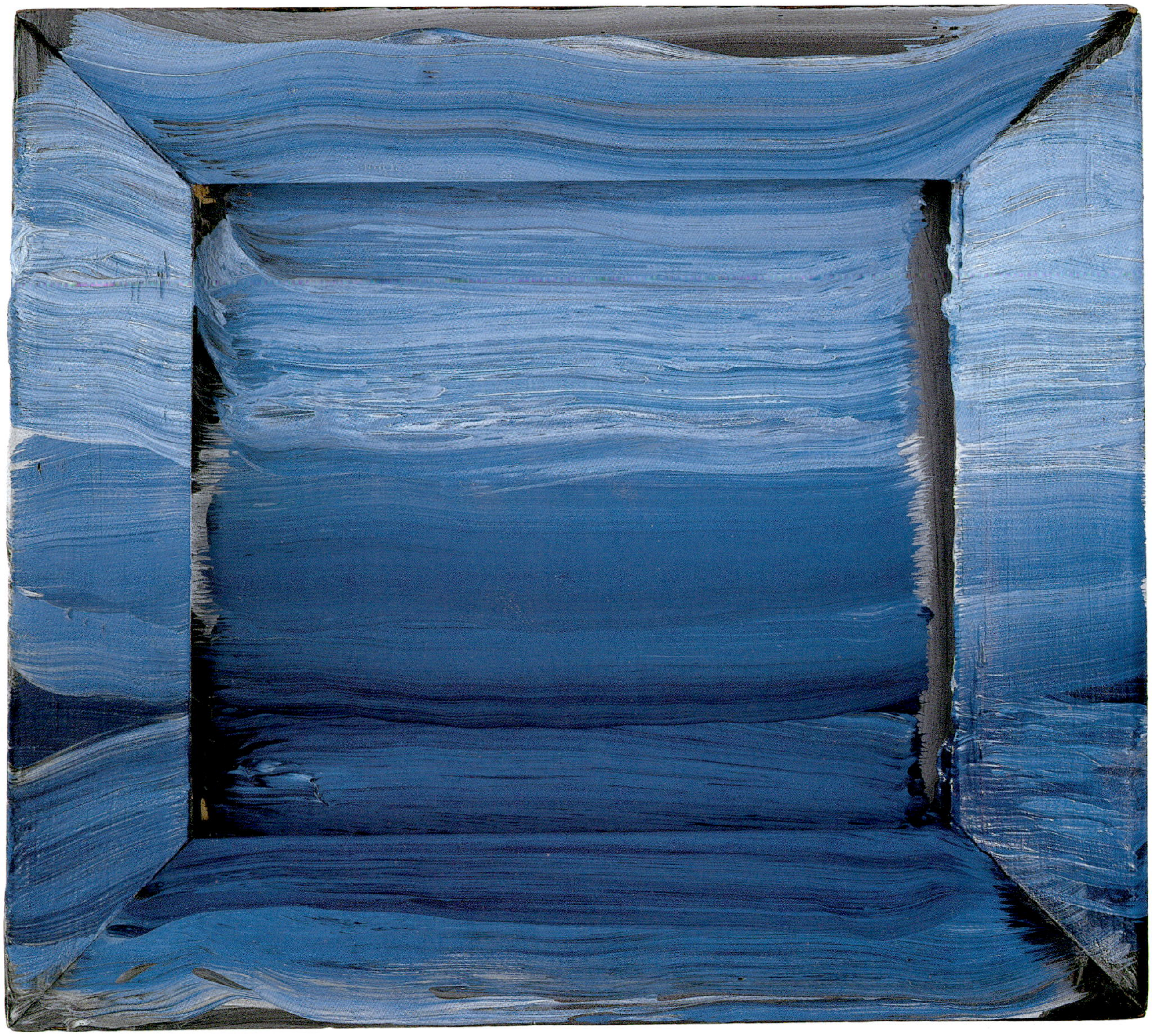

SEASCAPE
1996

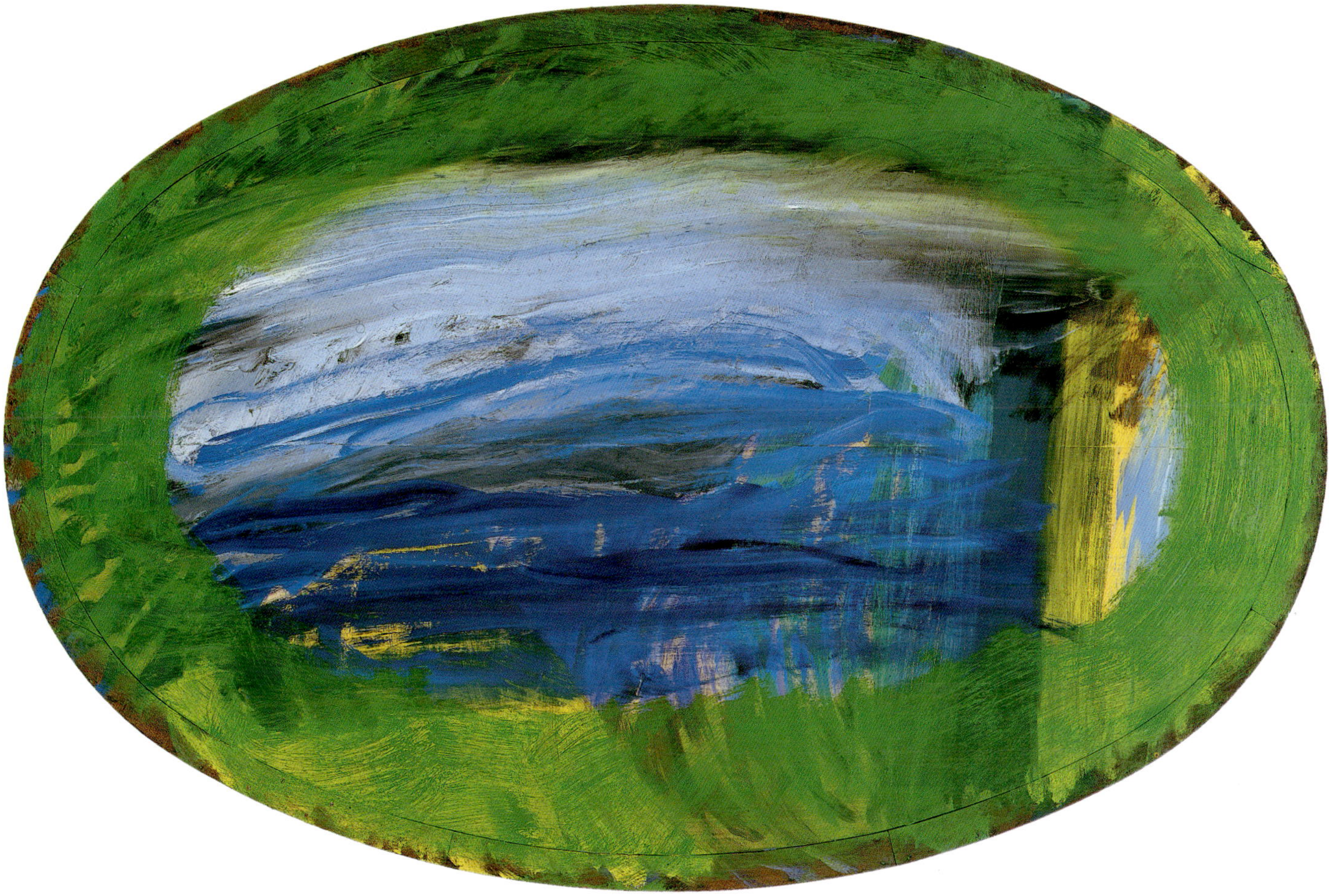

EVENING SEA
1998

'Whenever people talk to me about the weather, I always feel quite certain that they mean something else.' (Oscar Wilde, *The Importance of Being Earnest*)

The Heat of the Day (1995–96) is a brilliantly concise expression of its stated P. 187
subject matter – a few liquid stripes of red and green and yellow, swiped across a panel of wood, to conjure up noon-day shimmer. Many of the artist's later paintings have been straightforwardly pictorial in this way, particularly those – such as *Evening Sea* P. 181
(1998), *Twilight* (1995–96) and *Seascape* (1996) – that take experiences of landscape, PP. 202, 180

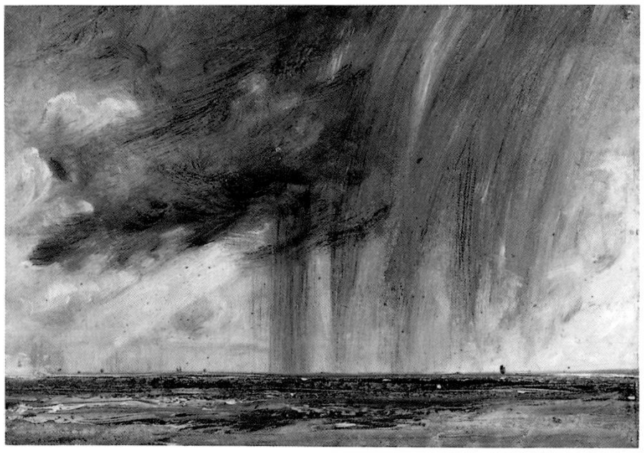

weather and times of the day as their themes. What you see is what you get, these works seem to affirm. But there may be more to them than meets the eye. *Old Sky* (1996–97), for example, is a picture that immediately complicates the relationship of these frankly meteorological pictures to nature, since it seems to distil an essence of skies not as seen in life, but in art. Looking into this essence of Old Masterly atmosphere we come face to face with, so to speak, the varnished truth.

Few of these later paintings of weather and natural phenomena could be said to be directly *mimetic*. They suggest a growing interest in landscape as a theme, while simultaneously embodying the painter's central preoccupation. They are among

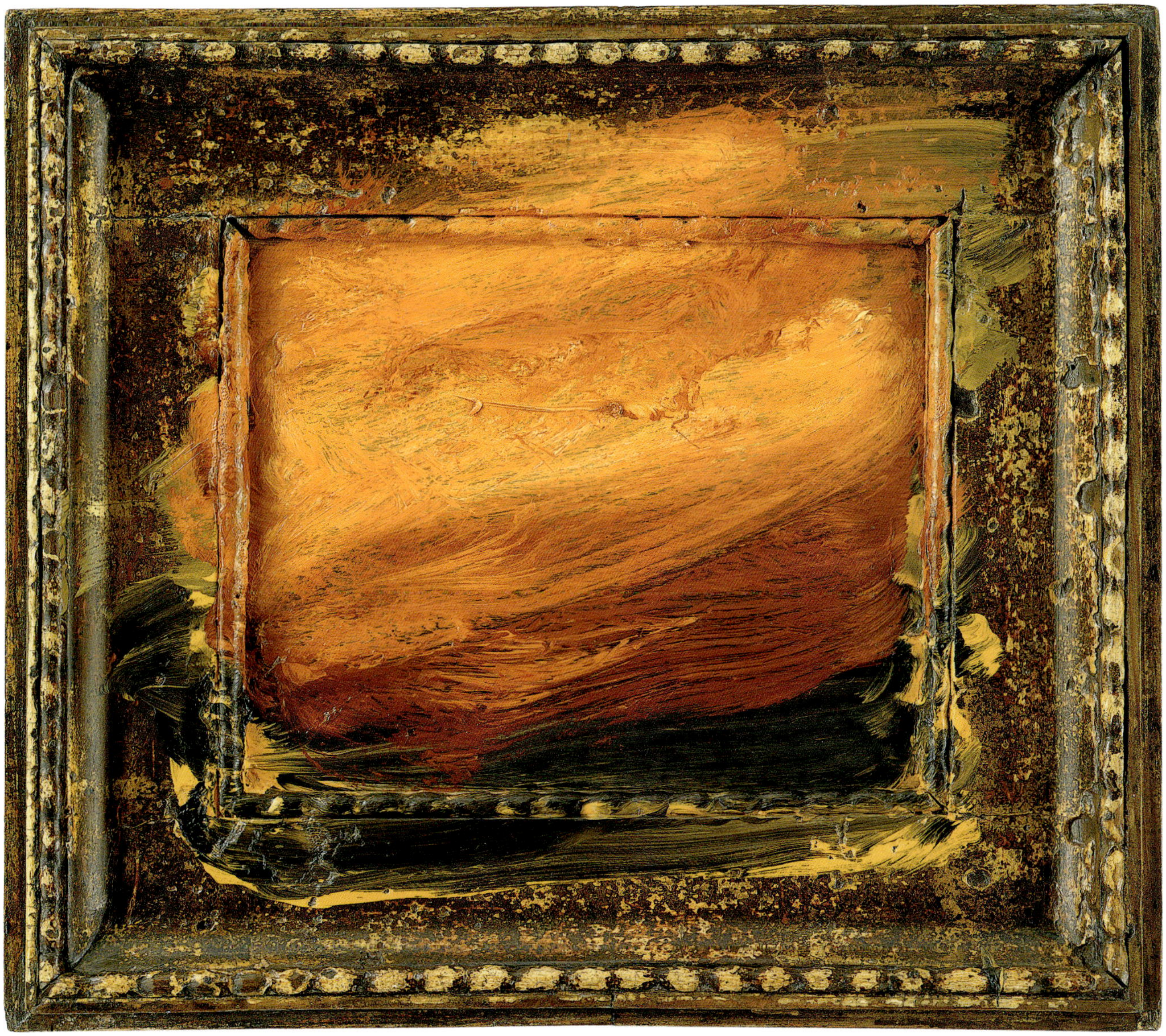

OLD SKY
1996 – 97

Hodgkin's boldest attempts yet to chart a particular part of the territory of selfhood, somewhere on the borders of memory and present vision. A picture such as *End of the Day* (1999) abstracts from perceived reality, while substituting its own equivalent reality of colour and form, in a considerably more extreme way than the pictures he was painting ten years earlier. P. 208

□ □ □

Goethe wrote in his diary one day in 1833:

'I had entered an inn towards evening, and, as a well-favoured girl with a brilliantly fair complexion, black hair, and a scarlet bodice, came into the room, I looked attentively at her as she stood before me at some distance in half shadow. As she presently afterwards turned away, I saw on the white wall, which was now before me, a black face surrounded with a bright light, while the dress of the perfectly distinct figure appeared of a beautiful sea-green.'

Goethe was interested in colour theory, and intrigued by the way in which the experience of staring at one colour can subsequently produce the sensation – once that first colour has been removed or, as in this case, has absented itself – of staring at its complementary. Thus, green being the complementary of red, the figure in the scarlet bodice still registers on the eye, after she has left the room, as an after-image of 'beautiful sea-green'.

But for all the acuity with which he describes the striking effects of complementaries, Goethe hardly emerges from the inn that evening as a model of empirical objectivity. He writes about staring at a pretty girl. In other words, he writes about what emotion can do to visual experience, and about the ways in which feeling – as well as the laws that govern perception – can complicate and alter what you see, or think you see. After all, if Goethe had not been staring so intensely (if the waitress had not been so pretty) he would never have experienced the phantom figure of the complementary. The experience doubtless changed in the remembering of it, too.

It is moments such as this, when vision, and inner vision, and emotion merge, that Hodgkin's paintings continue so powerfully to evoke.

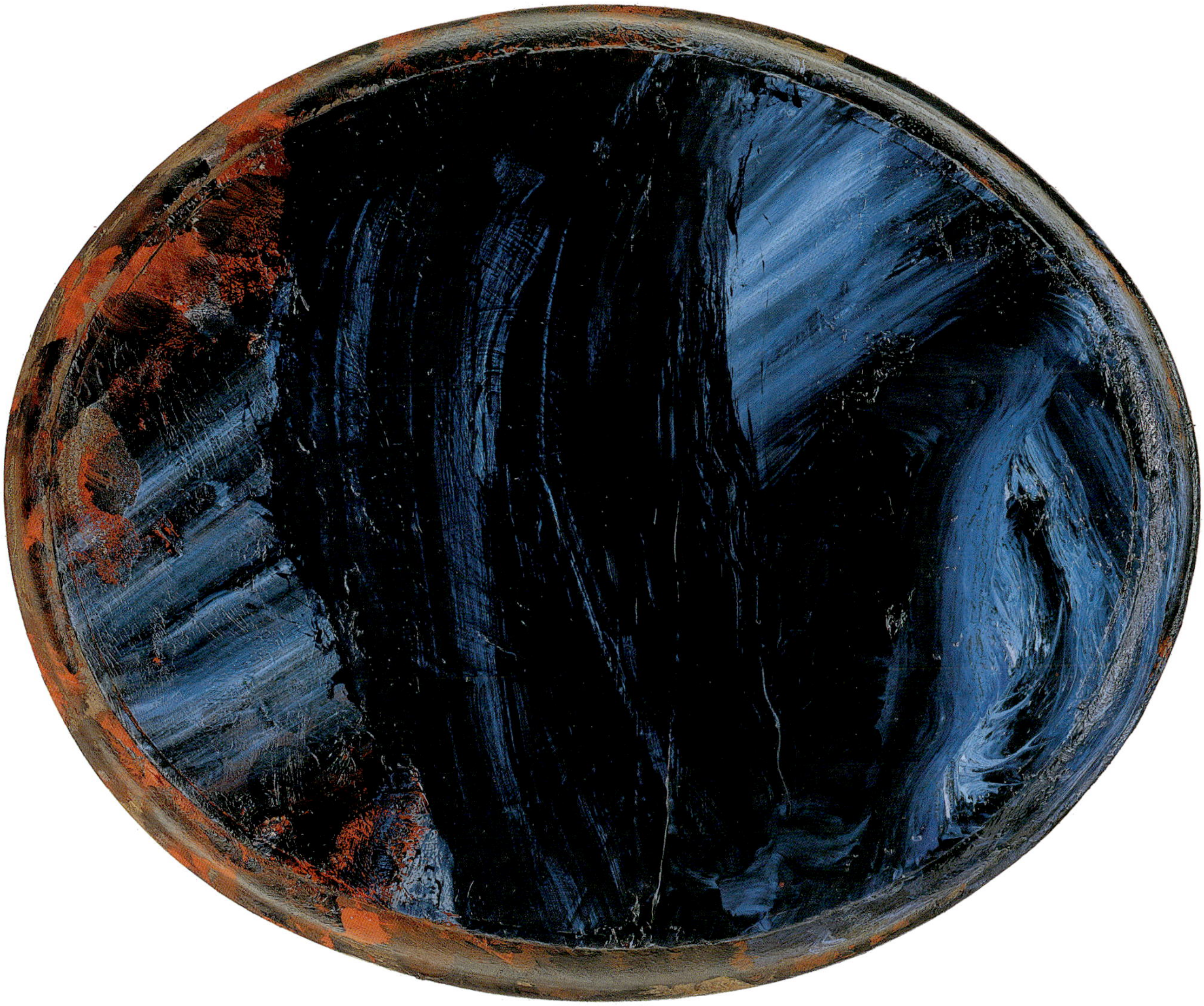

DARK MIRROR
1999

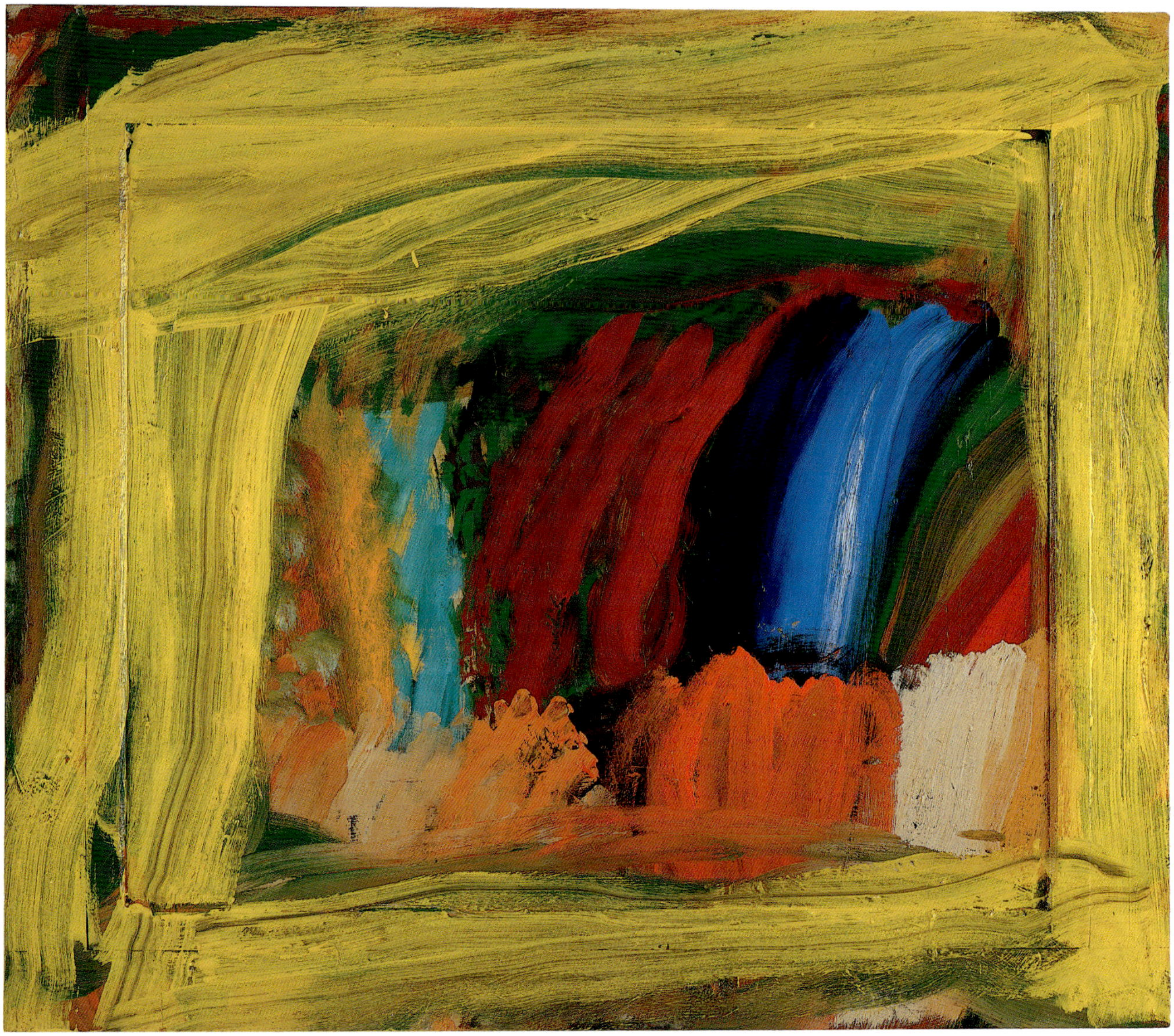

IN MIRZA'S ROOM
1995 – 98

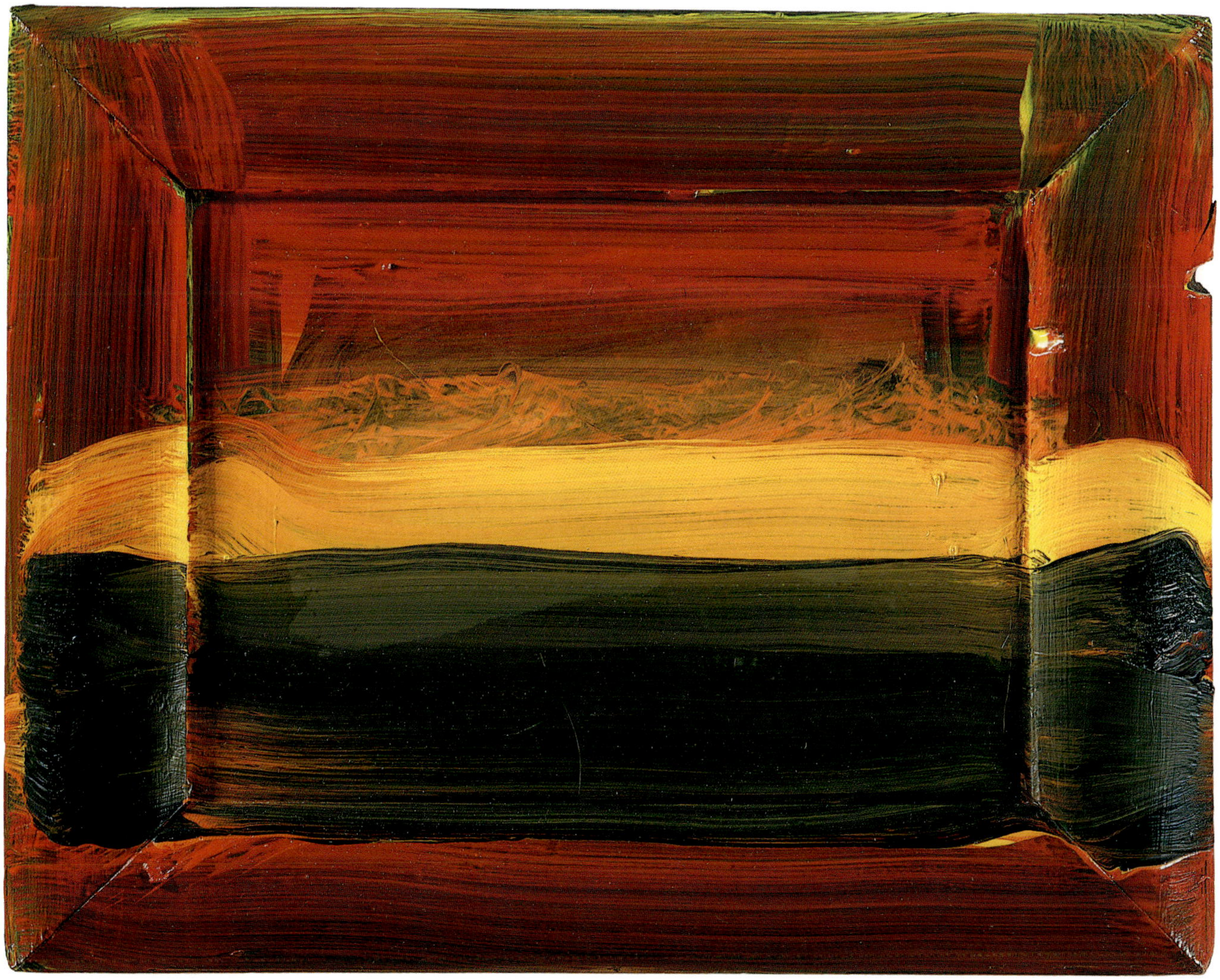

THE HEAT OF THE DAY
1995 – 96

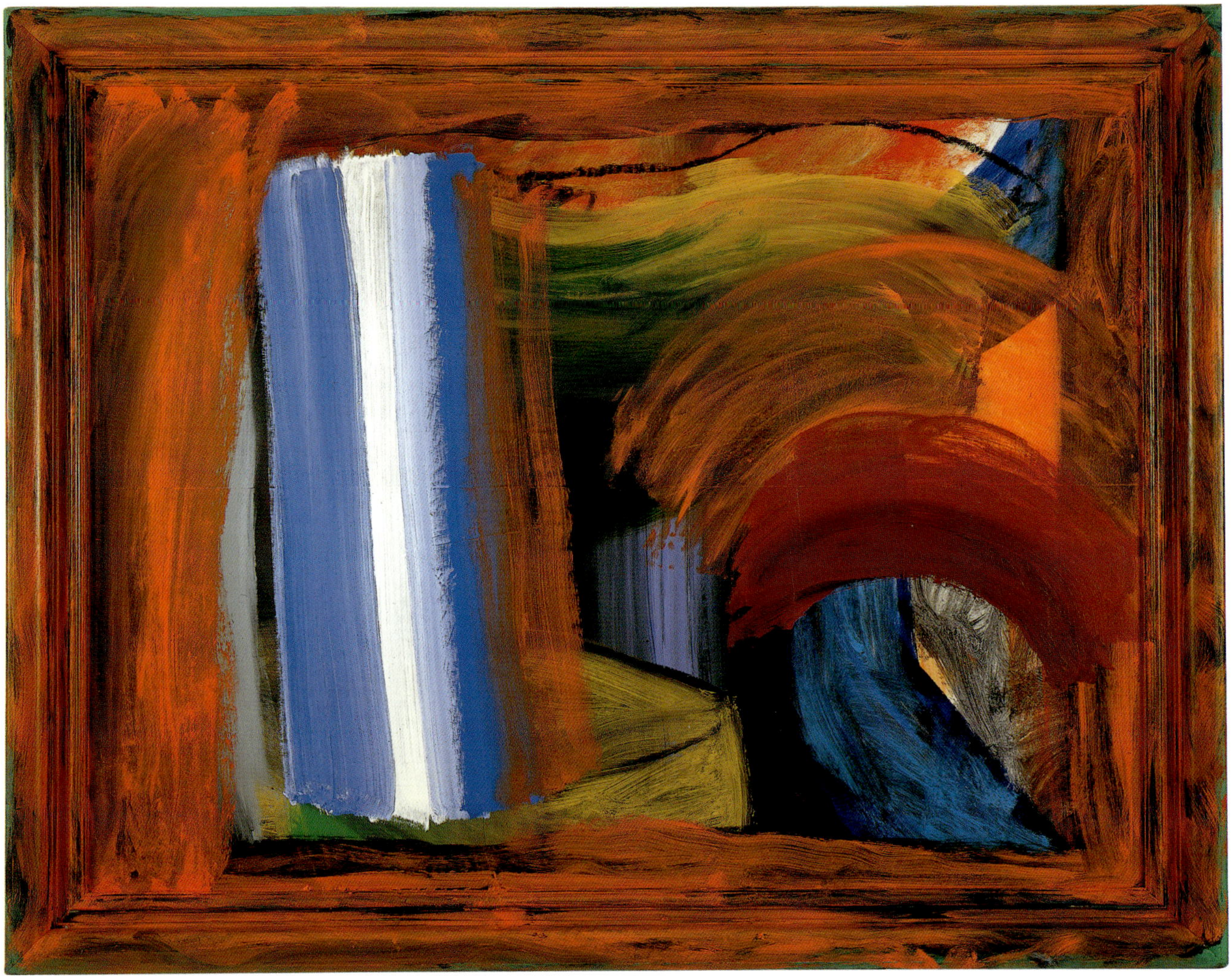

IN MEMORY OF MAX GORDON
1990 – 96

Many of the later pictures offer – as the title of one of them has it – a kind of *Dark Mirror* (1999). Looking at them can sometimes feel like trying to look at what you see when your eyes are closed. Perhaps Lawrence Gowing was on to an important truth about Hodgkin's work when he remarked – in a characteristically light but penetrating aside – 'His paintings make me dream about appearances...'

□ □ □

Ever-increasing directness of form and colour has been accompanied by an ever-decreasing interest in direct, one-to-one representation. In the 1970s and 1980s the artist would fairly often intrude recognizable shapes into his pictures: the outline of a figure or a building might emerge like a sudden apparition from the circumambient painted universe of bars, spots and veils. That practice has subsequently been more or less abandoned, so that every mark on the paintings is inimitably his own. It is as if the artist has come to accept the pictorial language that he has invented for himself in a new and fuller way. He has taken possession of his own devices more completely than ever before and has decided to allow them, and them alone, to carry his subject to the viewer. This has made it easier than ever to see that the experience which these pictures set out to capture is not vision pure and simple but contemplation.

There is evidently little point in trying to hunt out Max Gordon's face in *In Memory of Max Gordon* (1990–96). He is not present in the picture in the same way that Terence McInerney, say, is present in the artist's considerably earlier portrait of *him*. The memories that lie behind the later work have been too fully transformed into a language of visual equivalents for that to be the case. The painter's feeling for a friend has been translated into an object, and the kind of truth which it communicates is primarily moral and emotional. *In Memory of Max Gordon* is one of the largest of the artist's pictures, one of the most sternly ordered, and one of the most welcomingly three-dimensional. It is a painting which frankly invites the viewer to enjoy an experience of light, space and form. (Max Gordon, not incidentally, was an architect.)

The American novelist Nicholson Baker, in his book *U and I*, has some interesting reflections on the theme of memorials, epitaphs and obituaries:

'The intellectual surface we offer to the dead has undergone a subtle change of texture and chemistry; a thousand particulars of delight and fellow-feeling and forbearance begin reformulating themselves the moment they cross the bar. The living are always potentially thinking about and doing just what we are doing: being pulled through a touchless car wash, watching a pony chew a carrot, noticing that orange scaffolding has gone up around some prominent church... Even when the dead...have died unexpectedly and relatively young, we give them their moment of solemnity and then quickly begin patronising them biographically, talking about how they "delighted in" x or "poked fun at" y – phrases that by their very singsong cuteness betray how alien and childlike the shades now are to us. Posthumously their motives become ludicrously simple, their delights primitive and unvarying: all their emotions wear stage make-up...'

Hodgkin's memorials to his friends remain uninfected by the epidemic condescension of posterity – the 'official' tones of regret familiar from newspaper obituaries – because they are painted epitaphs which have been designed to allow the dead as much unruly, unpredictable life as the living. *In Memory of Max Gordon* does not solemnly remember a man who 'delighted in architectural form', as one of Nicholson Baker's patronizing biographers might express it. Instead, the painting *re-enacts* such delight, *embodies* it – and thus offers up a very different (and very much more alive) form of memorial.

The scale of the picture would once have made it exceptional in the artist's oeuvre – but not any more. One of the most distinctive characteristics of the painter's art in the late 1970s and early 1980s – an era of overweeningly large canvases – was its relatively modest scale. But many of the most impressive works of Hodgkin's later career – including such diverse paintings as *Evening Sea*, *Night and Day* (1997–99), PP. 181, 196 *Memories* (1997–99) and *After Matisse* – are large pictures, painted to the scale P. 192 traditionally reserved for mythological or biblical subjects. The effect, however, is not one of aggrandisement but of an enhanced intimacy.

The painter has taken as much care as possible to preserve the compression and concentration of his smaller works. Some of his stratagems have been purely practical.

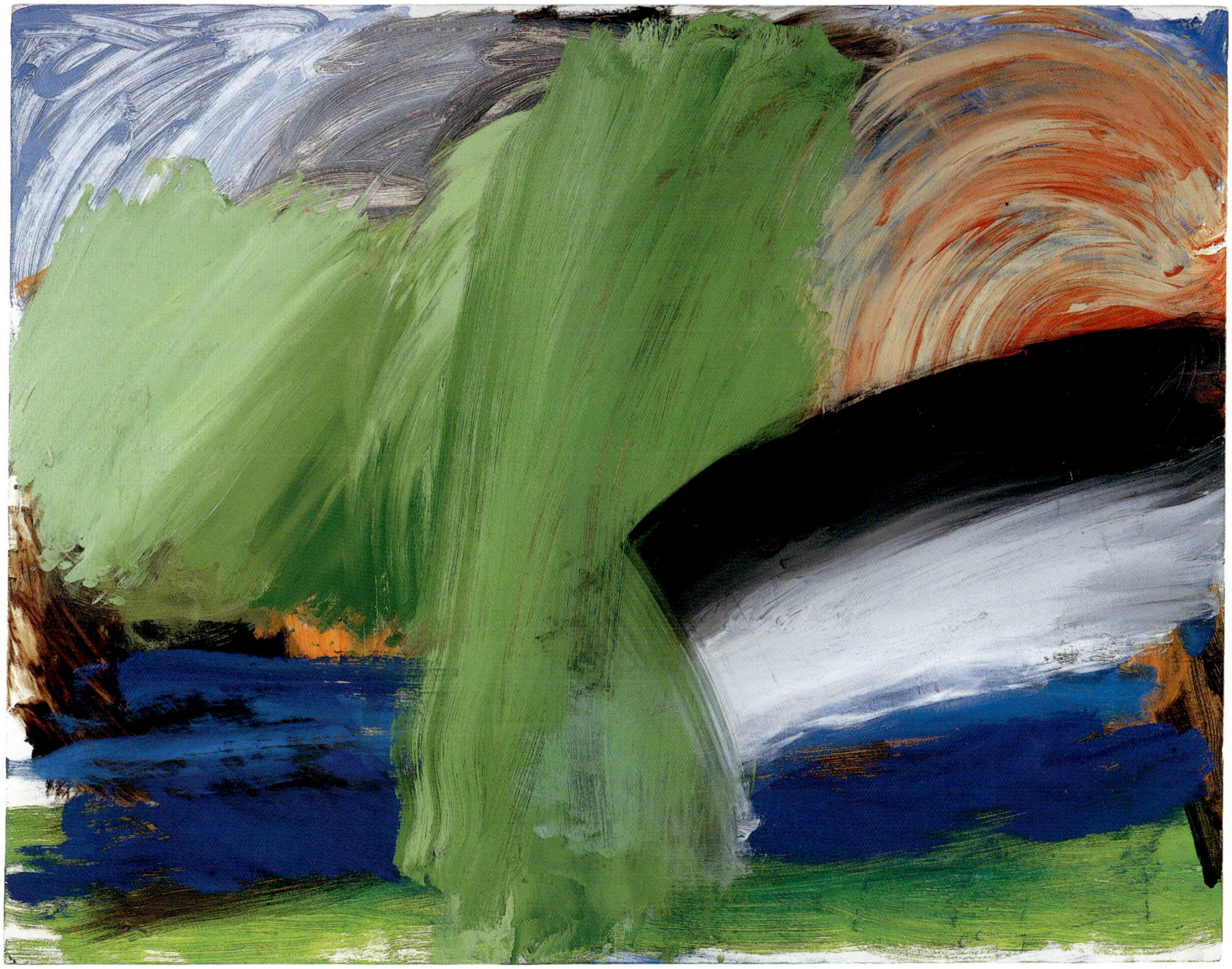

RAIN AT IL PALAZZO
1993 – 98

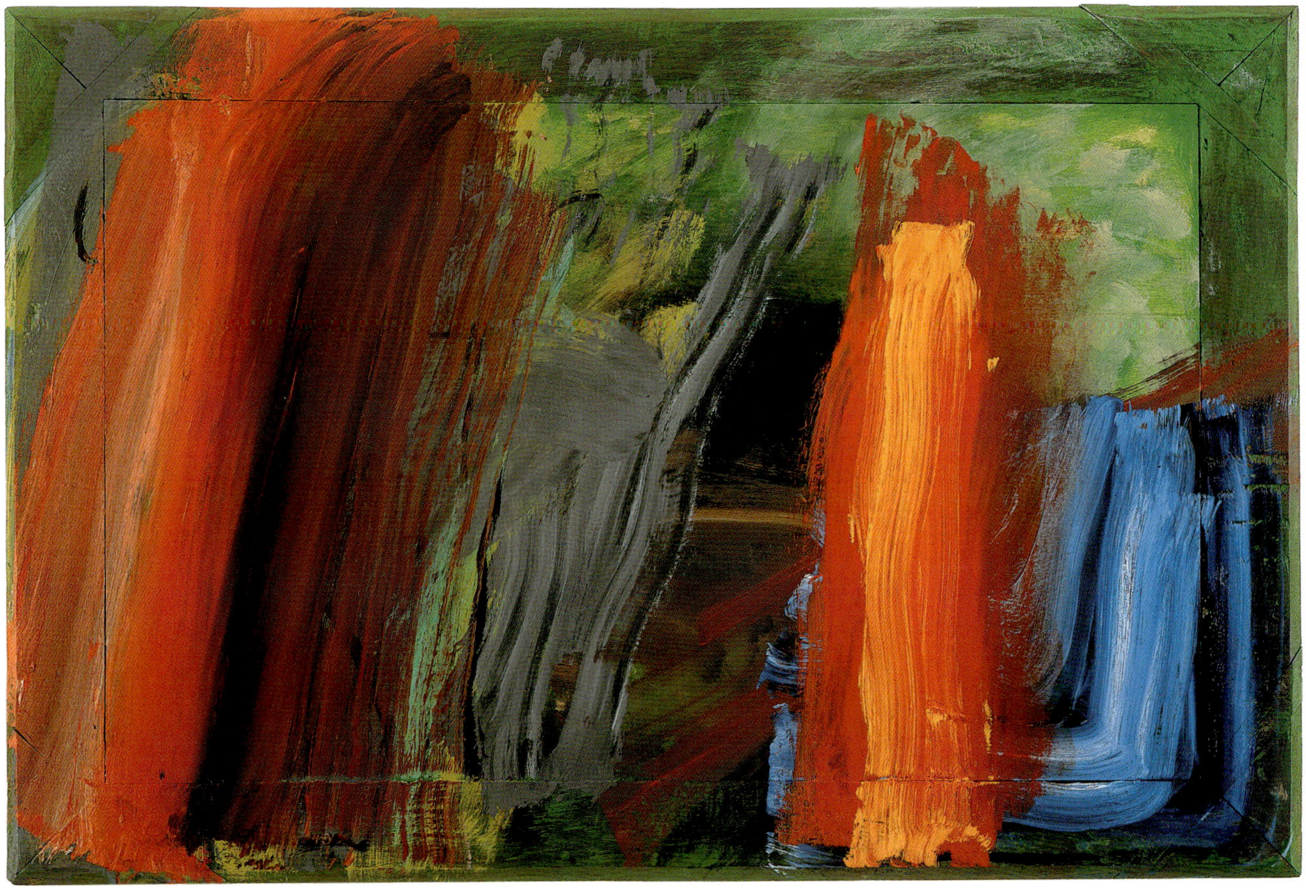

MEMORIES
1997 – 99

He has used much bigger brushes, for example, so that each individual brushstroke – such a vital element of his pictorial vocabulary – reads just as emphatically even though the scale of the painting might have been dramatically expanded. For many artists, painting large pictures is a sign of enlarged ambition. In Hodgkin's case that is manifestly not so because the ambition is always the same, to paint life. Enlarging the scale of his work is a different means to the same end, as well as a way of recognizing that large pictures can involve the viewer in certain ways that small pictures cannot do, because they are nearer to the scale of sociable human life. While Hodgkin's larger

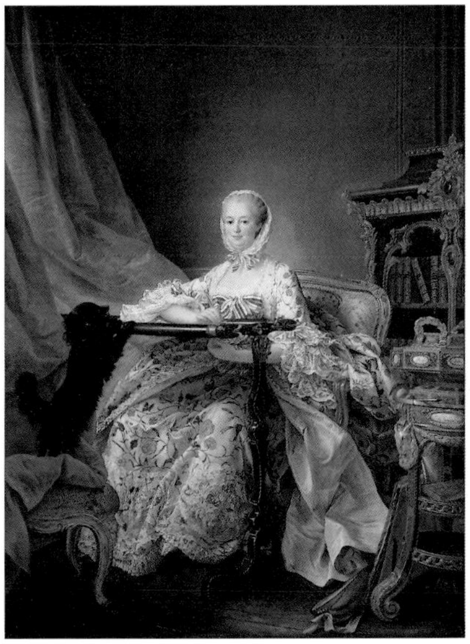

pictures may not offer the literal appearance of life-size figures, they do offer experiences, within them, which relate to human scale. They can be intoxicating, sensual and extravagant, in the manner of a Baroque altarpiece or Rococo fantasy; and it is fair to say that they expand the repertoire of his art considerably. But still the artist's old suspicion of the grandiose or the bombastic persists. In his own words, 'In the case of a successful large picture, it is as if *we're in this together*.' He was referring to Drouais's *Portrait of Madame de Pompadour* (1764), in the National Gallery, London, but the remark applies equally well to his own work.

In *Memories* the painter revisits once more the central theme of his art. It is a work that seems to belong to that category of pictures that represent not a moment of life but a particular aspect of consciousness – conjuring a state of mind, or a part of the way in which the mind works. Leaning columns of paint simultaneously animate and frame a recessive landscape at the centre of which we may fancy we see the opening to a cave. The handling of the paint is violent but expressive, almost suggesting a botch that has turned out, against the odds, to say what the painter wanted. Things in this world are mystifying but vivid, bright forms clustered and broken – seeming almost to dance and clamour, like versions of the figures in a Poussin bacchanal – around a void that is drawing them in. P. 192

Degas used to say he wanted to shoot all the industrious *plein-air* painters, toiling away *devant le motif* in Post-Impressionist Paris – not just because they were spoiling the view for everyone else, but because they had missed the point so badly. For Degas, the attempt to paint only what the eye sees was always doomed to failure (and dull failure, at that). Art's subject should be what the mind's eye sees, always a memory. Hence his opposition to nineteenth-century academic art education, which held that the more accomplished the student of painting became, the closer he should be placed to the model. Degas believed the exact opposite:

'If I were to run an art-school I should take a tall house, and I should put the model and the beginners in the top storey; and as a student's work improved I should send him down a floor, until at last he would work upon the level of the street, and would have to run up six flights of stairs every time he wanted to look at the model.'

Howard Hodgkin is a graduate of this imaginary art academy.

□ □ □

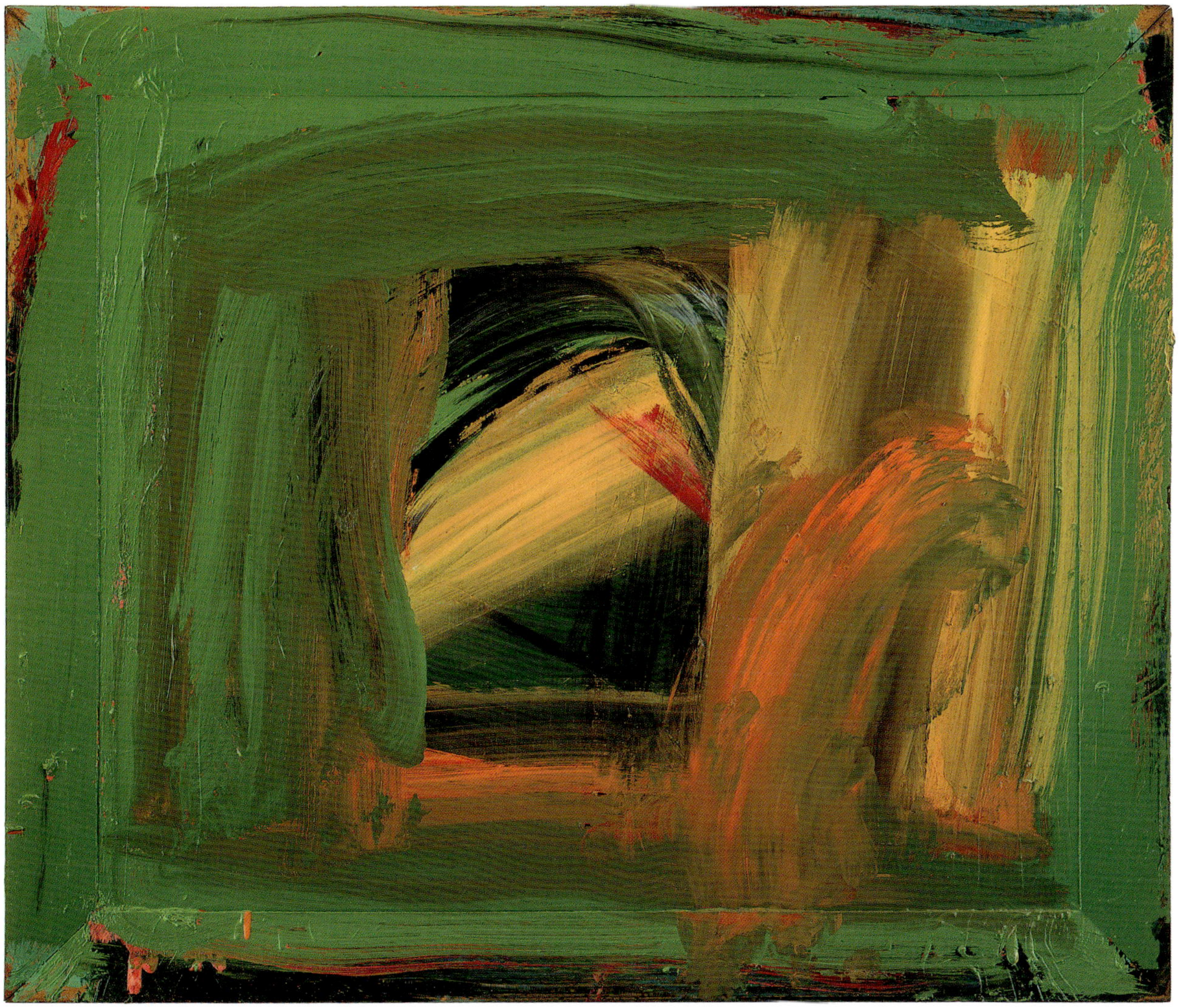

ONCE MORE WITH FEELING
1999

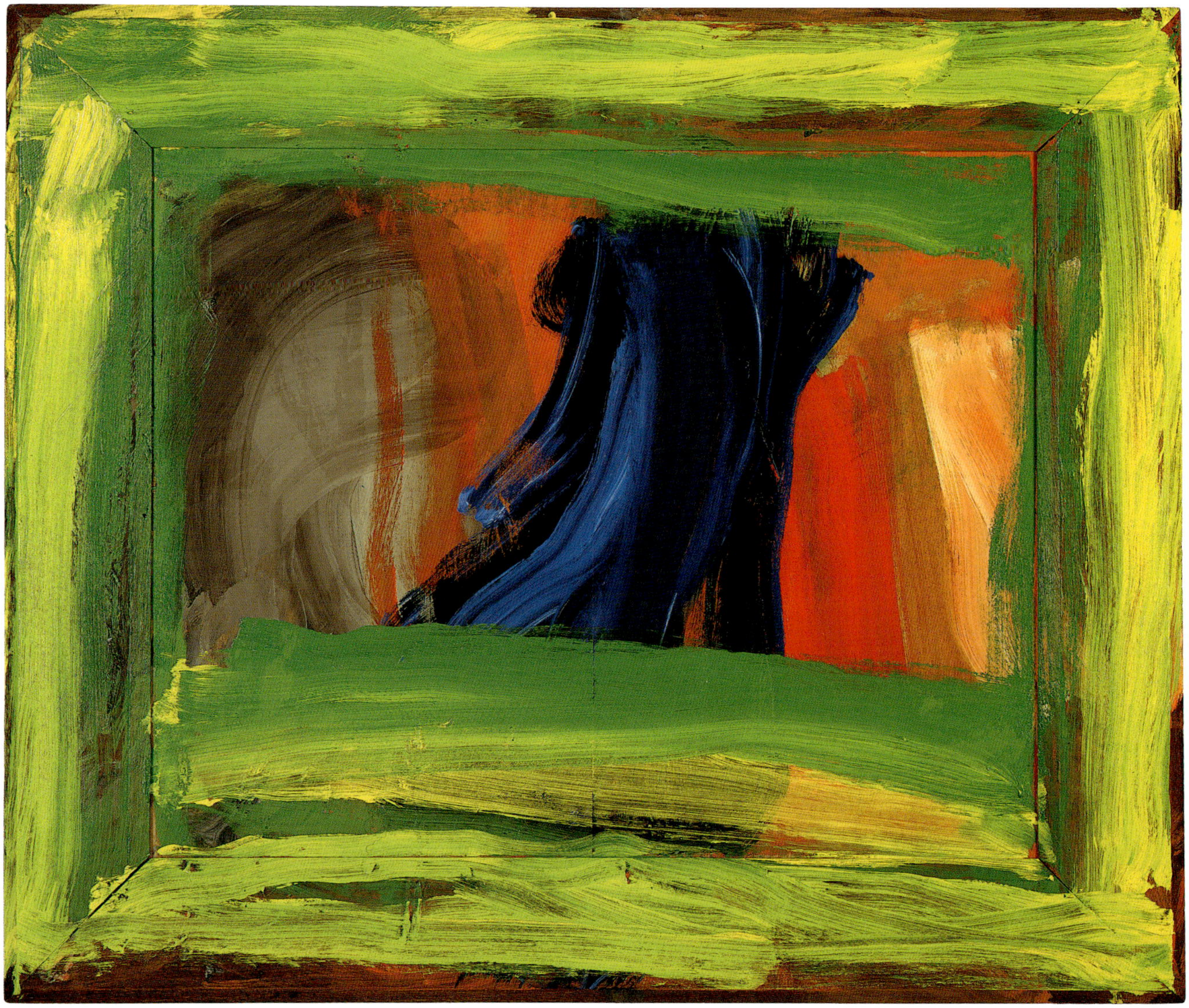

NIGHT AND DAY
1997 – 99

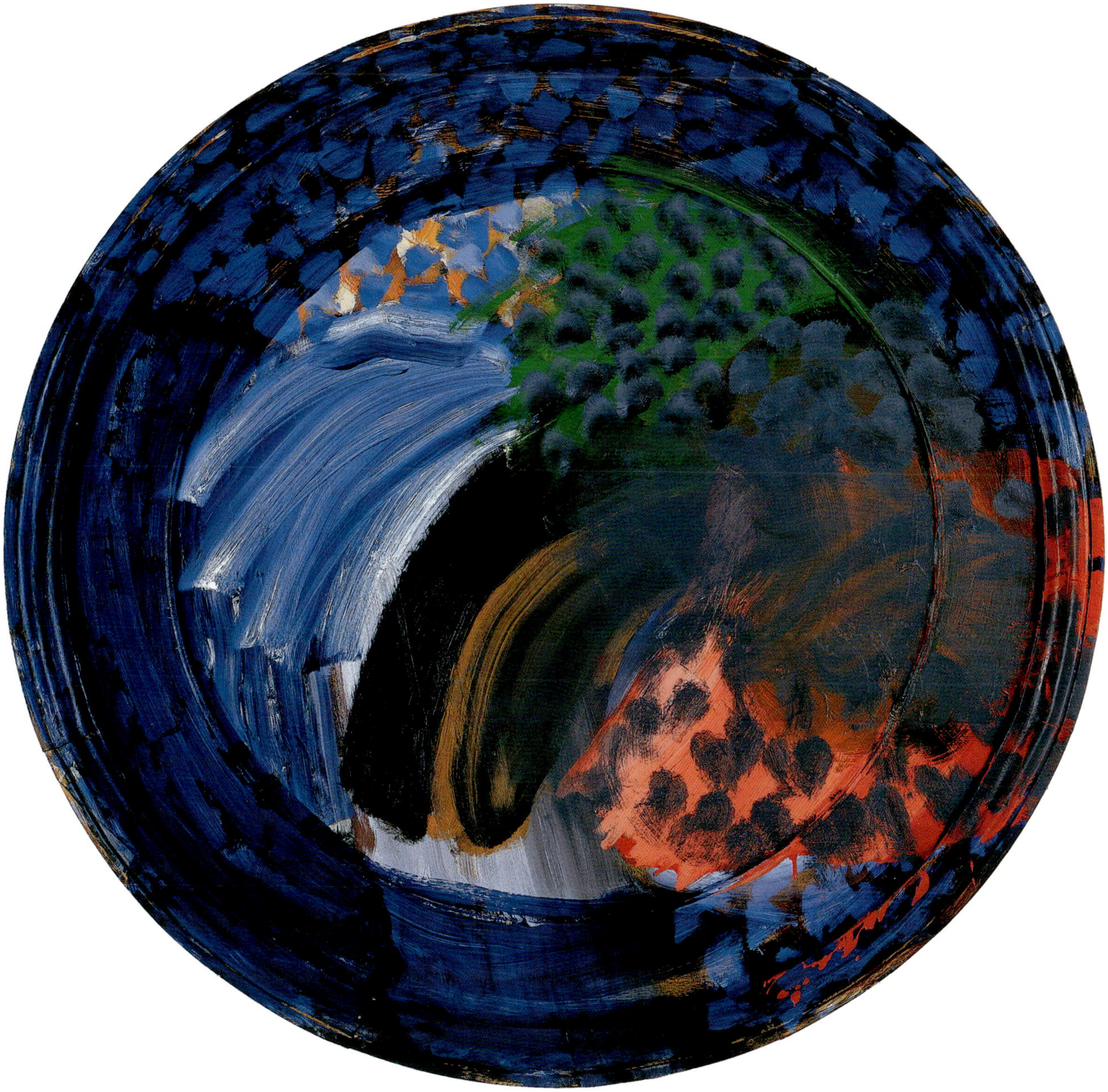

CHEZ MAX
1996 – 97

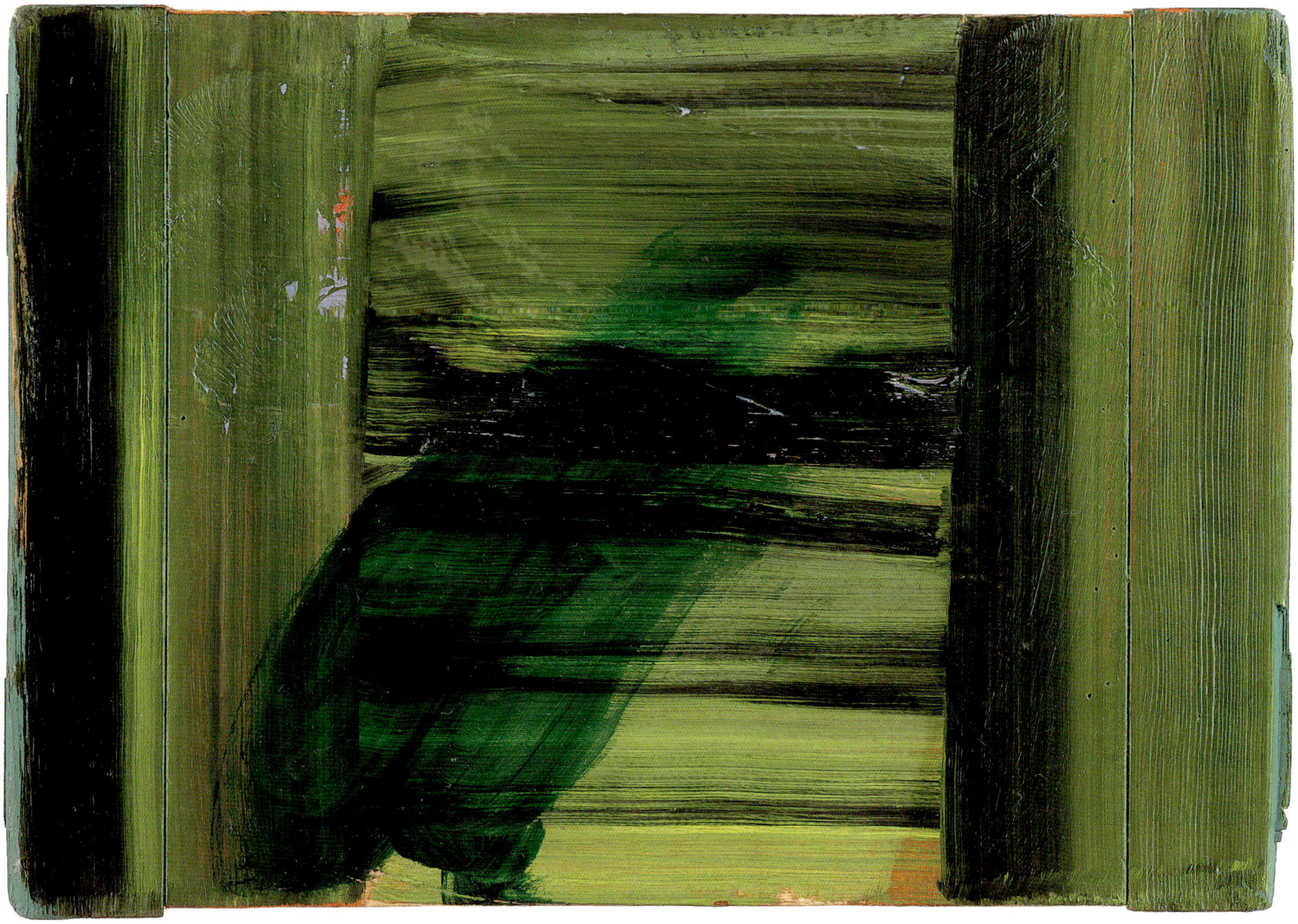

ESCAPE
1996

To the relative fixity and theatricality of traditional portraiture or narrative art, the painter continues to oppose his own more fluid and evanescent alternatives, painting PP. 198, 204 pictures such as *Escape* (1996) or *Fatherland* (1991–95) which attempt to make introspection palpable. The latter – part flag, part wound, part seascape – glancingly recalls Samuel Johnson's aphorism about patriotism being the last refuge of a scoundrel. Such paintings have, themselves, the living qualities of half-surfaced thoughts and feelings.

John Elderfield, in a correspondence with the painter subsequently published in the catalogue to his 1995 touring exhibition, asked him if he was familiar with the work of Proust and Freud. The answer was a fairly blunt no, which was not necessarily to deny that those writers have shaped his work in some way (after all, their ideas about memory, dreams and subconscious thought have been so pervasive that they are now simply part of the scenery). Nevertheless it may be more fruitful, in considering the notion of self to which his paintings give expression, to look back further in time than the late nineteenth and early twentieth centuries.

It is difficult (and not altogether advisable) to try to put a date to the origins of what might be called modern self-consciousness. The *Confessions* of St Augustine mark a great shift in the Western conception of identity, and it is possible that if they had never been written we should not talk about 'ourselves' in anything like the same way that we do now. But it was the French sixteenth-century writer Montaigne who, more than any other philosopher of the post-antique world, set the seal on a distinctively new and mobile conception of the self – and in so doing decisively reversed the direction of antique, classical thinking about human nature. Ancient thinkers were almost unanimous in the belief that beneath the ever-changing desires of the unwise soul, and standing firm against the flux of external reality, man's true nature, his reason, was an unshakeable foundation. But for Montaigne,

'There is no constant existence, neither of our own being, nor of objects. And we, and our judgement, and all mortal things incessantly change, turn and pass away... We have no communication with being; for every human nature is always in the middle between being born and dying, revealing nothing of itself but an obscure appearance and shadow, and an uncertain and weak opinion. And if perhaps you try to fix your thought to catch its essence, it would be like going to grasp water.'

Standing in a room full of Hodgkin's later paintings, it is tempting to believe that such a conception of existence has been given a visible form. There are other artists of whom this might be said, even one or two other British artists: Francis Bacon, for

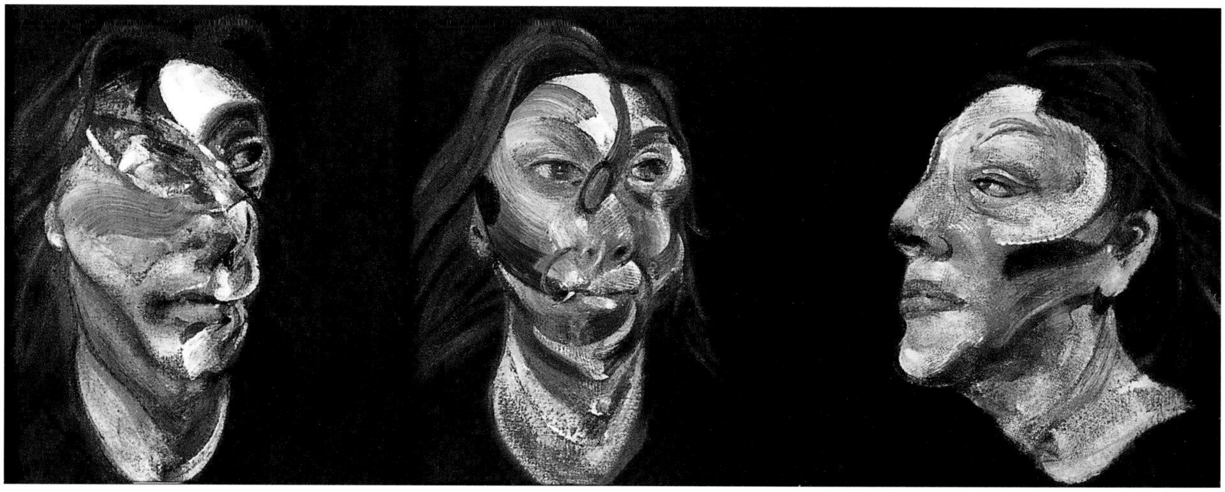

example, who in his most expressive works (his portrait diptychs and triptychs of the early 1960s, for instance) snared the truth of being caught 'in the middle between being born and dying'. But whereas Bacon painted what the truant sense of self or human identity might look like from the outside, almost as if in a cartoon or caricature, Hodgkin has set out to paint what it feels like from the *inside*. In other words, looking at his pictures we are presented not with images of man but with analogues for experience. This was true of much of the earlier work, but it seems even more intensely true of later pictures such as *Come Back Dull Care* (1999), or *Once More with Feeling* P. 195
(1999). Perhaps this is because they are works in which the traces of their own becoming are preserved with such delicacy and freshness. 'As if to grasp water': it is like seeing the shiftings of sensibility hung on a wall.

□ □ □

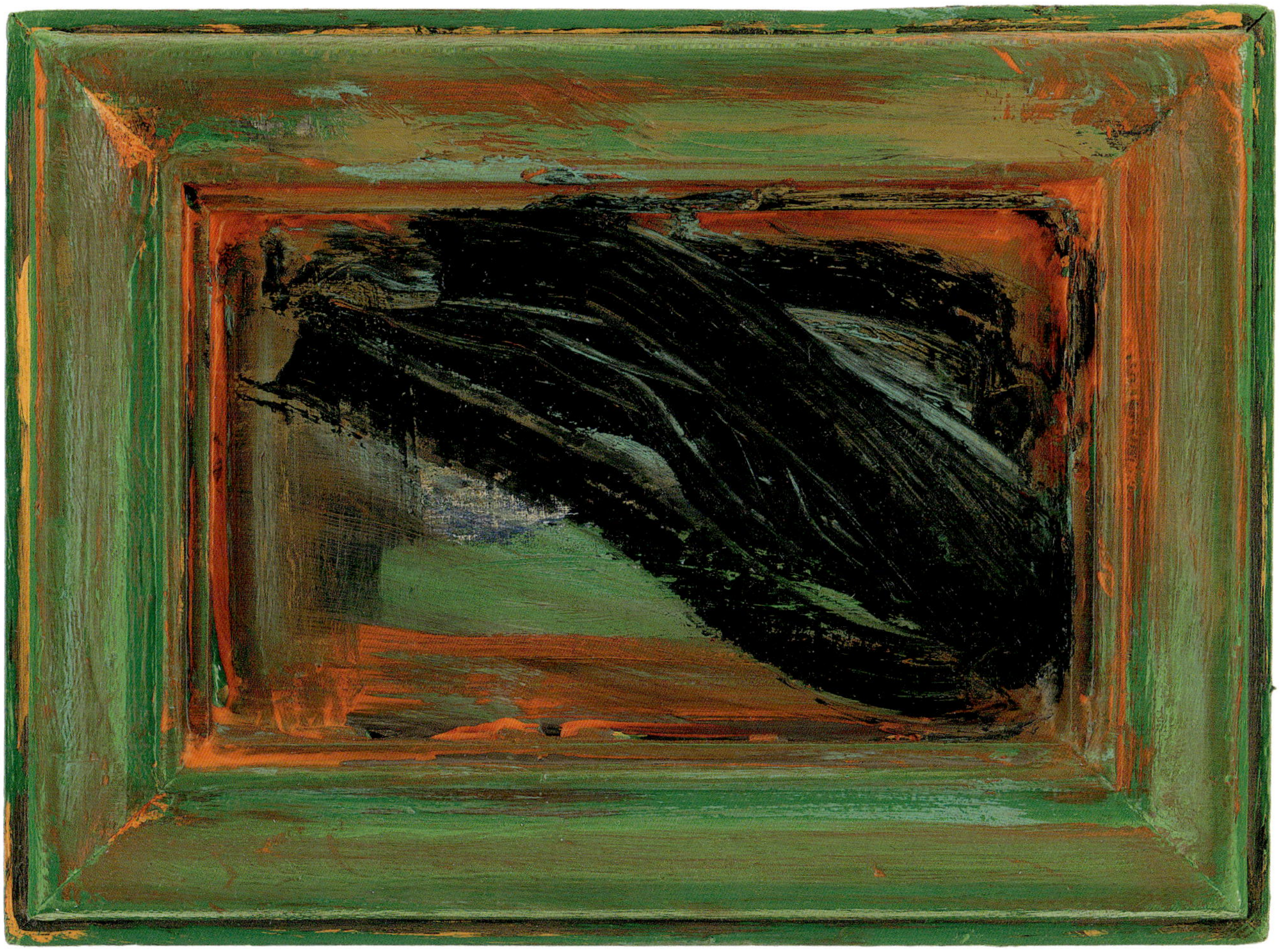

COME BACK DULL CARE
1999

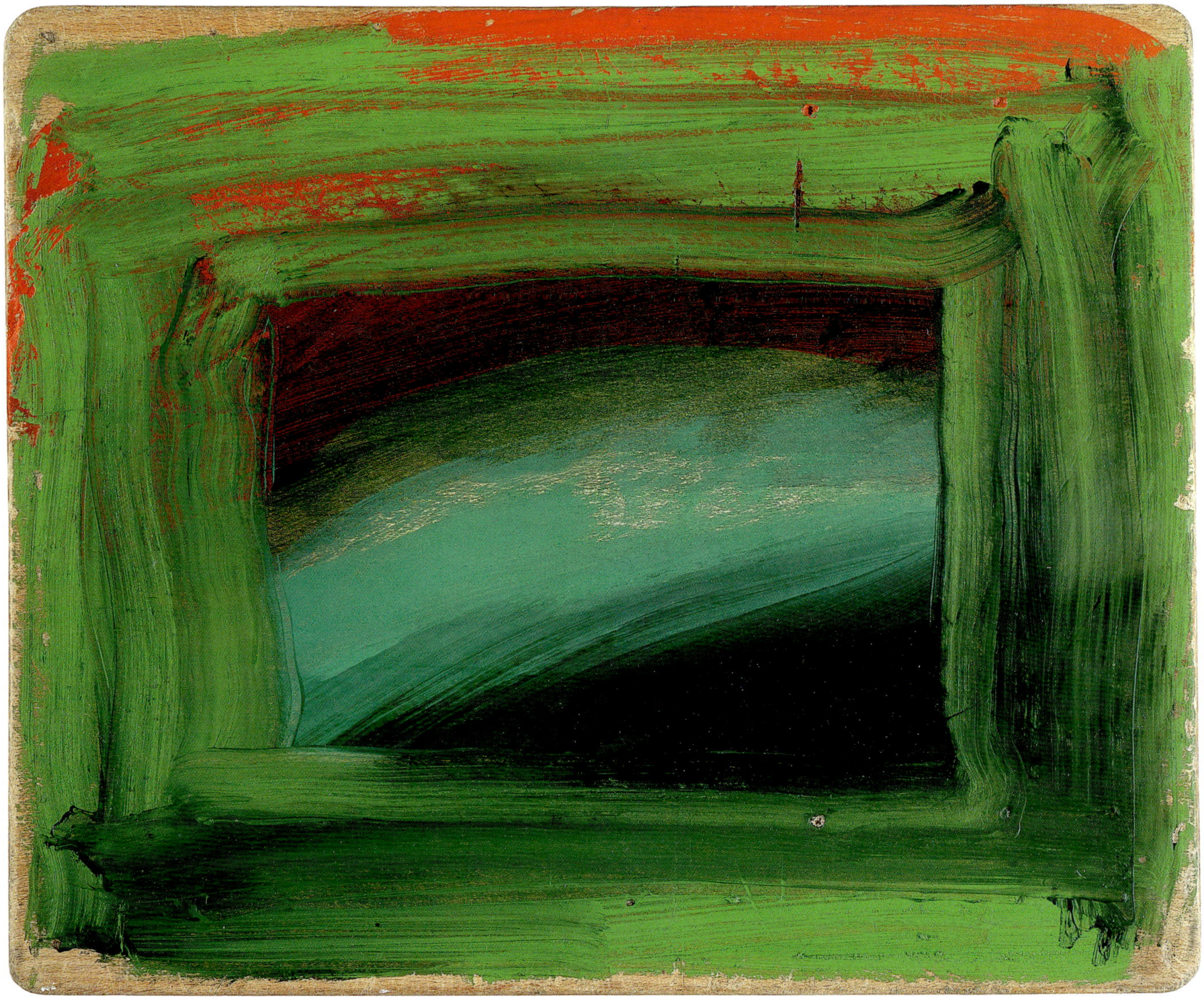

TWILIGHT
1995 – 96

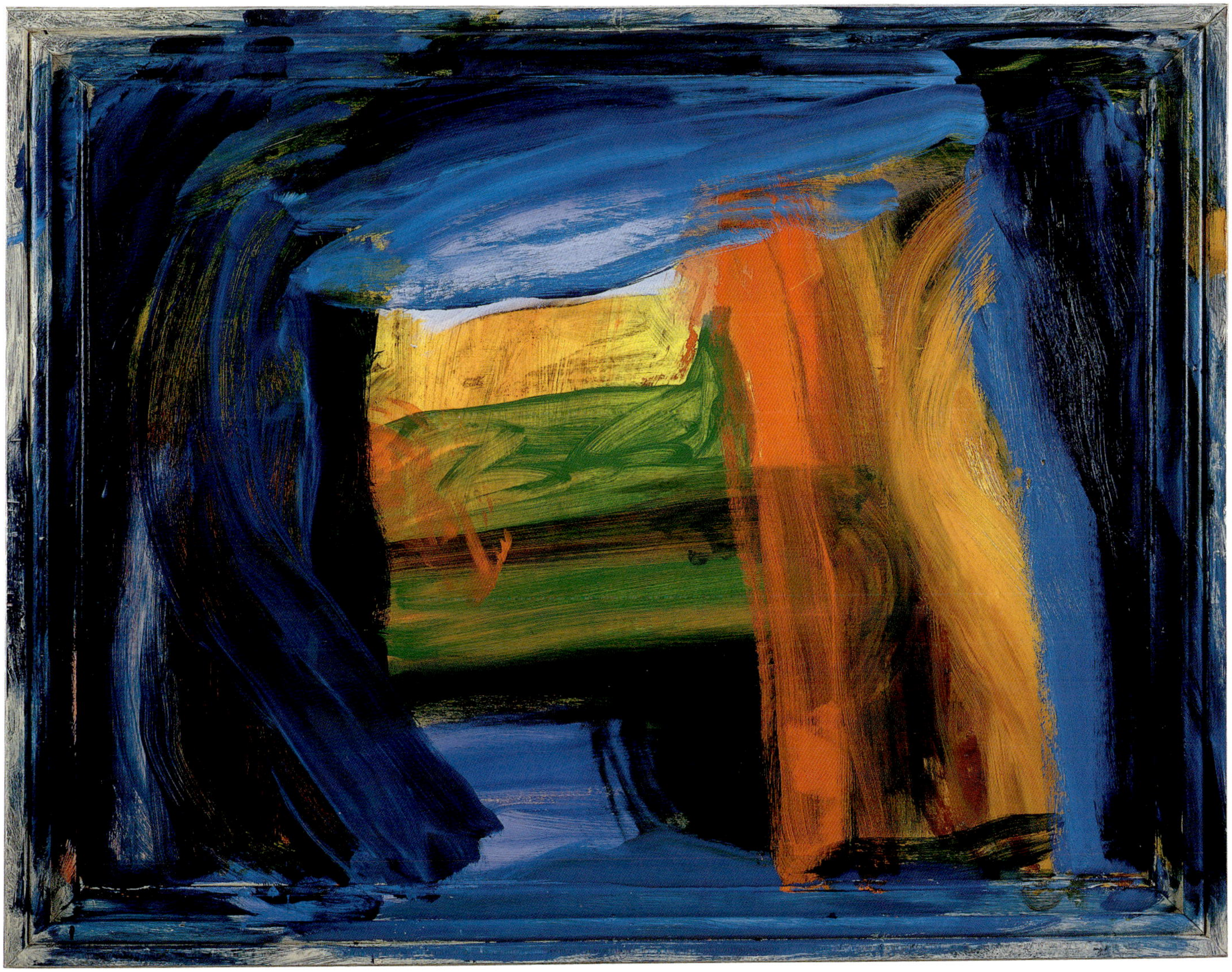

ANDREW ALLFREE
1994 – 98

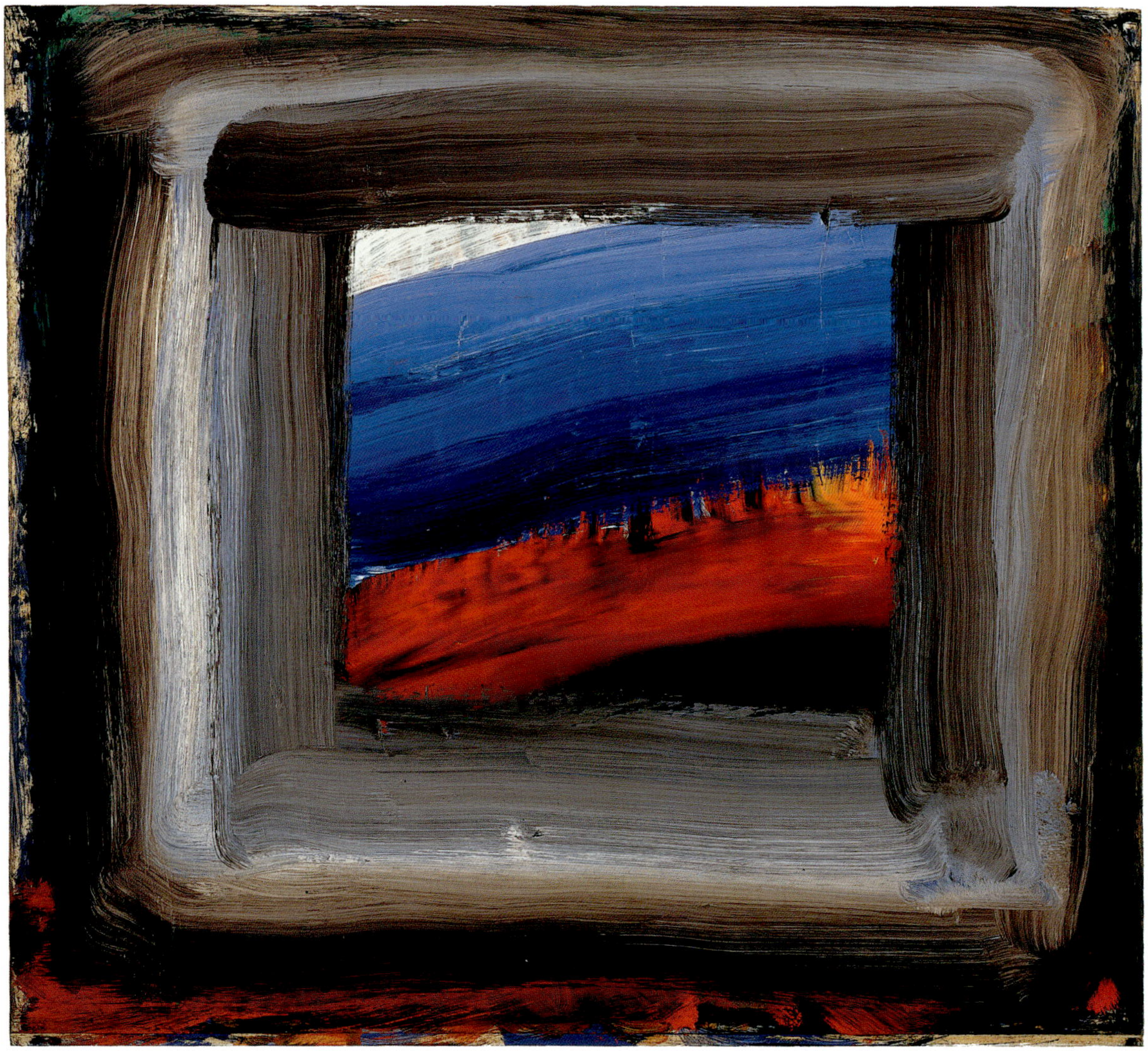

FATHERLAND
1991 – 95

I was in Rome a few years ago, sitting in a taxi with the window down, when a man and his girlfriend roared past on a motorbike. It was a moment that stuck in my mind. That couple speeding through the city, too fast for me even to fix on them, seemed somehow to embody life and hope and energy and pleasure.

How do I remember that moment, thinking about it now? I remember a warm wind blowing through the car window; a motorbike flashing past; people smiling in the street as if to applaud; the silhouette of Bernini's Triton fountain; and the green graffiti of the Hotel Bernini – BERNINI – shining in the sky. I remember all of these things, but merged and blended one with another.

Just as Turner taught us to look at sunsets, or at least taught us to pay them a different quality of attention, so too – I believe – Hodgkin has called attention to an aspect of human experience often previously overlooked. He has made us see the relationship between memory and feeling and vision in a new light. He has opened up a rather mysterious part of life and helped us to think of it afresh.

□ □ □

Charles-Nicholas Cochin, in his memoir *Essai sur la vie de M. Chardin*, published in 1780, tells the story of Chardin's growing annoyance with an artist of limited gifts and a 'cold, overworked style', who loved to boast about the purity and the perfection of his colours.

'Who told you that an artist paints with colours?' Chardin asked him.

'What else does one paint with?' came the surprised response.

'One uses colours,' said Chardin, 'but one paints with feeling.'

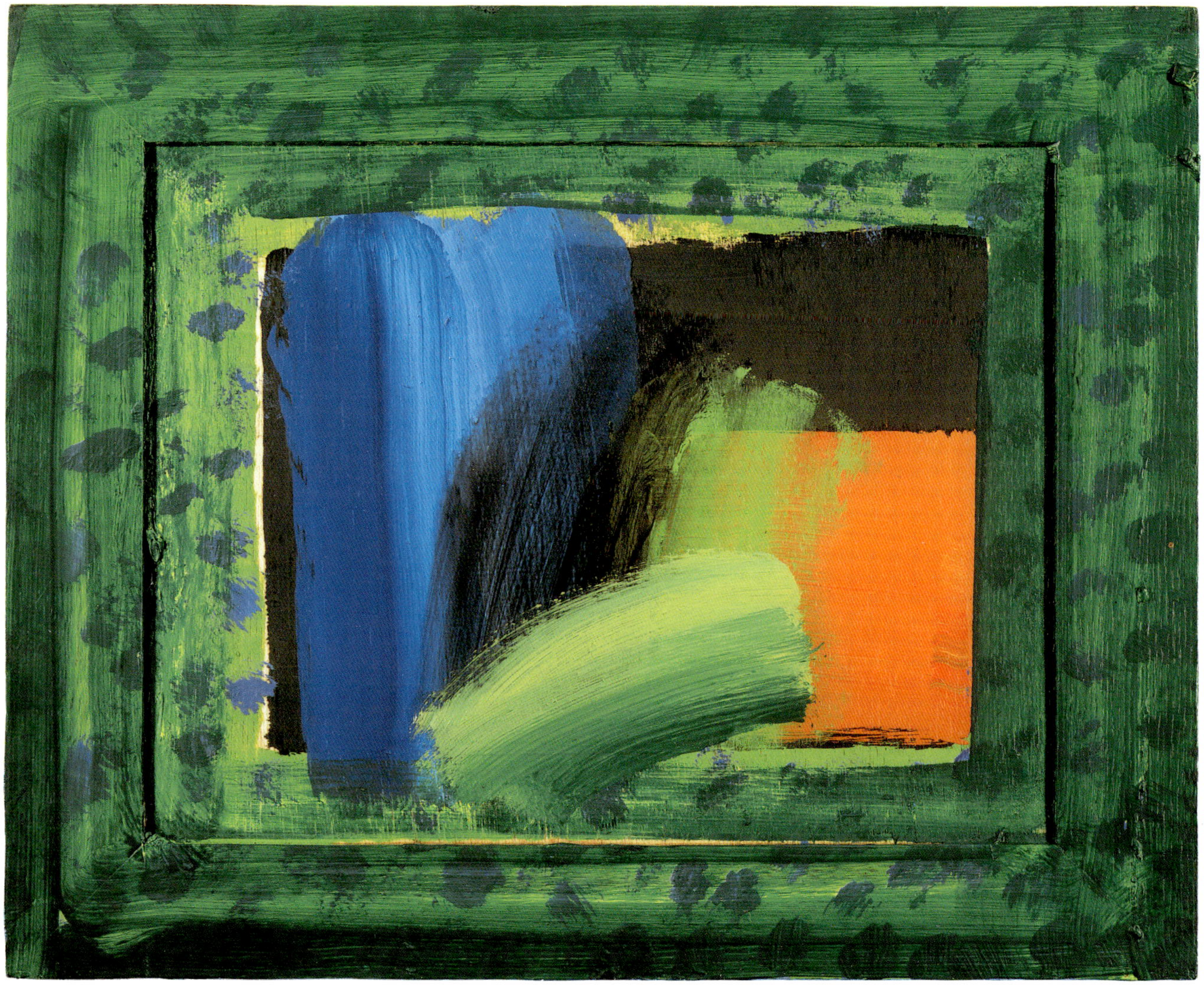

A LEAP IN THE DARK
1992

15
END

Picasso may have defined the predicament of the modern artist more succinctly than anyone. 'Beginning with Van Gogh,' he told Françoise Gilot, 'however great we may be, we are all, in a measure, autodidacts – you might almost say primitive painters. Painters no longer live within a tradition and so each one of us must re-create an entire language. Every painter of our times is fully authorized to re-create that language from A to Z. No criterion can be applied to him *a priori*, since we don't believe in rigid standards any longer. In a certain sense, that's a liberation but at the same time it's an enormous limitation, because when the individuality of the artist begins to express itself, what the artist gains in the way of liberty he loses in the way of order, and when you're no longer able to attach yourself to an order, basically that's very bad.'[24]

Howard Hodgkin has been forced, like all modern artists, to invent himself from scratch, to invent his own subjects, his themes, his language as a painter. In that project of self-invention he has had to find a way of bridging the gap that divides mere self-expression and genuine communication, to find a way of transforming personal experience into public statement. Beyond that, he has tried to evolve an art that is not cramped, not confined to merely one kind of statement, the dumb reiteration of a solitary theme. He has tried to devise an art that is never, merely, habitual, an art that can speak of loneliness and sociability and fear and beauty and idealism and pessimism and loss and memory and anticipation and jealousy and love. And he has succeeded.

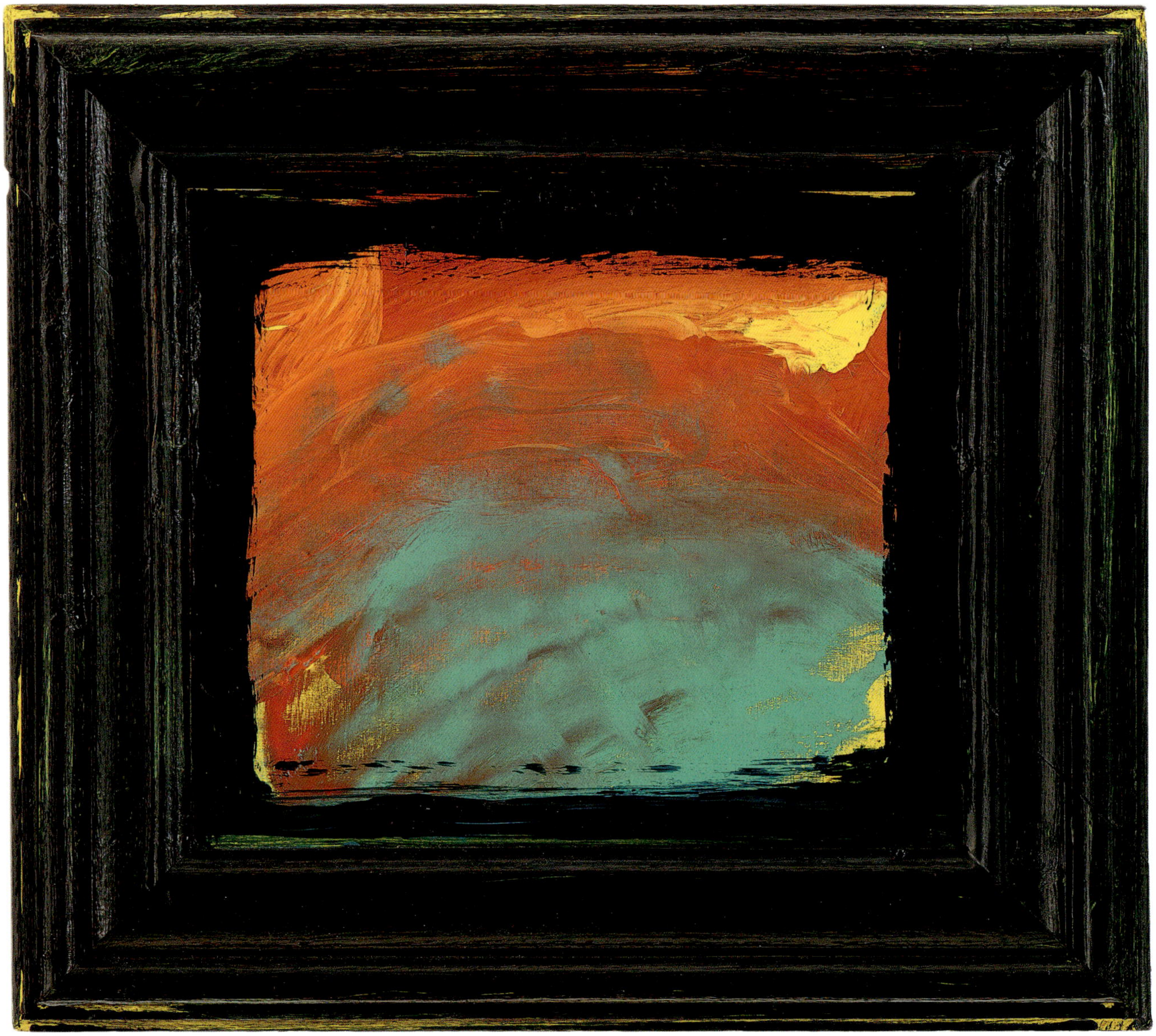

END OF THE DAY
1999

POSTSCRIPT

In 1992, when I wrote the first edition of this book, the existing critical literature on Howard Hodgkin's painting – notwithstanding a few honourable exceptions – seemed thin and disappointing. Most writing (I felt) had been plagued by a fatal combination of vagueness and reserve. It seemed to me that the painting was being put across by the majority of critics either as emptily decorative or as intellectually difficult, all of which seemed to me to be spurious. The work's true value lay, above all, in its blatant humanity. I came to believe that there was room for a book which tried, by contrast, to show how *easy* it was to appreciate the qualities of the paintings in question. I also thought that it might be practically helpful for someone to stick their neck out on the subject of these pictures. Once one person had done so, it might embolden others to come out with more definite and engaging ideas of their own. It might move discussion – which had been frozen – along. Sometimes the most important thing about the first book on a painter is the fact that it enables others to be written.

Recent writing has engaged with Hodgkin's painting in a much more interesting and deeper way. The artist himself has in my opinion been primarily responsible for this. His painting has got better as he has come to recognize himself and his own aims with ever-increasing clarity. The publication of this revised and expanded edition has given me the welcome chance to write a chapter about the new work Hodgkin has created since the early to mid-1990s. This appears as Chapter 14. I have also taken the opportunity to make several changes to my text.

Andrew Graham-Dixon, London, May 2000

FURTHER INFORMATION

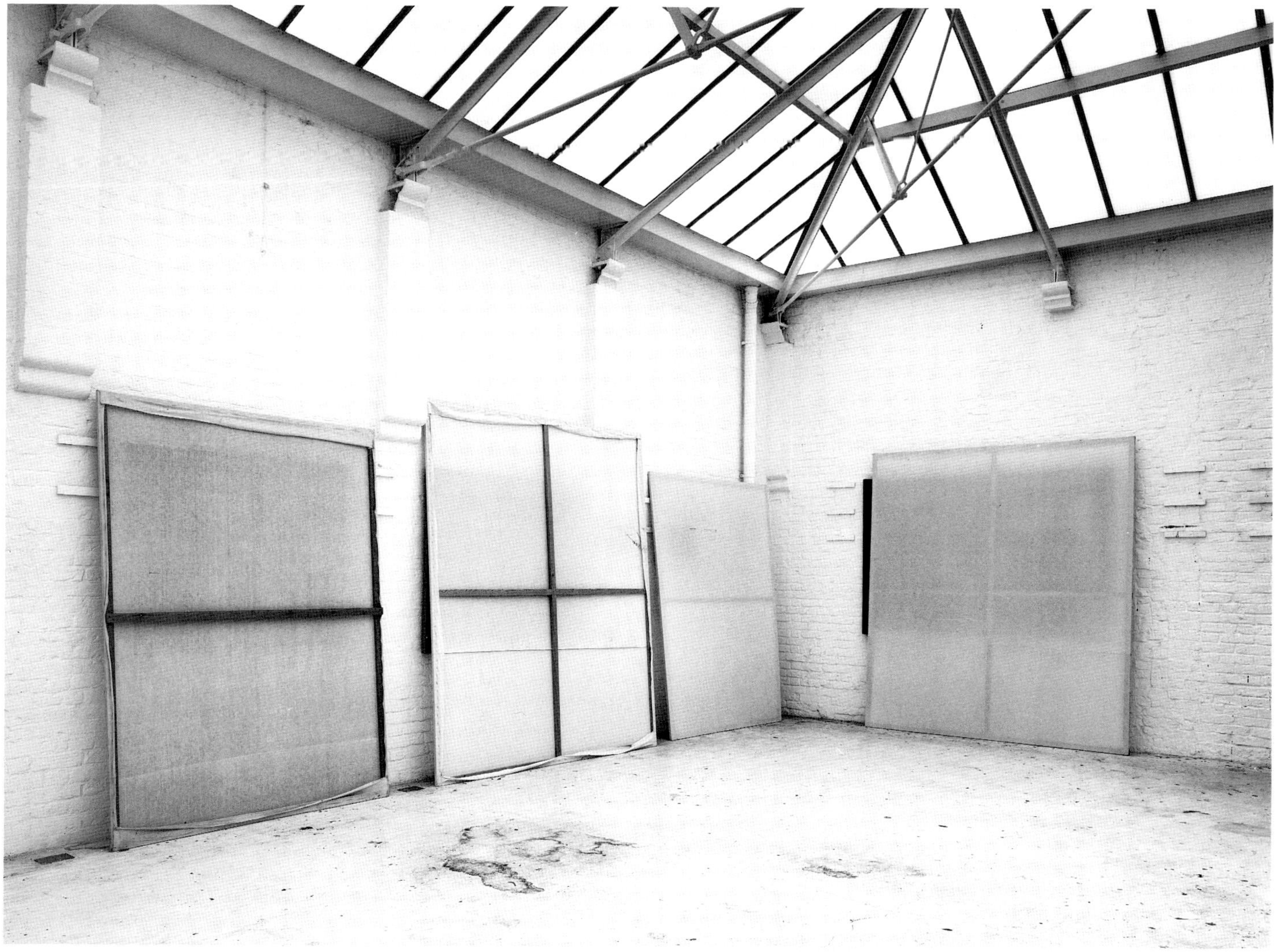

Photo: Keith Davey

NOTES

1 Virginia Woolf writing on the Ashmolean Museum version of Sickert's *Ennui* in *Walter Sickert: A Conversation*, London, 1934. Cited in *Sickert: Paintings*, Royal Academy of Arts, London, 1992, p. 232.

2 Bruce Chatwin, *Howard Hodgkin: Indian Leaves*, Petersburg Press, London and New York, 1982, p. 13.

3 Ching Hao, note on brushwork, tenth century, cited in Ian Crofton (ed.), *A Dictionary of Art Quotations*, Routledge, London, 1988, p. 114.

4 'On Figuration and the Narrative in Art: Statements by Howard Hodgkin, Patrick Procktor, and Norman Toynton' in *Studio International*, vol. 172, September 1966.

5 Edmond Duranty, 'Réalisme' in *Réalisme*, Paris, 15 November 1856, p. 1 (author's translation).

6 *Howard Hodgkin: Forty Paintings: 1973–84*, The Whitechapel Art Gallery, London, 1984, p. 97.

7 Ibid.

8 John Updike, cited in Nicholson Baker, *U and I: A True Story*, Granta Books, London, 1991, p. 38.

9 'Peter Blake and Howard Hodgkin in California' in *AMBIT 83*, 1983, p. 4.

10 Claude Roger Marx, transl. E.B. D'Auvergne, *Vuillard: His Life and Work*, Paul Elek Publishers Ltd, London, 1946, p. 48.

11 Adrian Stokes, *Venice: An Aspect of Art*, Faber & Faber, London, 1945, pp. 1 and 4.

12 P.E. Charvet (transl.), *Baudelaire: Selected Writings on Art and Artists*, Cambridge University Press, Cambridge, 1981, p. 403. Taken from *The Painter of Modern Life*, first published 1863.

13 John Elderfield, *Henri Matisse: A Retrospective*, The Museum of Modern Art, New York, Thames & Hudson Ltd, London, 1992, p. 66.

14 Maurice Denis, 'Definition of Neotraditionism', 1890, cited in Ian Crofton (ed.), *A Dictionary of Art Quotations*, Routledge, London, 1988, p. 67.

15 Adrian Stokes, *Venice: An Aspect of Art*, Faber & Faber, London, 1945, p. 4.

16 Bruce Chatwin, *op. cit.*, p. 14.

17 Paul Fussell, *Abroad: British Literary Traveling Between the Wars*, Oxford University Press, New York, 1982, p. 19.

18 Ibid, p. 17.

19 John Russell, letter to the author, 24 November 1991.

20 Paul Cézanne, letter to Emile Bernard, 1904, cited in Ian Crofton (ed.), *op. cit.*, p. 30.

21 Gaston Bachelard, transl. Maria Jolas, *The Poetics of Space*, Beacon Press, Boston, Mass., 1969, p. 155.

22 Charles Baudelaire, referred to in Enid Starkie, *Baudelaire*, New Directions, Norfolk, Conn., 1958, p. 294.

23 'Howard Hodgkin by Lawrence Gowing' (introduction to the catalogue), in *Howard Hodgkin*, Knoedler & Company, Inc., New York, 1981, n.p.

24 Françoise Gilot and Carlton Lake, *Life With Picasso*, Virago Press Ltd, London, 1990, pp. 67–68.

ARTIST'S STATEMENTS

To be a painter now is to be part of a very small, endangered species.

In conversation with the author, 1993

My pictures are finished when the subject comes back. I start out with the subject and naturally I have to remember first of all what it looked like, but it would also perhaps contain a great deal of feeling and sentiment. All of that has got to be somehow transmuted, transformed or made into a physical object, and when that happens, when that's finally been done, when the last physical marks have been put on and the subject comes back – which, after all, is usually the moment when the painting is at long last a coherent physical object – well, then the picture's finished and there is no question of doing anything more to it. My pictures really finish themselves.

Quoted in 'Howard Hodgkin interviewed by David Sylvester' in *Howard Hodgkin: Forty Paintings: 1973–84*, The Whitechapel Art Gallery, London, 1984

I want to get the sort of evasiveness of reality into my pictures. I mean, looking at you now, I don't see Ingres' portrait of Monsieur Bertin, for example. Because I'm always seeing something else and something more. I might be looking past you or looking at the light falling on part of you or thinking of you. So it's my idea of you as well as what I see that's in my mind. But this kind of realism which depends also a lot on illusionism, is, of course, evanescent, frail and difficult to establish.

Quoted in 'Howard Hodgkin interviewed by David Sylvester' in *Howard Hodgkin: Forty Paintings: 1973–84*, The Whitechapel Art Gallery, London, 1984

My pictures often include a frame which I paint on as part of the painting. I sometimes go to immense lengths to, as it were, fortify them before they leave the studio. The more evanescent the emotion I want to convey, the thicker the panel, the heavier the framing, the more elaborate the border, so that this delicate thing will remain protected and intact.

Quoted by Patrick Kinmonth in 'Howard Hodgkin', *Vogue*, June 1984

I would like to paint pictures where people didn't care what anything was, because they were so enveloped by them.

In conversation with the author, 1993

... when a picture of mine is going wrong it's when it's losing its meaning. But one can go back to the subject. That's the one thing I can do or the one thing I would claim I can do – I mean, even to the extent of going back to some love affair of long ago, or something like that. And, because for obvious reasons it was long ago and all gone and so on, the picture might well then be almost completely dead and finished with. To turn it into a picture, one has to go back to the original feeling and then start making new bricks or rather new choices of bricks to build it up again. Somebody once said to me that I always claimed that my pictures were about feelings, whereas he thought they were always resolved in terms of the picture, in terms of pictorial language and in terms of the physical object. And he's quite right, because they are pictures and they have to be resolved in those terms. But the impetus for that resolution comes from the feeling, which is what they're about. And if I've succeeded, I've turned the original feeling, emotion, or whatever you like to call it, into an autonomous pictorial object, which I look at in exactly the same way you do. I once described finishing a painting to somebody as where – this is obviously talking of an ideal situation – the picture is somewhere hovering in mid-air between myself and the spectator so that it looks as strange or as interesting or whatever to me as it does to any other spectator.

Quoted in 'Howard Hodgkin interviewed by David Sylvester' in *Howard Hodgkin: Forty Paintings: 1973–84*, The Whitechapel Art Gallery, London, 1984

I have never been able to think of either pastel colours or off-whites as being colours in the way colours I use in paintings are colours. But in England, strong colour in painting since the pre-Raphaelites has been almost disallowed. I think probably since Whistler no artist is truly taken seriously if he uses strong colour. There is an in-built puritanism about the English attitude to colour which is really quite bizarre. I was wondering in the National Gallery today how a Veronese in good condition and a Rubens in very good condition would be rated, in terms of moral seriousness and as great works of art, against paintings by Rembrandt for example. I think that the Rembrandts would get an overwhelming majority on the side of seriousness. Rubens has caused a lot of trouble. It's only that his drawing is so obviously miraculous that he's got away with it. And when one gets to an artist like Renoir, the tumescence of the colour in his later pictures makes it quite impossible for a lot of English people to recognise them as formal inventions at all.

In conversation with David Sylvester, quoted in 'Colour Dialogue', *Vogue*, January 1988

I have a feeling that it is only in the Anglo-Saxon world that sunsets are to be described as 'vulgar'. And I think the reason why is because of the connotations of the colour of sunset. Sunsets, after all, are very red, very orange, which at the red end of the spectrum are the colours of tumescence.

In conversation with David Sylvester, quoted in 'Colour Dialogue', *Vogue*, January 1988

I think a lot of people in England are afraid of pictures which have visible emotions in them. They feel calmer in front of pictures which are placid. They want to be distanced from the feeling, to look out at the storm through a window, or a frame.

Quoted by Patrick Kinmonth in 'Howard Hodgkin', *Vogue*, June 1984

Passion lies between one mark and the next, and also within all of them.

Quoted by Patrick Kinmonth in 'Howard Hodgkin', *Vogue*, June 1984

There are many aspects of the subjects which I paint pictures about that would lose their meanings if they were too specifically presented, and that's why I am forced into metaphor. That's one reason, but others are the nature of my language and the nature of the pictorial object I end up with. I'm forced into the use of metaphors, because, if you particularise too much, especially about private emotions, they would remain in the painting. In fact, the more I think about this, my pictures are totally metaphorical, but in a way that is of necessity rather than by design.

Quoted in 'Howard Hodgkin interviewed by David Sylvester' in *Howard Hodgkin: Forty Paintings: 1973–84*, The Whitechapel Art Gallery, London, 1984

The only way an artist can communicate with the world at large is on the level of feeling. I think the function of the artist is to practise his art to such a level that like the soul leaving the body, it comes out into the world and affects other people.

Quoted by Timothy Hyman in 'Howard Hodgkin: Making a Riddle out of the Solution', *Art & Design*, 1985

I no longer think it is possible for an artist to think of himself as part of history.

In conversation with the author, 1993

My titles are straightforward. People want to ask me questions, I think, because they want to ask all artists questions. My hope that painting pictures is all any artist needs to do – or dancing or writing or whatever – was dashed a long time ago. I don't believe in programme notes or explanations for paintings, since they come between the audience and the picture. It must have something to do with the times or the change in communications, but nobody seems to be able to respond to art without a gush of words.

Quoted from 'A Conversation with Howard Hodgkin' by Antony Peattie, in *Howard Hodgkin*, Anthony d'Offay Gallery, London, 1993

I am happy for people to talk about my pictures; but I wish devoutly that I was not expected to talk about them myself. The more an artist talks about his work, the more his words become attached to it. It is true that other people's words do as well, but not as much. I want people to look at my pictures as pictures, as things. When you talk about different categories, it would be better to say, 'This one is a large picture; this one is a small picture; this one is a middle-sized picture; this one has a lot of emotion, but is a small picture; this has less emotion, but is a big picture' and so on. Then people would feel more as if they were buying (or thinking of acquiring) some useful object when they looked at them. They could say, as they would say about furniture, 'This is a night table or a dining-room table' or, perhaps best of all, 'This is a kitchen table or a table where I would write letters of an intimate nature' or, 'This is a different kind of table, where I would write letters of a business nature.'

Quoted from 'A Conversation with Howard Hodgkin' by Antony Peattie, in *Howard Hodgkin*, Anthony d'Offay Gallery, London, 1993

Some pictures look enormous in real life, because they take up a lot of emotional or spiritual room. They give off a lot of energy. If you try to talk about that, it immediately sounds ridiculous... Large pictures, on the other hand, *can* be slighter than small ones or, because of their scale, tell a great deal more. Everything depends on the picture itself. Reproducing them simply gives readers a souvenir, if they have seen the original picture, or otherwise just a taste of what they will see. But they are *not* an accurate record. The more successful the scale in a painting, the harder it gets to guess how large the picture is. If all its parts relate to one another in a physically successful way, then it should be difficult to tell whether the picture is large or small. Or, equally, the pictures all look medium sized.

Quoted from 'A Conversation with Howard Hodgkin' by Antony Peattie, in *Howard Hodgkin*, Anthony d'Offay Gallery, London, 1993

In the museum culture in which we now live, small contemporary paintings don't rate. And yet a Morandi, a Mondrian, a Vermeer, a Chardin, a Fragonard, a small Picasso or a small early Vuillard, to take a few random examples, can knock you out across a room. One of the high points of my career as a 'public artist' came when I saw one of my smallest pictures hung in the Guggenheim Museum in New York. I had been taken by a friend who knew it was there. I walked round a column and saw it across the circular space – it was hanging on the other side of the void and I could see it from where I was standing. It did what it had to do from that distance. It confirmed for me that small pictures can be as large in a public sense as huge pictures. Sometimes more so.

Quoted from 'A Conversation with Howard Hodgkin' by Antony Peattie, in *Howard Hodgkin*, Anthony d'Offay Gallery, London, 1993

I don't like national schools. People inescapably belong to the country where they were born in some way or another, but I don't like it. Being an English artist may pose particular difficulties, however, because (for reasons which I suppose are partly sociological or even anthropological) most English painters have always thought that very little is possible. One of the most encouraging things about Francis Bacon, for other painters, was he thought of being an artist; to him, to be an artist was to be a great artist. I don't think the thought ever crossed his mind that what he did could be considered minor. He was working somewhere up in the empyrean. How rare this phenomenon is in English art. Francis Bacon was working in a way that was unheard of since...when? Since Joshua Reynolds perhaps, or Turner. Sickert, I think, knew just how good he was as an artist and also how impossible it was to be taken sufficiently seriously. He got round it by laughing and laughing and laughing. A pity that such a great artist could have fallen for that English habit of making light of things. After all, he wasn't very English.

Quoted from 'A Conversation with Howard Hodgkin' by Antony Peattie, in *Howard Hodgkin*, Anthony d'Offay Gallery, London, 1993

How irritating it is to be constantly told that my pictures are beautiful; this either suggests that they have no meaning and are therefore failures, or that no one cares whether they mean anything or not, or that if they look 'pretty' they cannot have any content. Also, particularly in England, a feeling exists that the use of colour as a pictorial device suggests a fundamental lack of seriousness; also that the overt emotions and feelings expressed in painting are in some way elitist... My subject matter is simple and straightforward. It ranges from views through windows, landscapes, even occasionally a still-life, to memories of holidays, encounters with interiors and art collections, other people, other bodies, love affairs, sexual encounters and emotional situations of all kinds, even including eating... All these subjects have one thing in common – seen through the eyes of memory they must be transformed into things, into pictures using the traditional vocabulary of painting, where scale and illusionism, among many other ingredients, play their part.

Letter to John Elderfield, 2 February 1995, in *Howard Hodgkin Paintings*

It seems almost impossible to talk about colour rationally or sympathetically, but nothing (for a painter) can compare with its infinite possibilities, its infinite seductions; the multiplicity of its possible meanings from the most profound to the exceedingly trivial. Can you imagine a serious pink next to a trivial blue or even a ridiculous black? All these randomly chosen colours can *be* any number of other things depending on shape, context, scale, etc... But I can't say another word about the pictorial uses of colour except to paraphrase a letter I wrote to a friend long ago talking about a visit to Naples, 'two or three smudges of blue and green paint rubbed into this wooden panel, and I begin to feel I am there.'

Letter to John Elderfield, 13 February 1995, in *Howard Hodgkin Paintings*

I have absolutely no desire to collect my own work, but do have what with age seems an almost unquenchable thirst for acquiring other things to look at. My only real collection is of Indian paintings and though the pictures themselves haven't influenced me very much, I think the art of collecting certainly has. One is continually making the kind of value judgments, asking the same old questions: is this picture better than that one? Why? Is it more expressive? Is it of better quality? And of course the best is the enemy of the good, etc. This is quite daunting as a way of looking at one's own work, and often discouraging. It also brings a new edge to the self-criticism essential to all artists. Sometimes I have felt that this critical eye for quality was an enormous handicap and probably more responsible than anything else for my small output. But once a picture is finished, I feel it should be strong enough to look after itself in the outside world.

Letter to John Elderfield, 13 March 1995, in *Howard Hodgkin Paintings*

One of my recurrent fantasies is to invent a formula, as many 20th-century artists have done. Then I could say, like the advertisement, 'One size fits all'. Wouldn't it be wonderful to find the ideal format? Then it wouldn't matter what you needed to express, the picture would always be the same size. Some artists seem to have taken this further: whatever they've got to say, whatever they feel, the picture is always the same colour... Unfortunately, the older I get, the more this doesn't seem to happen.

Quoted from 'A Conversation with Howard Hodgkin' by Antony Peattie, in *Howard Hodgkin*, Anthony d'Offay Gallery, London, 1993

CHRONOLOGY

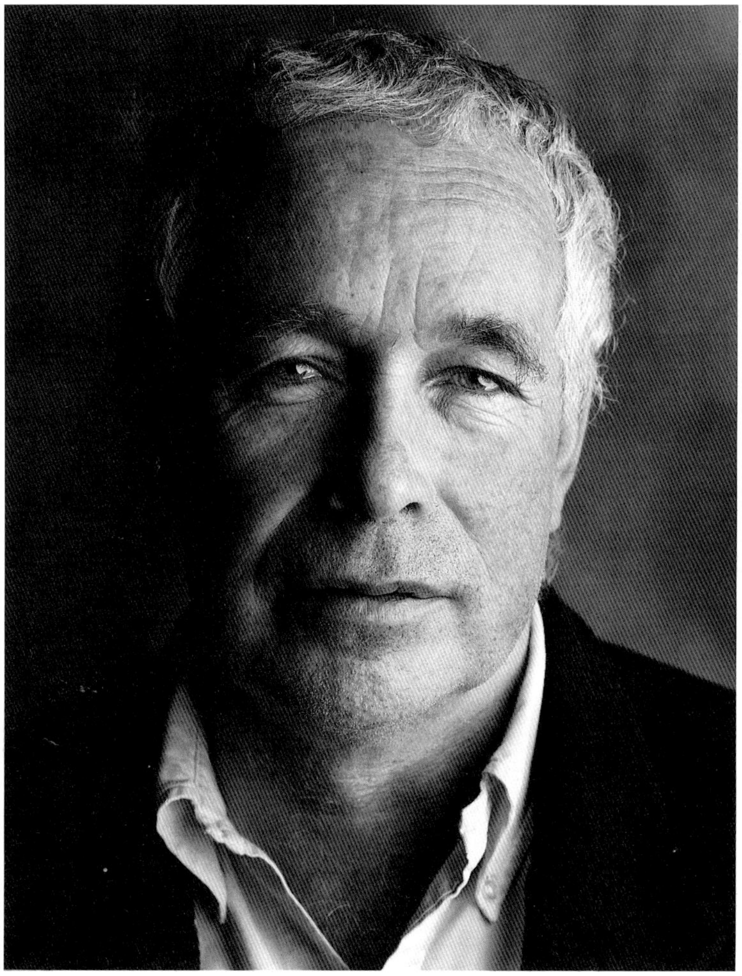

Photo: Terence Donovan

1932	Born 6 August, London
1940–43	Lived in the United States
1949–50	Studied at the Camberwell School of Art, London
1950–54	Studied at the Bath Academy of Art, Corsham
1954–56	Taught at Charterhouse School, Surrey
1955	Married Julia Lane (two sons)
1956–66	Taught at the Bath Academy of Art, Corsham
1966–72	Taught at the Chelsea School of Art, London
1970–76	Trustee of the Tate Gallery, London
1976/80	Awarded Second Prize at the John Moores exhibition
1976–77	Artist in Residence, Brasenose College, Oxford
1977	Appointed CBE (Commander of the British Empire)
1978–85	Appointed Trustee of the National Gallery, London
1985	Awarded 1985 Turner Prize Appointed D. Litt., University of London
1988	Appointed Honorary Fellow of Brasenose College, Oxford
1989	Committee, National Art Collections Fund
1992	Awarded Knighthood
1997	Shakespeare Prize (Alfred Toepfer Stiftung F.V.S.)
1999	Appointed Honorary Fellow of the London Institute

ONE-MAN EXHIBITIONS

1962 Arthur Tooth and Sons, London
1964 Arthur Tooth and Sons, London
1967 Arthur Tooth and Sons, London
1969 'Howard Hodgkin: New Paintings', Kasmin Gallery, London
1970 Arnolfini Gallery, Bristol
1971 Galerie Muller, Cologne
Kasmin Gallery, London
Park Square Gallery, Leeds (prints)
1972 Waddington Galleries, London (screenprints)
1973 Kornblee Gallery, New York
1975 Arnolfini Gallery, Bristol
1976 'Howard Hodgkin: Forty-five Paintings, 1949 to 1975', Museum of Modern Art, Oxford; Arts Council exhibition toured to Serpentine Gallery, London; Turnpike Gallery, Leigh; Laing Art Gallery, Newcastle-upon-Tyne; Aberdeen Art Gallery, Aberdeen; Graves Art Gallery, Sheffield
'Howard Hodgkin: New Paintings', Waddington Galleries II, London
Tate Gallery, London (print retrospective)
1977 Museum of Modern Art, Oxford (print retrospective); toured through England until October 1979
André Emmerich Gallery, New York
Galerie André Emmerich, Zürich
1978 Riverside Studios, London (prints)
'Howard Hodgkin: Indian Views' (prints); British Council exhibition touring India, Malaysia and Colombia
1980 'Prints by Howard Hodgkin: 1977–79', Waddington Graphics, London
Bernard Jacobson, New York (graphics)
1981 Knoedler & Company, Inc., New York
Bernard Jacobson, London (prints)
Macquarie Galleries, Sydney
1982 'Howard Hodgkin: Recent Prints'; coordinated by the University of Queensland Art Museum with the British Council's assistance: Melbourne University Gallery; Queen Victoria Museum and Art Gallery; Contemporary Art Society of South Australia; Art Gallery of Western Australia; Newcastle Region Art Gallery; University of Queensland Art Museum
'Howard Hodgkin's Indian Leaves', Tate Gallery, London; exhibition in collaboration with publication of *Howard Hodgkin: Indian Leaves*, Petersburg Press, London and New York
Jacobson-Hochmann Gallery, New York (prints)
'Howard Hodgkin: Paintings', Knoedler & Company, Inc., New York
1984 'Howard Hodgkin: Recent Work', Knoedler & Company, Inc., New York
'Howard Hodgkin Prints made in New York', Bath Festival Exhibition, Festival Gallery, Bath
1984–85 'Howard Hodgkin: Forty Paintings: 1973–84', touring retrospective exhibition initiated by the Phillips Collection and the Whitechapel Art Gallery, and supported by the British Council; toured to British Pavilion, Venice Biennale; Phillips Collection, Washington, DC; Yale Center for British Art, New Haven, Connecticut; Kestner Gesellschaft, Hanover; Whitechapel Art Gallery, London. Supplement to accompany Whitechapel exhibition, *Howard Hodgkin: Ten Paintings*
1985 'Howard Hodgkin: Works on Paper', LA Louver Gallery, Los Angeles
'Howard Hodgkin: Works on Paper', The Harcus Gallery, Boston
'Howard Hodgkin' (etchings), Bernard Jacobson Gallery, London
'Howard Hodgkin: Prints 1977 to 1983', Tate Gallery, London
1986 'Howard Hodgkin: Prints', Albright-Knox Art Gallery, Buffalo, New York
'Howard Hodgkin: Recent Work', Knoedler & Company, Inc., New York
'Howard Hodgkin' (prints), Odette Gilbert Gallery, London
1987 'Howard Hodgkin: Gravuras 1977 to 1983', organized in collaboration with British Council of Arts, London; Museu Nacional de Belas Artes, Rio de Janiero
'Howard Hodgkin' (graphics), Waddington, London
1988 'Howard Hodgkin: New Paintings', Waddington Galleries, London
'Howard Hodgkin: New Paintings', Knoedler & Company, Inc., New York
'Howard Hodgkin: Solo Prints', Solo Gallery, New York
'Howard Hodgkin at Bjorn Olsson Gallery', Bjorn Olsson Gallery, Stockholm

1989 'Howard Hodgkin: Etchings and Lithograph 1980–86', The Joanne Chappell Gallery, San Francisco

1990 'Howard Hodgkin: Small Paintings', organized by the British Council of Arts, London; toured to Musée des Beaux-Arts, Nantes; Caixa de Pensions, Barcelona; Scottish National Gallery of Modern Art, Edinburgh; Douglas Hyde Gallery, Trinity College, Dublin

'Howard Hodgkin: Recent Paintings', Galerie Michael Werner, Cologne

'Howard Hodgkin: Recent Paintings', Knoedler & Company, Inc., New York

'Howard Hodgkin: Prints 1980–88', Reynolds/Minor Gallery, Richmond, Virginia

'Howard Hodgkin: Paintings and Graphics', Ganz Gallery, Cambridge, England

1991 'Howard Hodgkin: Small Format Work', Matrix, University Art Museum, University of California at Berkeley

'The Way We Live Now' by Susan Sontag (exhibition of four hand-coloured etchings and hand-coloured endpapers); Karsten Schubert, London; Brooke Alexander Editions, New York

1992 'Howard Hodgkin: Seven Small Pictures', British School at Rome, Italy

1993 'Howard Hodgkin', Anthony d'Offay Gallery, London

1993–94 'Howard Hodgkin', Knoedler & Company, Inc., New York

1995–97 'Howard Hodgkin: Paintings 1975–1995', organized by the Modern Art Museum of Fort Worth, Texas. Tour: Metropolitan Museum of Art, New York, 1995–96; Modern Art Museum of Fort Worth, Texas, 1996; Kunstverein für die Rheinlande und Westfalen, Düsseldorf, 1996; Hayward Gallery, London, 1997

1997 'Howard Hodgkin', Galerie Lawrence Rubin, Zürich

1998 'Howard Hodgkin', Gagosian Gallery, New York

'Howard Hodgkin', Haas & Fuchs, Berlin

1999–2000 'Howard Hodgkin', Anthony d'Offay Gallery, London

SELECTED BIBLIOGRAPHY

BOOKS

1965 Russell, John, and Bryan Robertson, Lord Snowdon, *Private View*, Nelson, London

1967 Pellegrini, Aldo, *New Tendencies in Art*, Elek Books Ltd, London, p. 207

1968 Jones, Christopher, and G.D. Thorneley (eds), *Creative Method in Painting* (conference on 'Design Methods'), Pergamon, London

1970 Lucie-Smith, Edward, and Patricia White, *Art in Britain 1969–70*, J.M. Dent & Sons Ltd, London, p. 96

1971 Dypréau, Jean, essay in *Figurative Art since 1945*, Thames & Hudson Ltd, London, p. 166

1977 Shone, Richard Noel, *The Century of Change: British Painting since 1900*, Phaidon, Oxford, pp. 11, 34, 42, 219, plates 173, 196

1982 Chatwin, Bruce, *Howard Hodgkin: Indian Leaves*, Petersburg Press, London and New York

1990 Moszynska, Anna, *Abstract Art*, Thames & Hudson Ltd, London

1991 Sontag, Susan, and Howard Hodgkin, *The Way We Live Now*, Jonathan Cape, London

Hughes, Robert, *The Shock of the New*, BBC Books, Thames & Hudson Ltd, London

1995 *Howard Hodgkin Paintings*, catalogue of touring exhibition 'Howard Hodgkin: Paintings 1975–1995' with essays by Michael Auping, John Elderfield, Susan Sontag and a catalogue raisonné by Marla Price, Thames & Hudson Ltd, London, in association with The Modern Art Museum of Fort Worth, Texas

ONE-MAN EXHIBITION CATALOGUE INTRODUCTIONS

1962 Lucie-Smith, Edward, *Howard Hodgkin*, Arthur Tooth and Sons, London

1976 Morphet, Richard, *Howard Hodgkin, Forty-five Paintings: 1949–75*, Arts Council of Great Britain

1977 Marcus, Penelope, *Howard Hodgkin: Complete Prints*, Museum of Modern Art, Oxford

1981 Gowing, Lawrence, *Howard Hodgkin*, Knoedler & Company, Inc., New York

1982 Rainbird, Sean, *Howard Hodgkin: Recent Prints*, University of Queensland Art Museum

Compton, Michael, *Howard Hodgkin's Indian Leaves*, Tate Gallery, London

1984 McEwen, John, *Howard Hodgkin: Forty Paintings: 1973–84*, The Whitechapel Art Gallery, London

1985 Morphet, Richard, *Howard Hodgkin: Prints 1977 to 1983*, Tate Gallery, London

1990 Dickhoff, Wilfried, and Timothy Hyman, *Howard Hodgkin*, Michael Werner, Cologne, Knoedler & Company, Inc., New York

Clousseau, Henry-Claude, Timothy Hyman, Deepak Ananth, *Howard Hodgkin: Petits Formats 1975–1989*, Musée des Beaux-Arts, Nantes

Russell, John, *Howard Hodgkin: Graphic Work: 14 hand-coloured lithographs and etchings 1977–1987*, Lumley Cazalet Gallery, London

1997 Imdahl, George, *Howard Hodgkin*, Galerie Lawrence Rubin, Zürich

1999–2000 Fenton, James, *Howard Hodgkin*, Anthony d'Offay Gallery, London

ARTIST'S STATEMENTS AND INTERVIEWS

1966 'On Figuration and the Narrative in Art', ed. Jasia Reichardt, *Studio International*, vol. 172, September, p. 140

1968 *Recent British Painting*, ed. Alan Bowness, catalogue of 1967 exhibition, republished as a book, Lund Humphries, London

Forge, Andrew, Howard Hodgkin and Philip King, 'The Relevance of Matisse', discussion in *Studio International*, vol. 176, July/August, pp. 9–17

1971 *Tate Gallery Report – Acquisitions 1968–70*, p. 89

1972 *Patrick Caulfield, Howard Hodgkin, Michael Moon*, catalogue, Galerie Stadler, Paris, March/April

1976 *A Recorded Talk on his Paintings – Indian Views, Screenprints and Lithographs*, pamphlet published by the British Council, November

1977 *Towards Another Picture: An anthology of writings by artists working in Britain 1945–1977*, eds Andrew Brighton and Lynda Morris, Midland Group, Nottingham, pp. 76–77, 96

1978 'An Artist in Residence', *Oxford Art Journal*, vol. 1, October, pp. 36–37

Hyman, Timothy, interview in *Artscribe* no. 15, December, pp. 25–28

1979 *The Artist's Eye*, catalogue, National Gallery, London, June/August, p. 3

1981 Lucie-Smith, Edward, interview in *Quarto*, no. 19, July, pp. 15–17

1982 'How to be an Artist', *Burlington Magazine*, vol. 124, September, pp. 552–54 (edited version of William Townsend Memorial Lecture, given at the Slade School of Fine Art, University College, London, on 15 December 1981)

Six Indian Painters, catalogue, Tate Gallery, London, April/May, p. 8

'Artist's Notes' in *Howard Hodgkin: Indian Leaves*, Petersburg Press, London and New York, pp. 51–53

1983 *Indian Drawing*, catalogue, Hayward Gallery, London, February/April, pp. v–vi

1984 'Art: Howard's blend of images and textures. Alexandra Pringle talks to Howard Hodgkin', *Harpers & Queen*, June

'Howard Hodgkin and Patrick Caulfield in conversation', *Art Monthly*, vol. 78, July/August, pp. 4–6

'Howard Hodgkin interviewed by David Sylvester', *Howard Hodgkin: Forty Paintings: 1973–84*, The Whitechapel Art Gallery, London

1987 Asmund, Thorkildsen, 'An Interview with Howard Hodgkin', *Kunst Og Kultur*, University Press, National Gallery, Oslo, April

1988 Sylvester, David, 'Colour Dialogue', *Vogue*, January, p. 122

1990 Graham-Dixon, Andrew, 'Hanging in the balance', *The Independent*, 10 July, The National Gallery re-hang

1991 Simmons, Rosemary, 'Howard Hodgkin: New Hand-Coloured Prints', *Printmaking Today*, no. 2, Spring

'The Essence of Paris', James Hall in conversation with Howard Hodgkin, *The Independent Magazine*, 31 August

1992 Crane, R.H., Steven Vita, interview in *Veery*, 2, pp. 1–2

Spalding, Frances, 'An interview with Howard Hodgkin', *Charleston Magazine*, Winter/Spring

1993–94 Antony Peattie, interview in the catalogue to 'Howard Hodgkin', Anthony d'Offay Gallery, London, and M. Knoedler & Company, New York, pp. 63–70

1996 Gayford, Martin, 'The Lonely Artist', *The Daily Telegraph*, 23 November

Parker, Peter, 'Interview: Howard Hodgkin', *The New Statesman*, 29 November

1998 Woods, Alan, 'The Place Where Silence Becomes Objects: Interview with Howard Hodgkin', *Transcript*, vol. 3, issue 2, October 1998, pp. 1–30

1999 Barber, Lynn, 'Hodgkin's True Colours', *The Observer Magazine*, 31 October

Dyson, Jonathan, 'Howard's Way', *The Independent*, 6 November

Billen, Andrew, 'London's Only Old Master', *The Evening Standard*, 10 November

Jones, Jonathan, 'Desperate Pleasures', *The Guardian*, 11 November

PERIODICAL AND NEWSPAPER ARTICLES

1962 Thompson, David, 'Two Young Figurative Painters', *The Times*, 21 February

Mullins, Edwin, 'Two Painters at Tooth's', *Apollo*, no. 76, November, p. 714

1963 Lucie-Smith, Edward, 'The Impact Makers', *Vogue*, August

Hodin, J.P., 'Londres: Pop-Art of Art', *Quadrum* 14, pp. 161–64

1964 Coleman, Roger, 'Up with the Jones's', *Arts Review*, vol. 16, 25 January/8 February, p. 4

Lynton, Norbert, 'London Letter', *Art International*, vol. 8, 25 April, p. 73

1965 Lucie-Smith, Edward, 'Howard Hodgkin', *London Magazine*, vol. 4, March, pp. 71–75

1967 Robertson, Bryan, 'Howard's End?', *The Spectator*, 24 March

Russell, John, 'Hodgkin Colour Locals', *Art News*, no. 66, May, p. 62

1969 Melville, Robert, 'Problem Solved', *The New Statesman*, 4 April

Russell, John, 'London', *Art News*, vol. 68, May, p. 43

1970 Richards, Bryn, 'Bristol Art – Howard Hodgkin', *The Guardian*, 2 October

1971 Russell, John, 'The Life of Colours', *The Sunday Times*, 11 April

Feaver, William, 'Exhibitionism', *London Magazine*, vol. 11, August/September, pp. 112–20

1972 Hackney, Arthur, 'David Hockney, Howard Hodgkin', *Arts Review*, vol. 24, 26 February

1973 Russell, John, 'The English Conquest', *The Sunday Times*, 11 February

Vaizey, Marina, 'British Allsorts', *The Financial Times*, 19 February

Schwartz, Sanford, 'New York Letter', *Art International*, vol. 17, May, p. 42

1975 Hyman, Timothy, 'Howard Hodgkin', *Studio International*, vol. 189, May/June, pp. 180–83. Also *Studio International*, vol. 190, July/August, p. 88

Feaver, William, 'All This and Real Beer, Too', *The Observer*, 19 October

McEwen, John, 'Howard Hodgkin', *The Spectator*, 8 November

1976 Haworth-Booth, Mark, 'Salon and Workshop', *The Times Literary Supplement*, 19 March

Feaver, William, 'Hodgkin's Intelligence Tests', *The Observer*, 21 March

Morris, Lynda, 'Hodgkin and Caulfield', *The Listener*, 1 April

Cork, Richard, 'Every Blob Counts!', *Evening Standard*, 20 May

Vaizey, Marina, 'British Understatement', *The Sunday Times*, 23 May

Morphet, Richard, 'Howard Hodgkin: Assessment', *Studio International*, vol. 191, May/June, pp. 297–98

Reichardt, Jasia, 'Howard Hodgkin and Portraiture', *Architectural Design*, vol. 46, July, p. 444

Crichton, Fenella, 'London Letter', *Art International*, vol. 20, Summer, p. 14

del Renzio, Toni, 'Pop', *Art & Artists*, vol. 11, August, pp. 15–19

McEwen, John, 'Howard Hodgkin at the Serpentine Gallery', *Art in America*, vol. 64, July/August, p. 113

Feaver, William, 'England: Involvement, assiduity and an openness of mind', *Art News*, vol. 75, October, pp. 33–34

1977 Feaver, William, 'Full House', *The Observer*, 24 July

Shepherd, Michael, 'The Better Half', *The Sunday Telegraph*, 24 July

McEwen, John, 'Hardy Annual', *The Spectator*, 30 July

Vaizey, Marina, 'The Best of British', *The Sunday Times*, 31 July

Spalding, Frances, 'Hayward Annual Part II', *Arts Review*, vol. 29, 5 August, p. 508

Hilton, Timothy, 'South Bank-ruptcy', *The Times Literary Supplement*, 5 August, p. 960

Russell, John, 'Tenacity Keeps British Art Alive', *The New York Times*, 25 September

Faure Walker, James, 'Ways of Disclosing: Mapping the Hayward Annual', *Artscribe*, no. 8, September, pp. 20–26

Frackman, Noel, 'Howard Hodgkin/Stanley Boxer', *Arts Magazine*, vol. 52, November, p. 29

Kuspit, Donald, 'Howard Hodgkin at Emmerich', *Art in America*, vol. 65, November/December, p. 134

Rubinfein, Leo, 'Howard Hodgkin', *Artforum*, vol. 16, December, p. 68

1978 Hilton, Timothy, 'Anthologist', *The Spectator*, 16 September

Bolton, Linda Lee, 'Howard Hodgkin', *Arts Review*, vol. 30, 13 October, p. 155

Feaver, William, 'A Matter of Ways & Means', *The Observer*, 3 December

McEwen, John, 'Abstract Prizes', *The Spectator*, 9 December

Packer, William, 'Critics Choice at the ICA', *The Financial Times*, 16 December

McEwen, John, 'Four British Painters', *Artforum*, vol. 17, December, pp. 50–55

1979 Packer, William, 'Hodgkin's Eye at National Gallery', *The Financial Times*, 23 June

Lucie-Smith, Edward, 'Getting It All Together', *Evening Standard*, 4 July
Collis, Louise, and Lavinia Learmont, 'London: The Artist's Eye', *Art & Artists*, vol. 14, August, p. 43
Boorsch, Suzanne, 'New editions: Birthday Party and You and me', *Art News*, vol. 78, September, p. 42
Volsky, Glen Sujo, 'Narrative Painting 2: at Arnolfini', *Art Monthly*, no. 30, October, pp. 19–21
Muchnic, Suzanne, 'British Artists Painting the Town', *Los Angeles Times*, 9 November

1980 Searle, Adrian, 'Narrative Paintings', *Artforum*, vol. 18, January, p. 76
Berthoud, Roger, 'Howard Hodgkin behind the Enemy's Lines', *The Times*, 17 April
McEwen, John, 'Pastiches', *The Spectator*, 13 September

1981 Cork, Richard, 'Audacious, Outspoken – A spur for things to come', *New Standard*, 15 January
Bindman, David, 'The Good Old Avant-Garde', *The Times Literary Supplement*, 23 January
Levin, Bernard, 'Mammoth Footprints seen in Piccadilly', *The Times*, 28 January
Clarke, Michael, 'Art, Politics and Kitsch', *The Times Educational Supplement*, 6 February
Faure Walker, James, 'Awkward Moments', *Artscribe*, no. 27, February, pp. 12–15
Sweet, David, 'The Decline of Composition', *Artscribe*, no. 28, March, pp. 18–23
Gilmour, Pat, 'Howard Hodgkin', *Print Collector's Newsletter*, vol. 12, no. 1, March/April, pp. 2–5
French, P.D., 'Diluted Abstractions: Richard Phipps. Howard Hodgkin', *Artweek*, vol. 12, 25 April, p. 8
Kramer, Hilton, 'Howard Hodgkin', *The New York Times*, 8 May
Feaver, William, 'A "New Spirit" – or just a Tired Ghost?', *Art News*, vol. 80, May, pp. 114–18
Smith, Roberta, 'Fresh Paint?', *Art in America*, vol. 69, Summer, pp. 70–79
Murray, Jesse, 'Reflections on Howard Hodgkin's Theater of Memory', *Arts Magazine*, vol. 55, June, pp. 154–57
Howarth, Kathryn, 'Howard Hodgkin at Knoedler' *Art in America*, vol. 69, October, pp. 154–56
Phillips, Deborah C., 'Howard Hodgkin', *ARTNews*, vol. 80, November, pp. 200–1

1982 Bevan, Roger, 'Howard Hodgkin: Indian Leaves', *Event*, 22 September
Spalding, Frances, 'Howard Hodgkin', *Arts Review*, vol. 33, 24 September, p. 484
Feaver, William, 'Leaves from India', *The Observer*, 26 September
Geddes-Brown, Leslie, 'Painter of Perfection', *The Sunday Times*, 26 September
Vaizey, Marina, 'The Spirit of India', *The Sunday Times*, 26 September
Kapur, Geeta, 'Howard Hodgkin's Indian Leaves', *Art Monthly*, no. 61, November, p. 10
Russell, John, 'Art: Works of Hodgkin Displayed at Knoedler's', *The New York Times*, 19 November
Hughes, Robert, 'A Peeper into Paradise', *Time*, 29 November, p. 88

1984 Van Hensbergen, Gijs, 'Howard's Hues', *Ritz*, no. 86, March, p. 6
Russell, John, 'Maximum Emotion with a Minimum of Definition', *The New York Times*, 15 April
Brenson, Michael, 'Art: Howard Hodgkin and Paris Legacy', *The New York Times*, 27 April
McEwen, John, 'Finding Form at Fifty', *The Sunday Times Magazine*, 10 June, pp. 38–41
Vaizey, Marina, 'Dancing among the ruins', *The Sunday Times*, 10 June
Feaver, William, 'Copy, parody, variation, fake', *The Observer*, 17 June
Mullaly, Terence, 'Abstracts in abundance – and in setting to suit', *The Daily Telegraph*, 23 June
Carlson, Prudence, 'Howard Hodgkin at Knoedler', *Art in America*, October, pp. 192–93
McEwen, John, 'Late Bloomer', *Vanity Fair*, November, pp. 68–75
Stevens, Mark, 'A Palette of the Emotions', *Newsweek*, 3 December, p. 82
Lacayo, Richard, 'Returning to the Frame Game', *Time*, 3 December, p. 72
Fawcett, Anthony, and Jane Withers, 'Howard Hodgkin at the Venice Biennale', *Studio International*, vol. 197, no. 1005, pp. 16–17

1985 Feaver, William, 'England', *ARTNews*, February, pp. 57–59
Raynor, Vivien, 'At Yale, the "Afterthoughts" of Howard Hodgkin', *The New York Times*, 10 February
Galligan, Gregory, 'Howard Hodgkin: Forty Paintings', *Arts Magazine*, March, pp. 122–25
Gibson, Eric, 'The Hodgkin Paradox', *Studio International*, March, pp. 23–25
Sweet, David, 'Howard Hodgkin at Yale Center for British Arts', *Artscribe*, May/June
Higgins, Judith, 'In a Hot Country', *ARTNews*, Summer, pp. 56–65
Hyman, Timothy, 'Howard Hodgkin: Making a Riddle out of the Solution', *Art & Design*, vol. 1, no. 8, September

1986 Harrison, Charles, 'Hodgkin's Moment', *Artscribe*, December 1985/January 1986, pp. 62–64
Perl, Jed, 'Winter Notebook: Recent Abstract Painting', *The New Criterion*, April, pp. 57–58
Gill, Susan, 'Howard Hodgkin. Knoedler', *ARTNews*, September, pp. 115, 119
Galligan, Gregory, 'A Small Thing But Painting: The New Work of Howard Hodgkin', *Arts Magazine*, September, pp. 65–67
1987 Sylvester, David, 'Artist's Dialogue: Howard Hodgkin. The Texture of a Dream', *Architectural Digest*, March, pp. 54, 62, 66, 70 and 74
1988 Graham-Dixon, Andrew, 'On the Edge', *The Independent*, 5 April
Hilton, Tim, 'Hodgkin's quick start', *The Guardian*, 24 August
Dorment, Richard, 'Art: Drawn towards the light', *The Daily Telegraph*, 26 August
Hilton, Tim, 'Beyond the boundary', *The Guardian*, 31 August
Auty, Giles, 'Howard's Way', *The Spectator*, 3 September
Feaver, William, 'Whoosh in Venice', *The Observer*, 4 September
Packer, William, 'Overlaid with witty eroticism', *The Financial Times*, 6 September
Hicks, Alistair, 'Beneath the surface', *The Times*, 6 September
Graham-Dixon, Andrew, 'Drawing on life', *The Independent*, 6 September
Shepherd, Michael, 'Hodgkin's Venetian hours', *The Sunday Telegraph*, 11 September
1989 Adams, Brooks, 'Howard Hodgkin at Knoedler', *Art in America*, January, pp. 143–44
Moorman, Margaret, 'Howard Hodgkin. Knoedler', *ARTNews*, January, p. 129
Cyphers, Peggy, 'Howard Hodgkin', *Arts Magazine*, January, p. 106
Walker, Patricia G., 'Howard Hodgkin; M. Knoedler & Co., Inc.', *Cover*, 1 January, p. 16
Fuller, Peter, 'Howard Hodgkin and Robert Natkin', *Modern Painters*, vol. 1, no. 3, Autumn, pp. 76–77
Cooke, Lynne, 'Special Report: British Art in the Eighties', *The Journal of Art*, vol. 2, no. 2, November, pp. 24–26
1990 Hicks, Alistair, 'The Fire of London', *Art and Auction*, May, pp. 212–17
Russell, John, 'A Hodgkin Original', *The New York Times Magazine*, 11 November, pp. 56–62
Dorment, Richard, 'Howard's Way', *The Telegraph Weekend Magazine*, 24 November, pp. 50–55
Thomas, Michael M., 'He Behaved at the Pierre, Got Shocked at Bergdorf's...', *The New York Observer*, 26 November, pp. 1, 17
Stevens, Mark, 'Shades of the Past', *Vanity Fair*, December, p. 172
Crozier, William, 'Howard Hodgkin: The Artist's Eye', *Modern Painters*, December, pp. 16–21
Cork, Richard, 'Painting to ease the passing of time', *The Times Saturday Review*, 1 December, pp. 16–17
1991 Edelman, Robert C., 'Howard Hodgkin', *ARTNews*, February, p. 146
Morgan, Robert C., 'Howard Hodgkin', *Arts Magazine*, February, p. 78
Graham-Dixon, Andrew, 'Heavy Rain', *The Independent Magazine*, 16 February, pp. 36–37
1992 Heller, Zoe, 'Howard's Way', *Harpers & Queen*, April
1993 Russell, John, 'In New Delhi, Pursued by an Enormous Tree', *The New York Times*, 28 March
Levy, Paul, 'What's New From Freud and Hodgkin', *The Wall Street Journal*, 18 September
Lubbock, Tom, 'Howard Hodgkin: For Me', *Modern Painters*, Autumn
Lucie-Smith, Edward, 'In Profile: Howard Hodgkin', *Arts Review*, October
McEwen, John, 'Colour too deep for comfort', *The Sunday Telegraph*, 10 October
Graham-Dixon, Andrew, 'Truants of the memory', *The Independent Magazine*, 16 October
Hall, James, 'Souvenirs of life', *The Guardian*, 25 October
Sewell, Brian, 'The mark of a lesser spotted', *The Evening Standard*, 28 October
Smith, Giles, 'A stripe is a stripe, a splodge is a splodge', *The Independent*, 30 October
Cork, Richard, 'Painting from memory', *The Times*, 2 November
Farson, Daniel, 'Knight Errant', *The Daily Mail*, 7 November
1994 Shone, Richard, 'London and New York, Howard Hodgkin', *Burlington Magazine*, January, pp. 45–46
Wei, Lilly, 'Howard Hodgkin's Mandarin Pastimes', *Art in America*, April, pp. 92–97
1995 Smith, Roberta, 'Making the Abstract Light and Personal', *The New York Times*, 3 November
Pitman, Joanna, 'Showing His Colours', *The Times Magazine*, 4 November
Raine, Craig, 'What an Optic Nerve', *The Sunday Times*, 5 November
Stevens, Mark, 'Beauty and the Beast', *The New York Magazine*, 13 November
Kramer, Hilton, 'The Seductive Hodgkin Loses His Exotic Charm', *The New York Observer*, 15 November

Bernard, Bruce, 'Howard's Way', *The Sunday Telegraph Magazine*, 17 December
1996 Boyd, William, 'Abstract with Memories', *Modern Painters*, Spring Issue
Adams, Brooks, 'Hodgkin's Subtexts', *Art in America*, May
Gayford, Martin, 'The Lonely Artist', *The Daily Telegraph*, 23 November
Lewis, Matthew R., 'Abstractly Fabulous', *Gay Times*, December
Searle, Adrian, 'Howard's Way', *The Guardian*, 3 December
Packer, William, 'Loaded Brushstrokes', *The Financial Times*, 7–8 December
Feaver, William, 'Howard Hodgkin Shows his Colours (but not in a black and white newspaper, he doesn't)', *The Observer*, 8 December
Hilton, Tim, 'A World of His Own', *The Independent on Sunday*, 8 December
Robertson, Bryan, 'Light Fantastic', *The Independent*, 10 December
Dorment, Richard, 'When Colour Makes Life Sweet', *The Daily Telegraph*, 11 December
Januszczak, Waldemar, 'Too Bright for His Own Good', *The Sunday Times*, 15 December
McEwan, John, 'Tortoise Outruns Soulless Hare', *The Sunday Telegraph*, 15 December
Nicholson, Adam, 'Howard's Way', *The Sunday Telegraph Magazine*, 29 December
Gayford, Martin, 'Is That a Guest or a Gun Turret?', *Harpers & Queen*, December
Graham-Dixon, Andrew, 'Portrait of the Artist as an Older Man', *Vogue*, December
1997 Gottler, Christine, 'Die Farbe fluchtiger Emotionen', *Neue Zürcher Zeitung*, 27 January
Grishin, Sasha, 'A Leader Among Today's British Painters', *The Canberra Times*, 7 February
1999 Gayford, Martin, 'What's It all About, Sir Howard?', *The Independent*, 1 November
Januszczak, Waldemar, 'Shiny, Happy Pictures', *The Sunday Times*, 21 November
Packer, William, 'Abstracted Romantics', *The Financial Times*, 27 November
Gayford, Martin, 'Great Memories', *The Daily Telegraph*, 1 December
2000 Lucie-Smith, Edward, 'Critic's Diary', *Art Review*, January

FILMS, TELEVISION, RADIO AND AUDIO-VISUAL PROGRAMMES

1976 *Howard Hodgkin: Indian Views*, a recorded talk on his paintings with Timothy Hyman, The British Council
1981 *Howard Hodgkin*, London Weekend Television, The South Bank Show, 29 March
1982 *Howard Hodgkin*, colour, 37 minutes, directed by Judy Marle, Landseer. The Arts Council of Great Britain
1984 *Howard Hodgkin interviewed by Richard Cork*, Lecon Arts Enterprises, London (audio-visual)
Four Rooms, BBC Arena, 21 February
Howard Hodgkin, sponsored by the Phillips Collection, Washington, DC, broadcast on WETA-TV, Channel 26, Washington, DC, 11 and 14 November
1993 *The Late Show: Howard Hodgkin*, BBC2, directed by Bernadette O'Brien, 26 and 30 October
Arts Section, Entertainment UK: Howard Hodgkin, ITV, produced by Elaine Gallagher and directed by Fiona Adam, 26, 28 and 30 October
Nightwaves: Howard Hodgkin, BBC Radio 3, interviewed by Christopher Cook, 28 October

LIST OF COMPARATIVE ILLUSTRATIONS

Measurements are in centimetres followed by inches, height before width.
Figures in **bold** refer to page numbers

LIST OF COLOUR ILLUSTRATIONS

Measurements are in centimetres followed by inches, height before width.
Figures in **bold** refer to page numbers

59 *Memories of Max*, 1991–95; oil on wood, 170.5 × 223.5, 67⅛ × 88. Private collection. Photo Prudence Cuming

60 *Venice Evening*, 1984–85; oil on wood, 37 × 44.5, 14½ × 17½. Collection Nan and Gene Corman. Photo Ken Cohen Photography, New York

63 *House near Venice*, 1984–88; oil on wood, 50.8 × 56.2, 20 × 22⅛. Private collection

64 *Venice/Shadows*, 1984–88; oil on wood, 41.3 × 46.4, 16¼ × 18¼. Laura and Barry Townsley, London

65 *Fire in Venice*, 1986–89; oil on wood, 49 × 56.5, 19 × 22⅛. Ron and Ann Pizzuti, Columbus, Ohio

66 *Venice Grey Water*, 1988–89; oil on wood, 66 × 75, 26 × 29½. Collection Antony Peattie. Photo Prudence Cuming

67 *Venice Sunset*, 1989; oil on wood, 26 × 30, 10¼ × 11⅞. Private collection, England. Photo Prudence Cuming

68 *View from Venice*, 1984–85; oil on wood, 39 × 47, 15⅜ × 18½. Collection Antony Peattie. Photo Ken Cohen Photography, New York

70 *Counting the Days*, 1979–82; oil on wood, 55.2 × 64.1, 21¾ × 25¼. Private collection

72 *Grantchester Road*, 1975; oil on wood, 124.5 × 145, 49 × 57. Private collection, London

73 *Souvenirs*, 1980–84; oil on wood, 152.4 × 274.5, 60 × 108. Collection Robert and Jane Meyerhoff

75 *The Green Château*, 1976–80; oil on wood, 98.2 × 123.7, 38⅝ × 48½. Private collection, USA

76 *After Dinner*, 1976–77; oil on wood, 76.2 × 98, 30 × 38¾. Collection Mr and Mrs Gund

77 *Reading the Letter*, 1977–80; oil on wood, 45.1 × 50.8, 17¾ × 20. Private collection

78 *The Hopes at Home*, 1973–77; oil on wood, 91.4 × 106.7, 36 × 42. City of Manchester Art Galleries

80 *After the Shop had Closed*, 1992; oil on wood, 31.7 × 36.8, 12½ × 14½. Private collection, Davos, Switzerland. Photo Prudence Cuming

82 *After Corot*, 1979–82; oil on board, 36.8 × 38.1, 14½ × 15. Private collection, Los Angeles. Courtesy Louver Gallery, Venice, California

85 *After Degas*, 1993; oil on wood, 66 × 76, 26 × 30. Private collection, London. Photo Prudence Cuming

86 *Venetian Glass*, 1984–87; oil on wood, 34.3 × 42.5, 13½ × 16¾. Private collection, Davos, Switzerland. Photo Prudence Cuming

87 *Interior at Oakwood Court*, 1978–83; oil on wood, 81.3 × 137.2, 32 × 54. Whitworth Gallery, Manchester

88 *Tea*, 1977–80; oil on wood, 42.5 × 111.8, 16¾ × 44. Private collection

91 *In Paris With You*, 1995–96; oil on wood, 71 × 88.9, 28 × 35. Private collection. Photo Prudence Cuming

92 *The Moon*, 1978–80; oil on wood, 44.8 × 55.9, 17⅝ × 22. Collection R.B. Kitaj, London. Photo Jonathan Bayer

95 *Rain* (detail), 1984–89; oil on wood, 164.8 × 197, 64½ × 70½ (whole painting). Tate Gallery, London. Photo Prudence Cuming

96 *Fruit*, 1988–89; oil on wood, 33 × 40.6, 13 × 16. Collection Mary Tyler Moore and Dr S. Robert Levine

97 *Fisherman's Cove*, 1993; oil on wood, 28.3 × 38, 11⅛ × 15. Private collection, London. Photo Prudence Cuming

99 *In the Bay of Naples*, 1980–82; oil on wood, 137.2 × 152.4, 54 × 60. Private collection, USA. Photo Ken Cohen Photography, New York

100 *Rainbow*, 1983–85; oil on wood, 53 × 53.3, 20⅞ × 21. Collection Holly Hunt, Chicago. Photo Ken Cohen Photography, New York

102 *When Did We Go to Morocco?*, 1988–93; oil on wood, two panels, 196.9 × 269.2, 77½ × 106 overall. The Metropolitan Museum of Art Purchase, Lila Acheson Wallace Gift, 1994. Photo Prudence Cuming

105 *In Tangier*, 1987–90; oil on wood, 163.5 × 179, 64½ × 70½. Private collection

106 *Egyptian Night*, 1983–85; oil on wood, 49.5 × 59, 19½ × 23¼. Private collection. Photo Ken Cohen Photography, New York

107 *Dark Moon*, 1983–84; oil on wood, 31.4, 12⅜ diameter. The Luther W. Brady Collection

108 *In Central Park*, 1983–86; oil on wood, oval, 48.3 × 63.5, 19 × 25. Private collection. Photo Ken Cohen Photography, New York

109 *Goodbye to the Bay of Naples*, 1980–82; oil on wood, 55.9 × 66.7, 22 × 26¼. Private collection, USA

111 *Bombay Sunset*, 1972–73; oil on wood, 85 × 92, 33½ × 36¼. Private collection, London

112 *The Last Time I Saw Paris*, 1988–91; oil on wood, 113 × 127, 44½ × 50. Private collection. Photo Prudence Cuming

113 *Kerala*, 1992; oil on wood, 23.5 × 35.6, 9¼ × 14. Private collection. Photo Prudence Cuming

120 *Talking about Art*, 1975; oil on wood, 106 × 127, 41¾ × 50. Private collection

123 *The Cylinder, the Sphere, the Cone*, 1978–84; oil on board, 92.1 × 116.8, 36¼ × 46. The Museum of Art, Carnegie Institute, Pittsburgh (Gene Baro Memorial Fund and Carnegie International Acquisition Fund 1984)

124 *Paul Levy*, 1976–80; oil on wood, 53 × 60.3, 20⅞ × 23¾. Saatchi Collection, London

125 *D.H. in Hollywood*, 1980–84; oil on wood, 108 × 130.8, 42½ × 51½. Private collection. Photo Ken Cohen Photography, New York

128 *Clean Sheets*, 1982–84; oil on wood, 55.9 × 91.4, 22 × 36. Tate Gallery, London

129 *None but the Brave Deserves the Fair*, 1981–84; oil on wood, 62.8 × 76.2, 24¾ × 30. Private collection, New York. Photo Ken Cohen Photography, New York

130 *Patrick Caulfield in Italy*, 1987–92; oil on wood, 110.5 × 146, 43½ × 57½. Private collection. Photo Prudence Cuming

131 *Patrick in Italy*, 1991–93; oil on wood, 65 × 75, 25⅝ × 29¼. Private collection. Photo Prudence Cuming

132 *After Visiting David Hockney*, 1991–92; oil on wood, 48.9 × 61.6, 19¼ × 24¼. Barclays Bank Collection. Photo Prudence Cuming

134 *A Small Thing But My Own*, 1983–85; oil on wood, 45.1 × 54, 17¾ × 21¼. Private collection. Photo Ken Cohen Photography, New York

137 *Snapshot*, 1984–93; oil on wood, 150 × 225.4, 59 × 88¾. Private collection, London. Photo Prudence Cuming

139 *Rain*, 1984–89; oil on wood, 163.8 × 179, 64½ × 70½. Tate Gallery, London

140 *A Small Henry Moore at the Bottom of the Garden*, 1975–77; oil on wood, 52.7 × 53.4, 20¾ × 21. Private collection, New York. Photo courtesy of the Whitechapel Art Gallery, London. Used in its catalogue, 1984

141 *A Henry Moore at the Bottom of the Garden*, 1975–77; oil on wood, 102.9 × 102.9, 40½ × 40½. Saatchi Collection, London

144 *Like an Open Book*, 1989–90; oil on wood, 52 × 63, 20½ × 24¾. Private collection, England. Photo Prudence Cuming

145 *Indian Sky*, 1988–89; oil on wood, 54.1 × 70.2, 21⅜ × 27⅝. Private collection, New York

148 *Waking Up in Naples*, 1980–84; oil on wood, 59.7 × 74.9, 23½ × 29½. Private collection, London. Photo Ken Cohen Photography, New York

150 *The Moon* (side view), 1978–80; oil on wood, 44.8 × 55.9, 17⅝ × 22. Collection R.B. Kitaj, London. Photo Jonathan Bayer

153 *Sunset*, 1990–93; oil on wood, 57 × 65.5, 22½ × 25¾. Collection Sandy and Harold Price, Laguna Beach, California. Photo Prudence Cuming

156 *Down in the Valley*, 1985–88; oil on wood, 73.7 × 91.4, 29 × 36. Bruce and Judith Eissner, USA. Photo Ken Cohen Photography, New York

157 *Blue Palm*, 1985–86; oil on wood, oval, 27.9 × 33, 11 × 13. Dr and Mrs John T. Chiles, Toledo, Ohio. Photo Ken Cohen Photography, New York

159 *It Can't Be True*, 1987–90; oil on wood, 76.5 × 71, 30¼× 28. Janice and David Blackburn

160 *Leaves*, 1987–88; oil on wood, 50.2 × 65.4, 19¾ × 25¾. Renee Nelson. Photo Ken Cohen Photography, New York

163 *Small Durand Gardens*, 1974; oil on wood, 56.5 × 66.7, 22¼ × 26¼. Private collection, London. Photo Rodney Wright-Watson

164 *Dinner in Palazzo Albrizzi*, 1984–88; oil on wood, 117.5 × 117.5, 46¼ × 46¼. Modern Art Museum of Fort Worth. Photo Ken Cohen Photography, New York.

165 *Haven't We Met?*, 1985–88; oil on wood, 48.9 × 64.1, 19¼ × 25¼. Saatchi Collection, London. Photo Ken Cohen Photography, New York

167 *Mr and Mrs James Kirkman*, 1980–84; oil on wood, 103.5 × 121.3, 40¾ × 47¾. Sue and David Workman. Photo Ken Cohen Photography, New York

168 *First Portrait of Terence McInerney*, 1981; oil on wood, 128.3 × 127, 50½ × 50. Collection Nan and Gene Corman

169 *Second Portrait of Terence McInerney*, 1981; oil on wood, 128.3 × 139.7, 50½ × 55. Nancy M. O'Boyle, Dallas, Texas

170 *Italian Landscape*, 1990–91; oil on wood, 36.8 × 46.8, 14½ × 18½. Private collection, New York. Photo Prudence Cuming

172 *Autumn Foliage*, 1998–99; oil on wood, 99 × 118, 39 × 46½. Private collection. Photo Prudence Cuming

174 *After Matisse*, 1995–99; oil on wood, 110 × 126, 43⅜ × 49⅝. Private collection. Photo Prudence Cuming

177 *Seurat's Bathers*, 1998–2000; oil on wood, 185.5 × 282.6, 73 × 111¼. By kind permission of His Grace The Duke of Westminster CBE TD DL. Photo Prudence Cuming

179 *Chez Stamos*, 1998; oil on wood, 198.1 × 260.4, 78 × 102½. From the collection of Mr and Mrs Herbert L. Lucas. Photo Prudence Cuming

180 *Seascape*, 1996; oil on wood, 25.4 × 27.9, 10 × 11. Private collection, London. Photo Prudence Cuming

181 *Evening Sea*, 1998; oil on wood, 175.9 × 260.4, 69¼ × 102½. The Museum of Fine Arts, Houston, Texas, Museum purchase with funds provided by the Caroline Wiess Law Accessions Endowment Fund (2000.234). Photo Prudence Cuming

183 *Old Sky*, 1996–97; oil on wood, 39.4 × 43.8, 15½ × 17¼. Private collection, London. Photo Prudence Cuming

185 *Dark Mirror*, 1999; oil on wood, 36.8 × 43.2, 14½ × 17. Private collection of Marco Compagnoni. Photo Prudence Cuming

186 *In Mirza's Room*, 1995–98; oil on wood, 117.8 × 133.5, 46⅜ × 52½. Collection the artist. Photo Prudence Cuming

187 *The Heat of the Day*, 1995–96; oil on wood, 34.3 × 43, 13½ × 17. Private collection. Photo Prudence Cuming

188 *In Memory of Max Gordon*, 1990–96; oil on wood, 188 × 238.8, 74 × 94. Private collection. Photo Prudence Cuming

191 *Rain at Il Palazzo*, 1993–98; oil on wood, 150 × 189.8, 59 × 74¾. Private collection. Photo Prudence Cuming

192 *Memories*, 1997–99; oil on wood, 119.4 × 175.2, 47 × 69. Private collection. Photo Prudence Cuming

195 *Once More with Feeling*, 1999; oil on wood, 78.4 × 92.2, 30⅞ × 36¼. Private collection. Photo Prudence Cuming

196 *Night and Day*, 1997–99; oil on wood, 165.1 × 196.9, 65 × 77½. Collection the artist. Photo Prudence Cuming

197 *Chez Max*, 1996–97; oil on wood, 176.5, 69½ diameter. Private collection. Photo Prudence Cuming

198 *Escape*, 1996; oil on wood, 34 × 48, 13⅜ × 19⅞. Private collection. Photo Prudence Cuming

201 *Come Back Dull Care*, 1999; oil on wood, 23.5 × 31.7, 9¼ × 12½. Private collection. Photo Prudence Cuming

202 *Twilight*, 1995–96; oil on wood, 30.8 × 37, 12⅛ × 14½. Private collection. Photo Prudence Cuming

203 *Andrew Allfree*, 1994–98; oil on wood, 153.2 × 193.5, 60¼ × 76¼. James Erskine, Sydney. Photo Prudence Cuming

204 *Fatherland*, 1991–95; oil on wood, 76 × 83, 29⅞ × 32⅝. Collection of Luther W. Brady. Photo Prudence Cuming

206 *A Leap in the Dark*, 1992; oil on wood, 35.6 × 42.7, 14 × 16⅞. Private collection. Photo Prudence Cuming

208 *End of the Day*, 1999; oil on wood, 38.5 × 42.5, 15¼ × 16¾. Collection Mr and Mrs Lawrence Rubin. Photo Prudence Cuming

ACKNOWLEDGMENTS

My thanks to Leslie Heitzman for helping in the preparation and typing of the manuscript; to John Russell for sharing some of his thoughts with me; to my daughter Eleanor for helping me to clarify some of my ideas; and last but not least to *The Independent*, and in particular its editor Andreas Whittam Smith, for allowing me time away from my column for the newspaper to work on this book and also for permitting me to adapt one or two passages from my own articles for use in the book. Many thanks also to Jo Thornberry and Anthony d'Offay for all their help in preparing this second and revised edition.

INDEX

Figures in **bold** refer to the page numbers of illustrations